AN INTRODUCTION TO LIABILITY CLAIMS ADJUSTING

By

CORYDON T. JOHNS

THE NATIONAL UNDERWRITER COMPANY
CINCINNATI

ATLANTA	CINCINNATI	DENVER	NEW YORK	ST. PAUL
BOSTON	CLEVELAND	DETROIT	PHILADELPHIA	SAN FRANCISCO
CHICAGO	DALLAS	INDIANAPOLIS	ST. LOUIS	

Printed in the United States of America

To

Elizabeth Eddy Johns

ACKNOWLEDGEMENTS

This book, written as a text for one of its courses, grew out of the Educational Program in Insurance Adjusting of the Insurance Institute of America, supported by the National Association of Independent Insurance Adjusters. Were it not for this program, it is doubtful that this book would have been written. Should any merit be found in the book, due credit should go to the toughminded presidents of the Association who got the program under way, to a hard working educational committee, and to the members of the Association who voluntarily taxed themselves to underwrite this program.

Dr. John W. Hall, the Association's educational consultant, also had a hand in the book. He patiently edited and criticized the manuscript. I was told when I started the book, "All editors are tyrants." My experience supports the statement, provided that I am permitted to insert that John Hall is a benevolent tyrant. I had no idea what I had bitten off when I started to write and I am positive that John Hall had no idea how much work it would be to criticize, edit and assist an adjuster who had never written anything longer than a report on a claim.

This story may shed light on Dr. Hall's contribution. Last summer, I was wrestling on our back porch with a stubborn chapter. I got up to go into the house, possibly to open another can of beer. As I walked off, Mrs. Johns swears she heard me mutter, "That miserable John Hall is right again."

I cannot speak highly enough of his remarkable understanding of the claims business and his patience. If the book displays clarity, coherence and organization, I somewhat doubt that those qualities would have been attained without his help.

Dr. Edwin S. Overman of the Insurance Institute of America, read Chapters 3 and 4. Stewart C. Eggert of the Tampa law firm of Allen, Dell, Frank and Trinkle, read Chapter 2 and parts of other chapters. Their painstaking criticisms were very helpful.

Many of the secretaries in our company typed and retyped furiously and were often helpful. I hope I do not incur the wrath of Mrs. Doris Stearnes, Mrs. Jo Anne Roberts, Mrs. Joyce Hubbard and Mrs. Eleanor Federika when I mention that Miss Esther Israel went over some sections so much that she must be regarded as having a kind of proprietary interest in them. Her encouragement was always welcome and she was more than helpful in pointing out areas which needed to be clarified for the benefit of our trainees.

My own secretary, Mrs. Shelby Steger, suffered through more drafts of more chapters than one person ought to have to endure. I have, I am sorry to confess, a failing for what one of my high school teachers condemned as "purple patches of fine prose." I am grateful for the cold eye that Mrs. Steger gave these passages and for her assistance in finding a better way to say something.

"An Introduction to Liability Claims Adjusting" was read in manuscript by: Meredith K. Nelson, State Farm Mutual Automobile Insurance Company; H. L. Handley, Jr., Farmers Insurance Group; Glen F. Johnson, Travelers; Edwin B. Barber, American Re-Insurance Company; Frank P. Horner, American Family Insurance Group; J. Roy Nicholas, Royal-Globe Insurance Companies; J. E. Linster, Employers Mutuals of Wausau; Price M. McCulley, McCulley Adjustment Company; Chris G. Hume, Jr., Hume and Company; William C. Couch, Couch Adjustment Company; Thomas E. Foley, Foley Adjustment Company; and William E. Condray, Bierman-Condray Inc. I acknowledge gratefully the many helpful comments and criticisms from them.

I have observed that authors customarily acknowledge with gratitude, "coffee, sympathy, understanding, encouragement, etc." from their wives. I fear I dismissed these acknowledgements as perfunctory, an error for which I hope to be forgiven since I have now been able to identify and appreciate a wife's real contribution. To make clear this contribution, I must explain something of the technique by which an adjuster produces a book: First he writes, polishes and sends a section to John Hall. Hall returns it with copious marginal comment which translates, "You haven't made your point clear." Adjuster re-writes and asks his wife to read it. "What does it mean to you?" Wife's paraphrase indicates that the point is still hopelessly buried. Adjuster loses his temper.

For repeatedly enduring this monstrous injustice, for suffering through some sections until they *were* understandable, for giving up evenings and weekends that we both lost count of and for "coffee, understanding, etc.," I am indebted to my Eddy.

Despite the abundant professional help from John Hall, industry readers, and my fellow adjusters the final decision as to what to say and how to say it has always been left with me. Responsibility for techniques, philosophy and errors remains mine.

CONTENTS

CHAPTER 1

Introduction to Adjusting

It is a truism that every time creates its own institutions. The business of liability claims adjusting no less than any other business institution is a response to a need. To an unique degree, this business is an almost accidental accommodation to some conditions of modern life. To an equally unique degree it is a specific response to some widely prevailing attitudes about some of the aspects of modern life. It was said of the Austro-Hungarian Empire before World War I that it was so essential to the economic health of Central Europe that if it had not existed, it would have had to be invented. This book suggests a similar essentiality in the claims business.

The liability insurance business serves individuals, businesses and industry by assuming the risks that beset them, offering security and peace of mind at the cost of a relatively small premium. The *technical services* involved in the investigation and settlement of liability claims—services known collectively as *adjusting*—began as a collateral function of the liability insurance business. But these services are found where there is no insurance, an indication that the provision of the means of adjusting claims, the anticipation of the cost of this function and a way to spread the cost have a necessity quite apart from the insurance business with which they are associated. The features of the society which has called the institution of liability claims adjusting into being and which determine its characteristics require a brief look.

The Legal System

Highway hazards, their resultant damage, injury and death, and to a lesser degree the hazards of other features of life, came

1

somewhat unexpectedly on a country which already had a legal system for transferring the cost of injury from a victim to a negligent party adjudged to be legally responsible for that hurt. The legal system included, of course, laws, lawyers and the courts. This became part of the mechanism for coping with the results of highway hazards.

It would be a mistake, though, to consider the legal system as more than a *part* of the mechanism for dealing with the claims of accident victims. That legal system actually handles a mere trickle out of the flood of millions of accident victims, but it influences profoundly the practice of adjusting because the system, its lawyers, courts and juries are the destination of claims not disposed of by agreement; that is, claims not successfully adjusted.

A peculiar feature of the system is that nowhere does it provide a scale of values. In the matter of values, each jury is literally a law unto itself. The system as a whole does present a vague consensus of value, but the outline of this consensus is dim and its authority subject to some doubt.

The law, then, while it provides part of the mechanism, is far from the whole story. Courts could not possibly adjudicate all claims. The delay and waste of manpower would be intolerable. Furthermore, their scale of values, insofar as any outline or consensus can be designed, is unacceptable to many litigants, if indeed any scale can be discerned.

The System of Voluntary Agreements—and One Feature of That System

As the business of insurance grew, it developed that more claims, by far, were settled by *agreement* than were disposed of by *litigation*—and this situation continues to prevail. It seems both reasonable and obvious to infer that this is because claimants and the people against whom they make claims prefer it that way. What is not so obvious is that almost every such settlement is based upon a scale of values which has its own unique and highly respected sanction. It is not an imposed scale; it is an agreed value, even though agreed to by only two parties. This scale may be—usually is—different from that which can be discerned as the consensus of values which the legal system would apply. To the extent that each of the participants agreed to it, he rejected the values of the legal system and elected to value the claim on a scale personal to him.

Values—what little the industry knows of them—will be explored in greater detail in Chapters 9 and 10. The point made here is that adjusting is not a process of determining what courts would award in a given circumstance and then delivering that sum to a claimant. On the contrary, disposition of a claim by litigation and verdict represents the failure of the adjusting process.

Aggressive Claims Attitudes

The tendency to voluntary settlement notwithstanding, it is hardly giving away secrets to disclose that many claimants are something less than restrained in pressing their claims. Instead, they may be very aggressive and their aggression takes many forms:

Simple over-valuation (demanding $5,000 for a trifling injury for which the most liberal jury would hesitate to award $500)
Attributing to accident, pathology which is not, in fact, accident-connected
Exaggerating or prolonging injury
Claiming non-existent injury
Disputing or distorting facts about an accident so as to make "liability" out of "no liability"

Simple, innocent lack of knowledge, self-deception, honest but imaginary complaints, or outright cupidity may be involved, alone or in any combination.

Far from taking the position that all claimants are greedy and grasping, this book will consistently take the position that more claimants are honest than otherwise. Still, facts are facts and it is naive to write about claims without recognizing that both intent to make money on claims and the knowledge of how to do it are widespread. This combination of intent and knowledge is known to the industry as being "claims-minded." Claims-mindedness usually varies directly with the size of the community, claimants being more aggressive in the big cities and less so in rural areas. Few areas are now so rural as to be entirely free of some degree of aggressive claims-mindedness.

ADJUSTING: A PRODUCT OF FORCES

Having sketched in the nature of the world in which a claims man works, it is now possible to outline his job.

Adjusting may now be defined in part as the work of disposing of claims by agreement. It is influenced by a legal system which looms in the background ready, if called upon, to impose *its* rules and *its* values, and adjusters must prepare their cases for this eventuality. Adjusters' daily duties present them with some claimants who lean over backwards in a sincere attempt to minimize their claims, some claimants aggressive and anxious to capitalize accidents, and many claimants in the middle, ready to swing one direction or the other as the adjuster handles them wisely or unwisely, successfully or unsuccessfully. Some claims are inevitably headed for litigation because of a claimant's forthright attempt to pervert the courts into an instrument for his gain. Some head for trial because, with all its faults, the jury system is still probably the best and most equitable way for civilized people to settle their differences. Against this background of persons and attitudes the adjuster attempts to settle as many claims as possible by agreement; and where there must be litigation, he makes the preparations which he hopes will insure a successful defense.

The world in which he lives involves him in defense against fraud and aggressive claims attitudes, and brings him up against the idea that fraud and aggressive claims attitudes are, in a sense, simply costs, the control of which is his duty. It presents him with the problems associated with the distribution of funds to those who are not aggressively claims-minded, and it creates a dilemma for him because the actions necessary to the control of one class of claim may conflict with the attitudes he must instill in order properly to process claims of the other class.

Each of these ideas will now be considered.

Aggressiveness and Fraud, Costs to Be Controlled

An adjuster hopes to settle [1] every claim even though he recognizes that some may have to be litigated, and knows that at any time, any claim may take an "aggressive" course.

These possibilities to a high degree set [2] the nature of his work. (These are not the *only* factors which set the nature of his work. Others will be introduced later.)

It is for the reasons listed above that an adjuster investigates to determine where the truth lies, takes statements attempting to prevent stories from being changed later, and confirms and verifies much of what is told him. These are undeniably defensive moves against actual or potential aggressiveness on the part of claimants.

Experience discloses that claims-minded aggressiveness takes many forms: some situations that the most relaxed moral code would immediately identify as larceny, some situations that the sternest code would recognize as reasonable points over which honest men of good will might differ, and the usual broad middle group where it is difficult to draw a line. Drawing the line, however, is not the point. The point is that *it is not the adjuster's business to draw lines.* This may seem a strange thing to say when most of what is written about claims states clearly and calmly that fraud and claims of no merit should be resisted. Such statements imply that once fraud is identified, the problem is solved. This is not so. Whether fraud (one might prefer the broader term aggressiveness) consists of outright lying, exaggeration, or simple manipulation of innocent but ignorant tools, adjusters have no difficulty in identifying it. The problem is not recognition; the problem is to resist *effectively.* There is nothing so futile as to try to explain an adverse verdict with the excuse, "It was a miscarriage of justice."

Both the press and the pulpit deplore our deteriorating moral values. It is significant that the two things most cited as examples are cheating on income tax and lying on insurance claims.

---

[1] "Settle" in this sense must be taken to include the admittedly unrealistic hope of persuading all claimants to accept denials.

[2] "Set"—in the sense that a fishing pole, improperly supported, "takes a set" and acquires a more or less permanent bend.

Unless their experience and reaction to the business is quite extraordinary, most adjusters, as they become familiar with the techniques of sophisticated claimants and with trial results, will conclude that exaggeration is difficult to disprove and that what may appear fraudulent to the adjuster is often rewarded with cash by the jury. He may even conclude that he is out of step with the moral climate of his times. If he arrives at this point, it may be just as well for him to stay there, for an adjuster is not paid to praise, to condemn or to establish moral attitudes. He is paid to handle claims, to dispose of them as effectively as possible. His moral judgments will be sensed and resented by those with whom he must deal, and will interfere with the effective performance of his duties.

Viewed in this light, control of fraud and the control of aggressive attempts to maximize the value of claims becomes much the same thing. In either event, such attempts, to the extent that they succeed, tax the policyholder and affront the majority of claimants who follow a more restrained approach. Where an adjuster should draw the line between what to resist and what not to resist is peculiarly his own decision. It will presently be made clear that he does not approach these decisions without guidelines, both internal (his conscience, judgment, etc.) and external (the pressures of the several interests to which his work relates him).

This, then, is part of the climate that called into being the work known as liability adjusting.

Distributing Funds to Claimants Who Are Not Aggressive

Aggressive claimants are far from being the only citizens of the claims man's world. They are healthily outnumbered by people who do *not* expect to decorate every rear-end tap with a "whiplash," who do not exaggerate or inflate their claims. Many make honest and sincere efforts to minimize their claims, whether for property damage or bodily injury. Since these folks are in the majority, it follows that a substantial proportion of an adjuster's time goes into the processing of their claims.

Between these people and aggressive claimants lies a large body of claimants ready to adopt an aggressive or a restrained attitude according to their response to the treatment accorded them by an adjuster. The requirements of processing the claims of the non-aggressive and the undecided also has much to do with determining the set of an adjuster's work. These people are entitled to promptness, to a reasonable determination of the sums due them and to a recognition that they have met with misfortune, the obligation to ameliorate which the insurance business assumed when a liability contract was written.

Conflict Between Defensive Attitudes and Other Important Goals

The conflict between the moves he *must* make and the attitudes he *hopes* to create establishes the most fascinating and possibly the most important problem with which adjusters contend.

By words and attitudes an adjuster hopes to reinforce non-aggressive claims attitudes much as if he were saying, "I trust you and your intent to hold your claim within reasonable limits." But he must take statements and he must confirm expenses, for he can never know when a claimant is going to develop aggressive characteristics. He must perform these inherently defensive moves so that his actions do not convey mistrust and inspire a claimant to retaliate by resort to litigation.

In a way, an adjuster is like the mother who says to her daughter, "I trust you—but I am going to sit on the couch with you and your date." Her words try to inspire trustworthiness—but her actions will certainly inspire a red-blooded girl to try to outwit her chaperone.

The hallmark of a really good adjuster is the honesty and restraint of his claimants, and much of this is far from accidental. An adjuster does much to create these attitudes by dealing with the claimant so as to appeal to the more reasonable elements in his character. He does this while carrying out his defensive moves (statements, verifications, etc.) in such a way that the claimant is not challenged to outwit or overcome him.

DEFINITIONS

Before examining the interests involved and the nature of the adjusting process itself, it is well that certain definitions be reviewed.

Loss

A loss has been defined, for insurance purposes, as *"an unintentional decline in, or disappearance of, value resulting from a contingency."* [3] Although the liability insurance contract is a two party agreement (a contract between the insured and insurer), a third party—a person who is not a party to the contract and who has suffered damages allegedly because of the acts of the insured—is involved in every loss. This is why liability insurance is often spoken of as "third party insurance."

The "third party" may then attempt to transfer his *loss* to the insured, making a *claim* against him, alleging that the insured's negligent conduct was the cause of the "third party's" loss. It would serve no useful purpose to compensate a man with a broken leg by breaking the leg of the man who had injured him, therefore damages are defined and treated as the *money value* of the property damage, bodily injury or death loss sustained by this third party. If the claimant-third party is successful in his effort to transfer this loss, it becomes the insured's loss, and *this* loss is the loss against which a liability contract is designed to protect.

An insured is exposed not only to the danger of being required to pay for the damage he may do, but he may be required to pay sums levied against him by the application of one or another of the aggressive claims techniques mentioned earlier in this chapter.

The protection afforded by a liability insurance contract is twofold: a promise on the part of the insurer "to pay on behalf of the insured all sums which he is legally obligated to pay" by reason of those negligent acts which are covered under the contract; and the necessary collateral provision of service in the

---

[3] Robert I. Mehr and Emerson Cammack, *Principles of Insurance* (Richard D. Irwin, Homewood, Illinois, 1961), p. 22.

form of claims investigation, settlement and, where necessary, defense of lawsuits.[4] Except in workmen's compensation for industrial injuries, and sometimes in contractual and product liability situations, the meaning of "legally obligated to pay" is defined in the negligence law of the jurisdiction of the occurrence. Hence, *insured losses* include the *cost* of investigation and the defense of lawsuits and, where a valid claim arises, the amount (subject to the policy limits) which is determined to be the *money value of the damages* sustained by the "third party" claimant. Without liability insurance, the insured would have to bear all of these losses from his own resources, to the extent that he is able.

Claims

Strictly speaking, a *claim* may be defined as a *demand for damages due or allegedly due and based upon a legal right.* In liability insurance, a claim is made by the third party against the insured, alleging damages suffered through the insured's negligent act. Since, according to the terms of the liability insurance contract, the insurer agrees to defend, and pay on behalf of the insured "all sums which he is legally obligated to pay," the insurer acts as the representative of and for the insured in answering the claim.

In actual practice, claims are not handled quite this way. So universal is the knowledge of the principles of legal redress that all insurance companies upon the happening of any accident (unless the circumstances are such that it is all but impossible for the claimant to rationalize himself into blaming the insured), anticipate the assertion of a claim. Far from waiting for claimants to come and make their claims, adjusters may take the initiative. If a third party potential claimant does not have an adjuster on his doorstep within a very few days post-accident, he will likely be offended and resentful (and rationalize himself into suing for an injury when he might otherwise have been happy to limit

---

[4] The negligent acts complained of must be covered under the policy. This involves a distinction between "coverage" and "legal liability." This is discussed later.

his claim to property damage). Adjusting practice recognizes this likelihood. Hence, as a matter of practice, every reported accident is termed a "claim" by adjusters even though no demand is actually made, and procedures appropriate to the circumstances are initiated.

Adjusting—Adjustment

Adjusting refers to the entire process of investigating, evaluating and disposing of claims.

Adjustment refers to the disposition of a claim by agreement, the signing of a release, and the passage of money. Oddly enough, liability adjusters almost never use the word "adjust" or "adjusting." They say that they "settled" or "got together with him" or "got rid of" the claim. Fire men, too, by the way, seldom "adjust" a loss; they "close" their files.

The author offers no explanation for this strange reluctance to employ the word which describes his vocation.

Some Other Definitions

Investigation is the process of accumulating and recording facts. More specifically, investigation is the process of gathering and recording the facts with regard to:

1. The *insurance contract* in relation to the insured and the facts surrounding the claim, in order to evaluate the applicability of the insurance coverage.
2. *The occurrence* for purposes of evaluating the liability of the insured. Do the circumstances surrounding the claim indicate that the insured is legally responsible?
3. The *nature and severity of the injuries,* for the purpose of estimating the amount of damages.

Evaluation refers to the continuous process of forming an opinion regarding the *value* of a particular claim. Many factors influence value. A partial list could include:

Potential judgment values
The facts of the occurrence
The likelihood of a jury returning a plaintiff's or a defendant's verdict

The nature of the injury
The location of the accident
The attitude of the claimant
The quality and availability of witnesses, etc.

The disposition of a claim varies with the facts of each circumstance. In most instances, the adjuster negotiates with the third party claimant, and, where agreement is reached, the execution of a release relieves the insurer of any further obligation to the claimant and evidences the settlement thus arrived at.

Negotiation does not always lead to agreement. The third party claimant and the adjuster may not agree on the facts of the accident or occurrence. Doctors may disagree about the nature and extent of the injury. The adjuster and the claimant may agree on all these matters but disagree widely on the pecuniary value of the damage. The hope is that the adjuster will be able to persuade others to his point of view, even to that extreme, the acquiescence if necessary in a complete denial of liability.

If disagreements cannot be reconciled, the third party claimant may exercise his right to have the issue resolved in a court of law. The court's resolution of the issues takes the form of a *judgment,* an award of money, or a denial of any damages at all. It is true that the purpose of a claims department is to close claims—and trials do close claims, but this route is long, expensive, and in the end likely to be unsatisfactory to all parties concerned. A claim disposed of by litigation represents a failure of the adjusting process.

The peaceful disposition of claims—that is to say, adjusting— requires judgment, knowledge and techniques not otherwise found in business and industry. Thus, the technical, professional services of adjusters are required even by corporations so large that they assume their own risks and thus dispense with insurance. Even though financially able to sustain their own losses, such firms, in order to control the cost of the claims against them and to control and modify the aggressiveness and claims-mindedness of the day, maintain their own staffs or employ independent adjusters.

THE ADJUSTER AND HIS PUBLIC

Even this brief exposure to liability claim adjusting should have suggested seemingly unending conflicts. The nature of the hazard insured virtually guarantees controversy, and yet every effort must be made to reach an agreement as promptly as possible. Culpable negligence is often less than clear-cut. Injury and damage, seemingly unambiguous words, are frequently the subject of honest controversy. Negligence, injury and damage may be, although they rarely are, the subject of the most harmonious agreement; but, even if they are, there is no scale of values to turn this agreement into dollars and cents.

Many people, therefore, are involved in relationships with great possibilities for disagreement. The relationship between the claimant and the insured is adversative in nature. Doctors and lawyers may be in conflict with their fellow practitioners and with each other. Garage repairmen may disagree with other repairmen or estimators. Joint defendants dispute with each other, as well as with the plaintiffs. There are conflicts between the producing agent and his insurer, the agent and his insured, witnesses and even courts of law. The list seems endless, for conflict and controversy are daily facts of the liability business. Because of the controversy over liability, doubt as to damage, and the absence of a scale of values, *compromise* is a feature of many settlements. The adjuster soon learns that his world is neither black nor white; it is varying shades of gray.

Probably the most important skill of the liability adjuster is his ability to minimize controversy and achieve agreement. In his small way, he is a peacemaker. Peacemakers have been well spoken of by High Authority.

The Adjuster and the Defendant-Insured

When the insured causes injury or damage to another person, it is nothing less than good business that his case receive prompt and courteous attention by the insurer. But this is not enough. Although the company has obligated itself to assume his obligations, it helps that he be assured that his company is doing everything possible to protect *his* interests in the case. To be faced with the possibility of a lawsuit is a frightening thing. The insured's fright may be anything from mild concern to an outright case of "the shakes." It is the insurer's function to furnish the insured with the protection which he purchased; it will help the adjuster to see some of the broader aspects of his calling if he sees it as his *privilege* to bring the insured the assurance that his interests *are* protected in every phase of the adjusting procedure. Without this attention, the purchase of the insurance contract, while it may reduce the risk of financial loss, may not give peace of mind.

The adjusting service which an insured needs is more than a comforting pat on the back. Even if he has the money to pay for damage caused by his alleged negligence, an insured's notions of legal liability are usually rudimentary and often wrong. He has neither the time nor know-how to accumulate evidence upon which his liability may be determined, and is even less able to evaluate the evidence once it is collected. He does not know how to reach an agreement with a claimant on his damages. Very likely he does not know how to raise a question without provoking a battle. He has a technical problem. He needs the services of a technician.

The Adjuster and the Claimant

In the United States today, few claimants are less than keenly aware that they have a legal right to make a claim against a person who has caused them injury and damage through negligence. Along with much misinformation, knowledge of this legal right, increasingly present in our society, brings with it an increasing tendency to pursue this legal right to a conclusion.

The circumstances in which they meet place the adjuster and the claimant in a position in which they are essentially adversaries. Yet, if the claim is to be disposed of without the expense of litigation, some way to agree rather than to disagree must be found. The duty of finding this way rests on the adjuster's shoulders. The point has already been made that moral judgment of even so questionable a thing as fraud has no place in an adjuster's world. It therefore follows that an adjuster certainly cannot afford to criticize a claimant's decision to pursue his legal rights, or even to make unreasonable demands. While an adjuster may be required to *oppose* a claimant's demands, his course is to *persuade* the claimant into some more desirable attitude. Judgment, disapproval and condemnation, whether expressed or implied by his demeanor, are not for the adjuster. Restrained claimants—people more than willing to meet an adjuster halfway—still outnumber their aggressive brothers to whom a claim is an *opportunity*.

Successful adjusters do not hesitate to see their claimants as real flesh and blood and to sense the realities of their injuries. To be effective, an adjuster ought to see the claimant as a fellow-man, with feelings, faults and aspirations not greatly different from his own. This helps to establish and maintain the vital bridge of communication. It also protects the adjuster from zealous overreaching in the hard bargaining that is often a feature of difficult settlements.

Adjuster-Attorney Relationship

Because of the legal nature of the insurance contract and the liability situation, and the frequent need to settle issues by litigation, attorneys are often involved in the handling of claims. They may appear as representatives of the claimant (plaintiff) or the insured (defendant). The nature of the business demands that the specialized knowledge of attorneys be sought in many situations. The adjuster, therefore, negotiates with attorneys as adversaries, works with his own counsel in litigation, and often turns to attorneys for guidance in situations involving questions of law. In order that the respective responsibilities and duties of the adjuster and attorney might be clearly understood by both parties, the Conference Committee on Adjusters formulated for adoption on January 8, 1939, a *Statement of Principles on Respective Rights and Duties of Lawyers and Laymen in the Business of Adjusting Insurance Claims*. This document is shown in the Appendix under its even more lengthy current title. The standards which are detailed in the *Statement of Principles* are, in many ways, much broader in concept than merely explaining the "respective rights and duties of lawyers and laymen in the business of adjusting insurance claims." Complaints concerning insurance adjusters or attorneys respecting their conduct in handling insurance claims are referred to the Conference Committee whose duty it is to investigate such complaints and recommend or take action necessary to correct any practices contrary to public interest. This *Statement of Principles* should be studied with care. All reputable insurance and adjusting firms subscribe to and endeavor to enforce conformity to these principles.

Note that the *Statement of Principles* prohibits an adjuster from attempting to negotiate settlement with a claimant represented by an attorney, without consent of the attorney. Violation of this prohibition is a serious breach of ethical and professional conduct. It is probably in this prohibition that the *Statement of Principles* most often touches the daily work of adjusters. The marks of a professional are knowledge, ability and integrity. The last is not the least important of these.

The Adjuster and the Insurer

Since insurers are dealing in a service, a prime competitive weapon between them is the *quality* of the service rendered. Although the insurance contract is important at all times to an insured's peace of mind, once the covered contingency takes place that contract immediately assumes an importance that might easily surpass in value anything else that he possesses.

It is difficult to overemphasize that promptness and courtesy are not only good public relations; they are important (even essential) means of arriving at favorable adjustments.

The insurer's stake in the *amount* of settlement also requires examination.

Unrealistic under-evaluation and consequent refusal to pay claims may provide a temporary profit advantage for the individual insurer, but it may also lead to the establishment of an unfavorable reputation with the public and within the business. (In fact, if this practice were followed by a large number of insurers, it could undermine the institution of private insurance in a free-enterprise economy.) Such a reputation might result in loss of business, lower profits, and instability. Further, unwise denial of claims and unwillingness to recognize values encourage litigation. The profit advantage, if any, is short-lived, for if a claim is underpriced, it may be taken as a foregone conclusion that a jury will not be reluctant to rectify the error. This leaves the insurer obligated not only for a judgment—often in excess of the amount for which the claim could have been settled—but for an attorney's fee as well. The claims business knows no luxury so expensive as *unsuccessful* litigation.

Neither can insurers pay claims where there is no liability nor overpay legitimate claims. Insurers classify each loss exposure according to the likelihood and potential severity of the loss. Rates which are based upon the average loss experience of a particular classification are developed for each classification. Thus, rates reflect the *average* loss exposure for the class. If the insurer consistently overpays its claims (assuming proper underwriting), its loss experience will be worse than average for the class, and the premiums collected, based on such rates, will be inadequate.

Achieving the proper balance between underpayment and overpayment is therefore important to the competitive position of the individual insurer.

The Adjuster and the Insuring Public

In this review of the persons with whom an adjuster is concerned, the interests in whose behalf he exerts his efforts, and the pressures which they exert upon him, one more has to be considered: the insured—not in the sense of the man who has had an accident and whom the adjuster will probably meet in person, but a more remote person: the insured in the sense of the anonymous, faceless person who pays for it all, buys his policy annually, never has been and perhaps never will be involved in an accident. His principal contact with the insurance business is to pay a premium. He supports the insurance mechanism. He knows that accidents happen and that bent fenders and broken bones cost money. To him, insurance is only an item of expense—a cost—and while he does not mind pulling his fair share of the load, he certainly does not wish to pay more than necessary. Such a man is quite right when he says that, "It is not a big corporation's money that the adjuster is spending; it's my money."

It was observed previously that perhaps the adjuster has no right to criticize or ignore a claimant who may seem unreasonable or demanding, or who simply says, "More." Neither can he ignore or neglect the faceless insured on the sidelines, whose simple plea is, "Less."

It is not just for an insurance company that an adjuster raises questions, opposes built-up claims, bargains, and seeks newer and better ways of persuading claimants to moderate their demands. It is for the public that pays the bills that he does all of this.

HANDLING CLAIMS

Adjusting has now been considered externally, as it were, in the light of the society in which it takes place and certain features of that society, and in the light of the persons with whom an adjuster deals, the interests he represents, and the pressures exerted upon him.

In order to understand adjusting as a process, it is necessary to examine the work itself; that is, the goals sought, the actual progress of a claim, the nature of decisions made en route, the techniques employed by adjusters to attain their ends, and the peculiar nature of fact or reality as adjusters attempt to work with it.

Goals

The mention that has already been made of closing claims by settlement, closing by litigation, and closing by denial (a few other ways to close claims will be mentioned before this volume is finished) may already have conveyed the underlying purpose that pervades everything adjusters do. To state it simply, *an adjuster's purpose is to close claims.* It is to be regretted that the property insurance man's habit of speaking of "closing" losses has not more thoroughly penetrated the casualty adjuster's vocabulary.

"He moves his cases." This phrase in one form or another is one of the highest expressions of praise in the business. It implies not only that an adjuster "settles" cases, but also that he works to a purpose; that his investigations, his attempts to persuade others, and his decisions combine to advance his claims purposefully and with a minimum of misdirected effort toward the goal: a closed file.

Because there are many paths to this goal, decisions must be made both as to the goals to be sought and as to the methods to be employed to attain them. Since in many of his efforts an adjuster is actively opposed, and because much of his work consists of persuading others to his point of view, techniques to further the success of his efforts are needed. A look at the progress of a claim tells something of the decisions required.

The Progress of a Claim

The history of a claim as it progresses from an accident to its eventual disposition discloses the varied and shifting requirements of the work of liability adjusting.

One claimant leans over backward to minimize his claim. The next, no less honest, simply and good-naturedly wants to get everything he can for his injury. Clearly, one challenge is quite different from the other. Changing situations call for dramatic shifts in work functions, and in the results an adjuster attempts to achieve. The pressures of the various interests of the several people to whom his work bears a relationship also express themselves directly or indirectly on an adjuster's decisions to investigate or not to investigate, to settle or not to settle, or to change his ideas about value. The several different ways of closing claims, and the courses to each, color his decisions as he exerts his efforts in one direction or another.

One well-known authority [5] has outlined four general phases of claims handling procedures:

---

[5] Patrick Magarick, *Successful Handling of Casualty Claims* (Prentice-Hall, Inc., New York, 1955), p. 5.

1. Proper preparation
2. Prompt and thorough investigation
3. Decision and acting
4. Adequate reporting

It is interesting to contrast this with the diagram on page 20.

The author[6] of that diagram did not, I think, intend to create one, it seems to be something more than mere coincidence that the final shape of his figure approximates a circle, rather than a line. The circle demonstrates a feature of the business that this book will refer to repeatedly—the circular or interrelated character of claims work. Almost everything that is done is conditioned by what has gone before, and what one does in the beginning is influenced, if not determined, by what one hopes to accomplish in the end. The claims business is not a straightforward progression from phase 1 to phase 2, and 3, and 4; it is instead a continual process of information-getting, decision-making, and zig-zag progress toward a goal.

Decisions—Judgment

Decisions imply a need for judgment. Judgment in turn implies weighing factors and selecting between two or more alternatives, with no alternative wholly right and none all wrong. This is quite a different thing from learning that in Situation A one responds with Action 1.

Judgments are quantitative as well as qualitative. Each of us was taught in first grade that one does not add apples to oranges; yet in the claims business one must not only evaluate but do so by combining dissimilar elements. In effect, in the claims business one *does* add apples to hammers, or at least if this is not quite what happens, something very like it does.

An adjuster's work requires him repeatedly to balance one account of an event against another and to form an opinion not only of what took place but—and this is of more practical importance—an opinion as to what a jury will conclude took place. Disputed matters seldom permit clear-cut decisions; an adjuster

---

[6] John W. Hall, Professor of Insurance, Georgia State College, Educational Consultant to the National Association of Independent Insurance Adjusters.

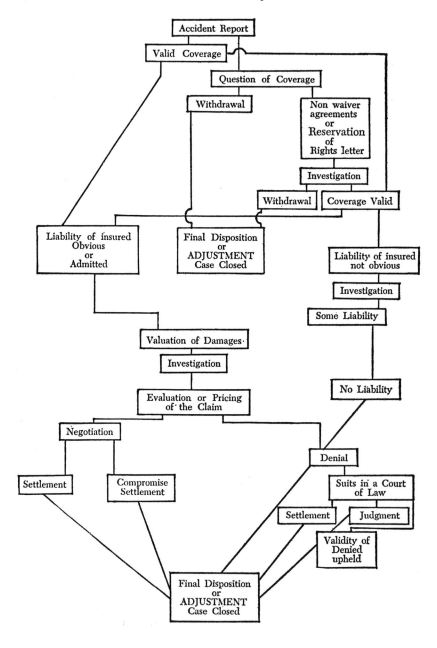

often has to work with opinions in the form of probabilities. "I think it is four to one that the decision will go against us," or to put it more laboriously, "If we had five cases like this to try, we would probably lose most of them, but some juries would see it our way—I judge that we would win once in five times." This is one aspect of judgment.

Injuries, too, present questions of judgment. Dr. A says there is no permanent injury, but Dr. T says there is. How much *will* a jury award?

The same claim may present questions of both liability and injury, and the opinion an adjuster holds after he has weighed these and possibly other factors must be expressed in terms of money. His opinion as to the claim's value governs his decision to pay or not to pay, or perhaps to pay but not more than a certain amount.

It would be premature to point out now the many other areas in which an adjuster is asked for judgment or experience. Experience will bring them to his attention. Later chapters will point out others. The adjuster's world, to repeat, is neither black nor white, but many shades of gray.

Common Sense

The emphasis so far placed on the lack of positive guidelines and of established precedents may at first seem discouraging. If this is so, this is not the result intended. The intent, of course, is to paint a picture—and the picture that this book intends to paint may differ from the conventional instructions to young adjusters. These instructions are usually so heavily larded with such adjectives as "prompt," "thorough," "complete," "detailed," that young adjusters can hardly be blamed for wondering, "How can I be prompt about everything? Surely something must come first, and something must wait." "How can I be thorough? A philosopher is said to have spent a lifetime studying a square foot of ground—and at the end to have felt that he had only scratched its surface. Surely even a simple accident must present enough complexities to tie me up for a month—yet I'll be expected to handle several accidents of considerable complexity in that time." This is a *truly* discouraging picture, and a young man could hardly be blamed if he quailed at such an impossible prospect. It may be helpful if for the impressive word "judgment" there be substituted, for the time being at least, the more comfortable term "common sense." Claims work places a premium on common sense, even if it is called for in a bewildering multitude of situations.

Some further observations may brighten a still possibly forbidding prospect. Supervisors and claims managers are familiar with the phenomenon of the young adjuster who, almost from the day he starts, seems to know instinctively what to do. It is not uncommon for such a man, in a very few months, to be handling death claims—the bulk of the really heavy work in an office. It is not easy to identify the qualities that make these neophytes so successful, but their progress is encouraging evidence that no deep mystery underlies this business. However, to avoid confusing those not so fortunate, it should be made clear that these fortunate ones are a minority. Many successful adjusters pass through a long period of advanced confusion.

The personal experience of even a very young adjuster should confirm another phenomenon that wholly refutes the proposition that effective claims action is necessarily based on a vast body of difficult knowledge, the understanding of which is given only to a chosen few and then only after a long novitiate. This common phenomenon is demonstrated every time an untrained claimant successfully manages his claims against an insurer. Even so short a time as a month should have exposed an adjuster to several persons who, completely without prior claims experience and often with little formal education, have sustained property damage or injury and have managed their claims skillfully, wisely and successfully. Their problems are an adjuster's problems, and their skills his; only the direction of their effort was reversed.

Common sense, judgment, the successful selection of alternatives, are commonplace in life and an adjuster should no more be dismayed than a mother is dismayed when she looks out the window and sees her toddler walking on the top of a brick wall. Does she let him climb? He may fall. Admittedly, the risk is remote, but he could be hurt. On the other hand, the last thing she wants to do is to make a "sissy" of him. She has no precedent to refer to. Decisions with no precedents to guide him, therefore, will be no new thing to a young adjuster; he has been making them all his life.

When the water is cold, one doesn't climb down the ladder; it's head-first and get it over with. There is no point in not making it clear from the first that the young adjuster will make endless decisions, and the shifting pattern of circumstances that presents questions to him will insure that judgment (or common sense) rather than knowledge as such, or precedent, will be his most frequent guide.

This book will attempt to identify the more common questions presented, attempt to point out contexts in which they occur, and suggest the factors to be weighed.

Techniques

Closely related to decisions are the *techniques* of adjusting. A purist might argue that techniques are only the application of a related body of decisions to some commonly recurring circumstances, as one might argue that the writing of a statement is nothing more than making a series of decisions—what to ask, how to ask it, when and how to write it. Whether such a process is a technique or merely a series of related decisions is unimportant.

Claims work does present a number of situations (writing statements and checking lost time and wages are only two examples), and for many of them insurers have, by trial and error, developed widely accepted procedures for efficient and successful handling. These techniques will be detailed as the progress of the text brings these several situations to light.

Salesmanship and Persuasion

The need to sell, to persuade someone to his point of view, is implicit in many claims situations. A witness is reluctant to tell what he knows; an adjuster attempts to persuade him that he has a conscientious duty to speak up. An adjuster tries to "sell" a body shop that he, the adjuster, will approve a reasonable estimate, that it is unwise and unnecessary to pad the estimate in order to come out with a profit on a repair job. The list is endless, and persuasion or salesmanship is an essential characteristic of a successful adjuster. An attempt will be made to identify the areas calling for persuasion, and some persuasive techniques will be explored.

Facts—Three Levels of Significance

The prevalence of contention and the frequent antagonistic relationship of the parties involved in a claim have already been made clear. These conditions, then, impose upon adjusters the frequent need to determine facts, to investigate, and bring us to one of the aspects of the business which laymen find most difficult to accept. Because a proper perspective in respect to it is an absolute essential, this aspect must be made clear.

What is so perplexing to someone not a part of the insurance business is the idea that there are various "levels" of fact—or reality, if one prefers. The proposition might be restated to this effect: A fact may appear to an adjuster on any of three levels, and the same fact will mean one thing on one level, something quite different on the second, and something entirely different again at the third level. An example from the field of fidelity bonding (even though bonding is significantly different from insurance) demonstrates the point.

To understand the account which is about to follow, it is necessary to understand that the usual fidelity bond provides that coverage for the dishonest acts of any employe ceases as soon as an employer has knowledge of that employe's dishonesty. This provides bonding companies with the defense known as "condonement."

It is also necessary to know that the law considers that knowledge by an officer of a corporation is the same as knowledge by the corporation itself. Consider now the same fact as it appears on three levels.

D stole small sums of money from his employer, a loan company. M, the company's treasurer, discovered D's dishonesty, and D admitted his thefts to M. Later D stole large sums of money and left the state, and the loan company entered a claim under its bond.

D consented to be interviewed (outside the state) and in fact was the person who disclosed M's role.

The fact of M's knowledge, then, was at the first level—a *truth* but useless without further developments.

M was located, furnished a statement and later a deposition confirming D's account in all details, and adding confirmatory embellishments. He agreed to testify when needed.

The "fact" of M's knowledge was then at the second level—it was *evidence,* and ready to be offered.

At the trial, since the bonding company resisted the claim, M did testify exactly as he had said he would, *but the jury returned a finding against the bonding company for the full amount of D's thefts.*

The "fact" of M's knowledge was then at a third level—a level of complete insignificance, for the supreme court refused to overturn the verdict. As far as being a "fact" was concerned, M's knowledge was of less significance than it would have been had it never happened.

Accordingly, in any disputed matter, an adjuster must learn that "facts," as he is accustomed to think of them, are really nothing more than *clues* until he can reduce them to evidence.

Having reduced fact to evidence, the adjuster has still to attain his goal, for, as older adjusters and attorneys will tell him, "A fact just isn't a fact until a jury says it's so," or, all the evidence of his senses to the contrary, if a jury says, "It's not so," then "It's *not* so."

In practical terms, this means that adjusters are interested not only in the question, "Was he hurt?" but in the deeper question, "Will the jury say he was hurt?"; not only in, "Who was to blame?" but in the attempt to forecast the really significant fact, "Who will the *jury* say was to blame?"

Many adjusters never do adjust their thinking to this shift in their traditional concept of fact. The problems presented by this shift are with an adjuster all his business life. They should, therefore, immediately be understood, grasped and accepted. They are an integral part of the business.

CONCLUSION

The adjuster's first duty is to do what is *necessary* so that proper disposition can be made of a claim at the earliest possible moment and at a money level satisfactory to the interests he represents. Ideally, ultimate disposition should be by agreement. (Here agreement includes successful denial of a claim.) This is a business where there are no absolutes.

An adjuster is not told to investigate every claim thoroughly —some claims he will not investigate at all.

An investigator is not told always to make a complete report —in many instances this is not desired.

He will be told that he should know something of the law, but that it is only part of the picture.

He will learn that people, their attitudes and emotions, are overwhelmingly important, but he may never forget the formal structure of the law in the background.

Some successful adjusters are back-slapping salesmen; others, equally successful, wear steel-rimmed spectacles and act the part. An adjuster is told, "Be yourself."

No adjuster can give every claimant everything he wants, but if he becomes a heartless automaton, he violates his conscience and he will be ineffective.

The adjuster is in a constant relationship to the defendant (insured), his employer (or client), the claimant (or his attorney), and the insuring public. Willingly or not, he is subject to all their conflicting pressures, and he will respond in some measure. These pressures, it may occur to him, are not really directed at him but at one another. He is only the means by which they resolve themselves. His participation is not passive. He has a great deal to do with the eventual outcome.

Undisturbed by exaggerated claims, he recognizes them as one of the world's imperfections and he deals with them as effectively as he can. He does his best for the "faceless insured" but he neither expects nor hopes to settle every claim for a nominal release.

This chapter has carefully avoided such terms as "fair value," "just claims" and "proper settlement" which have little meaning in and of themselves. They must be defined by each adjuster according to his own sense of propriety in relation to the circumstances of each claim.

The adjuster sees the claimant as a human being, complete with wants, needs, and suffering real injuries. The adjuster *will* be more successful if he has an active conscience and is responsive to his own desire to do justice.

The truly successful adjuster sets a formidable goal for himself. He seeks to satisfy his own conscience, tries to exercise sound judgment, desires to serve others and to be loyal to his employer; he is familiar with, and skillfully exercises, sound and efficient techniques, attempts to preserve his own integrity and a warm feeling for others. He tries always to be a persuasive spokesman on behalf of those he represents. Many of these qualities will at times conflict with one another. How he develops, uses and harmonizes them will also be the subject of this book.

CHAPTER 2

Legal Background

INTRODUCTION

Chapter 1 depicted adjusting as an activity deeply influenced by, but sharply differentiated from, law. It would indeed be difficult to adjust without some knowledge of law, for liability contracts themselves promise "to pay on behalf of the insured all sums [within the policy limits] which the insured shall become legally obligated to pay as damages."

In the end, claims not disposed of by agreement will be settled in the courts of law. The most careful reading of policies, however, fails to disclose any definition of the phrase, "legally obligated to pay," nor will a comprehensive definition be found anywhere.

Since an adjuster will be constantly dealing with the law, he should be capable of recognizing and applying some legal principles which this chapter will discuss briefly.

An adjuster's relationship to the law is not so much a matter of knowing what the law may be on a given point but, rather, a matter of knowing where an adjuster stands in relation to questions presented, what he attempts to prove or disprove, and the directions in which he decides to exert his efforts. For example, we may consider the question of *contributory negligence*— a concept to be explained later in the chapter. Contributory negligence has one effect on a claimant's right to collect damages in some states, and a quite different effect in others. However, whatever may be the *effect* of his findings, it is always an adjuster's duty to find out the extent to which a claimant's own carelessness contributed to his injury and to accumulate, if possible, evidence tending to demonstrate that carelessness.

One way for adjusters to look at legal principles is to see them as so many division lines. The adjuster will usually be found on one side of the line and the claimant on the other. Where the line is drawn may vary from state to state, from court to court, or even from jury to jury—in actual practice the location of the division line may even vary from case to case. Where the line is drawn may be a variable, but the adjuster's efforts in respect to the direction of the claims he handles will be reassuringly constant. Experience will, in a remarkably short time, acquaint an adjuster with some very fine points in respect to the law. By experience, he will learn with surprising precision where his jurisdiction draws some of the important dividing lines. But, the function of a text on the *fundamentals* of liability claim adjusting is to give simply the necessary orientation. It is in that sense that the principles of law to be discussed in this chapter will be taken up.

The law is constantly changing and seldom is there a ruling without exception or a ruling that is uniform in all jurisdictions. New decisions constantly limit or enlarge old concepts and new concepts are always being created. In seemingly clear-cut situations, the best legal minds may differ and arrive at different conclusions, or at the same conclusion by different legal avenues. Courts and judges sometimes reverse themselves and in the process overrule their prior holdings.

"Law consists of the entire body of principles which govern conduct and the observance of which can be enforced by the courts." [1] Law includes the constitutions of the national and state governments. It includes statutes adopted by the United States Congress and the legislatures of the various states. Further, each city and county has the power to adopt ordinances or local statutes.

Law also includes "common law" and "case law." *Common* law is a body of rules and principles derived from customs and usages or from court judgments which recognize such customs and usages. *Case* law is the aggregate of reported cases. The theory of case law is that a decision on a given point becomes precedent and hence influential, if not controlling, in respect to subsequent decisions on the same point.

---

[1] Ronald S. Anderson and Walter A. Kumpf, *Business Law Principles and Cases*, (South-Western Publishing Co., Cincinnati, 1958) p. 1.

There is a wealth of decisions of ancient vintage which are and continue to be the law of today. Newer case law may restate the old principles, alter them in some respects, make exceptions to them, and in some instances completely reverse those principles. As a general rule, older case law, or common case law, is recognized but exceptions are made to it by virtue of differing factual situations. Because of the great factual diversity involved in a seemingly infinite variety of situations, tort law relies heavily upon this case-to-case approach rather than the statutory approach to its problems.

At no time will this book attempt to state "the law" pertaining to a given situation. The law differs from jurisdiction to jurisdiction and the complications introduced by complex and shifting "fact situations" effectively prevent any authoritative over-all statement of the law. Both in reading this book and in day-to-day work, an adjuster should be cautious about drawing too many legal conclusions without competent legal assistance.

RUDIMENTS OF TORT LAW

Inasmuch as that field of law with which he will be most concerned is known as the law of *torts*,[2] the adjuster should be acquainted with those principles of tort law which will enable him properly to perform his work.

A tort is the *civil wrong* which arises from the violation of a legal right that is not created by a contract. The consequences of the wrong are *private*, and the redress for such a tort is a *civil action* seeking an award of *money damages* to compensate the damaged or injured party.

The person who has suffered a loss because of the wrongful acts of another and who seeks redress for it in a court of law is a *plaintiff*.[3] The person committing a tort is the tortfeasor or *defendant*.

---

[2] While a legal obligation to pay damages may arise from a breach of contract and thus involve the law of *contracts*, this rarely occurs with regard to the automobile liability situation, the principal subject of this chapter.

[3] Claimants come under legal terminology when their claims become lawsuits and they become *plaintiffs*, and insureds become *defendants*. For the balance of this chapter it will be assumed that the matters under discussion are before a court of law; therefore, claimants will be referred to as plaintiffs and insureds as defendants.

The basic elements of a tort are:

1. A duty owed
2. A breach of that duty
3. Injury or damage as a result of that breach
   (An important qualification of the third element, so important that it is sometimes considered as the *fourth* element, is that the injury or damage must be the *proximate* result of the second element, the breach.)

The burden of proving the elements of a tort rests upon the party making the claim. This is referred to as the "burden of proof," and it places on the plaintiff the duty of affirmatively proving the facts in issue or of establishing the truth of his claim by a preponderance of the evidence. This does not mean that he has to use more witnesses or exhibits than his opponents, but means that his evidence must be more *credible* or *believable* than his opponent's. One good witness or exhibit—such as a photograph—as opposed to many indefinite or confused witnesses has established this burden and won many lawsuits.

Although the burden of proving the elements of the tort rests upon the plaintiff, the opportunity of proving defenses (but also the burden of offering the evidence necessary to those proofs) rests upon the defendant.

Two particular aspects of the phrase "burden of proof," as it affects adjusting, may require explanation. One of these stems from a common misconception concerning the word "proof."

To a layman the word "proof" corresponds closely to the following dictionary [4] definition: ". . . the essence of logical proof consists in so combining propositions which we know, *that we finally see some other proposition to be a necessary admission . . .*" [Italics supplied.] "Proof" as lawyers use the term does not have the element of *compelling* a conclusion. For adjusters' purposes, the sense in which law uses the term can be taken as being synonymous with "evidence."

In the phrase "burden of proof," the word "burden" embraces the idea of weighing the evidence, deciding which is the more credible, determining whom to believe, etc. It is in relation to a subsidiary idea which derives from the "burden" that adjusters

---

[4] Funk and Wagnalls New Standard Dictionary, Funk & Wagnalls Co., 1913.

most commonly are concerned with this phrase and it is this subsidiary idea which in adjuster's vernacular is often conveyed by the phrase "burden of proof." To prove something by a *preponderance of evidence* requires the offer of *some* evidence. Plaintiffs may fail to sustain their burden by failing to offer *any* evidence. Testimony must sometimes be examined with a fine-tooth comb to determine whether it includes *any* evidence relative to the point the plaintiff has the duty to prove. Failure of the plaintiff to offer *any* evidence on a critical point may cause the judge to direct a verdict for the defendant. It is the failure or inability of the plaintiff to offer *any* evidence that adjusters usually speak of in connection with failure to satisfy the "burden of proof."

On the other hand, the offer of at least *something* satisfies the burden. The weight to be given to that offering is something which the court decides later.

To combine the two ideas, then: If in a law suit a plaintiff has the burden of proving that he was disabled, he is said, in adjusting parlance, to have satisfied the burden if he offers *any* competent testimony that he was disabled. It makes no difference that his opponent may have offered more or better evidence that he was not disabled. It is also beside the point that the court may find the evidence of disability unpersuasive and find in favor of the defendant. After the "burden" (in this sense) has been satisfied, the court may believe or disbelieve the plaintiff's evidence or it may find the defendant's evidence more believable, but if the plaintiff has failed to sustain the burden by failing to offer *any evidence at all*, then the court may *not* find for the plaintiff.

Each of the elements of a tort will now be considered briefly along with the qualification referred to as "the fourth element." The various defenses available to defendants will also be considered.

The First Element (Duty Owed)

Whenever a person moves among other persons, the law exerts pressure on him to compel him to attempt to conform to a minimum standard of conduct for the protection of the general public's security. A defendant cannot be held liable to a plaintiff to whom no duty is owed. The duty to use care is not a matter of moral right; it is a duty imposed by law [5]—a violation of which is an unlawful act.

The law does not demand of every person constant exercise of the highest degree of caution in order not to injure other persons. Such a high standard would result in complete inaction. Instead, *for different circumstances, the law imposes varying degrees of care.*

The duty owed by a driver of a motor vehicle to others on the highway is, in the absence of a special relationship between the parties, that of "ordinary care." That duty may change as the relationships change. The transportation of someone for a *profit* imposes a higher standard of care. A taxi driver cruising for customers owes a pedestrian crossing the street the duty of ordinary care; but if the pedestrian becomes a paying passenger in that taxi, the driver owes him a higher degree of care. [6]

The existence of a purely *social relationship* may lead to a diminished duty (a lower standard of care). If, for instance, the driver of a private vehicle picks up a friend, the duty owed may change to a lower standard or may remain the same, depending on the jurisdiction. If, as the ride continues, the car gets stuck in the snow, the passenger gets out to push and the car backs over him, still another question comes up: Is he a "pedestrian" or still a "passenger"? In some states he is one and in some he is the other. The important thing is to recognize that changes in fact may alter the duty owed.

---

[5] Here "law" does not necessarily mean statute law, such as a traffic code. The more usual violation is of the common law derived standard of care, which will be discussed shortly, when the question of the breach of the duty owed is considered.

[6] This raises a question: Suppose the pedestrian hails the driver, the driver acknowledges the hail and, while he is bringing his cab to a stop, the pedestrian foolishly darts in front of it to reach the door on the opposite side, is struck and injured. Was he a "pedestrian" or a "passenger" when he was hit? An experienced adjuster might call his attorney before trying to decide *that* question, but a raw rookie is expected to recognize that the shifting relationship between the parties may also change the duty owed, and therefore the particulars of the change in relationship should be covered carefully in his investigation.

Significance to Adjusters of "Duty Owed"

Identification of the concept of "duty owed" raises the next questions: What does this idea, and the distinctions it creates, mean to an adjuster? When, where and how does it influence his work? The significance is this: It requires the adjuster to bear in mind that circumstances surrounding the occurrence, and the relationship of the parties to one another, will bear on the legal obligation of the defendant to the plaintiff.

The factors which bear on this relationship may be commercial, social or personal. The plaintiff's representatives desire to do everything possible to show that a high standard of care is required; defendant's representatives—which is to say, adjusters —attempt to show the reverse.

Negligence (The Duty Breached)

In textbooks and in instructions given by judges to juries, there may be found many definitions of negligence. One such definition is, "The omission to do something which a *reasonable* man, guided by those considerations which *ordinarily* regulate the conduct of human affairs, would do, or the doing of something which a reasonable and prudent man would not do." [7]

This definition may be enlarged by emphasizing that the words "guided by those considerations" embrace not only the conduct of the "reasonably prudent man" but a consideration of the circumstances in which that conduct takes place. Therefore, definitions of ordinary negligence are frequently qualified by further language, "in the same or similar circumstances."

It is important to note that the words "reasonable" and "ordinary," which apply to conduct of the person whose supposed negligence is under examination, derive less from statutes [8] than from the standards established by *ordinary* people in the *ordinary* conduct of their *ordinary* affairs.

The law sometimes divides negligence into:

---

[7] Bouvier, Law Dictionary, Rawle's Revision, Vol. II, p. 478.

[8] Statutes do play *some* part at this point. The ordinarily prudent man doesn't go around breaking laws heedlessly. The part that infractions of statutes play will be discussed when the term "negligence per se" is examined.

1. *Ordinary* negligence
2. *Gross* negligence
3. *Slight* negligence

Ordinary negligence is defined not only in the terms of the *acts* of a possibly negligent person but also in terms of the *circumstances* in which the action occurred. Therefore an adjuster should recognize that a situation presenting great hazards calls for great care. It is conceivable, thus, that there might be a situation in which the only prudent course for the driver of an automobile to follow would be to stop his car, set the emergency brake and turn off the ignition.

For all practical purposes, *ordinary negligence* may be taken as the failure to observe that degree of care which a prudent man would ordinarily exercise under the circumstances in question.

The term *gross negligence* has a specialized meaning. It is something more than an extreme of negligence. It is a concept difficult to define; in fact, it can best be defined in terms of those circumstances which the courts of one's own jurisdiction have accepted as satisfying the conditions of gross negligence. In general, it may be said that gross negligence is predicated upon an indifference to consequences or a willful, wanton or reckless disregard for the lives and property of others. The concept of gross negligence finds its principal application in the guest statutes which are considered later in this chapter.

Certain situations arising out of the commercial or social relationships of the parties involved impose upon defendants the duty of a very high degree of care. This exacting duty may be breached by "slight negligence." It is usually seen in situations where someone is being transported by another for profit (as in taxicabs, buses, etc.). This high degree of care is often imposed by statute.

Significance of the "Breach" to Adjusters

What does this discussion of negligence mean to a practicing adjuster?

Since the adjuster's duty is not that of ascertaining how or where courts and juries in his jurisdiction draw the line between the conduct of a reasonably prudent man and the conduct of another who is not reasonably prudent, it follows that the adjuster's duty is to *develop evidence* [9] *which discloses and describes the defendant's conduct and the circumstances in which it occurred.*

The Third Element (Damage)

The third element of a tort is *damage*—either bodily injury or property damage. *Damages* are the sums (in money) recovered by a plaintiff as compensation for the damage which he sustained. There are, broadly speaking, two types of *damages: compensatory* and *punitive.*

Compensatory Damages

Since a tort is a civil wrong, compensatory damages are usually the only damages allowed. The injured party is compensated for losses actually sustained. As a matter of public policy, one is not permitted to profit from his loss, and the measure of his recovery is the award made by the jury, or by the court if there is no jury.

Compensatory damages may, again, be subclassified as *general* or *special* in nature. Perhaps the most important of the general damages is the financial measure of pain and suffering. General damages also include the loss associated with disfigurement, humiliation, embarrassment, loss of services and of consortium.

Special damages are those losses the principal characteristic of which is their susceptibility to measurement in dollars. The most notable examples are medical bills, actual loss of earnings

---

[9] "Evidence" is a kind of information. Most laymen are familiar with the classic requirements of courts concerning evidence—that it be competent, relevant and material. Evidence usually is oral, but it may be presented by any of the senses. Visual evidence (a picture) is commonly accepted, and physical objects are often received by a court into evidence. For the moment, it seems sufficient to say that evidence is any information which a court is willing to receive.

and the like. Determination of what are known as special damages is an important factor in the evaluation of a claim.

The distinction between general and special damages is often difficult to maintain. There follows a listing of types of general and special damages often encountered in liability claims adjusting:

1. Loss of earnings, past, present or future, where provable and probable
2. Loss of earning capacity (even though no earnings are lost)
   a. Impaired earning capacity of a minor (reasonably probable)
   b. Impaired earning capacity of married women (reasonably probable)
3. Medical care expense (actual and reasonably probable)
   a. Ambulance charges
   b. Doctor, dentist and specialist charges
   c. Hospital, clinic, or nursing home charges
   d. Medicine and drug expense
   e. Nurses' fees
   f. Prosthetic devices
   g. Travel expense to and from doctors
4. Funeral expenses (but not in all jurisdictions)
5. Loss of services or support
   a. Parent's loss of services of a child
   b. Husband's loss of services of a wife (including loss of consortium)
   c. Dependent's loss of support
6. Pain, suffering, disfigurement, deformity
7. Property damage
   a. Damage or destruction of property
   b. Loss of use of property

These various types of compensatory damages will be considered in greater detail later.

Punitive Damages

In negligence cases, punitive (or exemplary) damages are extra damages awarded in some jurisdictions over and above compensatory damages, as a matter of punishment—an example to society. To recover them, the plaintiff is generally obligated to prove, and attempts to prove, a degree of carelessness or recklessness going beyond mere ordinary negligence; and generally, this includes a reckless and willful disregard for the rights of others and such culpable acts that the facts would support a conviction of the crime of manslaughter.

What are, in effect, punitive damages may actually be awarded by a jury without labeling them as such. Therefore, although the obligation of the insurer to pay punitive damages on behalf of an insured has been questioned in several jurisdictions, from the standpoint of the insurance company and the insured, evidence of aggravated misconduct and highly culpable negligence is sometimes considered an influential factor increasing the value of a claim.

The Qualification (Proximate Cause)

Damage, the third element of a tort, *must* be the *proximate* result of the breach of the duty owed.

The "proximate cause" is that which, in the natural and continuous sequence of events, unbroken by some efficient intervening cause, produces the damage, and without which the damage would not have occurred.

To some, the concept is more easily understood by considering what it is *not*. An adjuster may find it more convenient to understand that an event is not the *proximate* cause of damage if between that event and its result there intervenes, as a necessary link in the chain of cause and effect, another event which is not the necessary result of the first. This intervening event is sometimes spoken of as an intervening *willed action*.

This concept is important to adjusters, for if there has been an intervening event between an act of negligence and the damage, it becomes at once an adjuster's duty to develop the evidence which describes the intervening event so that it can be determined which is the proximate cause (or possibly whether both might have been the proximate cause).

DEFENSES

Several defenses are available to the defendant (insured) in actions brought by the plaintiff (claimant) resulting from the allegedly negligent acts of the defendant.

In respect to all of the defenses now to be discussed, it should first be emphasized that if the plaintiff has failed to establish proof before the defense presents any evidence, the defendant need offer no defense. (Parenthetically it might be observed that modern judges are quite reluctant to rule that a plaintiff has failed to sustain his burden of proof. They are prone to let the jury decide whether this requirement has been met.) Secondly, the burden of proof—that is, the burden of offering evidence relating to these several defenses—*falls on the defendant.*

Contributory Negligence

The most commonly employed defense is *contributory negligence* of the plaintiff. Such negligence consists of the plaintiff's failure to use ordinary care under the circumstances where such failure contributed as a cause to the injury or damage which he sustained. Stated differently, the plaintiff is guilty of contributory negligence if his negligence, concurring and cooperating with the negligent act of the defendant, is a proximate cause of the injury. The standard of care required is identical with that required in any negligence action, i.e., the degree of care required of the *ordinary,* reasonable or prudent person under *similar* circumstances.

The doctrine of contributory negligence is followed in a majority of states. Theoretically, in these states any contributory negligence on the part of the plaintiff may defeat his cause of action. Even if the defendant is guilty of negligence which proximately caused the plaintiff's injury and damage, the plaintiff is not entitled to recover if he, himself, were contributorily negligent. Thus, if a jury feels that a defendant was 90% at fault and the plaintiff only 10%, the defendant is not legally liable for any amount. However, it must be realized that in most instances contributory negligence is a question of fact and hence *subject to jury determination.* Juries dislike to interpret this defense strictly and they enjoy a wide range in which to function in determining the existence or nonexistence of contributory negligence. They will sometimes go to great lengths to give recovery to a seriously injured plaintiff in a case where the defendant is financially responsible. There are legal doctrines recognized in some jurisdictions which modify or nullify the general rule of contributory negligence. These doctrines are discussed in a later section.

Avoidable Consequences

The defense of *avoidable consequences,* accepted in some jurisdictions, is related to the doctrine of contributory negligence. However, while the doctrine of contributory negligence is a *complete* defense (i.e., a complete bar to recovery) to an action based on negligence in those states which adhere to it, the doctrine of avoidable consequence is generally only a *partial* defense—a defense only to the extent that the plaintiff by the use of due care could have avoided some or most of the *effects* of the defendant's negligent act. It imposes a duty on the plaintiff to minimize damages. An example of this somewhat rare situation might involve a case where the plaintiff was injured through the negligent act of a defendant and, through his own negligence and repeated refusal to see a doctor, developed serious complications. The defendant might then argue successfully, under this doctrine, that the complications would not have occurred except for the plaintiff's own negligent actions which occurred *subsequent to the original injury.* When this defense is not available by name, much the same result might be obtained by raising a question of "proximate result."

Assumption of Risk

Another defense very similar to the doctrine of contributory negligence is "assumption of risk." In many jurisdictions it is part of the defense of contributory negligence. This doctrine applies when a plaintiff voluntarily assumes the risk of injury from a particular hazard. This assumption may constitute a complete defense and bar the plaintiff's recovery. The theory of this defense is that the plaintiff assumes the risk by voluntarily placing himself in a dangerous position with knowledge of the perils existing.

In most cases, consent to assume the risk is implied from the facts, e.g., where the plaintiff rides with a driver known to be intoxicated. Consent to assume the risk may also arise by express agreement, written or oral, between the parties.

Other Defenses

It should not be inferred that the defenses noted here are the only defenses to an action of tort. However, it is with them that the adjuster is most frequently involved, therefore discussion is limited to them.

To an adjuster the significant question is not so much whether a particular act would be accepted by a court as contributory negligence or assumption of risk; the question is what he does about it. His duty is to advance the cause of his defendant by gathering and placing in useable form, to the extent that he is able, all possible evidence demonstrating knowledge on the part of the plaintiff of the dangers to which he was exposed, his willingness to expose himself to those dangers, his lack of activity in removing himself from those perils, and his own carelessness in doing those things which any sensible or prudent man would have avoided, and demonstrating the relevance of those decisions, acts or omissions to the injury that subsequently befell the plaintiff.

DOCTRINES WHICH MODIFY THE LAW OF TORTS

In the sense that they alter the basic principles established and implied by the three traditional elements of a tort, there are a number of doctrines which from time to time concern adjusters. Two of the most important are known as "res ipsa loquitur" and "negligence per se."

Res Ipsa Loquitur

The plaintiff often has difficulty producing evidence to "prove" the elements of a tort. The courts hold that the burden of proof laid upon the plaintiff is, in certain situations, an unjust burden for him to bear. So, under certain circumstances, proof of specific acts of negligence may be dispensed with and reliance had upon the doctrine of *res ipsa loquitur* (the thing speaks for itself). The doctrine is usually applied where an inference of negligence can be drawn from the circumstances of the incident alone, and where the actual act or omission which caused the injury or damage is not apparent. The theory then is that negligence may be inferred from the happening of the event—but the plaintiff is obliged to show:

1. That the accident was of a kind which ordinarily does not occur in the absence of negligence.
2. That the accident was caused by an agency or instrumentality within the exclusive control of the defendant.
3. That the accident was not due to any voluntary action or contribution on the part of the plaintiff (contributory negligence).
4. That there is no direct evidence as to the cause of the injury.

If these elements are present the law creates a rebuttable presumption that the defendant was negligent. To rebut the presumption, the defendant may put on evidence that:

1. The accident could have occurred without anyone's negligence.
2. Someone other than the defendant was negligent.
3. The plaintiff himself was negligent.
4. Demonstrates lack of control of the agency or instrumentality by the defendant.
5. Proves due care by the defendant.

The adjuster's duty in respect to this doctrine is to develop on behalf of the defendant evidence tending to negate the propositions which the plaintiff is obliged to prove, and evidence supporting one or more of the contentions by which the defendant may overcome the application of this doctrine.

To be realistic about it one must acknowledge that "res ipsa" rarely comes into automobile work—and into some courts, it comes not at all.

Negligence Per Se

An adjuster's work brings him into constant contact with violations of traffic codes. It is essential therefore that he understand the relevance of these violations to his adjusting problems.

The common assumption is that violation of a law or traffic code automatically imposes civil responsibility on the wrongdoer. This is not so. The effect of a violation must be considered and put in its proper perspective.

The violation of a law may, in some jurisdictions, constitute what is known as "negligence per se." However, in order for a violation to constitute *negligence per se* it must be demonstrated not only that the law was violated but that the violation *contributed* to the occurrence of the accident and that the law was intended to prevent that which occurred. Hence, *negligence per se* is a law violation which *causes* the occurrence of an event which the law was intended to prevent.

An example of a violation of statute which would probably not be considered to be causative of an accident and therefore probably not *negligence per se* would be a car struck by a passing vehicle while parked on the wrong side of the street. It could certainly be argued—and the argument would probably hold—that this violation of law was a *condition* of the accident but not a *cause,* and hence irrelevant to the argument over liability.[10]

The next question to be considered has to do with the legal effect of *negligence per se.* Again, the lay notion is that a violation of law, or anything bearing so impressive a name as *negligence per se,* must certainly terminate the dispute. This is not so. The existence of *negligence per se* does not prove the negligence of the violator, let alone impose liability. It merely constitutes *evidence* of negligence.

In essence, then, violations of statute are not necessarily "controlling"; they may or may not be relevant facts. If they are relevant, the plaintiff has the burden of demonstrating that the violation caused the accident and that the law was intended to prevent the result which occurred. The defendant has the opportunity of rebutting the argument.

It is much more realistic to consider violations of law as mere parts of the general picture of responsibility around which the dispute, called a "law suit," revolves.

---

[10] If the operator of a motor vehicle hit another automobile parked at the curb, the accident could hardly be said to have been caused by the parked car's facing the wrong way. Presumably, had the parked car been facing the right way it would still have been hit but on the other end.

Significance to Adjusters of Violations of Statutes

Traffic violations and the decisions of traffic courts affect adjusting work in a roundabout but very practical way. This is despite the fact that in most jurisdictions, evidence relating to charges made before traffic courts, and even the decisions arrived at by the traffic judges, is usually excluded from those courts which decide civil litigation. (In other words, the usual situation is that in a trial of a civil suit, the court and jury may not be told of the nature of charges or of the conclusions arrived at by the traffic court.)

Whether it has legal standing or not, the decision of a traffic judge has great weight in the mind of the average member of the public. If the judge fined the plaintiff and let the defendant off, this has a decidedly chastening effect upon the average claimant. He may be less inclined to press his claim, or more willing to negotiate.

If, on the other hand, only the defendant was fined, the plaintiff feels himself to be in a stronger position and compromise settlements become very difficult, even in situations involving the most legitimate doubt as to real legal liability.

Granting further that the proceedings of traffic courts are highly informal (necessitated by the volume of cases they are obliged to handle), nevertheless the decision of the judge represents a view arrived at by an unbiased person, and if the traffic judge looked at the defendant's side of the picture with a jaundiced eye, this may be a modest preview of the reaction of a juror.

The opinion of the investigating officer, too, may be important to the juror. Officers commonly are not permitted to testify as to their conclusions, but even though their testimony may be strictly factual, their feelings, even if unspoken, usually convey themselves to the jury and, not without some reason, the jury is prone to believe that the officer, usually first on the scene and presumably unbiased, had an excellent opportunity to form a correct opinion as to who was "at fault." Once they think they know the officer's mind they are quite likely to adopt his conclusions as their own.

There is one important exception to the general rule (note the use of the word "general" rather than "universal"—these principles are not uniform from state to state) that proceedings of a traffic court are not admissible evidence in a court of civil jurisdiction. This exception has to do with a defendant's *plea* of guilty. The usual significance of a plea of guilty is that it is regarded as an admission against interest, and hence a record of this plea is admissible in the civil court.

Therefore, both because they are not attorneys and are forbidden to practice law, and because of the possible adverse effect of such a plea on the insurance company's interests, adjusters should be very cautious about—in fact, should refrain from ever—advising their insureds to plead guilty to a traffic charge. The sounder course is to seek advice from one's counsel as to the effect of such a plea in one's own jurisdiction, and to seek further advice as to what an adjuster may tell his insured without himself engaging in the practice of law.

PRINCIPLES AFFECTING THE APPLICATION OF THE LAW OF TORTS

In addition to the development of legal principles and concepts which have fundamentally altered the obligations imposed by the law of torts, there is another body of law, important to adjusters, which *governs the application* of the law of torts.

In the sense that this body of concepts may conflict with what he has hitherto assumed, and therefore may be something that he will have to *learn* (rather than being common sense application of what he has always generally understood about the obligations of people to one another); and in the further sense that he very *frequently* shapes his conduct to respond to these principles, they may be the most important facet of an adjuster's acquaintance with the law.

This facet of law revolves around the idea of "imputed negligence."

Imputed Negligence

In litigation over actionable torts, questions often arise: "Is A responsible for B's action?"—or "C's negligence undoubtedly contributed to the accident; does it interfere with D's right to recover, or only with C's right to recover?" These questions introduce the principle known as "imputed negligence."

Imputed negligence is a legal concept; it means treating the negligence of one person as though it were the negligence of another. This concept impinges on adjusting practice in three principal areas:

1. Vicarious responsibility
2. The obligation to absent property owners or innocent passengers in the adverse vehicles
3. The imputed negligence of a parent to bar a child's recovery

Before turning to this idea itself, it will be wise to identify some of the reasons why its application is so often confusing. Most of the legal concepts with which claims men work are met consistently in the same aspect. Contributory negligence, for instance, is consistently a defense and it is an adjuster's duty to bring out the evidence which establishes it, if he is to do his duty by his defendant. It is not always this way with imputed negligence.

Sometimes adjusters seek to establish imputed negligence as a defendant's doctrine. At other times, this same doctrine which they may have been *trying to develop* appears in another context and now, in discharge of their duty to defendants, adjusters find themselves investigating to develop facts which defendants hope will *overcome* the doctrine of imputed negligence.

As if this were not confusing enough, this doctrine (or frequent inability to invoke it successfully) provokes a violent conflict between legal principles and the preconceptions with which most adjusters are blessed (along with most other laymen). The preconception referred to is the seemingly logical notion that all the occupants of a given car will share an identical fate, liabilitywise. The occupants of the car which was in the right should recover—the occupants of the car in the wrong ought not to recover. Or at least, that is the way it seems to be until this notion is examined more closely.

This family of ideas, whose application has confused many adjusters, will be considered in each of the three aspects enumerated.

Responsibility of Owners When Their Cars Are Driven by Others

As a general rule an owner is not held responsible for the damages resulting from the negligent operation of his automobile *merely because of his ownership.*

To consider the circumstances under which an owner *may* be held responsible for damage caused by his car *while it is being operated by another,* it will be necessary to consider first the proposition that even though another person may have been at the wheel, an owner's negligence may still be a proximate cause of an accident, and for that negligence the owner must still answer just as he would have had to answer for negligence as a driver. Then there must be considered two important circumstances in which an owner, even though himself free of negligence, may be held responsible for the negligence of the *driver* of his car just as though that negligence were the owner's own.

Owner Negligent While Car Being Driven by Another Person

An owner may become legally obligated to a plaintiff if the latter is injured because of defective brakes, lights, tires, etc., provided the owner had knowledge of the defect. Owners may also be held responsible for lending their vehicles to intoxicated persons, people under the influence of drugs, or those with a reputation as dangerous drivers, provided the owner had knowledge of their incompetence. These circumstances, one has to admit, are rare compared to the very many situations where an owner is held responsible *for the negligent acts of his driver.*

Vicarious Responsibility by Agency

Possibly the most important extension of the owner's responsibility—in other words, imposition of vicarious responsibility—has been by the application of what is known as the doctrine of "respondeat superior"—the doctrine that when one acts as an agent for another, the principal for whom the agent acts is responsible for the agent's misdeeds. Therefore, if a driver, *acting as agent for the owner,* negligently injures another, the owner is held responsible for the driver's mistakes. This doctrine enters claims files most often via the principle known as "agency."

The legal relationship known as "agency"—which, it should be noted from the beginning, is not restricted to the automobile situation—exists in many business and personal relationships. *It may exist when an agent is doing something, or performing a service, even gratuitously, under the principal's direction or request, or with his consent.* (For practical purposes, no distinction need be made between the relationship of principal and agent and that of master and servant, or employer-employe.)

In determining the existence of a principal-agent relationship, courts generally apply one or both of two tests. Perhaps the most important is a determination of whether there was a reservation by the principal of the *right to control* the *conduct* of the agent. It is the *right to control* that is important, whether or not that right is in fact exercised. The determination of whether this right to control exists is a fact situation, and sometimes the evidence is conflicting. A finding by the court, however, that the right to control exists generally carries with it a finding that an agency-principal relationship is present.

Where the evidence as to control is in dispute, or a court is not satisfied that the right to control was reserved to the principal, a second test may be applied, namely, was the *act* or *function* performed by the agent *done in the principal's behalf?* When it is shown that the business of the alleged principal was being served primarily by the agent, this will serve to support a finding that the principal-agency relationship existed.

Agency may be created orally or in writing. It may be created by express contract or by implied agreement. The law may recognize an *apparent* agency relationship when a principal permits another to conduct himself in such a manner that it appears to others that an agency relationship exists, and where the principal raises no question as to this apparent relationship. This is possibly so close to agency by implication as to constitute, for all practical purposes, the same thing.

When an agent, in the course of his agency and acting within the scope of his authority, negligently causes injury, his action is considered to be the same as if it were the act of his principal, and the law may impose liability upon the principal for the results of the conduct of the agent. This imposition is known as "imputing" the negligence of the agent to the principal. The agent, of course, is also liable.

In addition to the tests mentioned previously (the right to control and the performance of the act in the service of the principal), questions dealing with the existence or nonexistence of an agency relationship may arise on the grounds of *deviation,* or upon an allegation that the relationship is not that of principal and agent but that of two *independent contractors.*

Significance to Adjusters of Agency Questions

Investigations of agency questions impose upon adjusters the duty of determining the purpose for which the alleged agent performed his acts, the reservation to the principal of his right to control, the extent to which the agent was empowered to act for his principal and whether he was acting within the scope of his engagement. Investigation may also disclose whether the relationship is that of principal-agent or of contractor-independent contractor. Investigation of the latter question is very similar to the question of investigating the right to control. In general, an independent contractor is characterized by enjoying a maximum of freedom as to the means adopted to accomplish his ends. An independent contractor relationship is generally characterized by lump sum payment rather than hourly remuneration. An independent contractor usually—but not always—furnishes his own tools, sets his own hours of work, is responsible only for the successful accomplishment of the work assigned. Investigation, therefore, seeks to uncover facts of this nature— the effect of which is for the attorneys and the courts to ultimately determine.

Deviation from the *scope* of agency may involve deviations in *time* or in *geography.* Investigation therefore attempts to ascertain what limits, if any, were applied by the principal; what limits were to be imposed by common sense or to be inferred from previous activity; and the extent of the deviation, whether the deviation be by selection of an unauthorized route or by a violation in time of the principal's instructions. Since the purpose of the deviation may be germane, it becomes the adjuster's duty to inquire whether the deviation was for the agent's convenience or pleasure or because of an intent to advance the cause of his principal; and also whether the deviation was slight or substantial.

The business world in general and the insurance business in particular often use the word "agent" to describe what is really an independent contractor relationship, a relationship in which the negligence of one is *not* imputed to the other. It is important for the adjuster to recognize this distinction. To make this recognition effective, he should concentrate on the *circumstances* which result in imposition of vicarious responsibility rather than on the idea of agency itself.

Agency has been treated here in a few lines. Most law schools devote an entire course to the subject. This is a sketch of the rough outlines of the subject as it pertains to claims work.

Agency has been considered as a doctrine which imposes on defendants responsibility for the acts of others. In this context it is usually the adjuster's duty to examine and if possible overturn it. Although it will be the same doctrine, agency will be seen shortly in another context, in which the adjuster will find that he will seek to prove agency as an affirmative defense to a claim.

Vicarious Responsibility by Statute or Decision

The dictionary offers as one of the definitions of the word "vicarious": *"suffered or done in place of or for the sake of another, or pertaining to that which is so suffered or done . . . substitutionary."*

In the light of that definition, therefore, the principal-agency relationship just discussed is a means of imposing vicarious responsibility. Many jurisdictions impose vicarious responsibility in other than agency situations. This imposition may be by statute or by common law decision. It may take the name of the "dangerous instrumentality" doctrine or it may not. In whatever way it may occur, the rationale appears most often to be that the automobile is a dangerous instrument—that the owner is liable for the negligent acts of one who drives it with his permission, knowledge or consent, express or implied.

Vicarious responsibility laws may be limited in their application to the operation of automobiles by minors; they may extend responsibility to the signer of the minor's application for license; or the responsibility may be imposed on an owner for any negligent act of any person operating with his consent—express or implied. General responsibility of parents for torts of minor children, imposed in some jurisdictions, may be applied to automobile situations.

It is the prompt duty of any adjuster, upon starting work in any jurisdiction, to ascertain the applicable laws of this nature in his jurisdiction. Once ascertained, he should keep abreast of them, for what is the law today may not be the law tomorrow.

Many jurisdictions impose a vicarious extension of liability known as the "family purpose doctrine." To be brief, this holds that when a car is owned by the head of a household and is used [11] by a member thereof, the owner of the car may be held responsible for the negligent act of the driver, as an extension of the law of agency. Whatever the rationale, the result is to increase the probability that a financially responsible person is available to pay for the damages.

OBLIGATION TO PASSENGERS IN OR ABSENT OWNERS OF ADVERSE VEHICLES

Distinctions must be made between the various persons whose claims may arise out of an accident. A layman commonly supposes that every occupant of an automobile has equal recovery rights. Widespread though this supposition is, it could hardly be further from the facts. The operator of a car involved in an accident has rights but the ability to recover of the passengers in the same vehicle may be quite different from the operator's and, particularly if he is not in the car, the rights of the owner may be something else again.

---

[11] In some jurisdictions the use must be with consent or permission of the head of the household.

In considering these distinctions, it may be wise to recall that the discussion of vicarious responsibility started with the proposition that "the owner of a vehicle is not held responsible for the negligent acts of his driver *merely because of his ownership.*" Similarly, determining the obligation to the owner of an automobile which has been damaged by the negligent act of another starts with the premise that the owner is not barred from recovery *merely* because the negligence of the driver of his car contributed to the accident; nor is the claim of an injured *passenger* against the operator of a vehicle other than the one in which he is riding barred *merely* because the driver of the passenger's car was contributorily negligent. In either situation, there must be *reason* for the law to consider the negligence of the operator as if it were the negligence of the owner (or passenger) himself. The frequent absence of such *reason* often makes "clear liability" out of claims of owners and passengers that would on superficial inspection appear to be "no liability."

Claims of Absent Owners (the So-Called "Bailment Rule")

The act of distinguishing between a vehicle's operator and its owner brings up the question of contributory negligence. How, if he was not the driver, could the owner have been negligent? Or, does the driver's negligence in some way affect the owner's right to recover as if it were the owner's own negligence? (Imputed negligence).

The answer is that in most situations,[12] the owner is not *negligent* and, unless there is a *reason* the driver's negligence will not be imputed to the owner. Three situations, two factual and one legal, often result in the driver's negligence being imputed to the owner and they will be considered shortly.

The freedom of the owner from the onus of the operator's negligence is the prevailing law in many states and where this is the case, the effect is to enable the owner of a car (if he was not a passenger in it) to come into court without the danger of a defendant successfully arguing that the negligence of the

---

[12] Save the rare exception—such as careless maintenance.

owner's driver contributed to the accident—that the owner should, therefore, be prevented from recovery. Unless there is some reason for imputing the driver's negligence to the owner, claims in this category are very difficult for the defendant to win, for usually all the plaintiff needs to do is to show *some* negligence on the part of the defendant in order to recover. The fact that the driver of the plaintiff's car may also have been negligent (may in fact have been more negligent than the defendant) is of no moment. The application of this rule thus deprives the defendant of one of his principal defenses.

Where this interpretation (freedom of the absent owner from the effects of driver's negligence) is followed it is often spoken of in liability claims jargon as "the bailment rule," and when the term is thus used, it must be remembered that it is a narrow, specialized application of a phrase. "Bailment" is an important term both in and out of the insurance business. Almost all forms of first party insurance (inland marine especially) have much to do with bailees (persons in lawful possession of the property of another), bailors (persons who have placed property in the custody of bailees) and bailment (the situation which obtains when a bailee is in custody of a bailor's property). A bailment, except in the narrow sense in which liability adjusters use the term, may be gratuitous, the bailee may be paid to look after the property or he may be the owner's agent.

Even though it may be a misleading use of a legal term, it should be clearly understood that *in a casualty claim office* the term "bailment" or "bailed car" refers to the operation of a car by someone other than the owner, with the further proviso that the operation is *under such circumstances as will not permit the negligence of the operator to be imputed to the owner* (usually this means the absence of agency).

Negligence Imputed by Permission

Some jurisdiction (but by no means all) do not follow the bailment rule. They hold that when a driver operates an automobile with the mere *permission* of the owner, his negligence, if any, is a bar to the owner's recovery. This is a point on which an adjuster new to a territory should promptly inform himself. When this situation prevails, its practical effect is to take the bailor-bailee's situation completely out of the claims vocabulary —an almost shocking change for adjusters who move from one state to another.

Negligence Automatically Imputed to Passenger-Owner

When the owner of a car is a passenger in it at the time of an accident, most jurisdictions almost automatically impute to the owner the negligence, if any, of the driver. It is possibly helpful to note that in such a situation *the right to control* (one of the criteria of agency) is virtually undeniable. The holding of his own jurisdiction on this point is one of the things about which an adjuster should inform himself without delay.

Negligence Imputed to Owner by Agency

The effect of the "bailment rule" (the right of the absent owner to be free of the effects of his operator's negligence) may be overcome by convincing a court that a negligent operator was acting as the *agent* of his vehicle's owner.

Previously this chapter identified agency as a plaintiff's doctrine—now it has appeared as a defense. An investigation to establish agency for defensive purposes seeks exactly the same facts as plaintiffs are obliged to develop in order to invoke agency—that is, purpose, right to control, scope of agency, deviation, etc. If a defendant can persuade a court that agency and right to control exist between a plaintiff owner and his driver, then the negligence may be imputed to the owner and that negligence pleaded as a defense against the owner's claim.

Significance of the Bailment Rule

What is the significance of the bailment rule to the adjuster? Well, it makes it, of course, his first obligation to find out where *his* state stands on the bailment rule.

He must also make it part of his routine to find out whether the claimant-owner is a passenger in his car at the time of the accident. Finally if the rule is in effect and the owner absent, then he must recognize that a showing of almost any negligence on the part of the defendant may permit a recovery. Therefore, he must be prepared to consider settling accordingly—but before he settles he must consider one more question: do the circumstances indicate a situation which would permit imputing the plaintiff's driver's negligence to the plaintiff-owner? From a practical standpoint, answering the last question means determining whether an agency situation exists—and the adjuster is thereby obliged to consider the advisability of investigating agency.

It would seem that a state which automatically imposes responsibility on an owner for the negligent acts of those driving with his consent would automatically impute to the absent owner the negligence of his driver for the purpose of barring the recovery of the absent owner, since these ideas seem to be virtual twins —only appearing in different contexts. It would also seem that other extensions of vicarious responsibility imposing obligations upon defendants for the acts of others would operate in reverse when automobiles are subjects of claims, the owners being absent from the cars at the time of the collision. *This is not necessarily so.* No attempt is made here to list the states following one form or another of the vicarious responsibility doctrines. An adjuster should find out for each doctrine, state for state, the extent to which it applies to a defendant and the extent, if any, to which the bailment rule or modifications of it, apply to a plaintiff. Sauce for the goose is not always sauce for the gander.

Passenger Claims (Similarity to Bailor Claims)

It was said that to evaluate claims of occupants of a claimant's vehicle, one must distinguish between the claims of passengers and the claims of their operator. Since many young adjusters fail in this situation to distinguish between passengers in an assured's car and passengers in the adverse car, *it is now stated with emphasis that the present concern is with passengers in the adverse vehicle—in other words, the claimant's passengers.*

In most jurisdictions, and in most situations, passengers have recovery rights *superior* to those of their operators. Their recovery rights are virtually the same as those of absent owners in the bailment situations just discussed, and for very much the same reasons. The reason for this superiority lies in the practical inability of the defendant to demonstrate contributory negligence as a defense. When one stops to consider it, it does seem difficult for two automobiles to collide without each operator contributing in some measure to the occurrence. As a defense against the claim of the claimant operator, a defendant may plead and argue contributory negligence and may thereby avoid or mitigate responsibility for damage. This opportunity does not exist in respect to passengers, for in the absence of some situation which would justify imputing the operator's negligence to the passenger, these claimants are probably free of negligence, totally and obviously. Hence they frequently recover upon the showing of the slightest negligence on the part of the defendant, and in spite of substantial negligence on the part of their own operator.

Significance to Adjusters

In addition to conferring a greater value, therefore, on passenger claims, the existence of this principle (or negative principle) imposes an investigational duty upon the adjuster. It becomes his duty to ascertain and reduce to evidence those facts which bear upon any relationship—agency, joint enterprise or otherwise—which would result in imputing the driver's negligence to the passenger in order to bar his recovery.

Again, the laws are by no means uniform from state to state. Ascertaining the holding of one's own state in respect to this point is of first importance.

Negligence of Parent Imputed to Minor Child

The mere fact that an unattended child is struck by an automobile does not necessarily mean that the parent was negligent. Parents are expected to exercise the care that is reasonably prudent under the circumstances. The law in some jurisdictions recognizes the obligation of the parent to look after the child.

Failure of the parent properly to see to the safety of his child may be negligence, and where this principle is recognized, this negligence of the parent may be imputed to the child to bar the child's recovery as if it were the child's own contributory negligence. In other jurisdictions, it may have the lesser effect of barring the parents' recovery for their derivative claims.

In all cases involving minors, it is wise to investigate carefully the facts surrounding the activities of the child and his guardian. Such questions as these can prove important:

How old is the child?
What was the traffic situation?
Who was looking after the child?
Where was the guardian?
How long was it since he had last seen the child?
What was the child doing when the guardian last observed him?
If the child was on or near a public way, had he previously been given to wandering out into the street?

DEPARTURES FROM COMMON LAW

As the reader may already have determined for himself, law is never in a state of being; it is always becoming something else. Whatever it may have been yesterday, it is today in the process of becoming what it will be tomorrow. It is necessary therefore to be wary of arbitrary statements of what the law is at any given time.

By judicial interpretation, and by statute, the principles of common law have been modified in numerous instances. Some modifications which are specifically applicable to automobile cases include the concept of *comparative negligence,* the doctrine of *last clear chance,* the *vicarious liability* statutes (already mentioned), *guest statutes,* and *survivor* or *wrongful death* statutes.

Comparative Negligence

It was stated that in those jurisdictions which follow the principle of *contributory negligence,* a plaintiff is not permitted to recover if his negligence contributed to his injury. One of the principal reasons for this rule is judicial reluctance to apportion fault—a very difficult task. Perhaps the best way to get at comparative negligence is simply to treat it for what it is, a retreat from contributory negligence.

Contributory negligence, by itself, is the simple idea that if a person has contributed to his own injury, he should not recover for that injury which he would not have sustained except for his own contributing carelessness. When the concept denied recovery to an injured man it tangled with sympathy. As is usually the case, emotion overcame reasoning and a concept which may have deserved better at the hands of its custodians was abandoned in many jurisdictions.

The Wisconsin Approach

Comparative negligence will first be considered in the light of the Wisconsin law [13] because there is a tendency to follow it in several states. The law is possibly more important in its application than in its principles. But first, to demonstrate its principles, a few examples:

1. Defendant guilty of greater negligence
   Two cars collide. Plaintiff is 40% negligent; defendant is, 60% negligent. Plaintiff's damage is found to be $10,000. Plaintiff recovers $6,000 ($10,000 reduced by 40%).
2. Plaintiff guilty of greater negligence
   Plaintiff damaged in the same $10,000 accident. Plaintiff is 60% negligent, defendant is 40% negligent. No recovery by plaintiff for his negligence is greater than defendant's.
3. Parties equally negligent
   Same damages. Plaintiff is 50% negligent, defendant is 50% negligent. Neither recovers. Defendant must have been guilty of greater negligence before plaintiff can recover.
4. Three negligent parties
   Plaintiff sustains same $10,000 damages. Defendant #1 is 10% negligent; defendant #2 is 50% negligent; plaintiff is 40% negligent. Plaintiff recovers nothing against #1 for plaintiff's

---

[13] The discussion of the Wisconsin concept, draws heavily on material prepared by Carroll R. Hefft and C. James Hefft, members of Hefft, Coates, Hefft, Henzl and Bichler of the Wisconsin bar. Messrs. Hefft are the authors of several articles and a book upon the subject. The examples are almost verbatim, however, some of the material on apportionment and contribution between tortfeasors has been omitted as inappropriate to an introductory text on adjusting.

negligence is greater than defendant's. Plaintiff recovers $6,000 against defendant #2 ($10,000 reduced by 40% of plaintiff's own negligence).
5. Three parties negligent, all equally negligent. No party can recover against either of the others.

Comparative negligence may also enter the picture to determine how much of an award each of two or more defendants are liable for when they have been found guilty of different percentages of negligence. These cases are quite rare. Discussion of this refinement is out of place in a text designed to be read in fifty jurisdictions.

The application of the Wisconsin approach was said to be important in its application. Now is the time to explain that statement.

In Wisconsin, and where her lead has been followed, a procedure leading to what is known as a special verdict is followed. Juries are asked to make specific findings as to whether or not parties are guilty of specific acts of negligence—look-out, speed, wrong side of road, failure to yield, etc. The jury is also instructed to reduce these findings to percentages of total negligence and to ascertain the total damage of all parties. Neither the court nor the lawyers may inform the jury of the effect of the jury's decision in causing one party to win or the other to lose.

The jury's findings having been made, the court then does the arithmetic; takes the percentages of negligence as found in the apportionment question and applies these percentages to the damages and reduces damages by the appropriate percentage when such reductions are in order.

Adjuster's Duty in Appraising Fault

To be effective in his operations where the Wisconsin approach is followed, an adjuster should think more deeply than the mere ascertainment of the facts. He should segregate and develop those facts into evidence bearing on specific negligent acts or omissions. His trial attorney will be thinking in terms of specific categories of fault such as lookout, speed, wrong side of the road, failure to yield, etc.

It is still more important to develop the evidence to enable the jury to weigh the fault of one party against the other. The percentages of fault will ultimately determine who pays and how much.

Mississippi Approach

The Mississippi Law Review, Volume 39, Page 493 speaks of that law as, "The first and only pure comparative negligence law of general application."

In two respects it differs markedly from Wisconsin's approach.

"All questions of negligence and contributory negligence shall be for the jury to determine," [14] and this is so to the extent that the special verdict device (by which in Wisconsin the jury finds the facts and the judge does the arithmetic) is not utilized.

There is no provision that a defendant's negligence must be greater than the plaintiff's. Thus, if a jury found a plaintiff 99% negligent and the defendant only 1%, it could avoid some damage— but the damages ought to be reduced to reflect the division of negligence.

The word "ought" is used intentionally. It reflects the lack of control over the jury's actions. In the absence of the special verdict device, it is difficult to see how one could determine just how the jury had divided the negligence and if it did divide negligence, whether it followed its own division in the award of damages.

Adjusters practicing under Mississippi rules report the statute as pretty much of a blank check to the jury. It should be remembered though that this result has considerable resemblance to practice in other states where *any contributory negligence* is still a *theoretical* bar to recovery. In those states, it is increasingly difficult to get juries to pay any attention to contributory negligence. As one lawyer put it, "Juries see 'good guys' and 'bad guys.' If they see you as a good guy, they are likely to rule with you and if you're a bad guy, you're out of luck."

---

[14] Mississippi Code § 1455.

Slight Negligence

Some states which adhere to contributory negligence as a bar to recovery soften the rule thus: if plaintiff's contributory negligence is only "slight," then such negligence need not bar his recovery. This ought to be expected to create litigation about the meaning of the word "slight" and it does.

Seat Belt Defense

This recently introduced legal concept is of occasional value to the defendants. It is well worth the adjuster's attention. He will not see many cases where he can use it but the few cases where he does are likely to be very serious—and very early in a claim's life he may have one (and only one) chance to gather and perpetuate evidence on which a successful defense may later be based.

The concept may be stated thus: *In certain circumstances, failure to buckle a seat belt may be considered contributory negligence and plaintiff's recovery denied or reduced.* In this situation, the opening phrase which was italicized probably has more to do with what adjusters do or ought to do than knowledge of the concept itself.

Merely showing failure to buckle up is not enough. The following elements may be considered as standard requirements of a successful defense. Although the courts of many jurisdictions have yet to ennunciate them, an adjuster should be prepared lest the courts in his state use his case to do so. Cases should be prepared with the idea that these elements [15] *will* be called into consideration.

1. The crash behavior of the car that the injured was riding in:
   What was its direction?
   What was its speed?

---

[15] This material on the seat belt defense is based upon two publications of the Defense Research Institute, Inc., Milwaukee, Wisconsin. The publications are: DRI monograph, *The Seat Belt Defense In Practce* (Vol. 1970, No. 6, July 1970) and *The Seat Belt Defense In Practice,* Defense Memo, 11 For The Defense 89 (Oct. 1970). The six criteria mentioned are taken almost verbatim from the latter article, which appeared in the DRI monthly newsletter, FOR THE DEFENSE. This material, published with permission, is copyrighted by the Defense Research Institute, Inc., all rights reserved.

What changes occurred in course and speed?
Did vehicle rotate on the surface or roll over?
2. Trajectory of claimant's body in the accident.
3. Relationship of vehicle crash events (1 above) to movements of the occupant's body (2 above) under the forces and stresses acting upon it.
4. The particular injuries suffered.
5. Trajectory which a restrained occupant would have taken.
6. The extent of lesser injuries which occupant would have sustained had he been restrained.

Additionally, one should anticipate a plaintiff's argument or a court's ruling that defense should be required to demonstrate that plaintiff knew or ought to have known that he should have buckled his belt. Whether or not such as argument might be made or sustained is also irrelevant to an adjuster's *duty*. Clearly, when he is on the job it is the time to show in statements, preferable the plaintiff's own, that he did know that the belt was available, that it had safety value and that he knowingly elected not to use it. If plaintiff did not know all these things, his statement should show as much knowledge on his part as possible.

The above considerations clearly go to the question of cause and their general thrust is to place on defendant the burden of showing that *failure* to use the belt was the cause of part or all of the plaintiff's injury.

To prove some or all of the elements cited, it may be necessary to resort to accident reconstruction experts. The expert may not be available at the time the original investigation was made or the decision to employ him may be made months later. Thus, if seat belt defense is to be invoked, it may fall to the adjuster to gather and preserve the evidence on which an expert can later base testimony. Therefore, having the six elements in the back of his mind, an adjuster should consider the physical evidence available to him with the thought in mind, "What do my observations indicate? Did the failure to buckle a seat belt contribute to the plaintiff's injury or to the severity of his injury?"

To illustrate the question, if plaintiff's car was hit on the side at right angles at a point adjacent to which plaintiff sat and if the injury were a crushed hip on the side presented to the oncoming car, one would probably conclude that whether or not a seat belt had been properly employed was irrelevant. If, on the other hand, two cars grazed one another and then one of them ran into a tree, throwing an occupant out of the window, one ought to suspect that the failure of the ejected occupant to use a seat belt might have contributed to his injuries. In this case the adjuster ought to set about collecting and preserving the evidence bearing on the six elements and on the question of the plaintiff's knowledge that he ought to have used his belt. Statements of participants and witnesses should cover their observations in relation to elements 1, 2 and 3.

The injured person should be queried (if he is alive to answer questions) on his own knowledge about point 4.

The scene should be considered in respect to 1, 2 and 3. If the physical layout shows anything or if there are skid marks, gouge marks, or crash debris tending to throw light on the course, speed and changes in course and speed of each vehicle or if adjuster observes anything that should be preserved, then his decision whether to expose hand camera and commercial photos becomes a matter of applying his own carrier's policy in regard to spending for such purposes.

The interior of the car in which the injured was a passenger should be inspected and photos considered. In the case of a very serious injury and a car showing evidence of particular importance, an adjuster might even consider having a friendly junk man buy the car for him and store it under appropriate safeguards.

Element 4, injuries sustained, is relatively straight forward and hardly likely to be suppressed but remembering the tendency of some parties interested in litigation to suppress and distort evidence it would be a good idea, if possible, to get plaintiff's doctors to commit themselves to their opinions concerning plaintiff's injury and particularly their opinion on "What hit him (or what did he hit) to cause this particular injury?"

Theorizing on points 5 and 6 and to some extent on point 4 is probably best left to the reconstruction specialist.[16]

The possibility of setting up a seat belt defense ought to be made an almost routine consideration in "head-on" collisions.

---

[16] See page 154, Preservation of Physical Evidence.

Here, claimant's injury usually results from the collision of some part of his body with the dash, windshield or windshield header. Many of these injuries would not happen if the passenger were properly restrained.

A claims man is only secondarily concerned with the law in his jurisdiction. His interest lies in evidence.

Does it show the claimant did not buckle his belt?
Does it show that the movement of his car and of his body inside it in relation to the car injured him?
Is it reasonably probable that the injury would have been lessened had a seat belt been employed?

If these questions are answered in the affirmative, then preserve the evidence to the carrier's best advantage whether by statements, photos, or preservation of the physical evidence itself.

Last Clear Chance

The doctrine of last clear chance was enunciated to avoid what was felt to be the harshness of contributory negligence as a complete bar to a plaintiff's recovery. Broadly, this doctrine states that the contributory negligence of a plaintiff in placing himself in peril need not preclude recovery from the defendant if the defendant, having the last opportunity to do so, through the exercise of reasonable care could have avoided injuring the plaintiff, even though the plaintiff himself may have been negligent.

Whether the defendant had a last clear chance—i.e., whether he saw or should have seen the plaintiff's danger—and whether he had the time and opportunity to avoid the accident, according to reasonable standards of conduct for a person under similar circumstances, is generally a question for the jury to decide.

Again, there is a difference of opinion between the various jurisdictions as to what facts and circumstances should be present so that the doctrine may be applied. Each adjuster should therefore be familiar with the elements required in his jurisdiction. Adjusters should be particularly alert to sense the possibility of the application of this doctrine to pedestrian cases. It is easy to overlook the possible applicability of the doctrine in a case which looks, on its face, to be a clear contributory negligence situation. By the application of the last clear chance doctrine, such a claim may acquire potential, particularly if it is exploited by competent counsel. Still, to be realistic, an adjuster should be slow to take alarm at the possibility of a plaintiff invoking this doctrine. The general feeling is that it is a hard way for a plaintiff to win a law suit. Reference to the doctrine may be a tip-off that plaintiff's attorney knows he is in a bad way; that he is grasping at straws.

Guest Statutes

The development of the common law in many states has permitted passengers injured while riding in a car driven by another to recover against their operators upon a demonstration of ordinary negligence of their own operator. In fact, they may in many jurisdictions elect to proceed against either their own operator, the operator of the adverse vehicle, *or both*. The usual elements of a right of action apply—that is, a legal duty, its breach, proximate cause, damages, etc.—and the injured party may not have to demonstrate any greater lack of care on the part of the driver of his car than for any other driver. The burden of proving negligence usually lies upon the plaintiff passenger. The two common law defenses—contributory negligence and assumption of risk—are still available to the defense of a negligent driver.

About half the jurisdictions have modified this common law relationship either by judicial decision or by statute—usually by statute—but at least one jurisdiction has attained the same end by decision.

These modifications have established a different standard of care, imposing upon a guest the necessity of proving that his host was more than ordinarily negligent. Although the statutes vary in wording, they generally require a guest to prove one or more of the following: Wilful and wanton misconduct, intoxication, intent to injure (if proven, this may let the insurer out—for coverage applies only to *accidental* acts), reckless driving, *or, the usual criterion, gross negligence.*

Clearly, the intent of these modifications has been to make a plaintiff's recovery more difficult, hence their reason for being. They were developed to prevent the assertion of fraudulent claims or the fraudulent padding of legitimate claims.

If the passenger does not come within the category of guest as defined by the laws, he is not limited to the provisions of the guest statute (or decision) and need prove only ordinary negligence on the part of his driver. Generally a passenger is considered a guest if he is riding in a car on a purely social basis and if the ride is provided gratuitously. There are many circumstances under which a passenger is not considered to be guest. For example, if the ride is furnished in connection with the *business* of the operator (as when an automobile salesman demonstrates a car to a prospect), or where there is a joint venture (e.g., two salesmen working from one car), or where the passenger's presence is for the benefit of the driver or their mutual benefit, or if the passenger has paid or agreed to pay for his ride, then the passenger is not considered a guest within the terms of so-called guest statutes. Close questions may arise when a passenger voluntarily purchases gasoline for the owner on a motor trip, or acts as a member of a car pool. The adjuster's duty is not to decide these close points; his duty is to collect the facts to enable an accurate decision on the law to be made.

A PROPER PERSPECTIVE

The foregoing brief discussion has not been intended to equip an adjuster to *decide* what is negligence or what is not, nor yet to understand what may be the plaintiff's or the defendant's duty of care in a given circumstance.

It is not intended that this chapter serve as a statement of the law. Any attempt to rely on it in that fashion would be unjustified. The intent has been to sketch the bare outlines of the legal framework which underlies and influences the mechanism for distributing and allocating the financial burden of accidents, which is to say, the claims business. These principles, so briefly introduced, are the legal outline within which attorneys' arguments and offerings of evidence take place.

An adjuster's approach to his duties will be on a sound basis if for the time being he discards the notion that any single factor, however clear-cut it may seem to him, is going to control the actual disposition of a given case, claim or law suit. While there are, from time to time, rare instances of these clear-cut situations, a claim or law suit more commonly consists of many claims, arguments, contentions and counter-contentions, all relevant but no one controlling, and so it is with the principles and concepts reviewed in this chapter.

An attempt has been made to demonstrate the legal significance of the evidence which the adjuster will be required to gather, and to point out those areas in which he should seek evidence in order to sustain his defendant's position.

It will not be too far from reality if he takes it as a foregone conclusion that in the end the whole dispute over any accident can be simplified into an argument, each party claiming that the accident was the other man's fault. The jury will, in the end, award damages less upon the instructions that it will receive from the judge as to the applicable law than upon its own subjective feelings—in other words, if a jury is persuaded (and it can be persuaded by convincing evidence) that a plaintiff is responsible for his own injury, it will likely send him home empty-handed; if not, it will probably award him damages.

The relevance of law to adjusters' duties seems also to be put in its proper perspective by the comment of a wise claims manager: "If the facts are on your side, you can usually find law to support you. If the facts are against you, the law will usually be against you, too."

CHAPTER 3

Relation of Coverage to the Adjusting Function

Every claim raises two questions:

"Is the *insured* legally obligated, and if so, to what extent?" (Except for this chapter, the major concern of this book is with one phase or another of this question.)

and (the concern of this chapter);

"Is there coverage?" or to restate the question, "Has the insurance company obligated itself to assume the burdens of the insured?" (This general question includes within itself such subquestions as, "Is the contract valid? Does it provide protection for the specified occurrence? Has the contract been rendered voidable?")

The question of coverage is the concern here. Because they are numerous, because many closely resemble others, and for the further reason that many policies undergo not one but often several changes during the working lifetime of any adjuster, memory is a treacherous foundation for a working approach to coverage. In fact, when a real question arises, an adjuster rarely relies on his memory. At first blush, this seems a bit strange, so a quick look at what he does do may be in order.

Most coverage problems involve one of two questions, "What does the policy say?" or "What does the policy mean?"

If the question boils down to "What does the policy say?" an adjuster's move is obvious. He reads the policy. The practice of going back to the policy is widely observed, so widely that it is probably correct to say that a confident, experienced adjuster, whenever he takes up a claim under a new policy makes this his *very first move* more than half the time. This chapter will attempt to give an insight into how one approaches this examination of the policy.

The question presented may, however, be one of *interpretation*—in other words, "What does the policy mean?" Now the adjuster goes to the *policy itself*, then to *reference sources* and in some cases beyond these to *judicial decisions* of which there are literally hundreds explaining and defining almost every word and phrase of every policy. Compared to questions involving only policy *language*, questions of *interpretation* are relatively rare; a busy adjuster may go several months without meeting one.

This chapter, therefore, except for an attempt to shed some light on how one goes about the examination of a policy, will have little to say about the content of insurance policies. It will try instead to show how one deals with them, records information about them and understands and analyzes coverage questions.

Coverage is the inescapable feature of every claim. Coverage information is received, recorded and reported in every file. Some suggestions will be offered as to how this may most easily be done and errors or ambiguity avoided.

Coverage must be examined to determine its applicability to the facts at hand. The approach to this examination should be accurate and sufficient so that the coverage may be correctly applied. To this end, and so that the examination when required will be efficient, the features of common policies will be outlined. In the hope that understanding and the ability to analyze will be promoted, some of the reasons underlying these common features will be explained.

Questions will come up, one's best efforts to the contrary notwithstanding. Techniques, therefore, for resolving them will be considered.

CONTRACT FORMAT

A surprising feature of liability insurance, considering the multiplicity of forms involved, is the basic similarity of their provisions. A quick look at the usual make-up of a policy will help the adjuster to know what to look for and how to find it; it may help him in his frequent need to analyze his policies.

Liability contracts are usually divided into the following parts:

1. Declarations
2. Insuring Agreements
3. Exclusions
4. Conditions

Declarations

Declarations are statements giving information which forms the basis upon which a contract may be written by the insurance company. The information provided is used by the underwriters for rating purposes and it is a basis for risk selection and identification.

The declarations page is usually the first page of the contract. Usually it is unsigned, but if a company's underwriting program presupposes an intent to deny coverage in the event of any discrepancy and a willingness to undergo litigation arising from that denial, then that company may require its declarations page to be signed. This furnishes a sounder basis for litigation than statements which may or may not have been answered accurately by the company's agent or other representative.

In most companies a duplicate of the declarations page is kept on file at the insurance company's controlling office, and in many cases at other locations such as the branch or agency office. This duplicate, known to the trade as "the daily," is normally the only part of the contract filed separately for each policyholder. The information contained in it, together with the policy contract and the endorsements indicated therein, make it possible to reconstruct an exact duplicate of the contract delivered to the insured.

From the standpoint of his daily work, the declarations are the part of the policy that most often concern the adjuster. This chapter will later discuss the two levels on which an adjuster works with coverage. On the first and most important level, his concern will be chiefly with the declarations and the information in them.

Insuring Agreements

The *insuring agreement* is that part of the policy which provides the coverage. This is where the company states what it is prepared to do. It is probably not too much to call it the heart of the policy, but the figure can be pushed too far. An animal has only one heart but many policies (automobile policies, for example) have several insuring agreements.

Ordinarily insuring agreements promise not only to *pay* but also to perform certain services. The typical automobile policy for instance promises, "to pay all sums which the insured may become legally obligated to pay." But, determining what an insured "has become obligated to pay" may require lawsuits, the purchase of certain bonds, and other related services; so in additional insuring agreements the policy enumerates many of these services and obliges the insurance company to provide them.

Insurance companies, even if it were not for these stated obligations to provide services, would be obliged to do—and undoubtedly would do—all the things required of them by these service features of the policy.

Other benefits—the payment of first aid expense, premiums on bail bonds, payment of certain legal expenses—may be provided.

Since the insuring agreements state the coverage extended, these sections of the policy should be examined first when the adjuster is obliged to determine whether a policy provides coverage in a particular event. An insurance policy is not designed for rapid reading—quite the contrary—and it is seldom that an adjuster needs to read more slowly or more painstakingly than in his examination of an insuring clause. Every word is there for a purpose. Each word should be read for its own significance and for its effect on other words in the same sentence and elsewhere in the policy.

Many words not ordinarily considered "limiting" have exactly that effect. An example is the word "accident" which appears in the insuring clause of many liability policies. When it appears, its effect is to exclude coverage for *intended* acts, and for those events which are not "accidental" within the meaning of that word as defined by the courts of the jurisdiction in which the event occurred.

"Accident" is only one word which importantly defines and limits the coverage provided. Where the policy writers have found it expedient to do so these words are often defined in a section labeled "definitions" which ought to be considered as a part of the "insuring agreement."

A common pitfall is the failure to recognize that insuring agreements (and exclusions too) can be quite misleading and baffling (wrong conclusions can be drawn from them) unless the definitions are studied. One way of thinking about the definitions is to recognize that they are employed to give a word or phrase a meaning that it *might not otherwise have*. The definitions tell what the word means when employed *in this policy*.

By all odds the most frequently invoked definitions in the casualty business are the definitions of "insured" as they appear in automobile liability policies. These definitions are sometimes referred to as "omnibus clauses" because they extend coverage to many people other than the purchaser of the policy. These extensions are so far reaching as frequently to amaze persons of even long experience in the insurance business. It should be noted that this particular "definition" demonstrates that the *definitions do not merely limit coverage, they may extend or expand that which was provided by the initial insuring clause*.

A typical automobile policy defines these terms: "insured," "named insured," "relative," "owned automobile," "non-owned automobile," "temporary substitute automobile," "private passenger automobile," "farm automobile," "utility automobile," "trailer," "automobile business," "use" and "war."

It is necessary that each of these words be defined, for usually in respect to the policy in which they appear the common or dictionary definitions would be either unclear or other than what the framers of the policy intended.

Policies providing comprehensive personal liability insurance define: "bodily injury," "property damage," "premises," "business property," "residence employe," "business," "automobile," "midget automobile," "undeclared outboard motor."

Other policies define those words or terms necessary to make clear the intent of their framers and to minimize repetition.

Exclusions

Insuring agreements, it has just been said, state the coverage provided by the contract. At first blush, an agreement may seem (at least after its modification by quoted definitions) to have provided clearly stated and properly defined protection; but the agreements are still generalizations. Experience brings to life many circumstances which the company never intended to cover. Since in the long run, the public always pays the bill, public interest requires still further provisions to narrow down the generalizations. *Exclusions* fulfill this function. Underlying virtually every exclusion will be found one or more fundamental ideas.

The insurance industry is unfairly and improperly maligned on the subject of exclusions. So long as there are policies and companies, uninformed laymen and some people who ought to know better will continue to insist that policies give coverage in the big print and take it away in the small. Understandably therefore, the public inclines to characterize exclusions as "loopholes." Because the adjuster needs not only to deal on a basis of sound knowledge with a confused and uninformed public, but also to maintain his self respect and his confidence in the industry he represents, he must understand the real reasons which underlie the exclusions with which he works.

It may aid his understanding if, as he studies specific policies, he will observe that the narrower the insuring agreement in a given policy, the fewer are the exclusions; conversely, the broader the insuring agreement, the more exclusions there will be. As he grows in understanding of the business, the adjuster will see more and more clearly that the broader the coverage provided, the more exclusions *there will have to be.*

A comparison between an insurance policy and the deed to a piece of real estate may be apropos. The deed to a house lot is short and simple. The deed to a large piece of property is long and complex—simply because it has longer boundary lines and takes more words to describe those lines.

Exclusions serve at least the following purposes:

1. They facilitate the handling of the moral hazard. In other words, they keep the company out of those situations where

there is no practical defense against misrepresentation, exaggeration or collusion by an assured and others in concert with him.

2. They help keep rates at a reasonable level, and the exposure within the rate structure. Unless, for example, "for hire" vehicles were excluded under most automobile liability policies, the obviously great cost of insuring them would have to be borne by distribution among all motorists. This general exclusion assists also in controlling the moral hazard. If there were no such exclusion, underwriters would try to avoid insuring "for hire" vehicles. Their owners would be tempted to try to beat the game by misrepresenting the real use to which their vehicles would be put. This misrepresentation would be difficult to detect without incurring unreasonable cost.

3. They eliminate coverage which would duplicate that of other policies which the insured may have, or may be able to obtain.

4. They eliminate coverages which though important to certain individual insureds are not needed by others.

5. They eliminate uninsurable perils.

6. They eliminate coverages of a specialized nature which the insurance company is not qualified to offer or which require special underwriting and rating.

These latter exposures will frequently be found to have been covered under some other form of contract.

When an adjuster observes that one of the foregoing purposes is threatened by the circumstances of a claim, he should suspect that his policy may provide an applicable exclusion. Reference to his contract often justifies this suspicion. For example, a claim under the basic automobile policy written for a corporation may involve injury to an employe of the insured, injured in the course of his employment. Whether or not he remembers the verbiage of the policy, it should occur at once to an adjuster that workmen's compensation insurance is intended specifically to cover this situation. If he pursues this thought and reads through the exclusions of the basic policy, the adjuster will find an exclusion —applicable to bodily injury liability coverage—of obligations for which the insured corporation is liable under workmen's compensation laws. This example illustrates another point—the difference between *liability* and *coverage*. The company may be *liable* for its employe's injuries; however, because of the exclusion just mentioned, it would have no *coverage* under the basic automobile policy.

Or, for further example, under the same basic policy the adjuster may face a claim for a broken connecting rod. It might then occur to him that if this claim were to be covered, there would be no practical limit to the subsidized maintenance that an insured could enjoy. This situation he will find was anticipated and provided for in the so-called "mechanical breakdown," exclusion of the physical damage section of the policy.

In some policies coverages are grouped under major headings, such as: Liability, Expenses for Medical Services, Physical Damage, etc. The insuring agreements, definitions and exclusions applicable to each coverage are then grouped together. This, it is felt, facilitates the study of and understanding of the contract.

Conditions

A large portion of any liability insurance contract is devoted to *conditions* applicable to one or more of the various insuring agreements. Generally these conditions are grouped together at the end of the policy in a section called "Conditions."

Many conditions impose obligations upon the insured which must be performed as a "condition precedent to recovery." These conditions refer to the duties and obligations of the insured after a loss has occurred, and include such things as "notice of occurrence," "notice of claim or suit," "assistance and cooperation of the insured" and "action against the company." Other conditions deal with "other insurance," "subrogation," "change of policy," "assignment of the contract," "cancellation," "limits of liability" and the significance of the declarations. Any of these conditions may become relevant to the adjustment of a claim.

Before he embarks on automobile work (the starting point for most people), an adjuster should read the policies with which he will be working. While reading each condition, he should attempt to imagine situations which may bring it into play. He should try to discern the reasons why a committee of men anxious to keep a long, complicated document to a minimum length found it necessary to retain each clause. While reading a condition about "notice" for instance, it should immediately occur to him that unless notified of an event which may give rise to a claim a company will be unable to conduct any investigation at all, let alone a sufficient or timely one. It may escape his attention that this notice should be "as soon as practicable," but he should fix it in his mind that the policy has a section dealing with "notice." When at a later date some policyholder appears to have been derelict in this regard, the adjuster should reread the policy. He will surely become aware then of the indefinite phrase "as soon as practicable." His search for its meaning may carry him to a reference source, such as *The Fire, Casualty and Surety Bulletins* (discussed later in this chapter) or to his company's attorney's office to learn what the supreme court of his state may have said constitutes "as soon as practicable."

ADJUSTER'S WORK WITH COVERAGE AT TWO LEVELS

An adjuster works with coverage at *two levels*. The levels merge into and affect one another.

First, the features of the policy under which he is adjusting determine to a high degree how an adjuster works, what questions he asks, and the questions that his work as a whole will be devoted to answering. Coverage is, at the *second* level, a feature of his work in that many phases of claims handling turn upon matters of policy interpretation (whether or not coverage extends to a given situation), or the application of a policy to a situation in which an assured's action may have voided a policy. Matters of the second category often involve the adjuster deeply, and they will be considered later in this chapter.

It may be stretching things a little to say that an adjuster might get along satisfactorily with no basic knowledge of how to deal with matters at the *second* level, but *he is helpless if he cannot deal with coverage matters on the first level.*

First Level Operation

Work at the "first level" is so basic that it is unlikely that any adjuster, even one with so little as a week's field experience, has not already gained a fair working familiarity with the subject. Nevertheless more time is lost and more outright mistakes are made because of sloppy operation at this level than because of inability to handle the more difficult features of coverage.

Therefore, it seems appropriate to spend a few pages at this very elementary level.

Preparing the Abstract

It may be easier to understand how coverage governs one's day to day decisions if these decisions are examined in the context of the conventional quasi-clerical method that the industry has developed for summarizing working coverage records for a field adjuster.

Although in many organizations the operation now to be described is done for him, it will be convenient for the moment to assume that an adjuster commonly prepares his working notes (some may refer to them as an "abstract") for himself upon examination of the "daily" (declarations). Even in those situations where the clerical divisions of his organization prepare these records, the adjuster in effect still has to "abstract" the coverage, for he must read the information that is given to him and then form decisions as to what he will do.

For recording necessary information, a place on the adjuster's worksheet [1] is usually provided. For a policy in common use, this space usually provides an appropriately identified series of spaces, thus reminding the adjuster of each item of information which it will be necessary for him to record. Here is one such form:

Pol#		Eff	Exp	BI	PD	MP
UM			Endorsements			
Year	Make		Type	M	S	
Fire	Theft	Limit	Compr	Collsn	Ded	

Examination of it and the declarations page from any standard automobile policy should make it clear that the abstract is actually nothing but a convenient shorthand for recording the information conveyed by the declarations page. Here is the

---

[1] *Accident reports* often provide space for this information. The accident report, then, or a copy of it, may become an adjuster's worksheet.

same form as it might be filled out to record information about a specific policy:

Pol# FAP-11-401-3074 Eff 3/1/65 Exp 3/1/66 BI 10/20 PD 5 MP nil						
UM Yes		Endorsements none				
Year 63	Make Chev	Type 2dr	M			S 1234567
Fire nil	Theft nil	Limit	Compr nil	Collsn nil	Ded	

The same information could be recorded equally well by writing "FAP-11-401-3074, 3/1/65—3/1/66 (family), '63 Chevrolet 2 DR Sedan 1234567, 10/20/5, med nil, UM yes, Phy D nil, endorsements none."

Because all of the automobile policies are complex forms, and because information about them is received and recorded daily by adjusters, forms for abstracting information about them are common. Except that they may differ in layout, these forms are much like one another.

For policies in less frequent use, adjusters usually have to abstract coverage without the convenient forms as a guide. Fortunately, other policies are usually (although not always) simpler. An abstract for the coverage provided by a comprehensive personal liability policy might be written "CPL-12345, 212 Park Street, Anytown, USA, 1/1/65—1/1/66, principal residence, above, Lia. 10M (single limit), med pay $500, Ph. D. to property $250, endorsements none." In general, therefore, to abstract coverage, one records: *policy number*, the *effective limits* for each coverage provided, a *description of the property* or location covered, and the presence of each *endorsement*. *A good abstract should make an outright statement about each of the coverages commonly afforded by the type of policy one is working with. If one of the common coverages has not been bought, the abstract should state unequivocally the failure to purchase it.*

Coverage as a Determiner of an Adjuster's Activities

The coverage involved determines the direction and much of the scope of an adjuster's activity. This will be more easily demonstrated than explained. Consider therefore this example:

Pol# 1234	Eff 1/1/64	Exp 1/1/65	BI 10/20	PD 5	MP 500
UM 10/20		Endorsements none			
Year 65	Make Buick	Type Conv.	M		S 56789
Fire nil	Theft nil	Limit	Compr nil	Collsn nil	Ded

Assuming that the automobile policy described above covered an accident in which a driver, unaccompanied, ran into a cut bank and was killed, an adjuster would analyze his work something like this:

1. No other car involved, no passengers, therefore no concern with the facts of the accident
2. Occupant of insured's car hurt (dead, in fact), therefore, make necessary preparation for processing medical payments claim
3. No physical damage is provided, therefore no concern over damage to insured's vehicle

Despite this being a very severe accident, therefore, it is simple from an adjusting standpoint.

Now let us deal with still another example:

Pol# 9875	Eff 1/1/65	Exp 1/1/66	BI 50/100	PD 10	MP nil
UM 10/20		Endorsements none			
Year 65	Make Ford	Type 2Dr.	M		S 432102
Fire nil	Theft nil	Limit	Compr nil	Collsn nil	Ded

Assume now that an insured has reported being struck in the rear while waiting for a red light. The report is silent on the question of injuries. There is severe damage reported to the insured's car.

An adjuster might think:

1. Liability: So clearly favorable to assured that it is probably best to leave claimant alone, lest I stir up a claim.
2. Medical payments:—No coverage. No action to be taken.
3. Uninsured motorists: Since coverage is provided, best to find out if other car is insured; if other car not insured, I may have insured to reckon with as a claimant.

4. Physical damage: Not provided, but (note this additional thought) since there is no collision coverage, it is all the more necessary to ascertain if the other car is insured; for, having no other means of repairing his car, insured, if the other car is *not* insured, may well have it suggested to him that he can claim a "whiplash" and collect enough under uninsured motorists coverage to repair his car.

The examples presented should make clear the point that an adjuster reviews coverage to determine the protection afforded by the policy. He then considers the accident he is investigating in the light of the policy provisions and identifies the losses to which his company has been exposed. He then does those things necessary to investigate, measure or control each of the potential losses.

Negative Information (The Surprising Importance of Recording It)

The point has been made that an adjuster's abstract should include an overt statement concerning each coverage. Note that in the examples cited the policies provided no collision coverage. Yet, in *each* instance, *an overt statement was made* indicating that collision coverage was not provided. Doing this saves time in the long run.

For example, when an adjuster first enters a claim in his notebook, he may understand that there are no injuries to persons in his policyholder's car. He may, therefore, record only that information which deals with coverages that he thinks are involved, possibly liability and collision. Some weeks later, his assured turns out to have been hurt and inquiries concerning medical payments benefits may arise. Does the blank spot in his notebook mean that the adjuster forgot to record it because he thought it would be inapplicable? Now time will be lost while he goes back to the beginning and re-ascertains what he ought to have recorded in the first place.

Failure to create a *complete* record, negative as well as positive, may lead to other mistakes with consequences more costly than loss of time, as the following correspondence, excerpted from an actual file, demonstrates.

May 18:   Accident report reports collision and comprehensive exposure.

May 27:   Field adjuster reports settlement of collision exposure.

June 7:   Home office points out that adverse [2] vehicle is a
motor scooter and asks, "Has the operator's statement been secured to rule out injury?"

(Note that the examiner has sensed the potential danger of
an injury claim from the scooter operator.)

June 11:   Memo passed to field adjuster raising foregoing
question.

July 10:   Same inquiry from the home office. Passed on to
the field.

August 15:   Regional office asks the field, "Please answer ours
of 6/11 and 7/10."

September 10:   Field adjuster finally responds, "Our file closed.
Do not have your 6/11 and 7/10 memos. What
did you wish?"

(The baffling silence from the field office is now explained.
Since its file was closed, the earlier memorandums were lost.
This illustrates a common phenomenon by no means limited
to coverage questions. Once a routine operation gets off the
track, its tendency is to get worse and worse.)

September 12:   Regional office sends photostat of the original
inquiry from the home office.

September 17:   Field adjuster responds, "Please check your file.
This is physical damage only. We are not con-
cerned with claimant's possible injury. Subrogation efforts were considered unwarranted due
to the small amount of this settlement."

(Note that the field is still assuming that there is no bodily
injury liability coverage involved.)

September 18:   Regional office responds, "Thanks. We thought
there was some liability exposure."

(Now the regional office has fallen into the same pit, for its
only coverage information came through the field office. The
home office however, gets its coverage straight from underwriting files. Note what happens next.)

September 24:   Home office, noting the foregoing writes, "Just
for the record, our file shows 20/40 B.I. and
5,000 P.D."

---

[2] In automobile work, particularly in accidents involving only two cars, the
vehicle other than the insured's is often referred to simply as the "adverse" car.

September 27: Regional office writes the field, "Note home office memo attached. Passage of time now makes it rather certain that we probably ought not to contact the operator of this motor scooter. However, we are concerned and think you should check up on your contact with the agent. How did it happen your file did not reflect the presence of applicable liability coverage?"

October 5: Field adjuster responds, "It appears that the agent's secretary was second guessing the facts of the accident. She reported only those coverages she thought were involved."

(Now what happened is clear. The agent's secretary checked the daily. Not being a claims person she failed to sense the potential injury claim inherent in a scooter operator being thrown to the ground. He must at least have been bruised. She made another mistake to which all persons who do not work professionally with liability claims are susceptible. She assumed the insured's story was true and she completely overlooked the possibility of the claimant's seizing on the incident to distort the facts. Therefore, although she clearly saw that bodily injury liability coverage was afforded, she assumed that it would be inapplicable and did not mention it to the field claims office.)

The exchange illustrated above, shows clearly that somebody "goofed." It will pay to spend another moment to ask, "Who?"

The guilty party is not the agent's secretary. Her hands are so full with her own duties that it is unreasonable to expect her to sense all the dangers inherent in the simple mishap she was reporting.

The personnel of the field office are at fault. It makes no difference whether the claim reached the field claim office by phone or via a written accident report. In the first instance, the adjuster (or the claim girl taking the call) ought to have asked in so many words, "Is there any liability coverage?" If the accident came in on a written report, someone ought to have phoned back to the agency to inquire about the liability coverage. This failure to sense inherent danger is a common failing. In one way or another, the field claims office should have required the agent's secretary to say whether liability coverage was or was not afforded. *Silence should not have been permitted to create the impression that liability coverage was not afforded.*

It is not stretching things to say that in the cited case the company was remarkably lucky. Any boy knocked off a scooter has at least minor injuries. Except in a few rural areas any injury can be expected to be the subject of a claim more often than not. Whatever the liability situation may have been, the four-month delay would have made the preparation of a defense difficult, if not impossible.

The Second Level

For the insurance adjuster, the ability to understand, work with and handle questions of coverage at the "first level" is a *sine qua non* of his profession. But adjusters are required to do more work with policies than simply to note that such and such a coverage is carried, or that limits of liability are $10,000/20,000 or some such figure. Adjusters are called upon to *interpret* policy language. They are often involved in investigation and contention over what coverage policies provide or do not provide. How an adjuster must proceed in this area must be studied.

Most field adjusters work out of an office where they have a manager or supervisor to guide them. In this environment an adjuster can earn his pay with surprisingly little ability to read, understand or interpret coverage. But he can never hope to manage, supervise, or even operate in a detached one-man office until he has developed an ability to work with coverage on the second level—that is, until he can read a policy and understand its language; go rapidly to a policy to determine what it provides in respect to a given question; determine his company's interest and see that its requirements are met in the event of violation of policy provisions; and finally, know how to apply to a factual situation the involved and ambiguous wording of a policy contract. Most of these skills he will acquire as he goes along.

Examination of Coverage

The purpose of the adjuster's examination of coverage is to determine the liability of the insurance company to or on behalf of the insured under a given set of facts and circumstances according to the terms of the insurance contract. This examination of coverage is a feature of every claim. To the uninitiated, in a routine claim it may seem to have been done so rapidly as to seem almost to have been ignored. This appearance is misleading. Actually, each claim is scrutinized from a coverage standpoint and each adjuster must learn that the practice of the industry never condones the omission of this scrutiny. Broadly speaking, in considering coverage the adjuster directs his attention to the following questions:

1. What is the extent of the coverage provided?
2. Have there been actions or omissions by the insured which would render coverage voidable?
3. Has the insured complied with all obligations imposed upon him? [3]

Each of these will now be considered.

Extent or "Boundaries" of Coverage

The following check list may aid an adjuster in determining the "extent" of the policy under examination or the "boundaries" of the coverage afforded.

Dates (Did the accident or occurrence take place within the *policy period?* Look on the daily for this information.)

Location (Is the occurrence within the *territorial limits* of insurance provided? Look now on the daily. If this information is not there, then look at the insuring clause or the policy conditions.)

Hazard (Does the loss come under one of the exposures for which coverage is provided? The answer to this one is probably in the daily or among the insuring clauses.)

Exclusions (Has the hazard been excluded?)

Limits (Is the coverage equal to the amount of the loss?)

Person (Is the person involved an "insured"?)

Vehicle-Premises-Operation (Does the policy apply in this particular?)

---

[3] Coverage may in rare instances be voided because of a violation of public policy. This is so rare that it need not be considered in a book on elementary adjusting.

Possibly the most frequent errors in checking coverage have to do with dates. These may be guarded against by making it habitual to give conscious thought, at the time coverage information is first received, to policy inception and expiration dates. The date of accident should be considered. Did it fall within the policy period? If an abstract of coverage is being prepared, the early establishment of the habit of entering information in *each* blank provided by the abstract will help to guard against this mistake.

Young adjusters are prone to a common error of technique in fixing the boundaries of the coverage within which they are to work. The error lies in questioning whether there is coverage, when really no question exists. An adjuster may recognize that he is courting this error if he finds himself thinking something like this, "I don't think it's covered, but I can't find anything in the exclusions about it."

This feeling may be the operation of the "coverage sense," "feel" or "intuition" whose development is encouraged elsewhere in this chapter. No one in his right mind, however, *decides* coverage questions on so flimsy a thing as intuition. The road to be followed should be clear to those who have read the earlier pages of this chapter. *Read the policy.*

And the problem itself provides a strong clue as to where the answer lies: the insuring clauses. The adjuster who has this problem makes the error of assuming that because he *expects* to come in the end to a *negative* answer, he will find the answer in the negative language of the *exclusions*. Possibly he has forgotten that there was no coverage at all until coverage was granted by the *positive* language of the *insuring clauses*. If the event being considered does not fall within the coverage provided there, there is no coverage and there is no need to mention the subject in the *exclusions*.

It is a rare office that fails to waste several hours a month debating questions like this. This would not happen had the practice of reviewing the policy been observed.

As a matter of self improvement, every adjuster should make it a rule never to approach his supervisor or manager to ask the simple question, "Is this covered?" without first having *read the policy.* The policy is his first and best source of coverage information. If having read the policy he still fails to understand his problem or to see it answered, then, and only then, should he seek help. If he will read the policy carefully and apply it to his problem, he will seldom have to look further for help.

If he cannot solve his problem to his satisfaction, the adjuster should discipline himself to see to it that he never approaches his supervisor without having read the policy; having located what he believes to be the pertinent sections; having made his own analysis of the question and formed a tentative answer to offer his supervisor for confirmation or amendment.

Repetition notwithstanding, the point is emphasized that if the adjuster has completed the steps listed above, he will rarely need further help. If he does, his supervisor will give it to him. If he approaches his supervisor without having completed these steps, he deserves a short and angry answer.

Developing Coverage Sense (and Using It)

It has been suggested that development of a coverage sense or a "feel" for coverage may be a good thing. How this "feel" may be developed and how it ought to be used will now be considered. Questionable coverage situations are comparatively rare. But although they are rare, they do arise. That is when an adjuster really learns about coverage. Then, in addition to reading what the policy has to say, the adjuster should consider *why* the policy is so framed. Why is the clause so worded? Why is this peril not covered? If these questions cannot be answered *within* the policy, the adjuster should continue his search until from some other acceptable source he learns the meaning of the policy section which he seeks to apply.

He should treat similarly his search for the meaning of an indefinite *phrase* or *word*—"cooperate" for instance, in the condition, "The insured shall *cooperate* with the company and upon the company's request shall . . ." This search may take the adjuster to some of the sources mentioned later in this chapter or beyond them to applicable court decisions.

An adjuster should try, as each situation presents itself, to attain complete understanding of the answer to the question presented. He should search for the reason for the answer in the logic, business practice, common sense or law which underlies each answer.

It may seem that this technique exposes an adjuster to the danger of knowing a lot about several unrelated questions. I can only say that this does not seem to be the way it works out in practice. The mind is an amazing instrument; relating these seemingly separate bodies of knowledge to one another, it makes them into a coherent whole with remarkable speed.

If in this way each question as it comes up is pursued to its foundations in the policy, the adjuster soon develops a feeling for what is and is not covered. This feeling, a valuable warning signal, will stand him in good stead. Its function is the same as that of the heat indicator on the dashboard that tells him when his engine is overheating. Reading the indicator doesn't cure the trouble, or even identify it, it simply tells the driver to stop and then look. If he looks long enough, he will find it.

Extension to Persons

An important question in establishing the extent of the coverage provided by any liability insurance policy is, "Who is an insured under this policy?" The young adjuster soon learns that liability insurance contracts extend protection to many more "insureds" than simply the "named insured." In the basic and comprehensive automobile liability policies this extension of coverage is provided by the section headed "Definition of Insured." In the family and other policies it is provided by the "Persons Insured" portion of the policy. Veteran insurance men refer to the extension as the "omnibus clause." Regardless of how this feature is labeled it is one thing about the policies with which he works that every adjuster should commit to *memory*.

The above advice may seem out of place here since hitherto so much has been made of the point that an adjuster should go to the policy when in doubt. An explanation is in order. It has been observed that the imagination of instructors and the memory of students is scarcely up to the task of giving a young adjuster a comprehensive and reliable picture of the amazing variety of situations that may invoke this provision or of the remarkable host of potential defendants who may be entitled to its protection. Memorizing enables the adjuster to "reread" his policy in the field without going back to his office where his specimen is filed.

Unless he is unique, a young adjuster will encounter many situations in his early years which he was unable to foresee when he first encountered this clause. He will usually find it easier to apply a specific situation to the actual language of the policy than to read the policy and form in his mind a picture of all the situations to which its language might apply.

In effect, therefore, the recommendation that the "definition of insured" be committed to memory is simply a reinforcement of the principle stated in this chapter that the adjuster should "read the policy."

The casualty adjuster should learn, lest he be unpleasantly surprised, that it is not enough for him to wait until each person entitled to coverage comes forward to ask for it. Potential defendants in a law suit may be unaware of their peril or that they are entitled to coverage. Their failure to report an accident or to seek coverage under the policy may well be excused by a court on the ground that the person entitled to coverage was not aware of his rights and should therefore be excused for failing to request them. Claimants on the other hand are tireless and resourceful in their search for the solvent defendant. The dominant American view is that if there is an injury, someone must be found to pay for it. Therefore, if there is a defendant whom the insurer may in the future be obliged to cover, it should be expected that the claimant will not rest until he has identified him. The time for the insured to face up to this situation is when something can be done about it.

An adjuster is *not* required to have at his fingertips the answers to all of the complex cases with which he will deal. What *is* required of him is to recognize potential trouble. He should try to develop the habit of considering all the theories of liability that a claimant may try to exploit. When he has identified those persons or firms against whom an injured person may possibly sustain an action, he should then consider whether any of these potential defendants is an insured or a potential insured under an omnibus clause. Where even the *possibility* of being called on to defend an apparently uninvolved defendant exists, the adjuster should take advantage of the availability of advice from his supervisor, home office or counsel. The time to dispose of this kind of potential claim is before it gets out of hand.

Policy Violation by Misrepresentation

A policy may be rendered *voidable* by reason of what is known as a *material misrepresentation*. Misrepresentation by itself does not void the policy or make it inoperative. It is only voidable by the company. If the company wishes to treat the policy as void, then there must be a formal rescission of the policy and refund of the consideration. To establish that there was, in fact, a misrepresentation, the company—in addition to showing *materiality*—must prove:

a. that the policyholder *made* a representation;
b. that it was in fact *false*;
c. that the policyholder knew or must have known it was false;
d. that the company relied upon it justifiably—i.e., did not have knowledge of the true facts or of the falsity of the representation.

Investigation of cases in which there is a suspicion of a material misrepresentation requires knowledge that these things must be established by *evidence*. Materiality can be determined by the company, but field investigation is the basis for proper and timely decision.

Because they imply the denial of coverage to an insured; because the policyholder is invariably disappointed and often enraged; because producers and the departments allied with them are inclined to identify with the policyholder, questions involving misrepresentation are upsetting and unpleasant to handle. They have been known to set different departments of a company at odds with one another. Questions of this category therefore should be raised only *for good reason*.

The test of *materiality* should always be considered. Upon examination many *apparent* misrepresentations prove to be quite *immaterial*. It is better to avoid raising questions in the first place than to raise them and then have to abandon them. The resolution of liability questions, disputes over injury and its value, and justifiable argument over the interpretation of necessarily complex policy contracts impose an abundance of strife upon the claims business. Careful thought to materiality enables the adjuster to avoid adding unnecessarily to this discord.

Policy Violation by Failure to Comply with Policy Obligations

Coverage may also be put in issue by failure of the insured to do some act or thing required of him.

Granted that a policyholder's principal obligation is the payment of his premium, nevertheless when an accident happens he does have duties to fulfill. Failure to perform them may void his coverage. Some of these duties are enumerated here:

1. He must give *notice.*
2. He must extend reasonable *cooperation* to his insurer.
3. He may not *settle* or *negotiate* "on his own."
4. In respect to medical reimbursement, he must *produce reports* and *submit to examination.*
5. He must *protect his property* from further loss and damage.
6. If a theft is involved, he must *notify the police.*
7. He must file *proof of loss.*
8. He must submit to *examination* under oath.
9. In many circumstances he must *arbitrate* otherwise unresolved differences.

These obligations of the policyholder are by no means clearcut. Often they have been watered down by a statute or traditional interpretation to the point where they mean considerably less than they seem to mean.

Notice

Disputes over *notice* outnumber by a wide margin all other questions raised regarding the insured's obligations. It is difficult to generalize as to what constitutes proper notice. Most liability policies among their conditions stipulate that notice shall be "as soon as practicable." This seems reasonably clear until one learns that at least one jurisdiction has held that a report delayed 18 months satisfied this requirement.

In serious claims the rights of the company may be gravely prejudiced by as little as 24 hours' delay. The key to the question of notice lies not in the time involved *per se* but in the prejudice done to the insurer's ability to investigate, defend and negotiate and in the extent to which it may be said that the insured ought to have recognized his exposure to legal liability.

Mere *inaccuracy* in the representations made by or on behalf of a policyholder when he buys a policy may not void coverage unless they have *materially* affected the company's decision to accept or reject the business. It may be helpful to regard the question of "prejudice"[4] in failure to comply with the policy's provisions as the counterpart of materiality. To put it in very simple language, courts in considering questions revolving about alleged failure to comply with policy requirements, when they apply the test of "prejudice" are saying, "In the end, what difference did it make?" If the court feels that the alleged failure to comply made no difference it is quite likely to disregard a failure to comply with the letter of the policy contract and to require coverage to be extended.

In like fashion, the adjuster should consider what circumstances may have influenced the policyholder in his consideration of the situation to which he was exposed. Was he in a position to recognize his liability to suit? Was he in fact conscious and able to report? In short, by what reasonable grounds might his failure to act be excused?

In the end, the adjuster will wish to acquaint himself with the pronouncements of his state supreme court in respect to interpretations of timeliness and those circumstances which they have regarded as excusing an insured for failure to act. However, this knowledge of the law is not necessarily prerequisite to handling the first case nor is it initially of paramount importance.

---

[4] Not all states require a demonstration of prejudice, but, even where prejudice is not required as a condition precedent to setting aside the policy, in any court *evidence* of prejudice makes a better case for the insurer.

It is one of many things, all important in the end but probably not essential to starting out on the job. If an adjuster were to stop to learn all matters of this order of importance, he might be middle-aged before he wrote his first statement. It will probably be sufficient if a beginning adjuster realizes that sooner or later these questions will come up. When they do, he will want to learn, if possible, the position that his state's courts took on the questions presented. Thus on a case by case basis he builds a unified picture of the obligations of the insured and the company to one another.

Before leaving the question of notice, it should be noted that there prevails in the business a widely accepted tendency to accept reports within 30 days of the occurrence as "timely." This custom has nothing to justify it in policy language nor in court decisions. It is best to regard it as a convenient "rule of thumb." The fact is that very few reports are questioned on the ground of timeliness unless they are 30 or more days old. Practice may vary from company to company and an adjuster will certainly wish to make it his business to ascertain at once the view of his employer on this question.

Other Obligations of the Insured

If an insurance company is to defend an insured, it seems only common sense that it must have his *cooperation*. This subject, too, is dealt with in policy conditions. An insured's cooperation is seldom lacking; in fact, it must be conceded that as a practical matter the insured's desire for vindication and his eagerness to inject himself into investigation, control and settlement often does more harm than good; and an adjuster is more often required to *discourage* an insured's activity than to seek it.

Overactivity, too, may conflict with policy provisions, for "except at his own cost [the insured shall not] voluntarily make any payment, assume any obligation . . ." (This language will be found in most liability policies.) The reason for this provision may not be obvious but it is only a matter of time until an adjuster has to handle a claim in which an insured, overanxious to preserve his underwriting record and rate or anxious to avoid prosecution under a traffic code, has tried to make his own settlement with a claimant. Unless his situation is quite out of the ordinary, the adjuster will find that his insured has taken an inadequate release (if indeed he took any at all), has possibly made what amounts to an embarrassing admission of liability, and may have angered the claimant to the point where the adjuster cannot deal successfully with him.

The reason for this policy provision will then be clear to the adjuster.

Whether he is trying to procure the cooperation of a reluctant insured or to discourage the meddling of an officious one, the adjuster's proper concern is not so much that of voiding coverage as to bring about the correct attitude and action from his policyholder.

When an insured is less than cooperative, it is usually because he does not know what is expected of him or what the policy requires, and the situation may have been compounded by his failure to understand the terms of advice given him by his lawyer. Often it is put, "My lawyer told me not to talk to anyone." A phone call to the lawyer will usually result in the attorney's willing assistance in bringing about the cooperation of the insured.

The assured who wants to be his own adjuster may be handled in much the same way. To him it can be explained that one of the things he bought with his premium is the privilege of sitting at his ease while the adjuster does his working for him.

Rarely, an insured may flatly refuse to cooperate. When this happens, the adjuster should first make certain that he has exhausted all means of peaceful persuasion. He should re-examine the situation to make sure of his own ground. Then he may make a clear demand in writing to his insured, setting forth the obligation imposed by the contract and the action which the adjuster desires him to take. Such a notice might also call to the assured's attention the fact that failure to comply could result in the voiding of his coverage.

This written demand for cooperation is regarded as an extreme measure and should not be undertaken except in unusual circumstances and then usually only after clearance from the home office. If an assured still remains unpersuaded, the company may as a last resort choose to go to its legal remedy, a suit for declaratory judgment to void the policy, citing as grounds for this action whichever of the policy provisions may have been violated.

It bears repeating that these and other maneuvers should be recognized for what they are, simply a legal means of requiring certain acts from an insured. In invoking these sections of the policy, the adjuster should be careful not to be too technical. He may win the battle and lose the war. The important thing is the procurement of compliance, not the voiding of coverage.

Procedure When Coverage Is In Question

That the coverage situation has been passed upon by others before a claim comes to an adjuster does not relieve him of the duty of raising a question if he himself discovers that coverage is in doubt. This does not mean that investigational steps made by another should be retraced; rather that the file should be scrutinized to make certain that these necessary steps have been taken.

The adjuster should immediately convey to his company any reasonable doubt which he may hold, *even though to him there may seem to be coverage.* At this point he is merely raising a question, which is to be distinguished from declining to cover.

Once the coverage question has been raised (and it makes no difference who raises it) the adjuster should realize that further steps in investigation or negotiation may seriously damage his company's ability to maintain its position if its rights have indeed been adversely effected. This damage may consist in the doing of something that will have placed the company in such a position that, in the eyes of the law, it will later be held to have waived its rights for defense against coverage or to have placed itself in such a position that the law forbids it to raise a question of coverage. In short, there are legal principles that add up to the homely admonition that the company must "fish or cut bait."

But the law may be a little shortsighted. Often the facts are unclear or disputed or (most common of all) neither company nor insured can predict whether on the facts at hand a court would rule "coverage" or "no coverage." This creates a dilemma. If the company withdraws, the insured (lacking know-how and resources to finance his defense) may wind up facing a much larger verdict than would otherwise have been the case. This could be a disaster to an insured if the coverage ruling goes against him. (It is hardly welcome to the company if the ruling goes against it!)

To resolve this not uncommon dilemma, the industry has developed two devices the intent of which is to permit investigation to proceed without damage to the rights of either party—the company or the insured. They are:

1. The sending of a reservation of rights letter.
2. The execution of a non-waiver agreement.

Examples of both documents are in the Appendix.

The procedures now to be outlined, although they are subject to the usual judgment exceptions, are as nearly universal as any to be found in this individualistic business.

Upon discovering a coverage question, the adjuster stops work on other phases of the claim not connected with that question. He does not resume investigation and negotiation until he has protected his company with a reservation of rights letter or a non-waiver agreement. He immediately advises his insured of the question at issue. All possible effort is made promptly to resolve the coverage question. While coverage is at issue most companies insist that no settlement be made without home office approval.

Upon decision by the company that "coverage is in order" [5] (or that the question cannot successfully be litigated), handling of the claim then proceeds without further reference to the coverage question and in the assumption that coverage is provided.

A negative decision on the other hand may result in a *denial of coverage*, or a decision to continue under a non-waiver agreement.

---

[5] Possibly this phrase is insurance jargon but its use is almost universal. It means that a decision has been reached that coverage is applicable to the loss or that the company has elected to close its eys to possible violation—in other words, to extend coverage.

A decision to deny coverage implies that a company recognizes the possibility (more likely the *probability*) that it will have to sustain its position in a court of law and further recognizes the company's willingness to attempt to do so. A decision to continue under a non-waiver agreement may simply imply a decision on the part of both the company and the insured to set the coverage question aside pending a resolution of other questions involved, such as liability, amount of damage, etc.

Of the two devices, i.e., reservation of rights and "non-waiver agreement," the non-waiver agreement is generally considered the stronger. The agreement exhibited in the Appendix is generalized to apply to many situations and is typical of the "non-waiver" form that adjusters are privileged to complete without conflicting with the restrictions imposed upon them by the "agreement as to the respective rights and duties." A "non-waiver agreement" drawn by counsel and particularized to the case at issue is stronger than a general agreement. Either is probably stronger than a reservation of rights letter. An individualized and particularized non-waiver agreement might be resorted to in the event that investigation of the coverage question leads to a decision to continue in defense of litigation, the coverage question notwithstanding—i.e., with the mutual agreement to leave the coverage question in abeyance.[6]

However, not even a particularized "non-waiver agreement" should be regarded as an iron-clad guarantee that the result sought—the unimpaired preservation of the company's rights— will indeed be accomplished.

If there is any one criterion about which the standard of a company's conduct revolves, it is probably that the company should do nothing that leaves the insured in a poorer position than he would have been in if the insurance company had not been involved in the matter at all. In other words, the insurance company cannot waive any rights or opportunity that would normally have been available to its insured. Neither by its words nor actions may it lull him into inactivity by permitting the

---

[6] Again the reminder, specific action in this area will be strongly influenced by the practices of individual companies.

growth of a belief that it will act on his behalf when in fact such activity is in doubt. That impression might induce him to remain inactive in a situation where he might otherwise protect himself.

In practice, therefore, the adjuster, even though operating under a non-waiver, should keep his insured fully informed and should secure his assent to any proposed course of action. This would be particularly true of a negative decision, such as that of passing up an offer to settle made by a claimant.

Non-waiver agreements notwithstanding, courts have been known to take the position that a company cannot continue to act indefinitely under a non-waiver. Thus, there reappears an idea expressed before, that there may well be a time when a company simply has to "fish or cut bait!" Hence, these situations, accentuate the usual obligation to keep the insurer fully and promptly informed, and to hold one's self ready to be guided by specific instructions.

To a young adjuster, the procurement of a non-waiver agreement often seems to be more of a problem than it ought to be. The insured should, of course, be promptly informed of the circumstances giving rise to the coverage question. This should be done unequivocally and in a manner that implies that the assured will certainly understand that the action is no less than he would expect to have taken in his behalf were his and the company's positions reversed. This is not a time to pussy-foot or to mince words. Neither is it a time to bluster, criticize or demand. Plain speaking need not be rude or unpleasant. Forthrightness best serves the insurer and will be best appreciated by the assured. It should then be pointed out to him that it will be to his disadvantage as well as the company's if investigation is delayed pending resolution of the coverage question. If it is further explained to him that there exists a device (a non-waiver agreement) by which the rights of each party, the insured and the company, may be preserved intact as they may exist at the moment, neither gaining the advantage over the other; and if, as he produces the document, the adjuster points out those phrases which *do* protect the insured, the signature of the non-waiver is not difficult to procure. The longer the procurement of a non-waiver is delayed the greater the difficulty encountered.

The foregoing discussion should be read with some qualifications firmly in mind. First, that all actions in this field are greatly influenced by individual company policy. The attempt here has been to set out what seems to the author as most nearly approaching the norm. An adjuster will, of course, always conform his individual actions to company policy and preferences. Secondly, companies—and the business as a whole—have two well-founded reservations about the use of non-waiver agreements.

The first reservation is simply the feeling (for which there is much justification) that using a non-waiver is such a formal procedure and places the company and the insured in such an "arms length" status that it may thereafter be difficult to get from the insured a truthful statement regarding the facts bearing on coverage.

Also, in some situations though by no means universally, it has been held that to request a non-waiver, to be refused, and then to continue in the defense and investigation of a claim is a waiver of the insurer's position. A reservation of rights letter avoids the possibility of being caught in this "corner."

Coverage Statements

Investigating coverage questions commonly involves "questions of fact." It is scarcely to be wondered at, particularly when facts are at issue as in the case of a delayed report, that an insured may insist that he *did* give a report as required and the agent to whom he says he reported may insist equally firmly that he never heard from his policyholder. Each obviously has a somewhat different version of the matter. It is therefore desirable to reduce immediately to writing the testimony of *all* parties concerned, particularly the testimony of the insured as to *when*, to *whom*, and *how* notice of the accident was given by him to a representative of the company. Notice is not the only point about which questions of fact hinge; it has simply been selected for discussion because of its frequency and to illustrate the way these questions should be handled.

Statements secured on coverage questions necessarily mention insurance. Because those statements which deal solely with matters of liability and injury may have to be introduced in a court action where coverage and the existence or non-existence of insurance is not at issue, those statements which do deal with coverage and which necessarily mention insurance should be taken separately. In other words, liability and damage should be covered in one statement and coverage questions in which there will be overt mention made of the fact of insurance dealt with in a separate statement.

The subject matter and techniques of statements in general will be discussed in detail in Chapter 6. The same care and technique employed for the more usual type of statement should be employed in coverage statements. It is particularly important that when an adjuster opens a point by writing anything about it the witness should be questioned until all his knowledge pertaining to the subject is exhausted. For instance, if a policyholder says that he "notified" his agent, he should be required to say when he notified him, whether by face to face conversation, by telephone, or through written communication or message via a third party. The substance of the conversation should then be detailed and if a third party was present or involved in the transaction, it will probably be desirable that his testimony likewise be fixed in statement form.

ACCIDENT VERSUS OCCURRENCE

Some liability policies contain in their insuring agreements the limiting words "caused by accident."

The determination of "what is an accident" as distinguished from an "event" or "occurrence" is one of the classic coverage questions. There are other questions of equal importance, some perhaps of greater importance, but to deal with each of them would make of this volume not a book about elementary adjusting but a book about coverage refinements.

Therefore it is only *secondarily* for the purpose of acquainting an adjuster with the "accident versus occurrence" question that a discussion from *The Fire, Casualty and Surety Bulletins* is reproduced in the Appendix.

The material is included because the question is typical of interpretational questions in the field of coverage. Parenthetically, it should be noted that this interpretational question, like most of its fellows, hinges on the definition, in its particular context in the policy, of a single word or phrase. Settling these points involves lawyers, judges and laymen and interweaves business law with the craft of policy writing.

The material quoted in that treatment shows an actual word in the process of acquiring its definition by the growth of decisions about it. It is unlikely that the last word has been said on the meaning of the word "accident," so the process is not yet at an end. It also shows one of the most popular and widely available references to which adjusters may turn.

REFERENCE SOURCES

Whether his office subscribes to them or not, an adjuster should familiarize himself with the common loose-leaf reference guides. Widely distributed, they will almost always be available to him in a nearby office if not in his own. Eventually and inevitably, an adjuster will find himself over his head in some coverage question. When he is, he may turn to:

1. *The Fire, Casualty and Surety Bulletins* (invariably abbreviated to its initials F.C. & S.)
2. *Policy Form and Manual Analysis* (abbreviated to its initials P.F. & M.)
3. *Adjusters Reference Guide*

The Fire, Casualty and Surety Bulletins are published by The National Underwriter Company, Cincinnati, Ohio. They are directed more toward *explaining* the meaning of various terms and provisions (many of which are common to many policies) than toward outright statement of the content of individual policies. The question of "accident versus occurrence" is a case in point. In reviewing the quoted material and also in referring to the *Bulletins* it should be remembered that the policies and the decisions which interpret them change constantly; hence what is true today and found in any loose-leaf service may be untrue tomorrow.

If he has access to F. C. & S. the adjuster should familiarize himself with his index which is unusually complete and very helpful.

P. F. & M., published by Rough Notes, Inc., Indianapolis, Indiana, consists mostly (though not entirely) of digests of very many policies. The language is simple, brief and non-technical. P. F. & M. is helpful when dealing with a non-standard policy. It furnishes an adjuster with a general idea of what the policy is about. It is of only limited use in answering specific coverage questions. Usually *when a coverage question is before him, the adjuster needs to get down to the actual wording and punctuation of the policy.*

The adjuster often needs neither simplification nor analysis. What he needs is something to give him the text itself. To satisfy this need he may turn to *Adjusters Reference Guide,* published by Insurance Field Company, Louisville, Kentucky (published in cooperation with the National Association of Independent Insurance Adjusters, Chicago, Illinois).

Adjusters Reference Guide prints verbatim specimens of current standard policies on a wide range of subjects.[7]

In addition to the foregoing, an adjuster will find it profitable, whenever he has occasion to deal with a new policy, to pick up a photostat of it and build his own private bank of policy specimens. Even though policies change with the years such a bank will be immensely helpful.

It is often more difficult than it should be for an adjuster to get his hands on a specimen of the policy under which he is attempting to adjust. When he is confronted with this problem, a specimen is usually closer than he realizes. I refer of course to the policyholder himself and his own policy. This may be examined and if necessary photostated.

SUMMARY

In relation to coverage, an adjuster's most pressing need is to develop simple, efficient and thorough techniques for ascertain-

---

[7] It also contains a compilation of articles dealing not only with coverage but with other phases of claims work.

ing the coverages provided by the policies with which he is working, and for applying those policies to the cases he is handling.

Perfecting those techniques will do more to keep him out of trouble than almost anything else he does with or about coverage.

In order to operate beyond the advice of a manager or supervisor or to function as a manager or supervisor which he hopes some day to do, an adjuster should develop the ability to read a policy, ascertain thereby the coverage that it provides, and apply it to a given situation. This will prove in the end to be his essential tool in working with coverage. This is what enables him to approach a claim under a completely unfamiliar policy with confidence.

To attain this goal, the adjuster should, therefore, study his policies and approach each coverage question as it is presented to him as an opportunity to discover the underlying reasons as well as the language governing coverage. He should encourage the growth of an intuitive ability to suspect the existence of coverage or non-coverage and of logical and necessary policy provisions. This intuition will lead him to his policy and there, in most instances, he will find the language to support him or to show him that he has been following a false trail.

Coverage sense develops from experience and a restless zeal to find the ultimate "why" of policy provisions as each one is called into operation by the need to apply it to a particular situation. Coverage sense is no substitute for reading a policy—it is a flag to tell one when he should go to his policy. The adjuster should cultivate the ability to read and understand policies and familiarize himself with the available authorities so that he may turn to them in need. By all odds, the most valuable advice offered by this chapter may be condensed to three words, "read the policy."

CHAPTER 4

Reserves

Remote though the subject of reserves may seem to be from his daily activities, there are nevertheless compelling reasons why an adjuster, even a beginner, should know what reserves are, how his activities relate to them and, possibly the least important, something about the theory of reserving since in some instances, he may actually be asked to establish reserves.

This section will introduce adjusters to this field of insurance activity.

What Is a Reserve?

If, when an accident occurs, it could be immediately reported, liability immediately established and the extent of loss determined, the insurance company involved would pay the claimant at once and by nightfall its funds would have been diminished by the amount of the loss. This would demonstrate the effect of that loss in their figures, the company's balance sheet and profit and loss statement would accurately reflect the claim and its effect on the company's financial standing.

If this combination of circumstances described realistic claim circumstances, there would be no need for the accounting device known as reserves. Claim, of course, almost never settle on the same day they happen and are reported. Damage may be difficult to measure; measurement may be impossible until an injury has healed and this may take years. Damage may be disputed and the dispute may take time to resolve. Liability may be unknown and unknowable until after investigation, and possibly not until after litigation. Claims, therefore, take time. Although carriers would prefer to pay losses as they occur, this is impossible. Never-

105

theless, an insurance company's assets are diminished as soon as it receives notice of any claim, and the amount of the diminution is the probable pay-out of the claim. The reduction has taken place but payment of the claim may not occur for days or even years. The diminution is immediate and to reflect the carrier's true condition, the books of account must in some way recognize that loss has been *incurred,* hence, the device we know as "reserves."

Reserves are an accounting device, a book entry, to record the fact that loss has been incurred and to subtract the dollar value of that loss from capital and surplus.

How should the amount subtracted from capital and surplus be determined? The amount, of course, should be the amount of the loss, but this is seldom knowable. Since the carrier cannot know, it must estimate. The loss reserve, therefore, is a bookkeeping entry to subtract from capital and surplus the amount a carrier *expects* to pay on a claim.

Incurred But Not Reported

In any month, a claims office will, by the end of that month, have received reports on only about half the losses which will have occurred in that month and which it will eventually handle. The same is true of the company which the office represents. Some reports will come in the following month but some will even be delayed for years. The courts, remember, are not inclined to void coverage on the argument that a report was not made "as soon as practicable."

All carriers, therefore, know that they are always faced with the certainty of paying for claims about which they know nothing except that they are out there somewhere. They do not know who had the accident, or where, or how, or why, but the claims are there and they will be paid eventually. To recognize this situation, carriers reserve a sum, usually in the neighborhood of the value of one month's average reported losses. This reserve is known as "incurred but not reported." In the trade, this figure is commonly referred to as "IBNR." Adjusters have virtually nothing to do with establishing or influencing this figure but they should know what the phrase and its initials mean.

Formula Reserves

Although adjusters have virtually nothing to do with them, it is well to know that many classes of cases are reserved by formula. These formulas are based on past experience. Claims of a given type will be reserved at an average figure—the same value given to each claim of a given category. Categories though, the adjuster should remember, may be determined on the basis of information he supplies. Except for this information, the adjuster has nothing to do with formula reserves.

How Reserves Are Established

Most reserves are established by the subjective judgment of adjusters. More often than not the actual reserve on a given claim is set by a supervisor or a home office examiner.

The figure selected will be the dollar result of a complex of ideas of which the following list is only a partial example:

The examiner's view of the claim's verdict [1] value.
His view of the possibilities of successful defense.
His estimate of the possibility of setting the claim at the subjective value level.
His view of the probable sum for which it can be settled.
His realistic recognition that sometimes his expectations will not be realized.

Time and the inflow of information from the field modify the dollar value of each of these concepts.

Sometimes an adjuster will establish reserves himself. This is likely to be done at the time a claim is first reported, but in many companies adjusters are requested to submit their reserve suggestions periodically on claims in their hands. These recommendations may be influential even though an examiner may modify them upward or downward as the following anecdote illustrates:

The adjuster was quite young and not accustomed to setting up reserves. His manager's illness thrust the duty of assigning

---

[1] "Verdict value" and "subjective value" are defined in Chapter 11, Evaluation.

initial reserves on him. The accident was reported by telephone and it was immediately obvious that the injuries were frightful and the liability probable. Although he had never seen a claim of such size he made a few quick calculations and assigned a $70,000 reserve and went out to investigate. Reserves of this size are not really everyday occurrences, even in a home office of the giant carrier. The next day the home office was on the phone and learned that the claim was indeed one of frightening potential. Alerted by the size of a neophyte's reserve, they were able to extend immediate advice and authority which resulted in eventually closing the claim at a substantial saving in the loss which would have been sustained had not prompt action been taken. The source of this anecdote is an executive who credited the saving, not to his home office staff, but to the sound, realistic action of the adjuster who assigned the reserve and drew attention to a problem when there was still time to do something about it.

How Reserves Relate to Adjuster's Activity

Reserves are principally established on the basis of information gathered by adjuster. Of all adjusters' faults, possibly the most common is to be slow or deficient in reporting information to file. A quick look at the 1970 issue of *Best's Key Rating Guide* may show why carriers take the subject so seriously and often dismiss adjusters who are habitually late in reporting.

This *Guide* discloses in reference to three large well-known carriers:

Company	Case Loss Reserves (000 omitted)	Net Premiums Written (000 omitted)
Liberty Mutual Ins. Co.	$868,519	$800,365
Travelers Indemnity Co.	633,430	808,902
State Farm Mutual Auto	785,926	1,477,629
Total	$2,287,875	$3,086,896

Taken together, therefore, this group of very large, very highly regarded carriers were carrying loss reserves aggregating 75% of their total business revenue at the close of 1969.

The same *Guide* reported the underwriting profits (the profits before considering investment income or gain or loss on investments) as follows:

Company	Underwriting Gain or Loss (000 omitted)
Liberty Mutual Ins. Co.	$ 9,754
Travelers Indemnity Co.	45,532 (loss)
State Farm Mutual Auto	82,371 (loss)
Total	$118,149 (loss)

Taken together, this group of exceptionally large, conservative, well-managed companies showed a loss of 3.3% on their aggregate writings.

If any member of this group was underestimating its loss reserves by as little as 10%, it suffered a major financial disaster in 1969. If, on the other hand, it was over-estimating its reserves by the same margin, it may have made a handsome profit.

The reserves of each carrier at the end of 1969 included many losses incurred in 1964 and earlier. Many of the losses incurred in 1969 will not be closed until 1974 or later.

None of these companies would have had the faintest idea whether it made or lost money in 1969 without the device we call "reserves."

Virtually all management's critical decisions depend on whether a company is making money:

Whether to extend or curtail writings.

Whether to raise or lower premiums.

Whether to emphasize or restrict a line or territory or some other phase of activity.

Presidents are fired (and adjusters' salaries are not raised) when profits are absent.

Clearly, reserves—and their determination— is a *vital* function as essential to insurance as any organ is to the body's health. Reserves are more vital to insurance than the leg to walking (one could always walk, after a fashion, on crutches).

Since adjusting generates the information on which reserves for the most part are established, it should be obvious that the accumulation and *reporting* of information about claims is the foundation without which reserves could not be accurately established.

Chapter 9 deals with reporting and will emphasize the theme that there is no part of the adjuster's work more readily subject to his control than the timeliness and adequacy of reports. The preceding paragraphs should have made it clear why such over-riding importance attaches to an activity so technical and so devoid of drama.

Anyone who can speak the English language can make adequate and timely reports. Now it is clear why in the long run the claims business deals harsely with those who do not.

SUMMARY

Losses are not paid as soon as they occur. Financial data must be up to date to guide immediate management decisions. In order that today's figure may anticipate the effect of payments to be made long in the future, case reserves are established. The accuracy of these reserves depends on information. To supply that information is one of adjusters' chief functions.

Chapter 5

Investigation

INTRODUCTION

Chapter 2 surveyed those legal principles with which adjusters are most concerned. These principles constitute the framework on which he hangs evidence and information and against which he forms decisions to act based upon that evidence.

The title of this chapter, "Investigation," suggests deep digging, exhaustive inquiry, and the patient unearthing of elusive fact. This might be somewhat misleading, when the real work of investigation is analyzed. The adjuster does, it is true, from time to time do some intricate searching for elusive evidence. He will, it is true, realize some of his deepest satisfactions from the successful unearthing of well-buried bodies. However, 90% of the adjuster's investigational activity involves the gathering of information from persons whose information is readily available for the asking and whose relation to the accident is obvious. This chapter concerns itself mostly with these obvious sources, when to search out the obvious facts, when not to, what to look for, and what the adjuster does with the information which he has obtained.

For the average claim, investigation means assembling, with maximum accuracy and minimum effort, the information and evidence on which the insurer can determine the position it should take in respect to its legal obligation—or to put it in practical terms, whether to settle, compromise or deny.

This is a book about the fundamentals of adjusting and it is in these fundamental terms that investigation is considered.

Although adjusters hope that they will settle every claim of merit and satisfy all other claimants that they should accept denials gracefully, they know that neither hope will be fulfilled.

111

Although only a few claims ever get inside the courtroom door, claims must be handled with the understanding that, efforts to settle notwithstanding, any claim may become a law suit. For the rest of his business life, therefore, the adjuster will be balancing his need to be prepared to defend his position against his need to process his claims with a maximum of speed and a minimum of expense.

These two antithetical requirements and the ways that he reconciles them are met in this chapter.

The office decisions which precede the assignment of a claim for field handling will also be discussed briefly, in the hope that this will make more understandable the work that is to come.

Then, since investigation is as much a matter of deciding what *not* to do and whom *not* to see as it is a matter of deciding *what* to do and *whom* to see, adjusters' decisions in these areas will be discussed at length.

Attention will then be directed to *techniques*—that is, how to accomplish certain objectives. Finally, consideration will be given to certain kinds of evidence and the problems related to creating, securing and preserving it; to certain special situations requiring special handling and to the question of cooperation between insurance companies.

This chapter will confine itself so far as possible to "investigation" in the sense of gathering information and evidence, but it is immensely important to recognize that this separation from such other adjuster activities as "control" and "settlement" is purely artificial. The separation is only a device to enable one to talk about one thing at a time. To emphasize the point, adjusters almost never speak of the number of claims they are "investigating"; instead they speak of the number they are "handling."

SOME NEW TERMS

Obtaining evidence and information, then, is part of an adjuster's job, but it is not a function which he carries out without reference to other phases of his work. It would be convenient if adjusters could always wait until investigation were complete to evaluate their claims and could wait again until evaluation had considered all relevant factors before beginning to settle them.

Unfortunately the claims world is otherwise arranged. Other adjusting functions impinge upon and to a substantial degree influence the way adjusters investigate (i.e., handle) claims.

This chapter, therefore, necessarily introduces terms not previously met—terms which will later be discussed at length but which ought now to be explained for the benefit of those whose work has not already made the terms commonplace.

The reason *why* these terms have to be made clear *at this point* is possibly more important than the terms themselves. It is that the claims business is one with seemingly separate operations inextricably inter-related. Almost everything that one does is so related to or dependent on what he has done before or will do in the future that it often seems that an *end* is indistinguishable from a *beginning*—that an adjuster meets himself coming in the door, as it were. No part of this business, therefore, can be considered without bearing in mind its relationship to other parts.

It is this quality of the business which will require this chapter to use the word "control," a word whose meaning in our business will be considered at some length in Chapter 12. For the time being it is enough to say that when an adjuster speaks of control, he is referring to something closely related to persuasion but in a context peculiar to our work. An injured claimant, actively or by default, must arrive at a decision whether to adjust his own claim or employ an attorney to adjust it for him. Creating in the claimant's mind confidence in the company, in the adjuster and ultimately, of course, in the claimant's own ability to negotiate in his own behalf, and all the things that an adjuster does to that end are referred to as "control." Control as an activity of adjusters will be seen in this chapter. It is a term whose use in the claims business is almost universal.

"Discounting," too, will be mentioned. Although this also is a procedure almost universally practiced in claims handling, it seems to have become widespread without in the meantime acquiring much of a name.

When, in our work, the practice is referred to by name, its most common name is "discounting," and in this book, "discounting" means *the process of evaluating a claim before all pertinent facts are known.* This is a rational process—quite a different thing from guesswork—and it, too, will be elaborated on in Chapter 12.

When an adjuster settles a claim and disburses the money involved, he often finds it worthwhile to do this in such a way that doctors, hospitals and other creditors are assured that the funds intended for them reach them, rather than being spent by an irresponsible claimant. This is essentially an exercise in public relations. It recognizes the debt of responsibility that business and professional people should feel toward one another. It is a gracious return of courtesies received by insurance adjusters and it enhances the standing of the adjuster, his principal and the insurance business to their eventual benefit in situations yet to arise, a clear example of an end being indistinguishable from the beginning. This practice is known as "protecting" creditors.

OFFICE DECISIONS PRECEDENT TO ASSIGNMENT

To a typical claims office, each day brings disasters as well as trifles, claims to be investigated, reports to be postponed or ignored. Before a claim reaches an adjuster, he should understand the selection process that has already taken place. Such an understanding clarifies the decisions which he must make in deciding where to go, whom to see, and what to do.

Upon inspection of the inital report, many claims may be classified according to the following categories:

Category	Disposition
a. Doubtful liability—minor property damage	a. Although files may be created for record, it is common to take no action on these reports
b. Clear or doubtful liability—property damage not sufficiently great to lead to the suspicion of bodily injury	b. File established, claim blank mailed to claimant
c. Report of bodily injury in claimant car	c. Assigned to adjuster
d. No report of bodily injury in claimant car but property damage or bodily injury in insured's car indicates violent collision; suspicion that there may be bodily injury in the other car	d. Assigned to adjuster

The decision to leave a claim alone, i.e., to take no action, is a calculated risk. In the business, this is known as putting a claim on "let rest" or simply, "letting rest." The willingness to run this calculated risk quite understandably varies from one insurance company to another and from person to person.

The typical morning mail also brings to the typical claim office some previously mailed claim blanks showing injury to a claimant operator or his passengers. These too are immediately assigned to an adjuster for active handling.[1]

It should be noted that the principal factors governing decisions regarding assignment turn more on *potential severity* than on *liability*. This may be the adjuster's introduction to one of the factors that perhaps most clearly differentiates liability adjusters from their property counterparts. A property adjuster tends to think in terms of the damage done, and his payment and non-payment decisions are generally more clear-cut. The liability man, on the other hand, looks at a claim in terms of its potentials; even a trifling or "no liability" accident may be the basis for a suit that will cost his principal thousands of dollars. His need to take action springs not only from actual damage done but often and very interestingly from a more shadowy consideration. The casualty adjuster is deeply concerned with whether the facts of the accident and the characteristics of the persons involved indicate an inviting base on which a dangerous claim may be built. He is obliged to assume that there is no lack of persons to exploit such potential if it exists and decisions to investigate or "let rest" are made accordingly.

If a claim is assigned for investigation or if an adjuster decides that it requires attention, it has, then, survived a "weeding out" process.

INVESTIGATION AS AN EXERCISE IN SELECTION

The most universal characteristic that observers have been able to identify in young adjusters is overwhelming confusion.

---

[1] The term "handling" is deliberately employed in preference to "investigation." It emphasizes the possibility that at any moment a decision to seize a favorable opportunity to settle may lead to the abandonment of further investigation.

There are so many things to do, so many people who perhaps ought to be seen, that the task of deciding seems all but impossible. The job is made no easier by a conscientious man's desire to be complete, thorough and accurate. The problem is compound, for an adjuster never handles "a claim," he is always responsible simultaneously for many claims. The result is often complete paralysis and a productive output equal to . . . nil.

Clearly some people must be seen before others, and some situations require certain actions while other situations require nothing.

The decisions now referred to are among the many alluded to in Chapter 1. It will be convenient to discuss them first in terms of the persons who are to be the subjects of adjusters' decisions and then in terms of situations—and the acts or moves that they call for.

It is not common to speak of adjusting as an exercise in selection (or better yet, discrimination) but, when one stops to consider the utter impossibility of learning everything there is to be learned about every claim under assignment, that is exactly what it must be.

Field Decisions—Persons Involved

Many persons are *immediately* involved in nearly every accident. These are the participants or witnesses. Others come in later in a service or professional capacity such as policemen, medical persons, garage people, attorneys. Still others will be *brought* into the picture perhaps even by the adjuster himself— photographers and various other technicians, for instance.

It is the persons *immediately involved* about whom decisions must first be made; it is about them that there is likely to be the greatest confusion. For these reasons, the people immediately concerned—that is the participants in and the eye witnesses to an accident—will be first considered and the factors influencing an adjuster's decisions about them identified.

In offering suggestions relative to these decisions, consideration will be given to the information an adjuster hopes to gain from and the influence he hopes to exercise on each of these individuals.

The persons to be considered will be taken up in the following categories: claimant *operators,* claimant *passengers, insureds, insured's passengers* and *witnesses.*

Claimant Operators

Possibly the first, but certainly not the last, of the paradoxes of this business is that a liability adjuster usually works backward from his claimant to his insureds. (Note the word is "usually" rather than "always.") Exceptions, and their justification will presently be seen.

The decision to see the claimant operator first is almost universal. His statement, even in the face of obvious liability, should be secured if possible.

The human tendency to "self-excuse" being what it is, it may be expected that courts and juries will be less than overwhelmed by insureds' self-excusing stories. Few items, on the other hand, offer more comfort to defense counsel than a claimant's statement incorporating his admission to an act or acts of negligence. Coaching and wishful thinking tend rapidly to improve a claimant's story from his own viewpoint with the ultimate intent to improve his position with the jury. For these reasons, a claimant operator's statement is an early order of business.

Besides recording the claimant's version of the accident in his statement, an adjuster should, at this initial meeting with the claimant, ascertain whether there were others in the claimant's car and whether they were injured. He should procure from the claimant, if there were any injuries, written permission[2] to procure medical information and hospital reports.

If the adjuster follows the statement techniques which are presented in Chapter 6 this procedure should assure that the interview yields the proper information.

Coincidentally with his investigative functions, an adjuster begins to exercise "control." Depending on how well or how poorly he handles his meeting with the claimant, he either establishes a relationship from which a satisfactory settlement flows easily and naturally—or he builds a wall that may later frustrate

---

[2] See page 318 for an example of a suitable permission slip.

his best efforts. He tries, therefore, to set up a workable person-to-person relationship and prepares, if need be, to determine the extent of the property damage. In the light of the claim's requirements, he makes suitable arrangements for future meetings.

Here are other practical hints for successful interviews:

1. Obtain phone numbers.
   If the residence is remote and difficult to locate, make copious notes. If you are transferred tomorrow, your successor will bless you.
2. Determine who wears the pants in the family—i.e., is the center of influence.
3. Be alert to recognize the person who, even though injured, wishes to make no claim. These people are rare in these times, but there are still some who are willing to recognize that an accident may be their own fault. Take care not to make a claimant out of one who is not so inclined.
4. Weigh carefully the advantages and disadvantages of attempting to pick up a release for a nominal consideration.

For aid in relocating the claimant or for deeper investigation, consider obtaining prior addresses, maiden name, names of permanently located relatives, etc.

Claimant Passengers

Until the possibility of an injury has been eliminated, seeing and securing the statements of claimant passengers is an almost universal necessity. Judgment may permit or even suggest the omission of this item if the claimant operator's statement reports "No injury to passengers," but an adjuster will be less inclined to "let rest" in this situation if he is in a neighborhood which he knows to be claim-minded. The test lies in the adjuster's subjective feel for the situation. If any doubt exists, he will usually elect to see the claimant passengers and get their statements. If he has reason to believe that the passengers will make no claim, he will probably "let rest."

The adjuster should remember that the passengers *in the claimant car* have recovery rights superior, generally, to those of the operator. In fact, these are often "clear liability" claims. Since the passenger is ordinarily passive and hence free of negligence and entitled to recover upon the slightest showing of negligence on the part of an insured's operator, no defense ought to be overlooked.[3] Because of the ordinarily superior recovery rights of claimant passengers and because of the facts which must be demonstrated in order to apply the principle of imputed negligence, statements of claimant passengers should stress the origin, purpose and destination of their journey. The answers to questions on origin, purpose and destination do not necessarily complete the job of demonstrating agency or common enterprise, even if that situation exists. These questions are intended to uncover situations permitting negligence of an operator to be imputed to his passenger. The statement-taking techniques for tying down the evidence necessary to demonstrate or prove the existence of these situations will be developed in Chapter 6. The development of the evidence necessary to this defense depends upon the situation. The fact situations that may be found are almost unbelievably numerous. To cope with them successfully, the adjuster will have to understand the legal principles involved and apply them resourcefully.

Concentration on claimant's passengers must not be permitted to obscure the obvious possibility that in addition to being a possible claimant, each passenger in the claimant's car is also a potential witness. In this role too, he is usually accorded a position of primary importance. It is only human for a person to lean, in doubtful matters, to the support of his friends and this common characteristic leads claims persons to expect that passengers will normally endorse the story of their own drivers. When, as sometimes happens, they do not, a statement of a claimant passenger—for example, to the effect that his operator *did not* stop at the stop sign—would be regarded as very valuable.

---

[3] A very brief review of the legal standing of passengers in claimants' cars may assist in understanding these paragraphs.

Passengers usually are inactive and therefore free of negligence, but if a driver is a passenger's agent, or if they are engaged in a common enterprise, then the driver's negligence may frequently be imputed to the passengers. That is, the driver's negligence may be held against the passenger as if it were the passenger's own negligence. Since agency or common enterprise is best demonstrated by the testimony of those who are engaged in that activity, an adjuster explores for these situations in statements of claimant driver and passenger and if agency or common enterprise exists, he attempts to make this clear in *their* statements.

This seems an appropriate place to make a few other observations that are particularly pertinent to the treatment of passengers in the claimant car.

Never have guests in an auto sign and agree to their driver's statement. Take a separate statement from each.

Most guests are passive; that is, they have nothing to do with the driving of the car. But this is *not always* so. Sometimes, there will be one who was asked to look to see if the way was clear. If this is so, and if he failed to see what he ought to have seen, *show in statements what his duty was, that he failed to perform his duty, and how and why he failed.* Such a demonstration may make it possible to defend or reduce the value of his claim on the ground that his failure contributed to his own injury.

Find out why the passenger was in the car. Did he pay for his ride in any way? If so, how? If he did, this may make his own operator liable to him, thus bringing in another insurance company to share the loss.

If passengers are interviewed separately from their operators, the chance of showing their driver's negligence or of uncovering discrepancies in their stories will be increased. Weigh this benefit against the value of the time saved by seeing all parties simultaneously.

Do not concentrate on statements to the point of forgetting to secure written permission for access to medical records. Procure a medical permission slip (to be explained in Chapter 8) from each injured person at the first meeting.

Since injured claimant passengers, in addition to being objects of investigation, are probably "claimants," the adjuster recognizes that in everything he does he creates impressions and attitudes that will influence his ability to control the claim and eventually to settle it. Every salesman knows that his sale starts the minute he walks in the door. An adjuster who for any purpose has any contact with a person who is or may be a claimant starts the process of settling when *he* walks in.

The Insured

For the purposes of this section, the word insured includes both the named insured and the actual driver of the named insured's car.

If an adjuster elects [4] to see his insured, it is usually for one or more of the following reasons:

1. To check declarations—in relation to possible misrepresentation.
2. To determine if the operator had permission from the named insured to use the automobile, or to investigate other coverage questions.
3. To arrange for the processing of medical payments claims, or other first party claims.
4. To learn the insured's version of the facts.
5. To complete, because of an uninsured motorist endorsement, those items one ordinarily takes up with any claimant.

In actual practice, face-to-face conference and the procurement of an insured's statement frequently are waived. When this meeting is held, it is usually for some specific reason. Situations in which one of the five foregoing reasons might call for a meeting with one's insured will now be considered.

Misrepresentation in procuring the contract (as recorded in the declarations) is rare, so an insured is seldom seen for this reason. When he is, it is *usually only because information turned up in some other phase of handling has raised a suspicion.* A statement, then, dealing with the facts as they affect coverage should be taken.

The question of whether the driver had the named insured's permission to use the car is seldom an issue. Permission is usually obvious on the first report and unless it is recognized as an issue it does not, by itself, call for a meeting. However, when it is identified as an issue, facts bearing on the subject should be developed in the statement from the driver and in the statement from the name insured. If the insured or his operator is seen for any other reason, then the issue of permission should be covered as a routine item in the statement of each or both.

When an insured has been seen on other phases of the claim, he frequently expects the adjuster to take an active hand in developing his medical payments claim. Ordinarily, this is a routine office function. A few minutes' explanation at the time of the interview enables the insured to understand what is expected of

---

[4] Some companies do not leave *this* decision to the adjuster's discretion; instead, they insist on an insured's statement as an almost invariable first move. Where management has laid down such a policy, an adjuster, of course, conforms rather than exercise his own judgment.

him, what he may expect the insurance company to do and avoids later misunderstanding.

An adjuster's decision to see or not to see his insured usually turns on the facts of the accident and secondarily on the uninsured motorist endorsement [5] potential. If the initial report has indicated admitted or probable liability, a meeting with the insured may be deferred; or, if the claim can be disposed of at a realistic value, perhaps dispensed with altogether. If the insured is obviously not at fault—e.g., if he were properly stopped at a light when his car was struck from the rear—seeing him may again be deferred, at least until there is some indication that a claim will develop. If, however, liability is disputed, then the insured should almost certainly be interviewed in person though even this interview may not be absolutely essential. Even when liability is disputed, seeing the *claimant* for control will probably take a higher priority. The adjuster on seeing the claimant may be offered such a favorable settlement opportunity that he can dispense with *all* further investigation, a type of decision that will be considered under the subject of "Discounting." If the insured is seen, the adjuster should follow the common rule, "If he is worth going to see, it's worthwhile to take his statement." Following the statement-taking techniques laid down in the chapter on statements, leads to proper development and recording of an insured's testimony.

Where the claimant's injury is serious, *regardless of the liability situation,* an insured should be visited and his statement taken. When the amount at stake is large, the governing principle is to "leave no stone unturned." Even if everything indicates that an assured's statement will only make the liability picture more dismal, the usual practice is to take his statement anyway. One never knows when by a remote chance the insured may introduce some new and wholly unexpected factor to improve the situation.

---

[5] When this book was first written, uninsured motorist coverage was relatively new. Few attempts were made to exploit it. Now it is well known and the public and their advisers are well aware of how easy it is to exploit. The subject, therefore, requires a much fuller treatment than is given it on this page. However, such a treatment, at this point would distort the picture. Here this chapter is interested in setting out the circumstances in which adjusters decide how to direct their work and the criteria which shape their decisions. Beginning on page 167 there will appear a fuller discussion of uninsured motorist coverage and how coverages under it are approached.

The pressure to process a volume of claims at minimum expense is so great that the industry can afford this kind of grasping at straws only in serious situations.

Two reminders in respect to the contact with an insured remain to be issued. First, for realism in pricing and to do justice to claimants the weak points in an insured's story should be brought out as well as the strong. Secondly, the uninsured motorist endorsement coverage is widespread, and because it is widespread and the first meeting may be an adjuster's only chance to record an insured's story before wishful thinking sets in, his statement should be taken while it is available. He is an insured today but if the other car is uninsured, he may be a claimant tomorrow. When an insured recognizes that shift in status, dramatic changes often result in his testimony. A careful statement may be an adjuster's only opportunity to hold his insured to the truth.

The uninsured motorist potential, of course, is no problem if the claimant is covered by liability insurance. If the claimant does not have liability insurance, and often if the issue is in doubt, the insured must be visited in order duly to record that information which may be needed if he eventually becomes a claimant.

A final warning remains with respect to uninsured motorist coverage: In most states it does not apply to *property damage*. This creates a problem when an insured who has purchased "U.M." coverage suffers property damage only at the hands of an uninsured motorist. The experience of the state of Massachusetts which has *compulsory* bodily injury liability insurance but *optional* property damage liability teaches us that when a man is balked at collecting a claim for property damage because that coverage is not provided, he readily shifts the grounds of his claim to injury. Similarly, it has been observed that insureds, upon learning that "U.M." coverage does not apply to property damage are prone to change their claim to one of injury. The best defense against this is a statement previously taken limiting the claim to property damage.

It is not the province of this book to deal with physical damage coverages and so, as far as possible, mention of them is intentionally avoided. Here, though, it should be noted that the adjuster often represents both the liability and the physical damage coverages—more often than not the coverages are in one company. Therefore, as a necessary part of processing his physical damage claim, the adjuster may be obliged to meet the insured, his operator, or both. If this meeting takes place, for whatever reason, the necessary *additional* time to cover the items discussed here in statement form is inconsequential. Under those circumstances, the insured's statement should almost invariably be secured.

An insured, a young adjuster soon learns, is often shaken by his recent experience. This is particularly so if the accident is serious. The numbing thought that he may have killed someone not infrequently sends a person to bed in near collapse. The after effects are usually in direct proportion to the severity of the injury. Something like the following words of comfort may prove helpful to the insured and also help to endear the adjuster to his producers:

"I'm sorry, Mr. .... I can't turn back the clock and wipe out the accident. But remember, this is the moment you paid for when you had the forethought to buy insurance. This is now our headache; you did your part when you paid your premium."

Along with reassurance, insureds often seek advice, some of which an adjuster may give if he keeps carefully in mind that as the representative of a corporation, he is forbidden to practice law.

A frequent question is, "What if somebody else wants me to make a statement to him?" The answer is:

To an officer of the law, an unqualified "Yes," only be sure he *is* an officer.

To an attorney (or his investigator) for the other side, an unqualified "No." (The agreement [6] on rights and duties obliges adjusters to conform to what are essentially the legal ethics. Most attorneys consider that they should exercise the same forbearance that they expect the insurer to extend to them—they will not see your insured.)

To an adjuster for the other side, "It depends." Practice varies from city to city and from one insurance company to another. The adjuster must learn the practice in his locale and the views of

---

[6] "Agreement" here refers to the *Statement of Principles,* discussed in Chapter 1.

his employer. The more serious the amount at issue the more likely the adjuster will be to require his insured to "talk to no one without checking with me." Routine injury predisposes the adjusting fraternity and carriers to a more relaxed attitude.

Closely related to the foregoing are the questions often asked by an injured insured, "Should I get an attorney?" and "Will you collect my claim?" The question of an assured's employment of an attorney will have to be deferred until page 177, when the subject of cooperation between adjusters will be discussed. Collection of an insured's claim, whether for bodily injury or property damage liability, is out of the adjuster's province completely. However, an adjuster may explain to the insured how the insured himself may phone, write or call in person in order to lodge his claim with the other party's insurance company. Again, the giving of legal advice and the expression of opinion as to the merits of a claim should be avoided. The line that separates friendly practical advice and the practice of law is probably not overstepped by such advice as is illustrated by this anecdote:

All adjusters take instant fright at the claimant who says, "All I want is what's coming to me." The author recalls an insured, a skilled laborer of intelligence and personality. This man said, "All I want, etc." He was advised, "For heaven's sake, don't say that. When you see the other adjuster, look him squarely in the eye, grin and tell him you want everything you're entitled to and as much more as you can get." This insured was kind enough to call back a few days later to say that he had collected his claim promptly.

Assured's Passengers

Passengers in an insured's car may be important as *witnesses* or as *potential claimants*. In either role, they may be quite unimportant. The reasons for their importance or unimportance must be considered.

As witnesses, it is often assumed, justifiably, that passengers will support the insured's version of the accident. Thus, they usually take a low priority in the order of investigation, for, of those witnesses who may support the insured's position, these are the least influential and from an insured's story one usually has a clear picture of the nature of his passenger's testimony. Therefore, if the insured's position can be determined satisfactorily without the help of his passengers, they often are not contacted.

But passengers may be *claimants*. In a state permitting passengers to recover from their operators upon the showing of ordinary negligence, they are potentially *dangerous* claimants. Contact, statement and control of these claimants are items for immediate attention. If the collision has been sufficiently violent to make injury a reasonable possibility, then it is usually in order to secure their statements and *if there is no injury, create a record to that effect*. The desirability of doing this before wishful thinking or collusion sets in seems too obvious to mention. The problem of controlling collusion becomes particularly acute in those states which permit wives and children to sue their husbands and parents. Hence, in these states, there is an even greater need for obtaining passengers' statements promptly.

In states requiring a passenger to show gross negligence as a prerequisite to his recovery from the operator, guest claims are not so fashionable. In these jurisdictions, one does not "expect" guest claims (with one exception soon to be noted). The usual practice is to take guest statements as claimants (as opposed to their statements as witnesses) only in the event of substantial injury—i.e., fractures or their equivalent.

However, whether in a guest law state or elsewhere, one-car accidents are prolific breeders of guest claims. The American view—"Somebody will pay for this"—whether one approves or not, is widespread. The search for a solvent defendant is persistent and ruthless. The adjuster who handles a serious one-car accident should prepare to meet claims from all of the insured's passengers. Every effort to secure their statements should be made before the conflict between truth and financial recovery begins to trouble the parties.

It should be implicit in the foregoing, but perhaps another aspect of his duty should be stated specifically: in the event an adjuster has occasion to see a passenger in his insured's car as a witness, the testimony that bears on that witness-passenger's claim, *if one should later be asserted* should be incorporated in the statement *whether or not the adjuster at that time anticipates a claim*.

Witnesses

In the true sense of the word, "witness" includes everyone who is in a position to give testimony relevant and material to a claim. The term in that sense includes insureds, claimants, doctors, repairmen and many others. For the purpose of this section, "witness" refers to those who are not themselves insureds or claimants but who are in a position to give testimony relative to the happening of the accident itself.

Because his work load does not permit and because *satisfactory* ascertainment of the insured's obligations is often possible without considering a witness's testimony, the adjuster must learn to select those witnesses whom he should see [7] at once and defer seeing or reject entirely others. Circumstances alter cases, so it should not be surprising that a witness, deferred initially, may later become important and this change will in turn call for a decision to see him after all. Since decisions regarding whom he will or will not see in person have much to do with an adjuster's efficiency, the rationale by which he arrives at these decisions will now be explored.

An adjuster should elect to see a witness if it appears to him that the witness's testimony will enhance his ability to defend the claim or yield information making a more accurate determination of liability possible. Thus, if one's insured has admitted liability in a clear fact-situation, then a witness's statement reinforcing the admission will not change the insurer's decision. There is no reason for the witness to be seen.

The adjuster should always ask himself, "Why am I seeing this man—to resolve a doubt, to reinforce my defenses?" If he cannot answer the "why" question, he should reconsider the move. Young adjusters, though, should be modest about their ability to see "why." Particularly until they have had an opportunity to demonstrate the soundness of their judgment, they may well elect to reinforce their conclusions by seeking the advice of their more experienced supervisors or managers. Young adjusters are

---

[7] The word "see" is used advisedly to imply those whom an adjuster *interviews in person*. Many witnesses one cannot justify going to "see" will justify a brief phone call. The word "see" is used to differentiate those whom one "sees" in person from those who are queried by phone.

often prone to question management's assignments—feeling that to see a certain witness may be an item that could well be omitted. Again, until a man has gained experience and demonstrated the soundness of his judgment, it is best not to question such an item if it should be *assigned* to him—it should simply be completed without question, and often the reason for the assignment will become obvious to the adjuster as he completes it.

Situations usually requiring witnesses' statements include:

Disputed liability
"No liability" claims that may have to be defended

Situations which may permit the waiver or deferment of a witness's statement include:

Clear liability
No liability (if the situation is so obvious that a claim seems unthinkable)
Doubtful liability (but adjuster is *confident* of arranging proper compromise)

The listing just made is a judgment matter; actual claims seem never to present clear-cut situations. Views on where to draw the line vary from insurer to insurer and from supervisor to supervisor. A candid supervisor must admit that one day he will require a witness to be seen, with cost no deterrent; yet the next day, faced with a seemingly identical situation, he may make the opposite decision.

Paradoxically, it may seem to an adjuster that he sometimes sees witnesses to prepare a *claimant's* case. This is not really so. The following example illustrates the point.

Assume a right angle collision directly under a traffic light with no passengers in either car. There is one witness to the accident. The insured's report says, firmly, "I had the light." The adjuster sees the claimant. The claimant states, "I had the light." There is no opportunity for compromise. Should the adjuster see the insured? Perhaps not yet. He should obtain the statement of the witness who saw the accident and who likely can be more objective. The witness's statement is positive and convincing, "The claimant had the green light." Decision: the adjuster should probably waive the insured's statement, settle with the claimant and go on with the next claim.

Field Decisions—Dependent on Other Factors

In addition to those factors which flow from his special relationship to certain persons, adjusters make their daily decisions according to certain general principles—and according to their desires to accomplish certain objectives. For the purpose of identifying them, it is convenient to distinguish this type of decision from those just considered which revolve around particular persons and their involvement in the matter under investigation.

The class of decisions now to be considered has to do with the desire for thoroughness and its conflict with the need for efficiency; with what might be referred to as the response to certain commonly encountered fact and law situations; and modifications of what one might call the conventional responses which changes in law from jurisdiction to jurisdiction bring about.

To discuss this class of decision, it will be desirable to consider and analyse the idea of *thoroughness* as it applies to adjusting; to consider the question of priorities, in other words, "What comes first"; to examine some situations which usually call for a standard response; to look at the effect of variations in local law on adjusters' management of their cases; and finally to consider the question of efficiency istelf as it influences the planning of the adjuster's day.

Thoroughness

There has been what seems to be a good deal of careless writing on the subject of thoroughness in the claims business. The effect of much that has appeared in print has been to confuse beginners. It seems obvious that the extent to which a claim is to be investigated *is* a matter for judgment. The tendency to waste time on interesting trifles is not a characteristic of the claims business alone. Recently, the head of one hospital's intern committee criticized the graduates of a prominent medical school as being too prone to lose themselves in some exotic phase of the blood chemistry of an interesting but non-critical patient, while less glamorously ill patients courted infection for lack of having their dressings changed. No matter how fascinating, trifles should be treated as trifles, and investigation limited accordingly.

When a conscientious trainee is exposed to unqualified exhortation that he must unfailingly be thorough in all regards, he can hardly fail to ask such discouraging questions as, "How can I ever remember all that? How can I possibly find time?" If he is of an analytical or imaginative turn, he may even suspect that over-emphasis on thoroughness is a little ridiculous, and he is quite right. The extent to which claims should be investigated is not an absolute—it is, it seems obvious, a matter of judgment.

A potentially serious claim calls usually for a thorough investigation; and liability, too, governs the extent of investigation. Cases of obvious liability are investigated scarcely at all (subject to the usual exception that if the injury is *very* severe, on investigation should be *very* complete). On the other hand, cases of *non-liability* or *questionable liability* are taken up with the initial intent of a complete investigation. If, however, the completion of a fraction of the work outlined discloses that liability is *probable*, the investigation is usually curtailed. In some insurers, this principle is stated: "Carry on the investigation only until you see that liability is clear—no further. At that point, concentrate on damage and settlement." The application of this idea is not uniform; some insurers go further than others. In fact, even within any given insurer, there may be variations from person to person.

Investigation may also be limited at times by consideration of settlement value and compromise. Outlined work may, for instance, be suspended pending efforts to settle a claim by compromise. If a satisfactory agreement cannot be arrived at, then work on the suspended items may be resumed.

As far as thoroughness is concerned, efficiency seems to be a limiting factor. The adjuster cannot afford to be thorough on *everything* regardless of importance. On the other hand a lack of thoroughness may make for inefficiency. If a job is to be done or an item investigated, it should be done thoroughly. *There is no "waste of time" so inexcusable as going back a second time.*

The checking of lost time and wages, to be discussed later in this chapter, is a case in point.

Priorities

The attention which has already been given to the various persons whom adjusters must see, and to their relative importance, has introduced the question of *priorities*. To bring the question of priorities down to a practical workday level, certain refinements have to be taken into account, although still further qualifications will be introduced when this chapter comes to consider that adjusters handle claims in volume (rather than one at a time). These qualifications will be taken up under the topic, "Planning the Day's Activities."

The industry would likely concur, perhaps unanimously, that the contact with an injured claimant is usually of *first* importance. Some companies have a special nomenclature for this type of assignment—"immediate" or "dispatch." In any event the idea is the same—for this type of assignment everything else is put aside. The adjuster discards his carefully worked out routing; *this contact takes precedence over all else.* The only consideration that lets the adjuster permit even one night's sleep to intervene is that of "good judgment." Only if for medical reasons or because he senses that it would be unwise to see his party until the excitement has died down, may the adjuster elect to wait until the next day.

But even the immediacy accorded his first contact with a bodily injury claimant has *its* exceptions. Upon receiving an assignment, the adjuster usually makes a few well-placed phone calls. If liability is probable, and the nature of the injury permits, the adjuster attempts to settle the claim on his first visit with the claimant. To enable him to evaluate the claim and to permit the protection of doctors, hospitals, etc., when he distributes the money he agrees to pay in his settlement, an adjuster should, before making his call on the claimant, determine the amounts of these several charges. To fail to do this is to tie his own hands, for he certainly cannot send a check to a hospital for the amount of its bill if he has neglected first to *learn* that amount.

From this maneuver may be derived another principle. Some items are prerequisite to the successful completion of others. Complete *prerequisites* promptly, so as to be ready to take the *next* step when opportunity presents itself. Checking special damages [8] falls into this category. *It* is prerequisite to evaluation and settlement. Usually all the sources of special damages—doctors, hospitals, places of employment, etc.—are well known to or discoverable by the adjuster. It is a commonplace error for an adjuster to fail to ascertain these items until the claimant's (or plaintiff's) attorney has presented a demand. The advantages of informing oneself in advance should be obvious.

Before leaving the subject of priorities, one other common error should be revealed. It is a familiar phenomenon that the "big cases" are apt to be neglected. It seems to be an all too human trait for the adjuster to want to dispose of the small claims—in effect to clear away the underbrush—so as to have a free hand with the serious claim that demands several days of uninterrupted attention. Unfortunately, the small ones have a habit of coming without interruption. If an adjuster senses that this situation is developing, the sternest self-discipline to divert attention to the big claim is required. In fact, possibly the situation should be brought to manager's or supervisor's attention so that the adjuster may be temporarily relieved of other duties.

Standard Investigative Responses to Standard Situations

The following tabulation lists some of the more common bodily injury situations. It by no means covers all of the exposures found in claims practice. The danger of a list is that one tends to think that if every item on the list has been considered, then all possibilities have been covered. A list long enough to cover all possibilities would be too long for practical use, and, thus, the equivalent of no list at all. Read this list with that qualification in mind.

The items enumerated are few enough to carry in a notebook. Deliberate reference to them may prevent overlooking important items.

---

[8] "Special damages" refer to a claimant's "out of pocket" expense or direct pecuniary loss—such as lost *wages*.

The claimant is:	To recover he must sustain the burden of proving:	Even if the claimant offers evidence showing negligence, the claim may be overcome if the jury finds more believable defense evidence showing:	To refute the claimant's alegations and to attempt to set up his defenses, the adjuster makes these moves:
1. Operator of claimant car	Ordinary Negligence	Contributory negligence	Gets statement demonstrating claimant's negligence and insured's due care
2. Absent owner	Ordinary Negligence	Contributory negligence plus agency	Gets statements of plaintiff operator and plaintiff owner demonstrating plaintiff's operator's negligence and agency or common enterprise
3. Owner of claimant car present in car at time of accident	Ordinary Negligence	Contributory negligence of claimant operator	In a jurisdiction where agency of an "in the car" owner is presumed, evidence of owner's presence usually suffices to demonstrate agency—otherwise agency must be demonstrated, so he gets statements of owner and operator
4. Passenger in claimant car	Ordinary Negligence	Contributory negligence of operator plus agency	Gets statements of operator and passengers in claimant's car to demonstrate negligence and agency or common enterprise
5. Passenger in assured's car (gross negligence states)	Gross Negligence	Contributory negligence and assumption of risk	Gets statements of operator and passengers covering gross negligence situations
6. Passenger in assured's car (states with no "guest law")	Ordinary Negligence	Contributory negligence and assumption of risk	Gets statements of operator and passengers demonstrating operator's freedom from negligence, passenger's negligence or assumption of risk. No injury statements from passengers

Local Laws Influence Field Decisions

Many adjuster attitudes and decisions vary from state to state. Basic decisions about whom to see or whom to avoid seeing hinge on local law, both statutory and common. An adjuster should inform himself at once of the local law on the following topics:

Bailor-bailee rules (They govern an insured's obligation to an absent owner)

The presence or absence of a "guest law" or its equivalent (and the strictness of its application)

Imputed negligence (the local position relative to imputing negligence of a claimant operator to his passengers as a bar to *their* recovery)

The law governing the taking of statements and the furnishing of copies [9]

Laws governing treatment of releases and covenants-not-to-sue and the effect of settlement on an insured's cross-action [10]

Settlement options in claims of minors (Although most states require court approval to make binding the settlement of a minor's claim, others provide that binding settlements may be made without court approval)

A knowledge of the local traffic code is obviously helpful but not so influential as the foregoing items in determining the types of claims to anticipate or restrictions on various adjusting activities—hence, the moves to make in an investigation. Traffic code violations usually boil down into only one of a number of factors, each influential but no one individually determinative of a jury's final view of liability.

PLANNING DAILY ACTIVITIES

The point has been made repeatedly that the adjuster must select his activities with an eye to their *ultimate* importance. But, the need for that kind of planning has left untouched another factor which has as much or more to do with the way an adjuster actually works. This factor, so easy to overlook, is that an adjuster almost never handles a *single* claim by itself. Instead, he handles *claims,* to an extent that in the course of a normal day he commonly handles from as few as five to as many as 20 claims, but if he *closes* two bodily injury claims per day, he may well be doing a very full day's work. Seldom may he follow an A-B-C order of procedure. His more usual course is that

---

[9] Some states prohibit the taking of statements in certain situations, or require copies to be given to those making statements.

[10] In most states, but not all, a release of one party is held to be a release of *all* who may have contributed to the injury. A "covenant-not-to-sue" releases only the defendant named in it.

of going from case to case as opportunity and efficient routing suggest.

As indicated previously, he must plan each day after considering the exigencies of each case but, since he must be efficient, he should, so far as possible, have a definite plan for arranging his day. The following observations are offered with the knowledge that towns and adjusters vary widely, yet the principles appear to be widely applicable.

The *office* may well be the adjuster's greatest waster of time. Unless he disciplines himself, he may find that it is his club, that he spends his day, or at least his morning, hanging around, wasting not only his time but that of his fellow adjusters and managers. Therefore, he should assemble his new work as quickly as possible, complete his dictation and leave the office so as to get on with his actual investigation and adjusting activities as quickly as possible.

A good rule is to plan one's activities for something like one and one-half times as much work as an adjuster thinks he can accomplish in one day. He thereby avoids backtracking and losing time while sitting in his car wondering what to do next.

Keep a watchful eye on items that seem to drag. Too often these are key items. It will usually pay to give such an item *whatever* attention is necessary to complete it, even if the work seems disproportionate to the result. There may be a good reason for the difficulty—e.g., the man may really be hard to find. There may also be reasons not so good: that is, the work for one reason or another may be distasteful or unpleasant and an adjuster may permit his reluctance to express itself in procrastination. He should therefore hold himself to such a job until it is completed. Even if it means literally sitting on someone's doorstep and being eaten by midnight mosquitoes, a good adjuster sits grimly until his man comes home. Procrastination only compounds the problem.

As much as possible, the adjuster works by appointment. *Appointments* should be scheduled during the middle of the day, for this is the time when those whom he *must* see *unannounced* are least likely to be at home. Some people should be approached *without* appointment. These calls should be planned for those hours when they would be expected to be at home.

When on a house call no one answers the adjuster's knock, the adjuster should go to the back door; perhaps the housewife was using the washing machine and thus could not hear his knock. If the occupant is not at home, the adjuster should check with the next door neighbors. He may learn from them that his party is only a few doors distant, or will be home in a few moments. At the very least, he is likely to gain some information about the habits of the person sought so that the next visit can be made at a more promising hour.

Even though a person is at work, often he can be visited during working hours. If the adjuster remembers that he is requesting a courtesy, not demanding a right, the usual employer will permit an employe to be interviewed. Remembering that time is money, the adjuster may offer to reimburse the employer for the time thus lost to him. This offer is seldom accepted but it should be made in good faith. The interrogation of the employee should then be as businesslike and as brief as possible.

An adjuster's day should be organized to conform with the working pattern comfortable to his personality, but a pattern is helpful. One such pattern known to have been successfully employed follows:

8:00 to 10:30 a.m. Housewives are generally at home at this hour. This is a time for calling on them.

10:30 to 1:00 p.m. People are moving around now; in these hours try to have one or two appointments established. Otherwise perform such items as calling on body shops or places of business.

1:00 to 2:00 p.m. Stop for lunch.

2:00 to 3:30 p.m. This is the worst time of the day for finding people at home, hence it is a good time to call doctors, attorneys, etc., and to complete telephone items.

3:30 to 5:00 p.m. Return to office, turn in completed work, pick up new work, dictate.

5:00 to 7:00 p.m. Most people are home at this hour and no amount of planning will enable the adjuster to avoid making some calls at this time.

The adjuster will observe that in his office the men who carry the biggest loads are not necessarily those who do the most night work. The reverse is usually true. The most productive man is usually the one who tends strictly to his knitting during the business day. He uses his head. By planning, he gets most of his contacts in before 5:00 p.m. When planning and forethought fail him, he gets his difficult witness by evening or morning calls. (It's a little rough on adjusters but almost everybody is home at 7:00 a.m.) Planning and strict attention to business during the day and the avoidance of time wasting are his secrets of efficiency. He enjoys a high percentage of dinners at home with his family.

TECHNIQUES

Much has been said up to now about whether to complete items of investigation and when. Whether and when are not the only matters that concern adjusters. Sometimes the word "how" presents its problems. In other words, what an adjuster wants to accomplish may be quite clear. How to accomplish it is another matter. Some ways to attain familiar ends will now be described.

In this section attention will be directed to:

a. Witnesses—that is, finding out who may be a witness, and the further problem of locating or relocating him once a witness has been identified;
b. The development of sources of information;
c. Information developed by field effort to limit or control damages; and finally,
d. Identification of the insured vehicle.

Witnesses

Where liability is an issue, witnesses are often decisive. They will be considered first from the standpoint of learning *who is* or *may be* a witness (often no small job in itself). Then, since learning the name of a witness is often only the beginning of the search to find him, means of locating and relocating witnesses will be considered.

Some witnesses are so obvious that they are easily overlooked. The *insured* is a source of witnesses. Contrary to legend, some assureds even obtain names and addresses at the scene. The insurance business does all too little to encourage this admirable practice. The names of witnesses are often found on accident reports and adjusters have been known to overlook them.

The insured's memory—in fact the memory of any witness—should be probed for clues. "Who was first on the scene? Whom did the insured see just before the accident happened?" A witness may be identified by his dress (a postman's uniform, for instance), or a truckman by his rig. Other witnesses may be identified by objects in their possession. One adjuster located two old ladies who "pushed a baby in a baby carriage across the street just before the light had changed." He reasoned that old ladies seldom have babies. A baby cared for by *two* elderly ladies is an oddity. He suspected they might be known to local storekeepers. Since they were on foot, they could not have come a great distance. At the first store where he inquired, the ladies were identified immediately.

In short, unrecognized but important scraps of information may be buried in the mind of each witness. He may have no wish to withhold them, but a witness must be helped to bring them out. It is for the adjuster to dig for and recognize the importance and significance of these clues.

Police reports (in some areas referred to as "blotters") frequently list witnesses. Policemen, however, investigate accidents and often reach conclusions about them. They identify themselves with *their* conclusions; hence it is common for a policeman to list as witnesses those who *concur* with his views of liability and to omit those who disagree. These unlisted witnesses may still be uncovered. In addition to their official reports, patrolmen often keep notebooks. Tactful questions may induce the officer to divulge information not a part of his official record. Further, policemen often work in pairs, one of whom prepares the official record. The brother officer may be a source of additional and divergent information.

An old painter said of paint removers, "When all else fails, there's always lye." Similarly, when more subtle means are of no avail, the adjuster may still fall back on door to door footwork or "cold canvass." Chances of picking up a witness will be improved if the adjuster makes it his business always to know the name of the householder of the door he is knocking so that he can address by name the person who answers the knock. Chances will be still further enhanced if instead of asking flatfootedly, "Did anybody in here see . . .?" he says, "Good morning, Mrs. Smith, I understand you can help me with. . . ."

In all situations, an adjuster enhances his chances if instead of asking for general information he makes his questions specific. Example: "I've been having trouble finding out if that Plymouth stopped at the stop sign or just slowed down."

Children are invaluable aids to a neighborhood canvass. In densely populated areas, there may be large apartment houses and tenements so situated that some 50 households have windows giving full view of the intersection. Canvassing here is looking for the needle in the haystack.

This is a place to take plenty of hand camera photographs. A skilled adjuster does this and, before he sets out, sees to it that he has loaded his pockets with penny candies. To the children following him like the Pied Piper of Hamelin, he explains that he wants to know who saw the accident. He takes snapshots not only of the scene but of the children, and promises to return with the prints. In a few days he does so. The children will have covered the neighborhood like a vacuum cleaner. If there are witnesses in the neighborhood, this move is almost guaranteed to turn them up.

Other means of turning up witnesses include newspaper advertising, route records of organizations such as bus companies, dairies, postoffices, etc.

The testimony of so-called "hostile" witnesses is frequently of unusual value to the defense, for, if a witness is hostile, it is usually because of some relationship which identifies him with the claimant (member of the family—fellow passenger, etc.). A jury recognizing that such a witness's prejudices, if any. will be in the claimant's favor, will often give any reluctant admissions that he may make more weight than the same testimony from an impartial witness. The testimony of "hostile" witnesses, and of others who for other reasons may not be readily available to the adjuster, may be secured when and if they are required to testify at public or semi-public proceedings such as traffic courts, autopsies, coroners' hearings, etc.

If a public hearing is to be held, and if the subject matter of the testimony is of sufficient value to his principal, the adjuster should make it his duty to ascertain whether or not an official record is to be prepared. If there is an official record, it is usually available to any interested party upon payment of the cost of preparing a transcript. Oftentimes, no official record is prepared of the testimony at such hearings. Then the adjuster should consider the employment of a court reporter to attend the hearing and to prepare a verbatim record for him. The court reporter's fee will naturally vary with the length of the testimony. Usually there is a per diem fee of at least $20, plus the cost of preparing the transcript. Hence, fees for the preparation of this kind of transcript will probably fall somewhere in a range between $50 and $200. The final decision about whether or not to make such an arrangement rests upon the economic value of the testimony, the cost of procuring it, and the likelihood of procuring it by other means.

Locating and Relocating Witnesses

Witnesses identified by name but with no address, or an inaccurate address, are a common problem. Locating them is a matter of common sense and resourcefulness. For those whose imaginations may need a prod, the following list may be helpful. It may also help in relocating witnesses who have already been interviewed but who have dropped from sight.

Drivers' license records
Automobile registration records
City and phone directories
Utility companies' customer lists
School records
Moving companies (some neighbor almost always knows who carted off the furniture)
Neighborhood canvass
Collectors for insurance and loan companies dealt with by the witness
Relatives
Janitors

Business, union, religious and fraternal affiliations
Registered letter to last known address requesting return of
delivery receipt
"Please forward" letter by first class mail to last known address
enclosing a stamped return envelope and the request that the
witness furnish his whereabouts

In rural areas, postal authorities may be a source of information. Post office rules forbid the giving of an address as such.
However where a rural post office may not be able to divulge
the address of John Farmer, if Farmer's route and box number
are known to the adjuster, the postmaster or any clerk may quite
properly give the directions for finding"Route 4, Box 357-B."

Person to person phone calls are an invaluable tool. The following story involves four cities. An area sufficient to encom-
pass all of them could not be fitted within the confines of
the state of Massachusetts, and of course the distance between
Florida and Oklahoma, a state which comes into the story, is
known to all. A much needed witness had moved from his former
Florida address in a certain city. The telephone operator inquired
at the place of business of his former employer and developed the
information that the witness had a mother living in another
Florida city. The mother's first name was, unfortunately, unknown. However, in the second city, only 14 persons in the
directory had the same last name as the desired witness. The
operator rang each in turn and one proved to be a cousin. He
knew that the mother had remarried, knew her married name,
and that she now lived in yet a third Florida city. The mother,
now located, still by telephone, immediately informed the operator of the address of the witness, now to be found in Oklahoma.
The operator promptly completed the call to the witness. All
of these inquiries were made from a city more than 50 miles
distant from each of the cities where the first group of inquiries
were made. The cost: one afternoon, one adjuster's slightly
bruised ear, and a five dollar phone call. On foot, this same work
would have taken a minimum of two days, and several hundred
miles driving.

The adjuster will soon have cause to wonder whether any
witness is ever identified by a really correct address. Hence, when

he finds an address incorrect, it becomes second nature for him to extend his inquiries at the very least to the next door neighbors.

Since litigation may take place anywhere from two to five years after the accident from which it arises, it is wise to record automatically in the body of a statement that information which may be helpful in the event it becomes necessary to relocate a witness. Such information may include:

Exact address
Age (birth date preferable)
Sex
Name and address of a person permanently located to whom the
    witness's whereabouts will always be known
Nationality
Phone number
Social security number
Military serial number
Physical defects
Occupation
Employment
Length of service in present employment

Field Investigation to Limit and Control Injury and Damages

So much has been said about investigating questions of liability that it would be easy to overlook "grass roots" question-asking as a valuable tool to limit *unjustified* or *inflated* claims or to confirm reasonable demands. This investigation, too, is an important part of an adjuster's duty.

Gathering Medical Information

Next to the interviewing of parties and the writing of their statements, gathering information from doctors, hospitals and other persons related to the medical profession probably requires more time than anything else that adjusters do. So important is this work that for proper discussion it requires its own chapter—Chapter 8.

Lost Time and Wages

The financial loss resulting from loss of or diminution in earning capacity is a recoverable item. It is part of the claim of nearly every wage earner. It is commonly referred to in the insurance business as "lost time and wages" or even abbreviated to LTW. This loss is part of what are known as special damages and should be ascertained directly from the employer in almost every bodily injury claim. A phone call usually completes this item. The following questions or their equivalent should be asked and their answers noted:

When did disability begin?
What was the employe's earning capacity?
When did he return to work?
What do the employer's records indicate as to the reason for absence? Was the employe laid off for lack of work? Discharged for unsatisfactory performance?
Did the employe return to his regular work or did he suffer a diminution in earning capacity?

Even though an employer may not have been given permission by his employe to divulge payroll information, it is somewhat rare for an employer to refuse an adjuster's inquiry along these lines. Even so, if the adjuster anticipates this difficulty, he should endeavor to obtain the employe's written consent to the release of the desired information. Payroll records are obtainable if necessary by subpoena; it is therefore usually considered unnecessary to reduce this information to writing.

Sums recovered in a claim through a judgment for damages are not considered taxable income by the Internal Revenue Service. With this in mind, many claimants recognize the injustice of considering their lost earning capacity as recoverable in its entirety. With them, the adjuster may negotiate a settlement based upon take-home pay rather than gross pay. Courts, on the other hand, usually recognize gross pay as "special damages." Whether he approves of this more generous approach or not, the adjuster must not overlook this possibility. It should be a special spur to him to come to an agreement.

Ascertaining the true earning capacity of self-employed persons, or persons employed in a family business, is often difficult. In a really substantial claim the investigation of this item can be so involved as to be beyond the scope of this text. For example, suppliers and customers may have to be checked. In fact the full resources of the accounting profession may be required to uncover the proper figure.

In holding seemingly inflated claims for lost earning capacity to reasonable limits the adjuster may find help from an unexpected source. The reference is to the annual tax return filed by the claimant in prior years. If the sums alleged by the claimant as lost earning capacity appear inconsistent with his mode of life and apparent earning ability, the adjuster may request him to produce certified copies of his tax returns of the last several years. Or, he may request that the claimant furnish him with a letter to the Director of Internal Revenue authorizing the examination of those returns. One of the rights available to the defendant in a lawsuit in most jurisdictions is the right to require the production of these records as part of the pre-trial discovery proceedings. Therefore, if a claimant refuses to make such disclosure, it can be pointed out to him that if he does not disclose these items voluntarily, he can be forced to do so at a later date. The hope is that an unreasonable claimant may grasp the idea that the enforced production of so serious a document as an income tax return possibly contradicting his sworn statements can be more embarrassing than simply to reduce his demands.

The request for the production of this type of record should be made tactfully and with full recognition that the alleged loss may be entirely in order. Honest claimants usually recognize the adjuster's need for reasonable verification and cooperate fully. If the claim has been inflated, it is common for the request to be denied. Denial is, if not an absolute give-away, a strong indication of what the records contain. Even though the return may not be produced, to request it frequently results in a reduction of the alleged loss of earning capacity, and often the claimant settles promptly at a reasonable figure. This is an entirely legitimate move for the adjuster who has reason to feel that his insurer is being imposed upon.

Activity Checks

If an adjuster suspects that he is getting less than the whole truth about the severity or permanence of a disability, he may resort to a neighborhood inquiry. If no more effective means of getting the facts is available, he can at least go from door to door, stating candidly his purpose and the object of his inquiry. In nearly every neighborhood there will be someone who will cover up for a claimant, but there are frequently others from whom helpful information may be gained.

Some of these will be persons who feel a sense of responsibility toward the truth. Others may be persons who for one reason or another harbor hostile or malicious feelings toward the claimant. The caution that one should take what is told him with a grain of salt and not be misled by those in the last category is too obvious to mention. This, however, is not the *real* pitfall.

The real pitfall is mistaking *information* for *evidence*. How to avoid that mistake, and the real purpose of neighborhood activity checks, are illustrated by a brief anecdote. A zealous young adjuster came one day to his supervisor. From a neighbor, so he reported, he had learned that during his period of alleged disability, a claimant had participated as a player in an out-of-town basketball game. It was with some pride that the adjuster reported that this time he had really gotten facts. The response crushed him: "To blazes with the facts! Get me the evidence."

The supervisor's point was that accurate though the information might be it was only hearsay and useless as evidence. This is characteristic of information developed by activity checks. Only rarely do they provide actual evidence, but they often disclose the truth and, once the truth is known, then an adjuster can figure out where to look for the evidence—as the continuation of this account demonstrates.

The same young adjuster, coached as well as chastened by his supervisor, located the scorebook, arranged for it to be subpoenaed, and secured statements of members of the opposing team. With the insurer thus fortified with *evidence*, the case was successfully tried.

The supervisor would have been the first to admit that in making his point, he might have gone a bit too far. Even hearsay has its place, provided one distinguishes it from evidence. Hearsay *may* be accurate. It is probable that most of what one "knows" is based on hearsay (consider for instance the date of one's birth). In addition to guiding the adjuster in that investigation which is directed toward reducing information to evidence, it may also furnish defense attorneys with ideas for cross-examination. Mere hearsay, if it happen to convey the truth, may also be of limited use in settlement negotiations if it is employed tactfully and with restraint,[11] for both claimants and attorneys have enough experience with life to know that in the end truth sometimes does get out.

Developing Sources of Information

The author once compromised a claim where liability was clear but injury a matter of contention. He was later upbraided by his insured, the proprietor of a local taxi service. The insured, it developed, had a wealth of information about the claimant. Furthermore, he knew where the evidence to substantiate his information was to be found. He thought the claim had been overpaid. Casual inquiry amply confirmed the insured's judgment. *The claim had been overpaid.* This experience left the author with an abiding respect for the principle that almost always *somebody,* to use the common phrase, "knows where the body is buried."

Such a person is not impossible to locate if an adjuster keeps it in mind that claims and the activities of injured claimants do not take place in a vacuum; they occur in a society with strands so numerous that it has become a common figure of speech to refer to "the fabric of society." An observant, imaginative adjuster locates many of these strands and follows them to the information he requires.

In almost every neighborhood, in almost every business activity, there are key persons who ought to and usually do possess a vast amount of information under the general category of "what's going on." As he goes about his daily work, an adjuster should encourage relations that go beyond a mere acquaintance with these people. The taxi proprietor above was such a person and

---

[11] If an adjuster is not careful, introduction of this type of information in the settlement negotiations will backfire. The claimant or his attorney may take it as a challenge.

after his initial misstep, this adjuster never again had trouble in finding what he needed to know in that town. If the taxi man did not himself know, he could usually make one phone call and find out.

Contacts of this nature are abundant if an adjuster only cultivates them. They include the operators and employes of garages, body shops and wrecker services. (One does not have to be a social scientist to observe that garages these days perform many of the social functions of the local club or the general store of earlier days.) Similarly, personnel managers of the plant where the adjuster handles workmen's compensation claims, doctors with whom the adjuster deals frequently, and proprietors of neighborhood stores are all "key" centers of information. In small communities, law enforcement officers are incredibly well informed as to what is going on in the community.

If the adjuster handles properly his relations with all the persons whom he meets, his former insureds, claimants and even witnesses, any of them may become important sources of information. It is proper to cultivate them as such. This is the adjuster's (and the insurance business's) reward for decent, forthright performance of duty.

In one neighborhood, one adjuster had a particularly long and difficult settlement to negotiate with the proprietor of a neighborhood market. It was the hardest kind of horse-trading to the bitter end. He wound up with his settlement and what, in the end, proved to be more valuable—the storekeeper's deep respect. From then on, that neighborhood held no secrets from that adjuster. It is a pleasure to renew and preserve these many contacts; among all of the things that an adjuster can do to increase his effectiveness, it is one of the most fruitful and satisfying.

Identification

Was the car that was involved in the accident the one the insurer covered in the contract? Determining the answer to that question is "identification," in claims parlance. This is another less-than-top-priority item of investigation. Only a few insurers now want the car identified every time. The more common practice is to require identification only in major cases or where a discrepancy is suspected. However, when "identification" is required, it is essential that an adjuster know what he is doing and why he is doing it.

When a call must be made on an assured for some other purpose and the insured vehicle is available for inspection, there is really no excuse for failing to identify the unit. Any candid adjuster would confess to missing more of these than he should.

Identification is called for if it is sensed that a coverage question exists. The question is usually sparked by a discrepancy in make, model, year or configuration (two doors against four doors, etc.).

The actual identification is made by locating the motor or serial numbers stamped on the block or frame, or on a plate riveted to some part of the body. Identification means *reading the actual number from the vehicle itself.* Reporting the number as it may appear on a registration or title certificate is not *identification.* If there is reason to suspect that the body or engine has been changed, or numbers altered, there are serial and motor numbers stamped in secret places. Police departments know these secret locations and will aid in making proper identification from them.

Discrepancies of one or two digits in a long serial number are regarded as an innocent typographical error and do not justify raising a serious question of coverage. Many insurers identify the insured vehicle on their policy only by the last five digits of the serial or motor number.

If the vehicle is identified, the adjuster should record the following information: make, year, model, body style, color, registration number, mileage, and general condition.

Many of these items are not germane to the question of identification, but the additional time to record them is slight—changed circumstances may, at a later date, make any of these items of information important. By recording them when he has a chance to do so, the adjuster may thereby save himself costly backtracking and develop information of real value to the underwriters.

SPECIAL KINDS OF EVIDENCE

In addition to the testimony of witnesses, other evidence is often introduced in court, or influences an adjuster's decisions relative to liability or damage.

Some of this evidence already exists. The adjuster's role may be to secure possession of it, or to preserve it. Some of it he may himself create or cause to be created (photographs, for instance). Acquiring this evidence, identifying it with the cause at issue, or developing it has its own body of technique.

Maps and Diagrams

Diagrams and their professionally prepared counterparts, maps and plats, are usually considered investigative items. Since diagram preparation is a function normally performed by the adjuster as part of his field work, it is convenient to discuss it in this chapter. In reality, diagrams serve an adjuster in three ways:

1. They are an important part of the *reporting technique,* for it is often easy to show in a simple diagram what would take several dozen or hundred words to explain.
2. *They provide a vehicle for lay testimony.* As an adjuster's experience soon teaches him, an untrained witness has more than a little difficulty in putting his observations into words. Such a witness, unable to locate a position verbally, may easily convey what's on his mind by pointing to a map, photograph or diagram. So employed, maps and diagrams are simply a means of helping a witness to express himself.
3. *They perform an element of investigation* in the sense of developing information that may govern a company's decision about its position on liability by disciplining an adjuster to find and record information which he might otherwise overlook. Of the three functions, this is probably the least important.

There is no limit to the amount of information that can be incorporated in a map or diagram. Examples include the location of buildings, property lines, rights of way, and principal landmarks.

Definite preparation must be made in order to place maps or diagrams into testimony. Whatever the purpose of putting them before the court, maps or diagrams must be introduced into evidence by the testimony of a witness, and the introducer must be a person prepared to comply with the rules governing such offerings. Maps should be prepared by professionally trained surveyors, engineers or the like. The preparer should be able to testify to the method employed in ascertaining measurements, the scale employed and his own qualifications. Competent evidence must be offered that the map or diagram is a faithful representation of what it seeks to portray.

Of course, care should be taken to see that the map is prepared in such a way that the court will accept it when it is introduced, if that is the purpose for which it is eventually intended. It is even more important that the adjuster, often with the help of the attorney with whom he is working, analyze the problems presented by the accident so that the map will accomplish its desired purpose. This requires asking such questions as: "Why did it happen? What are the conflicting contentions of the parties?" and especially, "How do topography and features of the landscape bear on the situation?" Forethought must be given to these points and the surveyor instructed accordingly; otherwise the map may fail to demonstrate the items of information that it is intended to convey.

By his own initiative or instruction from his examiner, an adjuster may be required to prepare a detailed diagram even though adjusters' diagrams are seldom offered in evidence. The result may crystallize the adjuster's understanding or, examined at the home office, permit the discovery of hitherto unrecognized factors bearing on liability. In preparing a detailed diagram the following aspects should be considered:

It should be to scale.
An arrow should indicate North.
The scale should be indicated.
A legend of symbols employed should be clearly indicated.
Landmarks—bushes, trees, buildings, other obstructions to view— should be scaled to size and positioned accurately.
Street lights, traffic control lights, and traffic control signs should be shown and accurately positioned.
The width and character of berm (shoulder) should be indicated and scaled.

The direction and grade of any slope should be indicated.
Diagrams should be dated and signed.

To maintain proper perspective, one should realize that a
diagram as detailed as that discussed here will only rarely be
prepared by an adjuster. This kind of diagram is usually the work
of a professional surveyor or the like. Occasionally, an adjuster
may be called upon for this kind of detail. When he is so called,
possibly the most important benefit to be derived from this exercise is the self-discipline that it imposes on him. He is required to
observe more closely and record in greater detail. If this cuts
down on backtracking, sharpens his eyesight, and improves his
records, it is worth while.

Photographs

Diagrams and photographs are, in a sense, both *competitive*
and *supplementary* to one another. Diagrams are superior to
photographs in their ability to explain *action*. Hence, a very simple diagram demonstrating how two cars came together may ob-
viate several photographs or several paragraphs of dictation.
Photographs, on the other hand, better record and convey the
details of the scene at which the accident took place. A simple
diagram showing camera locations helps an examiner to understand the exposures made.

Photographs are by far the most common and the most useful
form of demonstrative evidence. A distinction must again be
made between photographs for the purpose of demonstrating a
point—i.e., those intended to be introduced as evidence—and those
which are purely informative or a part of the reporting technique.

If it is feasible to do so, a photograph, taken with the idea
that it will later be introduced in court, ought to be made by a
professional photographer, although in an extremity the adjuster
need not hesitate to use his own camera. Most commonly, photographs are employed to demonstrate skidmarks, direction of
opposing forces, points of contact, final resting place and damage
to vehicles. Such photographs are often used in a negative sense.
For example, a photograph might be used to indicate slight damage, hence a minor collision incapable of inflicting injury. Last but

by no means least, photographs are an *aid to testimony* to assist witnesses in expressing their observations about what took place and to aid the court in understanding them.

Photographs must be placed in evidence by the *testimony of an individual*. The substance of the legal requirement governing their introduction is that the court must be satisfied that the photograph is a faithful representation of the scene portrayed. The best witness to introduce the photograph is the photographer who took it. He should be prepared to testify to the following points:

The date on which the exposure was made
The type of camera used
The film
The lens
The lens apertures
Prevailing weather conditions

It is desirable if feasible that he develop the negative and prepare the prints himself, for, in the event of a dispute over their admission, the fewer the people who have had a hand in the chain of exposure, development, storage and identification, the simpler it will be to get the prints into evidence.

Commercial photographers are ordinarily well grounded on these points and require no instruction. In remote areas, the adjuster may have to make impromptu arrangements with a local newspaperman or photography hobbyist. When this is the case, the photographer may need to be instructed on the foregoing points so that he will make appropriate notes at the time the exposures are made. It is common practice for this information to be written on the reverse side of the prints submitted by commercial photographers. If the adjuster will see to it that this is done, he will not be caught short at trial time by inability to place a photograph into evidence.

More often than not, commercial photographs are introduced into evidence "by agreement." In other words, opposing counsel agree that photographs may be offered without supporting testimony of the photographer, a common move to simplify the trial process. Nevertheless, the adjuster should remember that the opposing counsel's willingness to admit photographs in this fashion is entirely *voluntary*. If needed, testimony to support them must be available.

Free-Lance Photographers

Movie cameramen, newspapermen, newsreel photographers, hobbyists, etc., frequently cover serious accidents and their pictures are often prime evidence. The adjuster should be alert to this source of evidence and consider the purchase of prints. If the claim has a substantial potential and the photographs are crucial, he may also decide to purchase the negatives. He thereby assures that the photographs will be available only to his principal.

Where the adjuster is unaware of the existence of such photographs, and where the claim is potentially severe or liability is in dispute, the adjuster should consider *searching* for this form of evidence and the purchase of prints and negatives if there are any.

Physical Objects

Many facts are established more graphically by an *object* than by photographs or by testimony. Hence, in a claim involving a brake failure, the hydraulic brake line itself, showing its rupture, the broken edges turned outward, the whole unit showing no outward sign of wear or abuse; and the flaw in the metallic structure visible under low-power glass—all of these things speak more vividly than the testimony of any expert. The adjuster should arrange things so that the members of the jury may be permitted to see this physical object with their own eyes, even though an expert may also testify on the same point from the stand. The adjuster's duty is to preserve such pieces and to see to it that they are kept, identified and preserved in such a way as to permit them to be accepted into evidence.[12] As with maps, photographs, etc., there is a definite "technique" for doing this.

An object must be introduced by the testimony of a person. The witness must identify the object and be able to testify as to

---

[12] Other potentially important objects are liquor containers, narcotic devices, firearms, etc.

its relevance to the cause at issue. Testimony should therefore be available as to possession of the object and its relation to the accident. For example, a broken mechanism removed from an automobile by its owner might be retained in the possession of the owner and offered in evidence along with the owner's testimony that he had removed the article from the machine in question and retained it in his personal possession uninterruptedly until the moment of its introduction in court. If, however, the article is removed by the owner and placed by him in the hands of the expert who will testify concerning it, the testimony of both the owner and the expert should be recorded in statement form and be available so that an unbroken chain of testimony relating the object to the accident and identifying it may be offered. Each person in the chain should be able to testify *how* he came into possession of the object until there is an unbroken sequence of testimony linking the object to the accident under investigation.

Objects are preserved usually only in claims of some magnitude. Their preservation, then, may justify considerable expense. To make certain that the chain of testimony will be unbroken, articles may even be placed in a public bonded warehouse. When this is done, it is desirable that the placing of the object in the warehouse be the physical act of the owner and the party who will offer the object in testimony. Since it is usually considered desirable to avoid all mention of insurance at a trial—and insurance would almost inevitably be mentioned if an adjuster had to testify as a witness—the chain should be kept as short as possible and adjusters avoided as persons in the chain. The parade of witnesses should be kept at a minimum.

Expert Opinion

Experts are the exception to the rule that evidence concerns itself with actual observations and not with mere opinions. A duly qualified expert (the court is the determiner of who is qualified) is not limited just to his observations, as other witnesses are confined. He may testify to *opinions within his sphere of established competence* and is allowed to draw conclusions from his observations. Experts are frequently utilized to demonstrate:

a. That damage was or was not the result of a certain occurrence;
b. The proper conclusions to be drawn from a physical observation —e.g., skid marks, direction of travel, exact point of collision or speed as a determinant of degree of damage;
c. Methods and types of construction and whether construction was in accordance with established usage.

When an expert is employed, it is essential that he be made to understand the reason for his employment. He should understand the points upon which he will be expected to testify and the question in regard to which he will be required to give an opinion.

An electrical engineer, for example, was asked to furnish his opinion in respect to an accidental electrocution. He did not understand why he was employed or what to look for until it was explained to him that the electrocution had been preceded by a partial short circuit. This in turn started a fire, and a dispute prevailed as to whether the automatic circuit breaker governing the current on the line ought to have opened (thereby keeping the current off the line) before the deceased came in contact with the electrified object. Experts, almost without exception, are apt to require the same sort of "briefing."

Expert witnesses also require careful coaching as to how their opinions may be presented. This is almost universally true of experts who, while they may be competent enough in their own fields, probably serve as witnesses seldom if ever. The electrical engineer previously mentioned again demonstrates the point. Even though a highly competent man and the only one available in the territory, he had virtually no experience as an expert witness. He very nearly expressed in writing the opinion that the circuit breaker had functioned perfectly when in fact he felt that it had malfunctioned. He arrived at this odd conclusion because he knew that under certain special and rare conditions the best of circuit breakers cannot be expected to function.

This man, and many like him, need coaching as to the proper way of expressing an opinion and, since opinion is seldom a matter of absolute certainty, they need to be told how to cope with the various exceptions that their experience tells them have to be taken into account. To illustrate, with respect to an alleged event the expert may have a sound opinion that it *did not* occur. Logic, reason and experience, plus the opinion of his peers, may support him overwhelmingly. Nevertheless he may be aware that upon examination he may have to concede the "bare possibility" that the event *did* occur. If an adjuster is not careful, such an expert may then proceed to write his report, putting himself on record to the effect that it is his opinion that the event actually *did* occur when it is *in truth and in fact* his actual opinion that it did not. Reasoning at such times seems to go something like this: "I can't prove conclusively that it didn't happen; I must concede the possibility that it did; therefore, I must testify that in my opinion it did happen." This failing is common among doctors when dealing with questions of causal relationship.[13]

An expert witness needs to be instructed that he is expected to state his opinion, that it is no reflection on his sense of sound judgment to admit that the evidence is not absolutely conclusive, and that the responsibility for deciding which opinion will in the end prevail is left to the jury. It may also be necessary to explain to him that he has not only the *privilege* but also the *duty* of stating his opinion, and that he has the duty to his client to support his opinion with all the weight of his logic, experience and reputation. This is often a difficult point for a scientific or technical man to accept. It is almost impossible to be too careful in explaining properly the nature of the duties and responsibilities of an expert witness.

Laboratory Tests

Where laboratory tests are desired for evidence, the object or material examined must be properly identified, then placed in

---

[13] Questions of causal relationship or "causal connection" refer to questions turning on a disputed relationship between illness and trauma. For example, whether cancer can result from a blow is highly questionable. Therefore, if a cancer victim alleged that his disease was the result of an accidental injury and sought damages, the insurance company would very likely resist the claim and an adjuster would be required to investigate the question thus presented—one of "causal relationship."

the custody or control of the person responsible for the test. Provision must be made for preserving a chain of identification. This chain of identification is similar to that required for photographs, physical objects, etc. Laboratory technicians generally require the same instruction and careful guidance as other expert witnesses.

Autopsies

Death claims often present problems of causal relationship—in other words, disputes about the *cause of death*. A deceased's survivors may, for instance, claim that he was killed in an accident, but the defendant may reasonably believe that death was actually caused by a heart attack; in fact, it may even be contended that the attack was the cause of the accident.

The light that an autopsy (doctors speak of a post-mortem or just "post") would shed on this dispute is obvious. Therefore, an adjuster may wish an autopsy to be performed or to procure the report of an autopsy which has already taken place. In either event his procedure is the same. *Written permission of next of kin* is usually necessary before an autopsy may be performed or its findings disclosed. If he senses the need for this kind of information, an adjuster should attempt to secure written permission on the occasion of his first meeting with the survivors.

If an adjuster knows or suspects that an autopsy report contains information helpful to his position, and if he has been unable to procure the survivors' permission to obtain the report, then he should consider an attempt to enlist the aid of a cooperative public official. Such an official—a coroner or prosecuting attorney, for example, if he can be satisfied that *his* interests too will be served—may exercise his right of subpoena and thereby introduce the autopsy report into evidence at some public hearing such as an inquiry before a coroner's jury, in traffic court, etc.). Once such a public introduction is made, the adjuster may procure his copy from the official record of the proceeding.

In many jurisdictions, the governmental body supervising workmen's compensation affairs has authority to order autopsies. This authority may require a reasonable demonstration that the autopsy is necessary and relevant. More likely than not, the request for this type of assistance will have to come from an interested compensation insurer and should be requested as soon as possible. Therefore, if a compensation company is involved, an adjuster may wish to consider soliciting the cooperation of the compensation adjuster in requesting such a report.

The Case for Unsubtle Requests

Prior to publication, one of this book's friendly critics wrote:

"'Autopsies'—I read with interest to the point where you advised that permission must be obtained. . . . This point was left in mid-air. How do you go about this? What does one say to obtain this permission? The only one who could possibly benefit would be the adjuster (or his employer) who takes on an 'adverse' status."

The point *has* been left in mid-air and in the end, that is where it will remain.

One of the features of persuasion is that more often than not the offer of a rational explanation for what one wants another to do simply invites the requested person to attempt to refute the reasons advanced (and in refuting to convince himself still further that he should refuse to do whatever may have been requested of him). There are many situations—and this is one— where one does not attempt to support or explain his position, he simply asks. It is true that he may try by the words preceding his request to put the person of whom the request is made in a position where he will be *inclined* to respond favorably.[14] This might be attempted by asking, "Am I correct in assuming that you agree with me that it will be desirable to confirm the cause of death by an autopsy? In that event, will you please. . . ." In other situations an adjuster might prefer to put it quite simply, "This is the authority for the post-mortem. May I have your signature?"

The essence of the matter is neither in one approach nor the other but in the simple unadorned request. Adjusters frequently

---

[14] In a situation where an adjuster desires an autopsy there is usually a valid medical doubt. Often the attending physicians, for reasons of their own, wish to hold a "post." One of them will often be willing to ask the survivor for permission to make the autopsy and furnish a report to interested parties (including the adjuster).

face situations comparable to the request for permission for an autopsy, situations in which their best thought is incapable of developing any persuasive approach or suitable "angle." In fact, inability to conceive what one expects will be a successful approach accounts for a good deal of procrastination among adjusters. The answer then is simple. It is to forget salesmanship, disregard subtlety and abandon the effort to develop a means of motivation. Instead, simply go out and ask the question. If an adjuster had 10 survivors from each of whom he desired permission for an autopsy, and if he went to each saying simply, "My name is _____. I represent _____. Will you please execute this permission slip so that a post-mortem may be performed?" It is probable that he would encounter more turn-downs than successes. It is also probable that he would have *some* successes. Even one out of 10 is better than none at all. Delay almost certainly means that the opportunity is lost forever, so it is better to ask, even without finesse, and have a few autopsies than to delay and guarantee no autopsies at all.

The philosophy of the painter, "When all else fails, there's always lye," recommends the unsubtle, unadorned question when nothing better offers. An adjuster is almost never criticized for inability to persuade others to grant a request. He ought always to be criticized if he has not at least asked the question.

SITUATIONS REQUIRING SPECIAL HANDLING

Certain claims situations require special investigative efforts or techniques. Some of the more common of these situations, familiarity with which seems to be most important to the new adjuster, are considered below.

Child Pedestrians

Children as claimants, particularly as pedestrians, present unique problems. The investigation of their claims recognizes those problems.

Many jurisdictions hold that the *character of a neighborhood* may constitute notice to a driver that children may be at play. The driver is held responsible for knowing that it is the nature of children to dart out unexpectedly, and he is required to drive so that even if this occurs, a child will not be injured.[15] Clearly this makes the claims of children difficult to defend effectively. Most jurisdictions hold that a child of tender years is *incapable* of exercising care, and hence incapable of being negligent. This deprives the defendant of an important defense, *contributory negligence*. The age at which this distinction is applied varies from jurisdiction to jurisdiction.

Some courts even the scales by applying the doctrine of *imputed negligence*. As applied to the claims of children, this doctrine may be sketched briefly as follows:

> A parent or guardian has the duty of guarding the safety of one too young to look out for himself. Therefore if the guardian is negligent (e.g., letting a child play on a sidewalk from which he might be expected to dart into the street) by engaging himself in conversation with the postman, then the guardian's negligence may be imputed to the child to bar recovery as effectively as if the negligence were the child's own.

If, in the state where he works, the courts apply the doctrine of imputed negligence to minors, then an adjuster must shape his investigation accordingly. The guardian's duties in the care of the child and the way he discharged (or neglected to discharge) those duties becomes a relevant item and should be covered in the statements of witnesses and guardians. People who may not have witnessed the accident may be witnesses to the guardian's actions. For instance, if the mother left her child on the street while she went into a store to shop, the shopkeeper might not see the accident take place. However, his testimony that the mother had been 20 minutes in his place of business, that there were no windows affording a view of the street, and that the mother was still inside negotiating with him when a passerby came in to inform her that her child had been injured would all be relevant to the mother's neglect of her duties—a neglect which might then be imputed to the child.

---

[15] At the same time, well-investigated "dart-out" cases often lead to sound defenses resulting in directed verdicts, jury verdicts upheld on appeal, etc. Often investigation establishes clearly "no negligence" by the motorist. Here thorough investigation may pay off handsomely.

In all jurisdictions, an injured child is a thing to pity. Veteran adjusters have been known to shed tears over them. Children, therefore, enjoy the sympathy of courts and juries to an extent greater than adults. This factor must be considered in evaluating their claims, especially if there is a question of liability.

Medical Payments Claims

The obligation to indemnify an insured or his passengers for medical, hospital and related expenses involves very few adjusting problems. The insurer's obligation is without regard to fault or legal liability. Since usually the insured does not himself profit from exaggeration of these claims, there is little temptation to inflate or pad them. Most claims settle routinely.

Usually the insured is instructed to hold his bills until treatment is completed and then submit them for reimbursement. If this is done orally, confirmation in writing is desirable to provide a record and prevent later misunderstanding. Under medical payments coverage, most insurers dispense with closing documents where claims are not large. They rely on the bills submitted and cancelled checks to demonstrate the complete satisfaction of their obligation. There is usually a dollar limit applied to this waiver of what is known as the medical payments release. An adjuster should acquaint himself with his employer's (company's) policy concerning the dollar level below which medical payments receipts may be omitted.

Unless the amount claimed is very small, most insurers require at least a brief report covering the diagnosis, describing treatment and relating the injury to an event for which coverage is provided.

By the terms of the policy, the insurer may require the insured to authorize his doctor to divulge information and may also required the insured (now a claimant) to submit to examination. This right is seldom invoked.

When medical claims do present a problem, it is usually because an insured, eager to increase the value of his claim against the adverse party, has deliberately prolonged his treatment at his own insurer's expense in order to increase special damages. The threat of requiring an examination sometimes puts **a halt** to this.

Expect for a minority of policies, payment of medical payments claims confers no subrogation rights on the insurer. Except where subrogation is involved, a claimant may therefore collect his claim in full—special damages, lost earnings, and pain and suffering from a tort feasor—and then collect his medical expense *again* from his own insurer. This has its good as well as its bad aspects. The adjuster should refrain from judgment and simply accept this situation as a fact.

Mechanical Defect and Sudden Illness Defenses

The defenses of "mechanical defect" and "sudden illness," two seemingly unrelated defenses, call for special investigation. The same reasoning supports each of them. The governing principle is that a man is not responsible for the happening of that which he had no reason to foresee or whose cause he had no obligation to discover. Hence, if the brakes fail or a man faints at the wheel, the law imposes no obligation on him unless he had reason to anticipate the brake failure or to have foreseen his illness.[16]

It must be conceded that many "my brakes failed" excuses are nothing but feeble excuses, and fiction at that, and the adjuster, who is obliged to do justice to his claimants and to avoid embroiling his principal in needless litigation, may be pardoned if he approaches these stories skeptically.

The investigation may be brief. A policeman or adjuster tests the malfunctioning part and, if the part works satisfactorily, the adjuster simply proceeds with the rest of the claim. Extensive investigation, on the other hand, may be required where preliminary tests do disclose a malfunction. An inspection should be performed by a qualified appraiser or engineer, and this inspection should be continued until the reason for the malfunction is found. If the malfunction is explained by a broken part or a faulty subassembly, the offending part or subassembly should be identified by the owner and then removed and stored in such a

---

[16] Or unless he is negligent *after* the occurrence.

way as to guarantee the ability to offer it in evidence after appropriate identification.

The key to the defense of "mechanical defect" is the ability to demonstrate that the failure, by its nature, was such that the insured neither *knew* nor in the exercise of reasonable care *ought to have known* what was about to happen.

The kinship of mechanical failure claims to claims involving fainting or sudden death at the wheel should now be evident. The key is what one might call the *surprise* factor. This defense will probably fail and ought to fail if the insured by reasonable forethought ought to have anticipated his illness or the failure of the mechanism for which he is responsible.

Investigation of sudden illness defenses involves careful questioning of the insured's family and associates to uncover or rule out premonitory symptoms—e.g., dizziness, prior attacks, etc. In the case of unexplained death at the wheel, a post-mortem may be needed to determine whether death was the cause or the result of the accident. Where a post-mortem is indicated, the need should be recognized promptly. The request must be made early, usually before interment, and with the utmost tact.

To be realistic, it must be recognized that defenses of this general category are not easy to uphold. Sympathy for the innocent victim is natural, and courts (particularly small claims courts and those devoted to rapid disposition of minor claims) and juries are prone to overlook what they regard as a mere technicality. Even if the claim is "air tight," it is not uncommon to lose the case at the jury level and to win it, *if at all*, on appeal.

If a claim is modest, therefore, and a reasonable compromise can be reached, many insurers consider it good policy to settle these claims, reserving these defenses as a last resort. This does not mean that the adjuster can leave his investigation to be completed later at a more convenient time, because *this type of investigation usually must be done promptly or not at all.* Promptness, a desirable quality in almost any work, becomes an absolute necessity here. Usually the evidence is soon destroyed; that is, the wrecked car is scrapped, or the body is buried. If there is any evidence helpful to an insurer's position, positive steps have to be taken to secure, identify and preserve it. Despite the possibilities of settlement, investigation should be complete. The company can then decide to settle or not as it chooses. Without prompt investigation it will be unable to mount any defense, hence it will have no option and will be forced to settle.

Handling Suit Papers

Although suit papers are usually handled by a claims manager or by his supervisory staff, a brief word about their treatment may not be out of order in an introductory text. Crises relative to unexpected suits have an exasperating way of coming up at the most awkward times.

The guiding principle is that to let a suit go into default is one of the unforgivable crimes of adjusting.

Suit papers, regardless of filing procedures, should always be brought *immediately* to the attention of a manager or supervisor.

Adjusters should be familiar with the requirements in their courts relative to filing answers to suits and the time allotted to defendants to do so. In the unlikely but not unheard of event of being unable to receive instructions from management in his own organization, an adjuster should, if faced with a possible default date, consider and adopt one of the following alternatives:

1. Refer to his company's regular counsel in the area if regular counsel are known to him.
2. If obliged by pressure of time and circumstance to refer to strange counsel, do so but arrange for counsel to "protect" the return date by making a filing appropriate to local practice subject to later withdrawal when regular counsel can arrange to take over.
3. Request agreement from plaintiff's attorney to assent to a late filing by defendant.[17]

The matter of filing an answer can be immensely complicated if there is any doubt as to coverage. If there is the slightest doubt, this doubt should be conveyed to counsel who are to file the

---

[17] Memory fails to disclose a single instance of a claimants attorney failing to live up to an oral agreement as to late filing. Nevertheless, claimant's attorneys almost unanimously agree that it is "better business" and avoids misunderstanding to make such agreements in writing. To make a *tactful* request for a confirming letter should not be beyond an adjuster's skill.

answer with the request that an appropriate reservation of rights letter be sent by counsel to the insured. In a doubtful coverage situation an agreement with claimant's attorney to assent to late filing after the adjuster has had time to consult his management would be more desirable than an answer under reservation of rights.

Young adjusters are more prone to err by failing to recognize the necessity of "protecting the return date"—by failing therefore to bring the suit papers to management's attention—than by using poor judgment when the manager is out of town. Except for the strict injunction that suit papers should always be brought at once to the attention of the manager or supervisor, the rest of this section should be read as procedure to be followed only in desperate emergency, when no representative of management is available, either locally or by long distance telephone.

Quasi-Fraudulent Claims

It is hardly divulging a secret to say that an adjuster's work involves something more than reasonable debate over different views of liability and injury. Much of it has to do with outright honesty and dishonesty.

It is the author's conviction that more claimants are honest than dishonest; that fraud in the sense of outright fabrication is rare; that the best way to get the truth from a man is to give him credit for being truthful and treat him accordingly, a principle the soundness of which ought not to obscure the inevitable observation that a substantial fraction of the public *will* take liberties with the truth. It is beside the point and beyond the purpose of this book to try to determine whether these liberties are deliberate or accidental, the product of wishful thinking, outright deceit, spontaneous, neighbor-inspired or lawyer-instigated. It is also beside the point to try to determine whether outright lying is involved or just favorable shading. These departures from strict truth are facts of life. *The adjuster's duty is not to pass moral judgments.* He is paid to deal with other problems and, it is hoped, control them to some degree. His hands will be quite full attending to this limited duty. Whatever they may be called, fraudulent or quasi-fraudulent claims reach into the pocket of every insurance buyer. The adjuster is often the buyer's only defense against this illegal tax.

It would be futile to list all the dishonesties that the adjuster meets; the limit is the limit of human imagination. A common variety involves "twisting," where a person distorts the story of an accident. This is a prevalent feature of automobile adjusting, since no great imagination is required to make liability or non-liability out of almost any collision. Thus, a collision on the wrong side of the road may be cheerfully explained, "I was driving along on my side when this fellow came toward me over the center line. I did the only thing I could do, and turned to my left and at the last instant he turned back into me." To excuse one's responsibility, similar twists for right angle collisions, pulling-out-from-the-curb cases, and even rear-end collisions are not difficult to arrive at.

Some cheerfully brazen souls almost admit these fabrications (but not in their statements). These folks, and the self-righteous ones who delude themselves into the most fantastic tales of self-excuse, are common. Adjusters usually find the former not only easier to stomach but easier to deal with than the latter. The defense against both consists of statements obtained as soon as possible. A sense of humor helps—people who are righteously mistaken are almost impossible to reason with.

In some areas, it is a neighborhood joke that any quick-witted bystander will attempt to involve himself in an accident. The departure of the street car which thoughtfully provided doors at either end has almost done away with a colorful folk custom practiced in some areas; everybody in sight climbed aboard through the back door after an accident and registered his name with the conductor in front. Sometimes there were more recorded passengers than the car was capable of carrying.

Occasionally the scene of an accident may be deliberately "moved" from the mid-block to an intersection, simply to place the pedestrian on a crosswalk. Smaller and more subtle moves, perhaps in the position of vehicles at rest, are more common.

Modern claimant practice recognizes tacitly that it is more profitable to attempt to increase the recovery in a clear liability claim than to try to make a "no liability" claim into "liability."

In a way it is a pity that the shift of emphasis to damages rather than liability makes these various forms of skulduggery less prevalent. They furnished some of the most colorful folklore of the business.

This book has no wish to urge wide-eyed innocence as the proper approach for a well-trained adjuster, but it insists that the best defense against these practices continues to be promptness and a forthright willingness to discharge cheerfully the insurer's true obligation—in short, to treat each claimant as a person of honor and worthy of respect. Prompt and carefully taken statements obtained before imagination, advice and wishful thinking set in are not for the purpose of trapping or harrassing a claimant. They may be the only way he can be held to the truth. For his own peace of mind, an adjuster should possess a sense of humor. For the soundness of his thinking, he should cultivate a sense of wry realism about the probabilities of the law suits that threaten his principal.

UNINSURED MOTORIST EXPOSURE

In several places [18] in this chapter uninsured motorist coverage has been mentioned. This coverage has become so important and so dangerous that fuller treatment is now required.

The coverage is important because, the effect of financial responsibility laws notwithstanding, there are still a great many cars on the road without liability coverage, probably a higher percentage than official figures indicate.

The coverage has been described as dangerous because the arbitration provisions by which disputed claims are decided tend to render decisions exhorbitant in amount and often with too little recognition of such factors as plaintiff's negligence. In many areas, plaintiffs' attorneys, when they handle claims under this coverage, tell adjusters that they simply regard the coverage as an open invitation to help themselves to policy limits.

How does uninsured motorist coverage distort and affect traditional claims handling? By making it incumbent upon the adjuster to:

---

[18] Pages 121-122.

Make immediate and positive efforts to ascertain if the adverse vehicle is insured, or in the alternative,

Discover *and tie down* the non-injury of insured and his passengers if that is the case and,

Discover and evaluate any other policies which may provide joint or excess uninsured motorist coverage to the insured and,

If there is injury or claim of injury and the adverse vehicle is not demonstrably insured, to proceed with great caution in managing all aspects of the insured's claim (collision, medical payments and the defense of the claim against an insured, as well as the outright uninsured motorists exposure).

Insurance On the Adverse Vehicle

The existence of a liability policy covering the adverse vehicle will usually enable one to dismiss the possibility of an uninsured motorist claim from his attention. Therefore, it is necessary to scrutinize the accident report for evidence that the third party is insured. A statement by the third party and repeated by hearsay to the adjuster that the third party is insured with an insurance company is probably accurate, but this information must be evaluated and often further work is necessary before one can rely on it. A statement, for instance, that a third party is insured for liability with an agency or finance company identified either as the insurer or as the source of the coverage has to be checked back to the alleged seller. Possibly the coverage is only for physical damage. Many people still do not know the difference between liability and physical damage coverages, and a good many more bury their heads in the sand hoping to evade their problems by ignoring the distinction. Information that liability coverage is carried with the insurer's name garbled may or may not be accurate. The identification of the carrier by a name or names almost unique to the insurance business (viz. State Farm, a combination of words almost never heard except in reference to the insurance companies in whose names these two words appear) is likely to be accurate but ought to be confirmed with the carrier or its responsible representative.

Information that coverage is available may still leave the adjuster with a problem on his hands. There may be a dispute over the applicability of coverage or, if the carrier is financially shaky, it may go under before adjusting insured's claim against it. Even if a supreme court in an adjuster's state has ruled that this does not invoke uninsured motorist coverage, one can never be sure that the court will not change its mind.

If there are no indications on the accident report that third party is insured, the conservative course is to assume that he is not, but go to work to find out if he is or to discover some policy under whose protection a third party could come.

To Find Out If a Third Party Has Coverage

To find out if a third party has coverage, ask him. If he says he is covered, confirm what he says to the extent of checking with his carrier or agent and checking to the point of ascertaining that he has not been cancelled.

Examine the police report, if any.

Inquire of a garage or body shop to which the third party has gone. The operator will usually know who is on the risk or where he bought his insurance or who the finance company is and through one or more of these, coverage, if it exists, can be traced.

Failure to find a valid policy with reasonable promptness, especially if one encounters avoidance or an apparent attempt to avoid by the third party, is usually a fairly reliable indication that no direct coverage is afforded. Once this situation is sensed, steps to control the insured should be instituted.

If direct coverage has not been purchased by the third party, he may still be an insured and entitled to coverage under someone else's policy. Steps to uncover such insurance should be simultaneous with the steps outlined above. Applicable coverage may be available under:

A policy issued to his employer if a third party's driving was on an employment connected journey, or with his principal if he were someone's agent.

A policy or policies issued to another member of third party's family or household under one of the provisions defining and broadening the term "insured."

The sooner one starts his inquiries to uncover such coverages, the easier they are to find, and conversely, the greater the delay, the more one's sources of information grow suspicious, defensive and cover up. Consequently, explore carefully on the first contacts with the third party—or anyone connected with him—for evidence that his trip may have been associated with his employment or as someone's agent or as a joint venturer. Inquire also into the ownership and use of the third party's car and explore his family relationship, including with whom he lives, their ownership of cars, insurance policies, etc. Do not stop with learning that there is a policy with XYZ Co. Examine the policy, record its dates, policy number, full name of insured, place and date of issuance. This information should then be confirmed with the carrier itself or a responsible agent. While doing this, see that full information about the accident is given this carrier so coverage may not be avoided on the excuse that a timely report was not made.

Tying Down Non-Injury in Insured's Car

The mere fact that insured's report makes no mention of injury simply leaves the question open. An outright statement to that effect is usually acceptable as sufficient evidence that no one is hurt. More often than not claims departments will now require something in the way of a statement—signed or recorded verbatim—negating injury. This operation is often performed by inside telephone adjusters who screen incoming reports by phoning insureds, recording conversations and pointedly inquiring about injury in their insured's car. A statement by an insured or his operator that no one in the car was hurt is generally accepted as disposing of the question. Obviously a more conservative course is to record the statement of each passenger to the effect that *he* was not hurt. Practice in this regard varies from company to company and an adjuster will, of course, follow policy as laid down by his employer or client.

If first contact indicates injury (and even more, if it indicates no injury but insured is unwilling to put himself on the record), the adjuster should immediately govern his activities to control the claim until the existence or non-existence of third party coverage can be settled.

Discovering Other Available Uninsured Motorist Coverage

If an adjuster finds that his principal is exposed, and if he can then uncover another policy to share in or contribute to the loss, he has served his principal well. The sooner this coverage can be found the better. This is so not only because people tend to become secretive and defensive with the passage of time (this phenomenon was previously referred to) but also because promptness pays off here in another way. When an adjuster walks into another insurer's office to say that he is faced with an uninsured motorist claim and says, "I think you, too, are involved so you ought to contribute," he will be, in the hackneyed phrase, "as welcome as the illegitimate child at the family picnic." The adjuster should expect that he will be resisted and resented even if this means that somebody else is hiding his head in the sand. It takes time to get carriers to agree on sharing a loss. Since this inability to agree may interfere with settlement negotiations which ought to be instituted, efforts to concert the carrier's position should be started as soon as possible.

Policy writers tried to deal with these situations by the provisions in uninsured motorist cover, making some policies primary and others subordinate, but, in many jurisdictions ,the courts have intervened and placed on an even footing, policies which by their language would be secondary and, hence, non-contributing. Therefore, mere knowledge of the wording of the polices involved may not answer the question. An adjuster must have available to him the findings of his courts or competent local advice.

So that settlement of claims which ought to be settled can proceed as efficiently as possible, one should in approaching another carrier to invoke its coverage:

Be prepared to display his own policy.
Be prepared to read the other carrier's policy thoughtfully, avoid fishing expeditions and try never to bother another carrier unless he is on solid ground. If recent decisions support his approach, prepare himself with copies or citations for the other carrier.
Offer to cooperate (and do cooperate) in exchange of medical and similar information. Attempt to reach an early agreement as to who will negotiate with the injured insured-claimant.

If an adjuster is approached by a second adjuster who feels that the first's principal should share in a loss, the man approached should:

Remember that tomorrow the shoe may be on the other foot.

Try to avoid a blindly resistive attitude; try instead to decide the question on its merits.

Read the policy and acquaint himself with current decisions of his court in this area. This will usually make the decision clear-cut. If it does not, try to work out an agreement that permits the claim to be adjusted peacefully (to the benefit of both carriers) and leaves the intra-industry dispute to be ironed out in private, perhaps by some method of intra-company arbitration.[19]

Managing the Claim When the Insured Is Hurt and Third Party Is Not Insured

The moves just described should smoke out most of the available third party coverage. Even in states with compulsory insurance there will be the occasional "hit and run," the adverse vehicle in the hands of a thief, and the out of state car. Therefore, even in those states and quite frequently in other jurisdictions, one should expect to find some of those injured insureds and their passengers developing into outright claimants under uninsured motorist coverage. In some areas one can expect that as many as 40% of the vehicles on the road will be uninsured and the adjuster should expect that 40% of his insureds are potential uninsured motorist claimants. Frequently the conduct of some of these drivers is a mixture of naive aggressiveness and sophisticated exploitation of the claim situation.

What does all this mean in practical terms to the man working these claims in the street? It means these things:

That if he is not careful, he can lose his principal a lot of money.

That if he is wise, understanding and diligent, he can save his principal a lot of money (an accomplishment which may not be recognized by the man who buys insurance but ought to be appreciated by him).

How he goes about attaining these admirable generalities will now be considered.

---

[19] This is an informal but efficient and very successful way to resolve such questions, particularly if the dollar involvement can be held to modest levels.

Before the Claim Happens

Some of the most important things an adjuster can do about his uninsured motorist claims ought to be done before the claim happens. Since this is something like the instruction for catching sheepshead (you strike just an instant before you feel him nibble), a little background information will help to understand "why" and, therefore, "what."

Retrospective examination of uninsured motorist claims that *did* get out of hand will disclose, in many instances, that insureds engaged attorneys because they were advised by their agent or sales representative to get a lawyer and go after the other guy. This was, no doubt, done with a pure motive—probably the hope of mitigating the collision loss. Nevertheless, the result is to transform a situation that can usually be handled on a gentleman-to-gentleman basis into an aggressive attempt to exploit the arbitration machinery.

Therefore, an adjuster should never miss an opportunity to explain to sales personnel that the insurance industry subscribes wholeheartedly to the general principle that differences can be adjusted by reasonable people and that negotiation between gentlemen rather than hardnosed litigation is the way claims should be resolved.

Just how far an adjuster should go along these lines depends on the policy of his company (client). Almost any carrier will endorse its sales representatives telling their insureds that if the adverse party is covered, his carrier will be anxious to make contact; that many flaws in information channels often induce deplorable good-faith delays in getting word of any claim to a claims person who should act on it and, indeed would, if he only knew about it. In consequence of this situation, the sales person, instead of advising the almost irrevocable step of engaging a lawyer, might well suggest that his insured be patient in order to give the other carrier a chance to receive its report from its insured and the sales person might well counsel his client to ask his own adjuster for advice as to whether the third party is covered, how to find out if he is, and how to proceed if the third party turns out to be truly uninsured.

Some carriers may permit and desire that their sales and claims representatives go even farther. Probably the most active measure to be taken is to advise the insured immediately on learning that he has had an accident that uninsured motorist cover is available; that so far as his injury is concerned, he need have no concern over the third party's coverage; that insured's own adjuster will discover any coverage that may be available and, if none is found, will proceed under the uninsured motorist provisions of the insured's policy. Such advice might invite an uninsured motorist claim where one would otherwise not have been presented, so it has its obvious drawbacks.

Insured's Statement

One takes statements from his insured to tie down "non-injury." These parts of an insured's statement which deal with injury used to be dismissed as academic. But now that uninsured motorist coverage is almost universal and a large segment of the public is aggressively aware of how easy it is to exploit these claims, there are obvious and immediate reasons to:

Describe and limit injury;
Describe the injured's symptoms, symptom complex and exclude the later imagination of other significant symptoms;
Secure information as to employment and earning capacity;
Cover post-accident activity tending to demonstrate the trifling nature of the injury if there is such activity;
Secure permission for access to medical and other records.

Procedure—Insured Is Represented By Attorney

The standard uninsured motorist endorsement contains language substantially as follows:

9. PROOF OF CLAIM; MEDICAL REPORTS. *Part IV.*

As soon as practicable, the insured or other person making claim shall give to the company written proof of claim, under oath if required, including full particulars of the nature and extent of the injuries, treatment, and other details entering into the determination of the amount payable. The insured and every other person making claim shall submit to examinations under oath by any person named by the company and subscribe the same, as often as may reasonably be required. Proof of claim shall be made upon forms furnished by the company unless the company shall have failed to furnish such forms within 15 days after receiving notice of claim.

The injured person shall submit to physical examinations by physicians selected by the company when and as often as the company may reasonably require and he, or in the event of his incapacity his legal representative, or in the event of his death his legal representative or the person or persons entitled to sue therefor, shall upon each request from the company execute authorization to enable the company to obtain reports and copies of records.

There are two difficulties arising under this section.

The procedure is so unlike the procedure in the usual B. I. liability claim that it must be recognized as an odd-ball—not really hard to handle but because it is inherently different, easy to forget. The danger in forgetting lies in the tendency of arbitrators to rule that if a carrier fails to furnish proof of claim forms and fails to demand the rights guaranteed in the above forms at an early date, it has voluntarily waived them. This poses a typical adjuster's Scylla-Charybdis choice. What to do about an insured (or insured-attorney combination) who is not really interested in exploiting the claim. Does one demand proof, examination under oath, etc., at the risk of putting the matter on an arms-length bargaining status when, left alone, it seemed likely to develop nothing more than the request for reimbursement of a few doctor bills?

The only answer has to be the adjuster's subjective feel for the situation.

To dull the horns of the dilemma, an adjuster can at least have a telephone conversation or face to face meeting with counsel, possibly culminating in a frank question about the insured's intent.

The horns of the dilemma just recited may be sharpened when the insured has no attorney. He has given no indication of anything but a modest undemanding attitude—and yet:

Again there are two courses and possibly the adjuster should follow both. The first, the frank discussion. The second, pull out a Proof of Claim form, fill it out and hand it to the insured for his signature and then hope to proceed to a placid disposition.

Medical Payments, Collision, Uninsured Motorist

The uninsured motorist endorsement was originally written to prevent a person from collecting medical expenses under medical payments coverage and then turning around and collecting the same sum again under uninsured motorist protection. There has been considerable judicial disruption of that intent. Therefore, how an adjuster proceeds in this situation depends upon what the courts in his area have done and the instructions he receives from his employer.

In any event, when uninsured motorist coverage is exposed, an adjuster should consider handling medical payments exposure by personal or telephone contact. This will, at least, give him feed back from which he can guage his insured's intent.

If the claim seems likely to exceed the limits of medical payments cover, or includes items (transportation to and from the doctor, for instance) which do not fall within the limit of medical payments, recognize this as an opportunity. Pay the insured the overage on an Uninsured Motorist Release and Trust Agreement.

In handling a claim under collision coverage, remember that, in most states, uninsured motorist cover provides no property damage coverage. If it is necessary to oppose some element of the collision claim, the adjuster should first be certain to have tied down "no injury" as firmly as possible. His employer-client then will at least enjoy some protection, for there is usually no lack of persons to advise an insured-claimant to see a doctor, have a whiplash and proceed under uninsured motorist coverage, if he cannot get that new fender which he can by no means justify.

Contributing Coverage

Do not take too literally, the wording of the endorsement about excess and contributing uninsured motorist cover. Many states, by the acts of their supreme courts, have in effect voided the language. This is usually found in areas where legislation makes an offering of uninsured motorist cover mandatory. The reasoning usually is that policy language, if it violates or restricts legislative intent, must be set aside and rendered void.

This book is not a law treatise so it makes no attempt to describe the law in the several states but urges that each adjuster acquaint himself with the law in his jurisdiction.

A word of cheer. After emphasizing that uninsured motorist claims are exceedingly dangerous, this text wishes to close the subject with the observation that if an adjuster is prompt, see his insured before control is lost, proceeds responsibly to make available to his insured those sums which may be due him and is diligent about promptly discovering the facts as to third party coverage and contributing uninsured motorist cover, most of these claims can be negotiated to prompt, modest and peaceful disposition.

Subrogation

A carrier's expenditures under this coverage may be recovered from third party tortfeasors. This possibility requires prompt inquiry into the financial condition of the third party. It is well to remember that this inquiry should not be restricted to the third party himself. It should go also to the origin, purpose and destination of the journey. A third party may be insolvent but may have been acting as an agent for some person or organization who is solvent and well able to respond to a claim. The ultimate need for this information should be remembered as the adjuster makes his early investigation to discover whether the third party is insured. The answers to financial responsibility lie in the same places as the information about coverage. There is no excuse for having to cover the same ground twice.

COOPERATION BETWEEN ADJUSTERS

Laymen often entertain what may, at first, seem to be a naive notion that adjusters, claimants and insureds get together and decide liability. Since each party's claim is a separate entity and since all parties have access to the courts to reconcile their disputes, the idea that adjusters decide who will and will not be paid is clearly erroneous.

In a sense, however, the necessities of the day, litigation-ridden as it is, have produced a situation which in its workings is not too different from the layman's misconception. In a case where liability is subject to question, an insured frequently asks his adjuster what to do about his own injury. Should he get a lawyer? Should he try to negotiate a settlement? The adjuster's answers to these questions should carefully avoid advising a person against the exercise of his right to counsel. Such advice may place him in conflict with the agreement on respective rights and duties. While an adjuster should not *advise against* the retention of counsel, it seems equally questionable for him to recommend that an attorney be employed, and it may be contrary to his principal's interest. The employment of counsel by one party is usually regarded by his opposite number as a hostile move, and the claimant is influenced to go and do likewise. In other words, if an insured rushes to get a lawyer, the claimant with whom the adjuster has been carefully negotiating is quite prone to feel that he must do the same in self-defense.

Therefore, this request for advice is properly met by reasonable assurance, first, that the other adjuster is a reasonable person, and secondly, that if negotiations fail there will still be plenty of time to retain an attorney.

It is not unusual, therefore, for opposing adjusters to assist one another in promoting a spirit of trust and willingness to negotiate. Many claims are less than clear-cut. They call for compromise rather than absolute decisions. The lawyer's phrase, "A poor settlement is better than a good law suit" is apropos, and this is one area where insurers and their representatives can better expend their energies in cooperation than in fighting one another.

In summary, then, an insured employing a lawyer and starting a suit usually provokes a similar reaction from the claimant. Adjusters can and should cooperate with one another in order to encourage a healthy spirit of negotiation.

"LIABILITY"—ITS AMBIGUOUS USE IN CLAIMS WORK

The word liability appears in the title of this work and frequently in the text. To avoid confusion it must now be made clear that the claims business uses this word in two senses.

To a claims man, the word "liability" in the phrase "liability claim" means a claim that rests on the legal obligation of one person to pay damages to another. Thus a "liability claim" includes claims under auto liability policies and under the several kinds of personal, business and professional liability policies. "Casualty claims," on the other hand, describes a somewhat broader class of claims and would certainly include workmen's compensation claims and probably claims under the various classes of burglary policies and fidelity bonds.

However, once one begins to handle liability claims the word liability gains increasing prominence in his vocabulary. Now, in its second sense, the word refers to a characteristic of an individual claim. Specifically it refers to the claimant's probable chance of demonstrating legal liability of an insured to pay damages. Thus in speaking of a claim in which one's own assured was obviously at fault, an adjuster might be asked, "Is there any liability?" and he might answer, "There certainly is!" On the contrary, where the insured is clearly not to blame, an adjuster would speak of the claim as one of "No Liability" or if he were inclined to recognize that there is hardly ever an absolute "No Liability claim" he might characterize it as one of "Questionable Liability"—and if the legal obligation were difficult to discern he might say that the claim "Presents a question of liability."

In this book, the word, "liability," is used principally to refer to characteristics of individual claims, thus "Questionable Liability" refers to one's judgment about a claim; expresses the thought that one believes it to be quite doubtful that the claimant could prevail in court.

CHAPTER 6

Statements

The claims business thinks so well of signed statements that it often calls them the backbone of investigation. It is the purpose of this chapter:

a. To make clear why this is so;
b. To identify and explain the many decisions that have to be made about statements;
c. To discuss the contents of statements together with some useful hints about obtaining a witness's story and presenting it in writing;
d. To examine some general problems in the examination of witnesses;
e. To consider the application of conventional skills to the taking of verbatim statements; and
f. To explore some miscellaneous statement problems.

IMPORTANCE

Because superiors can always tell him whom to see and tell him what to pay, it is not until an adjuster has learned to write an acceptable statement that he really begins to earn his salary.

There are many other reasons why this skill is considered so essential. *Preparing a statement is good discipline.* By writing a statement the adjuster conducts a better interview. The routine of question and answer, the following of a sound outline, all aid in the development of information that might otherwise be overlooked. Even a young adjuster's experience will soon enable him to recall statements which developed a kernel of information which, seemingly insignificant at the time, later proved to be critically important.

A statement preserves and authenticates testimony. From its contents, any claims person or attorney handling a file knows the nature of the witness's testimony as he evaluates the claim or prepares the case for a law suit. Many cases do not reach trial until years after the event at issue. Upon arrival in court, the witness is upset because, as he says, he hardly remembers the accident. He is presented a copy of his statement. As he reads, he smiles in relief: "Yes . . . yes . . . oh, yes, I remember that . . . yes, that's just the way it happened."

The taking of a statement is a businesslike procedure. It flatters the witness by demonstrating that his testimony is important enough to be preserved. Often it leads, logically and gracefully, to settlement by organizing the factors on which a settlement should be based.

But there is another and more important reason for statements. In many situations, it is difficult to escape the conclusion that a person's real reason for declining a statement is to preserve his freedom to lie. If it is necessary for a lie to be told there should be no recovery. This point is made bluntly because many beginning adjusters suffer qualms of conscience when their consciences ought to be clear and unconcerned. A statement is one of the best means yet invented to hold a person to the truth.

Properly taken, a statement puts truth in black and white and hangs it up for all to see. Controversy surrounds this objective of fixing testimony. From those whose business it may be to distort facts, there is a constant strain of propaganda. This propaganda is plausible and, until one stops to think about it, superficially appealing. "He didn't realize what he was signing," or "He never should have signed that statement" have an almost irresistible appeal to the thoughtless. However—and this is easy to overlook—if a person signs a truthful statement and thereby his own or someone else's claim is denied, the fault was not in the making of the statement. It was the circumstances of the original occurrence that frustrated the recovery—not the statement.

While there is no such thing as an air-tight statement, nevertheless a statement carefully and objectively taken by an adjuster who uses good technique and conscientiously tries to reproduce on paper what is in the witness's mind, is a rugged thing.[1] The statement has given unscrupulous witnesses more than one anxious moment; more than one defense attorney has been thankful for an adjuster's midnight penmanship.

The taking of a statement to fix testimony is a basic and justified purpose. Adjusters should be forthright about this common-sense, essential procedure.

The adjuster should remember that the time to weigh the importance of a statement is *before* he invests time and mileage in it—not after he has found the witness. Then, just by being there, an adjuster has incurred the bulk of the cost of procuring a statement, so he should take it. It was stressed in Chapter 5 that statements have an order of importance. Those of lesser importance may often be omitted. The need for statements increases with the seriousness of the claim and the degree of dispute over liability. The need for statements decreases when the claim is less serious or if liability is obvious. The time to make decisions is *before* the interview is scheduled.

PRECAUTIONS IN THE TAKING OF STATEMENTS

There are certain situations in which a statement is neither permissible nor advisable. Further, there are some common misconceptions about legal restrictions.

Competence of Witnesses

As a general rule, a statement should be taken from a person who is competent to give information. It goes without saying that an adjuster should not approach a person who may be in pain or under medication without first clearing with the patient's doctor. "May I see him?" "Will his welfare be endangered by

---

[1] A plaintiff's attorney once made a flat assertion as to what his clients, mother and daughter, were prepared to testify to in a falldown claim. That same morning he put the mother on the stand, the defense counsel laid the mother's statement on the table before him and mother "went down the line" with the statement—the exact opposite of what her attorney had said she would testify to. Daughter repeated the performance. Neither statement was offered in evidence. The court directed a verdict for the defendant, whose counsel was not obliged to offer the first bit of evidence.

questioning?" "Is he under the influence of drugs or narcotics?" "Is he competent?" Once this clearance has been secured, an adjuster may proceed to visit with a witness. Often it is good judgment for the adjuster to obtain *written* certification of competence from the doctor or nurse.

After having started his questioning, the adjuster may himself doubt that the witness is able to carry out sensibly his part of the question and answer process. To render worthless a statement taken at this time, it would only be necessary for opposing counsel to put the adjuster himself on the stand. Certainly no jury would give weight to a statement if the adjuster himself were to testify that it was his own judgment that the witness was confused or irrational. So, of course, that statement should be discontinued, to be taken up at a later and more appropriate time.

Similarly, an adjuster may sense or observe that talking or the mental labor of trying to recall is painful or exhausting. Where this is the case, it is usually better to break off the interview and try again when the witness is more nearly himself.

To generalize, then—and this point, being no trifle, comes up often—on the grounds of expediency an adjuster should not take a statement if his own testimony cannot support it as the witness's own, sensible, self-expression. On the grounds of decency, he should forbear where he observes that the process is inflicting pain or strain.

Taking statements from persons whose competence may be questioned involves more judgment. Of this and many other situations which he faces, a conscientious man may well suspect that if he cannot look back on some instance of overreaching, where perhaps a statement was not warranted, he convicts himself of one of two crimes, either he is heartless and unable to recognize a possible previous error, or he is simply not trying.

Children as Witnesses

Children as witnesses call into question the matter of *their* competence. It is frequently thought that a statement may not be taken from a child or that a child's statement may not be taken except in the presence of his parents. Neither idea is correct. A child may be a witness, and his competence is for the court to decide. Whether or not he may make a statement becomes a matter of common sense and judgment. Children are innocent and lacking in some defenses of the adult. It is not surprising therefore that considerations peculiar to children govern their statements.

Generally, the younger the child the more desirable it is for an adjuster to protect himself from an allegation of undue influence or coercion. Strong protection is the presence of the parent (preferably signing as a witness), but this is not obligatory. Any third person furnishes some protection to such an allegation—the more responsible the witness, the better. A statement which is an earnest search for the truth usually proclaims itself for what it is. The language should be simple and within the child's ability to express himself and to comprehend. If a parent or impartial witness is not available to help authenticate a child's statement (and even if the parent is on the scene), the statement's best support is the care and objectivity with which it is written.

Two Imaginary Hazards

Although beginning adjusters may be prone to question the taking of a statement from the claimant whose account they justifiably discount in advance as adverse, the prevailing opinion in the industry is that the statement is still important, if for no reason other than to let the defense counsel know exactly what he must cope with. There is, one must concede, always the possibility of uncovering some point whose importance the adjuster had overlooked. Finally, even though it contains no information to advance the liability phase of the claim, a properly written statement from an injured party may well contain information relative to injury which may later serve to control an exaggerated claim.

Often beginning adjusters question the wisdom of taking of a statement from the claimant because of the thought, "If I take his statement, I may frighten him. Maybe I will lose control."

This fear should be subdued for what it is—a creature of the adjuster's imagination. It illustrates the maxim that the salesman's biggest obstacle is in his own head. The young adjuster would be well advised never to permit himself to yield to the temptation to avoid taking a statement from a potential claimant until he has at least three years of experience. He may sweat out a few anxious moments and may even scramble back from some wobbly limbs, but he will, in the end, make few mistakes.

Litigants Represented by Counsel

An unwritten rule, formerly widely observed as a matter of courtesy, has been formalized by an agreement between insurers and the bar. Known as the *Statement of Principles on Respective Rights and Duties of Lawyers and Laymen in the Business of Adjusting,*[2] the agreement has this to say:

> The companies may properly interview any witnesses, or prospective witnesses, without the consent of opposing counsel or party. (Note: at meetings on September 8, 1940 and February 20, 1955, the Conference Committee adopted the following interpretation: "the word 'witness' shall be construed to include 'parties,' *but this construction shall not authorize an interview of a party after he is represented by an attorney.*"

From this agreement it may be stated that an adjuster may interview any witness, or the parties to the claim, but this right to an interview does not extend to a party who is represented by an attorney.

Miscellaneous Legal Restrictions

In passing, attention is also called to the language in the *Statement of Principles* which imposes on the adjuster the obligation to furnish the witness with a copy of his statement upon request. At least three jurisdictions have imposed this obligation as a matter of law.

---

[2] This agreement is discussed in Chapter 1 and is reproduced in the Appendix under its later title, "Statement of Principles on Respective Rights and Duties of Lawyers, Insurance Companies and Adjusters Relating to the Business of Adjusting Insurance Claims."

Other legislative enactments require that a stated period elapse "post accident" before a statement may be taken from an injured person. In still other jurisdictions, the taking of statements in a hospital is forbidden.

Compliance with these requirements is a matter of learning the law in one's own jurisdiction, for they are not universal.

Slanted Statements

It has been suggested that an objective statement is often its own best support. A look at the other side of the coin is in order. Is it desirable or feasible to write a statement so as to make a witness appear to testify at variance with his own convictions? A statement that did this would, of course, be a slanted statement.

There is no need to debate this point. The *Statement of Principles* indicates that an adjuster "will scrupulously avoid any suggestion calculated to induce the witnesses to suppress or deviate from the truth. . . ." The slanted statement should not be taken. To emphasize the point, the author seriously suggests that each adjuster owes it to himself to try, at least once, to induce a witness to say something other than what the witness honestly believes. Having tried it once, the adjuster will never try it again. A witness who is trying to get away with something will from time to time trip himself up in a statement, but the honest witness is protected from overbearing adjusters by the dictum of the philosopher: "You can't cheat an honest man."

For those who find the practical realities (as outlined above) unattractive, it is simply suggested that a defense built on a distorted view of the facts is a house built on sand. It is hard enough for the defendant to win the cases which he should win, without wasting time trying to defend the indefensible.

SIGNED STATEMENTS

The signed statement is a true statement of the witness, prepared by the adjuster in longhand, or typed, and signed by the witness. Before giving his signature the witness reads the entire statement, writes a closing sentence, "I have read and understand this statement on ... pages and it is true," and then signs his name.

Legibility and Format

Since it is intended to be read, it is basic that the statement should be *legible*. Most statements are handwritten, and it must be conceded that adjusters as a class are not noted for their penmanship. The adjuster who does not write naturally in a clear and legible hand is hardly disqualified from the business, but he cannot remind himself too often that his product is intended to be read. Perhaps examiners and supervisors, sympathetically recalling their own problems as field adjusters, are too disinclined to call this point to the field adjuster's attention.

In the interest of legibility the field adjuster should observe a few practical points:

1. He should avoid writing in his lap. Rather he should ask for permission to use the dining room or kitchen table.
2. He should take his time in writing the statement.
3. If he has reasonable proficiency with a portable typewriter and is able to think while using it, typed statements are desirable.

As various forms of *recorded* statements become more acceptable to the industry, the adjuster should train himself in the skills necessary to this form.

In order that their authenticity may be preserved free of alteration, statements should be written in *ink* or some other unalterable material such as an *indelible pencil*. More than one copy should be prepared with each copy signed by the giver in the same manner as the original, the number of copies depending on company policy.

Most adjusters and their employers prefer that the statement be unparagraphed. Each line starts at the extreme left edge of the page, or the left margin line, and continues all the way to the right edge of the page. One sentence follows another without a paragraph break, and the only blank in the page is the bottom line of each page (which is left blank for the witness's signature) and the remainder of the page at the end of the statement.

Those who believe in this technique feel that they are thereby protected against a possible subsequent charge that a blank space had been filled after leaving the witness's presence—that the statement was not the authentic statement of the witness. Of course, changing one or two key words *might* alter the entire sense of the witness's testimony, and thus this argument is valid.

Other authorities prefer conventional paragraphing. Their position also deserves consideration. All agree that a statement is intended to convey information. Paragraphing is a device of written language intended to clarify the message. Its purpose may be grasped more readily, it is argued, if a statement is paragraphed. Moreover, the result is less repellent to the eye.

The adjuster should follow the preference of his employer. Once the basic technique of writing a statement is grasped, it is not difficult to switch from one style to the other. It is enough that the adjuster should understand the "why" of each technique and be able to make the most of it.

Statements are almost invariably written in the first person, as if the witness is telling his own story.

Content of Statements

The contents of the statement are indicated by the following check list and the samples which follow:

Address
City and State
Date
Hour

1. Name—age—residence
2. Occupation
3. Driver's license—ownership of vehicle
4. Date, time and place of accident
5. Weather—locus

6. Passengers
7. Origin of trip—purpose—destination

8. Description of accident

9. Positions at rest
10. Skidmarks
11. Name—identifying information—adverse party
12. Admissions—allegations at scene
13. Injuries
14. Witnesses

Jones' Statement
Interrogation Diagram

ORANGE AVENUE

Possible witness
Ba-bee Dy-dee Service

other CAR at rest
position,
can't say color,
light tan

SECOND STREET

my CAR

10, 15 MPH
can't say
how far
when hit

STOP

Congregational
Church

Sample Statements

There follow now several examples. These statements, by fictitious characters Jones, Smith and Brown (pages 192 to 200), relate to the accident described in the exemplary report cited in Chapter 9. Each statement should be read carefully and, an important point, should be related by the reader item by item to the diagram which accompanies it. At a later point this chapter will explain how the diagram may be developed first, as a repository for information, its information later to be reproduced in the statement. Chapter 7 will also point out how a diagram is used as a critical tool, and that by it an adjuster satisfies himself on the sufficiency of a statement and learns how to criticize his own work to his and his employer's benefit. It will also be shown how the diagram is an invaluable tool in the hands of a supervisor as he performs his essential function of seeing that his file contains all needed information and that his field men are properly trained.

STATEMENT OF JOHN JONES

108 Allamanda Street
Sarasota, Florida
4/11/63 [3]
2:45 p.m.

I am John Jones, age 79, a widower, retired, living at the above address. I hold Florida driver's license No. 259038765, expiring 2/1/64. I own and register in my name a '62 Chevrolet convertible, identification number 21344321. The accident I am about to describe took place April 1, 1963, about 4:00 p.m. The weather was clear, the streets dry. I was on my way from my home to the post office to pick up my mail. I was alone. I don't know directions in this town by north, south, etc., but I do know that I drove away from my home and in the direction of the Congregational church.[4] I was driving in the center of Second Street as I approached Orange Avenue. I stopped my car at the stop sign

---

[3] Notice the date on this statement, and notice also the date on the statement of the claimant Smith. It is standard procedure to get the claimant's statement first. Except that the witness could not have been found except by a clue furnished by the insured, he too would have been seen before the insured.

[4] Notice this method of dealing with direction and a witness who is not properly oriented. As a matter of fact, to describe directions in terms of prominent landmarks—"toward the red church," "away from downtown"—is *preferable* to the use of the compass terms north, south, etc.

which faced me as I came to Orange Avenue. By "stopped," I mean that I applied my brakes and brought my car almost, if not entirely, to a dead stop. I do not remember if my automatic transmission "downshifted." I made this "stop" or "near stop" with my car's front end even with the near curb of Orange Avenue. I looked both ways.[4a] I saw nothing coming. I do not remember whether there were parked cars or bushes to obstruct my view to the right. After I was certain that there was nobody coming, I drove across Orange Avenue, my speed I judge about 10 to 15 miles per hour and my car still at the center of Second Street. I don't know how far across the intersection I had gotten [5] —whether a quarter, a half or farther—when suddenly there was a horrible crash. I learned later that this was my car colliding with another, but at the moment I had no idea what happened, for I never saw the car I collided with until after the accident. My car stopped after the collision but whether it was due to the collision or the application of the brakes, I do not know.[6] I do not know whether I stopped at the place where we collided or if my car continued forward and if so, how far. I was not hurt but I was confused and frightened. A young man—I remember the odd name, Babee Dydee Service, on his jumper [7]—helped me from my car. The other car, which I remember only as light tan, was stopped somewhere to the left of the intersection and to the left of my car, but I did not see its driver. I remember that the tan car still stood on its four wheels but where it stood on the road-way, whether headed east, west, north or south, I do not know. A policeman came to the scene. I do not know his name. I described the accident to him, just as I am doing now. I was arrested and posted $25 bond. I did not discuss the accident with anyone but the policeman. I did not see or talk with the other driver nor did I overhear anything he said. I was not hurt. I have read and understand this statement on . . pages, I understand it and it is true.

Witness: WM. ADJUSTER   JOHN JONES

[4a] The statement would have been improved had it disclosed how far the witness was able to see when he looked.

[5] Notice that it is insufficient to say that the witness does not know how far across the intersection he had gotten. It was made specific that he hasn't the

[6] The statement lacks information as to where Jones' car stopped. If, as is likely, he does not know, this should have been made clear.

[7] Notice that the adjuster has inquired carefully here for buried bits of knowledge that may serve as clues to locate a witness. Notice too that the use of the active voice—"A young man helped me from . . ."—almost forced the adjuster to identify the young man. If the adjuster had permitted himself to write, "I was helped from my car. . . ." it would have been very easy to have overlooked this important clue.

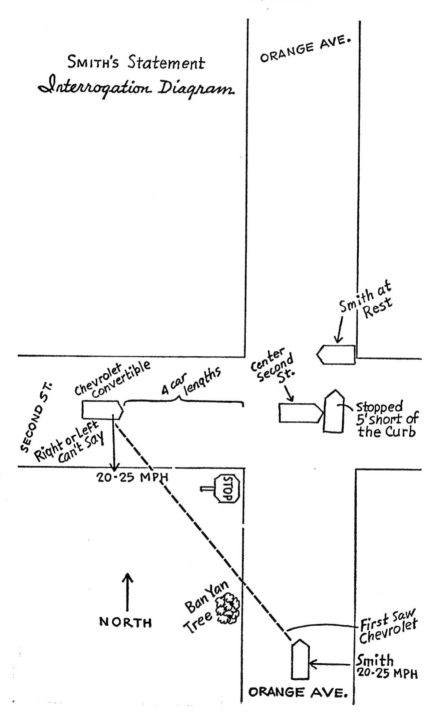

STATEMENT OF RICHARD SMITH

2969 South Tamiami Trail
Sarasota, Florida
4/10/63
5:20 p.m.

I am Richard Smith, born 3/15/34,, married and living with my
wife Jane at 140 Siesta Key Road, Sarasota, Florida. I am president and, except for a small fraction of the stock owned by other
members of my family, sole stockholder in Smith Candy Company. My remuneration as president is $200 per week. I am not
otherwise employed. I drive a 1962 Buick Special, serial number
22334455, Florida registration number 16-W-2920, a vehicle
owned by my corporation and used by me as a personal
and business car. April 1, 1963, was a clear day, pavement
dry. On that day I made a trip to inspect my branch office
at Fort Myers. I was alone, returning to the Sarasota plant,
when I drove north on Orange Avenue at about 4:00 p.m.
I was driving at approximately 20 to 25 miles an hour as
I approached the intersection of a street which I have since
learned is Second Street. I was driving so that my left wheels
were almost exactly at the center line of Orange Avenue and my
car was directly opposite a large banyan tree [8] which stands
on the west side of Orange Avenue, when I looked to the left
and for the first time saw a Chevrolet convertible headed east
on Second Street. From my angle I could not tell whether this
car was on the right side, left, or in the middle [9] of Second
Street. Its speed was about 20 to 25 miles an hour and when I
first saw it I judged that it was about four car lengths [10] back
from the west curb of Orange Avenue. I continued straight
ahead, my speed unchanged, expecting the convertible to stop

---

[8] Notice that the adjuster fixed this person's distance from the corner by
reference to a prominent landmark. Actually this is better technique than requesting him to estimate his distance in feet. If it becomes necessary to reduce the
information given to feet, it will always be possible to go out and use a tape
measure, thereby ascertaining beyond any doubt the distance of the banyan tree
from the corner, and likewise the distance from the corner at which this witness
first saw the other car.

[9] Notice again the care with which a negative statement is spelled out.

[10] The witness here describes the distance separating the adverse car from
the corner in terms of car lengths. It might be argued that cars are of varying
lengths. However, a layman's judgment of feet, yards, etc., is usually so unreliable
that to resort to "car lengths" is probably more realistic and, in the end, more
nearly accurate.

at the stop sign. Instead of stopping, the convertible came straight ahead at about 20 to 25 m.p.h. and before I could react in any way, the front end of the convertible struck the left rear side of my car.[11] My car was turned counterclockwise and I was thrown forward and against the door and window opening at my left. My car did not overturn. It came to rest facing due west, its left side in line with the north curb line of Second Street and its rear against the curb at the north-east corner of the intersection. The other car stopped, headed north, approximately in the midline of Second Street and with its right side about five feet west of the east curb of Orange Avenue. I saw it only from the left front quarter. I saw that its left front was damaged— whether or not there was any further damage across the front, I am in no position to say. I had no conversation with the other driver, and if there were any witnesses I am not aware of them. White Funeral Home's ambulance took me to Sarasota Hospital.[12] Dr. Green treated me and kept me overnight at the hospital. He tells me I have a broken bone in my right wrist; he applied a cast which I understand he will remove next week. I have a four inch cut in my scalp, covered by hair, and a number of minor cuts and bruises about my body, all of which have healed. I consider that I am quite well except for the right wrist.[13] I returned to work one week after the accident and, in spite of the cast, have been able to carry out my duties. My car was damaged at the left side and rear, where it hit a corner post, and is currently at Sarasota Body Shop awaiting repair. Although I did not learn it at the time, since the accident I have learned that the driver of the other car was John Jones of 108 Allamanda Street, Sarasota, Florida.

RICHARD SMITH

Richard Smith has read this statement on .. pages. He says he understands it and that it is true and, since his right hand is in a cast, he signs it with his left hand.

Witness: MARY OFFICECLERK   Witness: IMA SECRETARY
        10 Loma Linda   4110 South Trail
        Sarasota, Fla.   Sarasota, Fla.

---

[11] The place in the intersection where the cars collided is not made clear.

[12] Notice again the use of the active verb. "I was taken to the hospital" would permit the adjuster to slough over his duty in finding out by whom. The use of the form "took" disciplines the adjuster into asking the name of the ambulance and writing it down.

[13] This statement would be improved by the addition of "except for the injuries I have described here, I was not hurt."

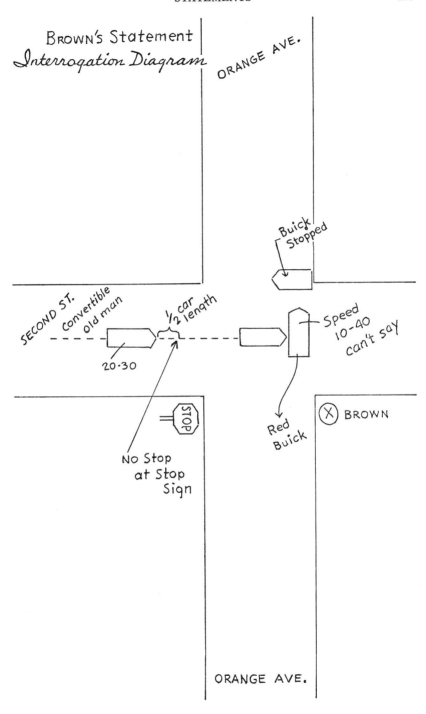

Brown's Statement
Interrogation Diagram

ORANGE AVE.

Buick Stopped

SECOND ST.
Convertible
Old man

½ car length

Speed
10-40
can't say

20-30

No Stop
at Stop
Sign

STOP

Red
Buick

(X) BROWN

ORANGE AVE.

STATEMENT OF ROBERT BROWN

220 North Palm Avenue
Sarasota, Florida
4/13/63, 8:30 p.m.

I am Robert Brown, age 23, single, living at the above address, a rooming house. My brother, John Brown, 239 Hawthorne Street, Malden, Massachusetts, an accountant in business for himself, is my only living relative.[14] I am employed as route man and general handyman at the Babee Dydee Service, 100 Main Street, Sarasota, Florida. April 1, 1963, about 4:00 P.M., I had just finished a pick-up and was about to return to my truck, which was parked headed west at the north curb of Second Street, facing Orange Avenue. I was alone and had gotten as far as the south-east corner of the intersection of Orange Avenue and Second Street when I looked to my left across Orange Avenue. What made me look I do not know, but when I looked my attention was immediately drawn to a '62 convertible driven by a very old man. He was then about a half car length west of the stop sign which faced him, and my attention was particularly attracted because he was going at a speed of not less than 20 though probably not more than 30, and at that speed I was already beginning to wonder if he would stop for the stop sign. He did not stop. He continued straight ahead, right along the middle of Second Street and across Orange Avenue at a speed of between 20 and 30 miles an hour. I was so surprised at this that I did not see a car coming north on Orange Avenue until, just as the convertible reached the center of Orange Avenue its front end struck the rear right side of a red Buick which was north-bound on Orange Avenue. Since I did not see the Buick until the collision, I cannot judge its speed. I do not know whether it was going 10 miles an hour or 40. The Buick was turned counter-clockwise by the blow and came to rest, its rear against the curb and corner marker at the north-east corner of the intersection, its front headed due west and its left side lined up with the north curb line of Second Street. The convertible stopped headed east. It was headed straight down the middle of Second Street, its front end, as I remember it, approximately at the east curb line of Orange Avenue. I went over and helped the old gentleman out of the convertible. He asked my name but I did not want to be involved. Immediately after that, I saw that there were a

---

[14] Cases are often reached for trial months and years post-accident. By this means the adjuster has provided himself with a way to relocate the witness.

number of other people around. Who they were or where they
came from, I don't know. I saw nothing about any one of them
to identify him as to occupation.[15] I left immediately. I did not
look and cannot say whether there were any skidmarks or scuff-
marks on the pavement. I did not learn the name of either
driver. I do not know if anyone was hurt. I did not observe the
damage to either car except to see that the convertible was
damaged at its front end, and the Buick on its right side and
rear.

I have read and understand these . . pages and they are true.

ROBERT BROWN

Witness: ELIZABETH LANDLADY
220 N. Palm Ave.
Sarasota, Fla.

Witness: NEXTDOOR ROOMER
220 N. Palm Ave.
Sarasota, Fla.

STATEMENT OF JOHN A. BLANK
(A Horrible Example)

Withalachobee, Rhode Island
July 1, 1963

I am John A. Blank, 16, live with my parents, Mildred Mae
Blank and Richard D. Blank, at 3300 Main Street. I am a student
at Withalachobee High School. Yesterday, June 30, 1963, about
4:00 p.m., I was driving my dad's car, headed north on 15th
Avenue, when I was involved in an accident at River Street. I had
a passenger in the front seat, right side, Tommy Brown of 1802
Catalpa Street. Tommy was bruised rather badly on the right
shoulder and he had x-rays at the hospital but I understand he
had no fracture. Apparently he just had a big bruise. I was not
hurt. I had no medical attention. I went to school today. Tommy
went to school but he was rather sore and uncomfortable. I was
driving and headed north on 15th Avenue. As I approached
River Street, I had stopped at the previous intersection one block

---

[15] Notice that at this point the adjuster is probing for hidden clues to still
further witnesses. By this time the sense of the accident is pretty clear to him;
probably further witnesses, if any, do not need to be seen, but this is the time
to dredge out of Mr. Brown's mind any clues that may be buried there.

south of River Street. I looked at my speedometer and then looked up and saw a truck on my right, headed west on River Street. I am sure that the other driver was moving over 30 mph and it might have been 35 miles per hour. My foot was on the brake and I did not have a chance to apply brakes. I was intending to go north but when I saw the truck I attempted to turn left to avoid the impact. I was unable to avoid the collision and my right front fender and wheel were hit by the left front of the truck. The impact knocked my foot off the brake and I went across the intersection up into the yard at the north-west corner of the intersection. The truck spun to its right and ended up facing roughly north. I was not cited because I was in the intersection first. The other driver was cited for failure to yield right-of-way. My car was not driveable and was towed to the Withalachobee Paint and Body Shop. The truck was not drivable. This is a true and complete statement containing 3 pages and I have retained a copy of all 3 pages.

(Signed) JOHN A. BLANK

The statement of John A. Blank has been presented as a horrible example of how a statement ought *not* to be taken. Except for the alteration of the names and the invention of a fictitious city, this is an actual statement taken by an experienced adjuster.

No diagram was made.

Instead of interrogating to the diagram and then writing the statement, the adjuster tried to interrogate and write simultaneously.

The adjuster's use of hearsay in talking about Tommy Brown's injury is probably forgiveable as a means of recording Blank's knowledge. One wonders, though, if the adjuster really understands the difference between evidence and hearsay.

His most glaring errors come when he starts to describe the accident. This was a claimant's statement—if there was contributory negligence, it was the adjuster's duty to bring it out.

Note these other errors:

1. Blank looked at the speedometer but he didn't say how close he was to the corner when he looked.
2. *He doesn't even say what the speedometer showed.*

3. He saw a truck coming from his right. He doesn't say how near the corner his (Blank's) vehicle was then.
4. He doesn't say how near the other unit was to the corner.
5. He doesn't locate it on the street.
6. He doesn't say which unit entered the intersection first.

There are other errors, less important.

Blank's negligence may have contributed to the accident. Any attorney who tries to get it out of Blank by cross examination will get precious little help from this statement.

Much of what has been written about statements may be reduced to a check list of items which, depending upon the cirstances, should be covered. Many such check lists are formidable indeed. If such lists were the answer to the question, "How do you write a good statement?" the next few pages of this text could be omitted entirely and all that would be required in order to write a perfect statement would be to compile one master check list—unless, of course, the resultant check list might be too bulky to carry into the field.

Instead, it has been observed that the *technique of reducing a physical event to writing* is not dealt with adequately by any statement outline. It has been noted further that many adjusters have difficulty developing this technique—many never master it. This text will bear down heavily on this point.

Adjusters whose training goes no farther than their being given a statement outline often tend to write six pages on related but unessential detail, and two lines about the accident itself. Sometimes they even leave the reader in doubt as to whether or not two cars collided. The adjuster who wrote the "horrible example" statement was unquestionably trained (or left untrained) by a statement check list.

This text attempts to shed some light on (1) *how to draw from the witness* those observations that, taken together, constitute *his picture of the accident;* (2) *how these observations may be organized* so as *to form a related whole;* and (3) *how this information,* once drawn from the witness's mind, *can be reduced to writing.* If the adjuster can master these techniques, he should find that he is able to deal with a check list of almost any magnitude and can go easily from one field of investigation to another.

Often more intelligence is required to ask a question than to answer it. As the adjuster gains experience in investigation it should gratify him to develop the capacity to analyze an accident, for himself. Thus, he himself constructs for each accident, a check list appropriate to it. This reduces his dependency on check lists. It increases his efficiency and satisfaction in his work.

Note again the content of the check list. A statement is always identified by the *date, place,* and frequently the *hour* of its writing by superscription in the upper right corner. The sample statements demonstrate the manner of dealing with items 1 through 7 of the check list and, except for a few points which will be discussed later, items 9 through 13 inclusive. These items are generally regarded as routine. It is not in their writing that the real problem of preparing a statement arises.

Item 8, description of accident, is the real heart of statement taking. Note the large blank space devoted to the subject in the check list. This was intentional, to emphasize the importance of this item and that the adjuster—at this point—is on his own.

"Any statement that has the position and speed of both cars when the witness began his observations, the effort made to avoid the accident, where they hit and where they came to rest, is a good statement." The supervisor who said this would in the next breath have agreed that this is an over-simplification. Nevertheless, many an examiner and supervisor would grant him the essence of his statement and forgive him the over-emphasis. *Preparing an accurate description of the accident, as the witness saw it, is the heart of statement taking.*

Assuming that the adjuster has negotiated successfully items 1 to 7, inclusive, on the check list, he is then ready to obtain the witness's story. Now he should lay aside his statement pad. It will be quite a while before he is ready to take it up again.

OBTAINING THE WITNESS'S STORY

The statement taker's goal is the creation of a written account from which an actual reconstruction of the accident may be made by the reader. This reconstruction is not necessarily that of the event that took place. Rather, it is a reconstruction of what the *witness recalls as having taken place.* The account should describe this recollection completely and so definitely that it permits only one interpretation. It should be written so that any enlargement on, or departure from, what has been written requires an outright contradiction of the statement.

A statement should be a faithful attempt to mirror exactly what is in the witness's mind. To reproduce faithfully and in writing what is in the mind of another is no easy thing, but it may be this goal of faithful reproduction that accounts for a misconception often found among beginning adjusters, a misconception which now requires exposure and destruction. Regardless of what he may formerly have believed, *an adjuster does not write along with the witness. He does not reproduce the witness's words as he says them.* To recognize and understand why this technique is not feasible is the beginning of sound statement-taking technique.

This chapter will recommend a *step between* the spoken word from the witness's lips and the written page of his statement. This intermediate step, a crude diagram, the use of which will be described, is a way to record and organize otherwise disconnected and unorganized information. To understand why this seemingly roundabout route is necessary, some characteristics of witnesses and the nature of the information sought from them will be explored.

Characteristics of Witnesses

With relatively few exceptions, witnesses as a class, even those who desire to cooperate, suffer from one or all of the following disabilities:

1. They are disorganized.
2. They are not responsive.
3. They do not think objectively.
4. They are inarticulate.

A witness often starts out half-answering one question, switches in mid-sentence to another that the adjuster had intended to inquire upon later, wavers off into irrelevancy and then, before stopping for breath, drops in another pertinent fact. This has its bright side. His spontaneous remarks may even divulge important information which the adjuster might otherwise have overlooked, some nugget that will change the whole complexion of the subject. This flow of disorganized information must be put together by the adjuster so as to make a sensible whole. "Where were you when you first saw the other car?" a common question, may draw from the witness, "What do you mean? The cop never would have arrested me if he had a brain in his head."

This blatantly non-responsive answer is possibly an exaggeration but only in the sense that some witnesses are not so wide of the mark. Clearly the question must be answered, later if not sooner, and this will have to be managed without antagonizing the witness. The valuable bits in the flow of volunteered information must be recognized and noted, to permit later examination and development.

Most witnesses are preoccupied with what took place after the accident, to the exclusion of the accident itself. Their tendency to dwell on that point has to be curbed and attention directed to more significant matters.

Much of the information sought by adjusters from witnesses is in the nature of judgments: "How fast?," "How near?," "How far?" and the like. Most people fail to think of such things in other than subjective terms; they do not readily recognize that "very fast" may mean one thing to them and a very different thing to another person. To complicate the problem, they often find it difficult to see that an inability to be precise in a question of judgment is an entirely different thing from lying. The nature of judgment and their ability to form estimates has to be taught them, patiently and carefully.

Distance, speed, etc., should be stated objectively. Witnesses' *subjective* nature notwithstanding, the adjuster must write his statement in *objective* terms. "Slow" or "Not too fast" must be reduced to a judgment in miles per hour. This is a real problem when the witness is uneducated and has no concept of miles per hour.

Discussion of the adjuster's responsibility to record information objectively recurs throughout this chapter.

"What do you mean, where was I? I was on Sixth Street, wasn't I?" Now the witness is responsive but he is inarticulate. Such a response indicates that he has a picture in his mind's eye; possibly he could even walk to the scene of the accident, stand at some point and say "This is where I was." What he lacks is the ability to *translate that picture into words*. He needs help. It is the adjuster's responsibility to provide that help.

Problems of Description

The characteristics of witnesses are not all that make the writing of a statement something more than a straightforward task of simple reproduction. The *nature of the information* which the adjuster must find buried in the witness's recollection, then transfer to the written page, poses its own difficulties.

Automobiles move in a two-dimensional world. In colliding, each of two cars occupies an almost infinite number of locations. To locate all of them is an obvious impossibility, but *each point necessary to be located must be located,* and *locating* a point for statement writing purposes has a very particular meaning.

Each position discussed should be located so that no other position corresponds with the description. Direction and course should be made so clear as to permit of no other interpretation than that which is the one in the witness's mind.

Describing an accident may require the location of positions suggested by the following abbreviated list—and it may require many more:

1. Location of each car when the witness began to observe
2. If there are changes in course and speed, the places where such changes occurred, and the nature of the change
3. The location of the collision
4. Positions at rest

Furthermore, many of the locations the adjuster will deal with are important, *not so much for themselves as for their relation to another event occurring simultaneously.* For example, a trainee adjuster once had the duty of describing an accident in which his operator pulled part way out into the intersection, said that he stopped, and then noticed the other car bearing down on him. In the statement which he wrote these words appeared, "To my best judgment, the Ford was 14 feet distant from me before we collided." By itself, true though it undoubtedly was, this bit of information meant nothing. Before the cars collided the other car was, at one instant, 15 feet distant and, at another instant, 15 inches. Probably what the adjuster was trying to write was that *at the time the witness first saw the other car* it was 14 feet distant from his car, and *that* information may well have been important. As the trainee wrote it, the sentence made only nonsense.

To write a satisfactory statement, its author must analyze each accident, determine those factors, movements and positions that are important to its description, and then extract the information describing the witness's recollection. Then he must write the words necessary to record the witness's recollection. The organized procedure necessary to this end tends, unfortunately, to interfere with another equally desirable objective.

Accidents do fall into patterns and one "pulling from the curb" claim seems soon to be quite like any other. The similarities notwithstanding, each accident has aspects peculiar to it. For each accident, there is usually an essential "Why." A stereotyped search for positions, speeds, distances, etc., should not be permitted to interfere with bringing out and recording what the witness has to say in regard to this important point. If one is not careful, this is exactly what the standard interrogation tends to do. An adjuster should balance the close questioning which enables him to bring the witness back to the pattern of the accident against letting the conversation flow unchecked for the possible development of further valuable information. Not infrequently, the most valuable items are not only volunteered, they come as a complete surprise. Often an adjuster has the feeling, "Boy! If he hadn't blurted that out, I never would have thought to ask him." In fact, *if this doesn't happen* to a busy adjuster at least once in every few months, it should cause him to suspect that his careful questioning has smothered such spontaneous revelations. They are easy to lose sight of if they are a little "off-beat." This point will be elaborated later in this chapter and further demonstrated when the use of various recording techniques is considered.

To a certain extent, therefore, a witness needs to be given his head, but the organization of what he is saying into a coherent whole can never be far from the adjuster's mind.

FROM WITNESS'S MIND TO THE WRITTEN STATEMENT

To accomplish the transfer from the witness's mind to a coherent statement—to organize and make objective that which has hitherto been subjective and disorganized—calls for an adjuster armed with certain attitudes and equipped with an adequate technique.

Adjuster's Attitudes

An adjuster has many goals. One of them is that proper balance between the silence that lets the witness say what he wishes, and the determination which brings him back to his point. Neither adjusters nor the insurance business are going to change human nature. Since this is the way witnesses are, an adjuster copes with the problem the way it is, not the way it ought to be. He needs tact, understanding and (carefully cushioned by these desirable qualities) *a generous measure of stubbornness to bring the witness back to the question.* Adjusters should expect witnesses to leave the point. They must be brought back or the statement will not be worth the paper on which it is written. *Without antagonizing his witness,* an adjuster must hold him to the question until he gets his answer, and mix patience with a grim determination not to leave the job until all the essentials have been obtained and jotted onto his diagram. He brings the witness back to any point as often as necessary until it is answered.

Many words are employed to describe qualities desired in an adjuster, but one which seems to have been unjustifiably overlooked is *patience.* Patience is the answer to many statement-writing problems. It is not unusual for a witness to have to be brought back as many as 10 times in order to elicit an answer to a single question. It is important to stick with the first question until an answer is obtained. Once this has been done, the idea usually communicates itself to the witness and later answers come more easily.

To stubbornness and patience, adjusters are also called on to add insight, the ability to analyze an accident and sense those questions which must be asked to lay bare the heart of the matter. The witness may volunteer this information—but only a rash man relies on this kind of assistance.

The Technique (a Diagram)

If by now the technique to resolve the problems presented by the nature of witnesses, and the character of the information to be gained from them, is already painfully plain, that plainness will not be mourned here. One of the sad things about education is that it is charged with furnishing answers; but the students to whom the answers are given often fail to grasp the lesson because, lacking familiarity with the question, how can they be expected to understand its answer? [16]

The technique, of course, is to lay aside the statement pad, construct a rude diagram of the scene on which the accident took place (on a separate sheet, preferably of generous size), and use the diagram as a reservoir—a means of recording quickly, by means of symbols and *brief* written entries, the information being accumulated. Some of the information will be volunteered, some will be unearthed by patient digging. How it is gained is, for the moment, of no importance. The briefest of entries will suffice to get it on the diagram. The whole idea is to interfere as little as possible with the questioning. If digging is required the questioner is free to dig.

The chain through which a witness's information passes is, therefore:

His mental image
His words
Entry on the diagram
The diagram's entries organized into a statement

There are, it is true, good adjusters who take good statements without employing this diagram techique. Omitting the diagram is *not* recommended to trainee adjusters; for them it seems better to recognize that the technique is omitted only at considerable risk. It invites just such a horror as the John A. Blank statement.

---

[16] The attempt here has been to emphasize the *question* and thereby make the *answer* obvious.

Many an old hand, as a matter of preference, interrogates to a diagram. The diagram guides him by reminding him as he goes along of the points necessary to be covered. This, however, is not all that a diagram does. It maintains a quick record of information *as it issues* from a witness's lips, and at the same time performs another essential function. This chapter has spoken frequently of the need to *organize* a witness's otherwise random information. This is exactly what the diagram does for the statement writer—and does it without further effort on his part. When he has finished his questioning, there is his information, laid out before him and ready to be written up in whatever order will make the sense of the several items most understandable.

The diagram an adjuster creates as the witness talks is a storage place, a reservoir, to record and store information so that later it may be properly organized and written into narrative form. It may be crude but with its aid questions may be broken down into bits small enough for the witness to handle as he tries to verbalize the picture in his mind's eye. "How far were you from the corner?" may now bring "About a hundred feet," or "Right opposite the big banyan tree," producing a quick entry on the diagram.

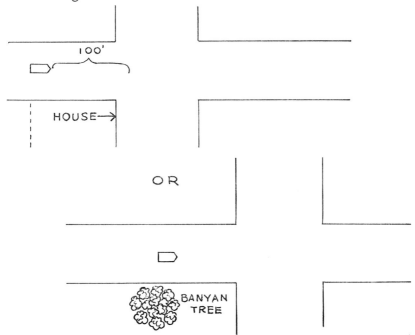

But—the car has not yet been completely "located," so the point should be followed by ascertaining its position relative to one side or the other of the street on which he was driving. This interrogation may change the diagram by forcing a relocation of the symbol representing his car, yielding something like this:

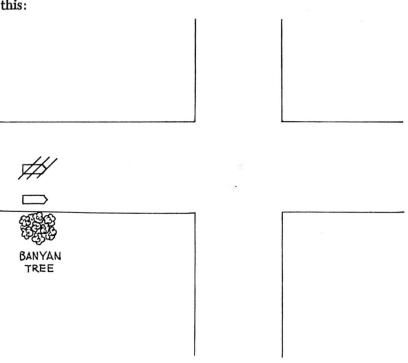

BANYAN
TREE

The change is no cause for concern; there will be others. *This diagram is not part of "the record." It is only an aid, a device to store information until it can be organized into a coherent narrative. The diagram needs to make sense to the adjuster but only to him.*

Started in this fashion, the statement continues, developing first the position of one car when the witness began his observations, continuing to its speed and direction, picking up then the location, speed and direction of the other vehicle, and continuing in this fashion until the two have collided and ground to a halt.

The interrogation has not been properly concluded, the description of the accident is not ready to be written, until the diagram, crude and messy though it may become, discloses the course of each car, their changes if any and where they occurred, the speeds and changes in speed of each until the vehicles are at rest. Then and only then is it time to take up the statement pad and continue writing on it.

COMMITTING THE STORY TO WRITING

The interrogation apparently finished and all necessary and significant information entered on the diagram, it is time for the adjuster to record this information in the written narrative statement. He again picks up his statement pad and resumes writing. He will still be unable to use the witness's own words. The witness was the source of all the information now entered on the diagram, but it is an exceptional witness who, even now, can assemble the information coherently.

Now it is time to review again the sample statements and abbreviated diagrams from which they might have been derived. These statements are imaginary. The accidents they describe never occurred. These statements are intended to demonstrate important elements in the interrogation and statement-writing technique. They are not intended as examples of the *best* statements that could possibly be written. Certain important items of a good statement are demonstrated by their omission. These are, in the Jones statement, footnote 6, and in the Smith statement, footnote 11.

Jones' statement reads, in part:

> "I stopped my car at the stop sign which faced me as I came to Orange Avenue. By 'stopped,' I mean that I applied my brakes and brought my car almost, if not entirely, to a dead stop. I do not remember if my automatic transmission 'down-shifted.' I made this 'stop' or 'near stop' with my car's front end even with the near curb of Orange Avenue."

This elderly gentleman thought he did "stop." He is essentially honest but probably confused. Questioning developed that he probably didn't stop at all, but even if he did he will be vulnerable to cross examination.

Readers should notice that the positions dealt with are described, each with two points of reference. Speeds are dealt with objectively, and other matters of judgment similarly.

Now notice the sentence structure. They are short, simple, and usually convey but one idea. Notice, too, that the flow of thought is even and the sense of the witness's mind is obvious even though the sentences are simple and many. Ungainly and overlong sentences trap many adjusters, possibly a natural consequence of trying to deal with a complex idea. It is a sound rule to keep sentences as short and as simple as possible.

Notice, too, that the statement writer stuck with a critical point—"stopping at the stop sign"—until he had *exhausted* his witness's testimony on that point. Contrast this with the expression in the Blank statement, "I looked at my speedometer," and then the glaring omission—the failure to record the speed shown by the speedometer.

By way of digression, it should also be noted that it is impossible to construct a sensible diagram from the statement of Blank. This is an excellent test of whether or not a statement has been properly taken. If an adequate diagram cannot be constructed from it, the statement is almost surely inadequate.

Here is another test. If, using the material in his statement, an adjuster cannot stand in a piece of roadway and say, "This is where my witness said he was when . . ." the statement is almost surely inadequate.

It may seem that this discussion has been elementary. It is usually recognized that the best football teams are those which block and tackle crisply. Dotting the i's and crossing the t's of one's statements are the blocking and tackling of statement writing.

As the adjuster translates his diagram notes to sentences on his statement pad he will, unless he is unusual, find himself in a continuing dialogue with his witness. He will usually inform the witness as he goes along as to what he is writing and how he is phrasing it. This enables him to secure the witness's assent, item by item, and shake out errors. It gives the witness confidence. Further, the witness has a reasonable chance to reconsider and amend what may have been inadvertent misstatements.

In some situations it may be desirable to use a witness's own words. A witness may have a particularly graphic phrase for describing some phase of the accident. If his language is better than the adjuster's, the adjuster should employ it. Further, many witnesses employ characteristic colloquialisms and unique turns of phrase. This colorful language should be reproduced in the statement, if this can be done without offense to good taste. The author once interveiwed a witness who habitually concluded his sentences with the words, "He did," or "So I did." A statement embodying such an idiosyncrasy has high authenticity, especially if a witness attempts to deny its contents from a witness stand. He usually employs the same mannerisms on the stand, and juries are prone to make the obvious connection. However, except for the working in of such idiosyncrasies, the statement is the adjuster's *own* composition. Recognizing this, he should consciously abandon any notion that he is going to "write it down as the witness says it."

If this discussion seems to underestimate the intelligence of the average witness, such is not intended. The adjuster should never permit himself to forget that to render in words an account of a physical event is a language feat of no mean proportions. It may be a healthy reminder that he himself had to "learn how to do it" if he will save a copy of his first statement attempt.

MECHANICAL POINTS OF STATEMENT WRITING TECHNIQUE

It is desirable that a statement demonstrate, so far as possible, that nothing was or *could have been* added after the witness had given his signature. The use of *paragraphing* has been discussed. Except for the final line of each page, which is reserved for the witness's signature, there should be no blank spaces.

All corrections should be initialled by the witness. All interlineations should be initialled—long ones at both the beginning and the end.

Some authorities believe it is good technique to make one or two errors or corrections on each page. The witness then initials them, thus, so it is thought, demonstrating conclusively that he was acquainted with the contents of the page. This seems something of a refinement of cunning. In reading a statement a witness may discover an error or wish to change what has been written. If he will write the change or interlineation *in his own hand,* then, whether or not initialled, this is good authentication.

If possible, avoid ending a sentence on the bottom of a page.

Sooner or later the adjuser may be tempted to let two witnesses sign the same statement. This temptation is almost irresistible when the witnesses are all passengers in the same car and the adjuster already knows that the stories are identical. He should always resist this temptation. The adjuster should write the second, third—and the sixth, if necessary—statements as carefully as the first, taking his cold comfort in the thought that at least, with each writing, he finds more ways to telescope the facts and cover the ground with fewer words. The experience is universal; no adjuster has ever been known to enjoy it.

A statement is terminated by having the witness write, in his own hand, an acknowledgment which should always convey four principal ideas. Though the language conveying the four ideas may vary from statement to statement, the ideas themselves are constant:

> I have (1) *read* and (2) *understand* this statement on (3) X pages and it is (4) *true.*

This entire subscription (as it is called) is to be written in the witness's own hand. If he is illiterate or has a language or other handicap, then an appropriate authentication should be prepared. The techniques for this are described later in this chapter.

Many witnesses sign the last page, then inquire why corrections are to be initialled. It is a mistake to treat the inquiry as an objection to be overcome. The witness is simply puzzled. Low-keyed reassurance is in order. An explanation that this is a routine matter, done so that he may know that nothing can be added or deleted or altered after the statement has left his presence, will usually be acceptable.

PROCURING THE SIGNATURE

The adjuster should *expect* every witness to sign the statement. Making the statement objective, letting it be obvious that he is trying faithfully to mirror what is in the witness's mind, and cultivating and displaying an air of routine carefulness, tend to put the witness in a proper frame of mind to give his signature.

Having finished writing, the adjuster should hand the statement pad to his witness and simultaneously place the ballpoint pen in his hand. The adjuster watches as the witness reads. As the witness nears the end of the statement, the adjuster should indicate with his finger the place where the witness is to start writing. Rather than letting the witness consider *whether or not* he will write, the adjuster fixes the witness's attention on the place where the witness *is* to write. Pointing, he tells him, "Now, right here, write 'I have read and understand . . . etc.'" and continues dictating the subscription. When the subscription has been completed, the adjuster continues in the same tone of voice, "John Witness." The *tone of voice* tells the witness that he is to continue writing. The adjuster should never *ask* a witness if he will sign. He avoids, if possible, the words "sign" or "signature."

If this simple technique is followed, the adjuster should have little difficulty with unsigned statements. The technique is designed to avoid giving the witness an opportunity to say "No." It may be used with equal facility by adjusters who possess the gift of persuasion and by those to whom this gift was denied.

In Chapter 1 it was observed that there are successful adjusters who are backslapping salesmen and others who wear steel-rimmed spectacles. The important thing is that the adjuster develop a *comfortable* technique. This will be the effective technique for him.

Salesmen vary techniques to fit the client, and adjusters must vary theirs to fit their witnesses. Self-brainwashed though he may be, the successful adjuster sees no respectable reason for anyone to decline to sign a statement. He is honestly surprised when a witness refuses, and most witnesses do sign for him.

GENERAL PROBLEMS IN THE EXAMINATION OF WITNESSES

In addition to the problems just discussed, which are peculiarly those of *writing* statements, the preparation of statements involves other, broader, questions concerning the interrogation of witnesses in general. Although these are not really problems of cross examination, they come close to it. They have to do with *leading questions, negative information, objective terms, sense of the accident—the "real reason," conclusions, obvious error (how to cope with it), injury.*

Leading Questions

A *leading question is one that suggests its answer.* "Dinner at six thirty tonight?" suggests, and in certain circumstances demands, a particular answer. It is a leading question. "When will dinner be served?" is not a leading question.

An attorney in the court room may not lead his *own* witness. He may, however, ask leading questions in cross-examining a hostile witness. Neither law nor custom limits the use of leading questions in outside-the-courtroom activities.

An adjuster is trying to get at the truth. A leading question may, by imposing his views on the witness, tend to obscure the truth. On the other hand, if a witness is inarticulate or is trying to obscure facts, a leading question may be the only way to obtain the truth. The adjuster's job is to reproduce truthfully on paper what is in the witness's mind. He may and does use leading questions to the extent that they help in attaining that end.

The adjuster is not a minor league Perry Mason, wringing the truth from a lying world with brilliant questions. Adjusters who hold this romantic view are no strangers to the business, but they seldom last long. Their work is often poor, their judgment unsound, and they have a deplorable tendency to get their principals involved in litigation that a more prosaic approach would have avoided.

Leading questions are often asked simply to save time. Leading questions should not be employed to force a witness to say that a car was on the left side of the street when he really believes that it was on the right. Leading questions may be used to help him say something that is in his mind but which he cannot put into words. This saves time. In fairness to the witness, if what he has been attempting to say leads to the conclusion that he was traveling in the middle of the right-hand half of the roadway, it is better to ask him in so many words, "Do you mean that you were driving in the middle of the right-hand half of the roadway?" This is a leading question, but if the witness is having trouble expressing himself, it is better to use such a question than to confuse him by further beating about the bush, or by wasting ten minutes in trying to avoid asking the question in a manner that suggests its answer.

In other words, an adjuster does not need to lean over backwards to avoid asking a leading question. He does not, for example, have to go to such ridiculous extremes as to ask, "Who chased whom how many times around the whats of what?" Almost any judge would forgive an interrogator who lightened the witness's burden a little bit by rephrasing his question, "How many times did Achilles chase Hector around the walls of Troy?"

Despite his care to avoid doing so, an adjuster may suspect that he is imposing his own ideas on the witness. If this is so, he should offer the witness alternatives—"Or do you mean that you were closer to the right-hand curb? Or to the center line?" The important thing is to get at what is in the witness's mind and render that thought into words properly transferable to paper.

Certain witnesses, usually insureds and their passengers, are eager to cooperate with an adjuster. With them he must be especially careful that he does not, in effect, wind up putting a self-excusing story in the witness's mouth. In fact, his greater effort will be directed usually to bringing out the weak points, if any, in his insured's version. A case investigated in a spirit of realistic skepticism is much more likely to withstand shrewd cross-examination in a courtroom. The process of evaluation is constant, and to improve a witness's story is to run the risk of covering up fatal weaknesses in one's own case. This in turn could lead to a lost settlement opportunity and undesirable litigation. Therefore leading questions should be used warily and sparingly on one's own witnesses. Care must be taken to *avoid* coloring their evidence by wishful thinking.

Care is also to be employed in using leading questions in interrogating *hostile* witnesses, but for other reasons, such as where the "prosecuting attorney" approach will be recognized and resented. It is seldom effective, anyway, outside the courtroom where the judge's discipline requires a witness to stick to responsive answers. Furthermore, although an *insured* may be anxious to follow what he conceives to be a lead from his adjuster, a *claimant* or a witness allied to the claimant by circumstances will resent such a lead. Necessary rapport can easily be damaged.

Therefore the adjuster should take great care that the leading questions that he does employ are not argumentative but are bona fide attempts to assist the witness in phrasing what is really on his mind.

If a witness is obviously exaggerating, it is ordinarily futile to attempt to expose his exaggeration by cross examination or to get him to change his story. It is usually better to give him his head. At this point the guiding principle is, "Give him enough rope and he will hang himself."

In summary, leading questions are a necessary device to save the adjuster's time. It is improper to use them to "improve" the story of a witness. They are legitimate but dangerous tools in obtaining the truth from a hostile witness.

Leading questions may illuminate or obscure the truth. The adjuster's real goal is to bring the truth out into the open. He should use leading questions only with that goal in mind.

Dealing with Negative Information

To record the fact that there is something a witness *does not know* is frequently as important and usually more difficult than what he does know. The simple statement "I don't know" seldom does the job. Observe how easy it is for a witness to distort what some adjuster might have thought to be a good statement. The attorney rises, displays a statement, asks the witness to identify his signature, and indignantly asks him, "Didn't you say right here, 'I don't know how fast the other car was going'?" The witness answers, "I sure did. This nice young fellow came out and asked me a lot of questions, and he was real careful. I remember thinking that he was a real good workman. He asked me if I knew how fast the other car was going, and I thought he meant did I know right down to the last mile or fraction of a mile per hour. I sure didn't, so I told him I didn't know. If he'd have explained to me that what he wanted was my judgment, I'd have told him, just like I do here, that I judged that car was going between 40 and 50 miles an hour."

This attorney will receive no help from the statement on *this* point, and it should be obvious that the adjuster gave the witness a blank check.

If a witness honestly does not know whether the car he observed was going 10 miles an hour or 50, he should say so, and it should be clear that *this,* and not something else, is his testimony. The statement of Brown, as he describes the speed of the red Buick, demonstrates the proper method of setting out an "I don't know" situation: "Since I did not see the Buick until the collision, I cannot judge its speed. I do not know whether it was going 10 miles an hour or 40."

The Use of Objective Terms

Witnesses are not accustomed to talking in objective terms—"fast," "very close," "right in front of," must be reduced to miles an hour, feet, or some other objective criterion of measurement.

Even though the adjuster knows well the difference between "objective" and "subjective," making this distinction apparent to his witnesses is a problem that will be with him all his days. "How fast was he going?" "Well, I don't rightly know, but the law said he shouldn't have been there anyway, because. . . ."

Tenacity and patience are important. This *is* a *hard* question. This may be the witness's first accident. He is not used to judging speed. He is not familiar with the use of exact language in expressing his judgment. Moreover, the witness may be unable to distinguish between outright lying and making an honest estimate with reasonable leeway for error.

It is a rare witness, though, who is unable to grasp the point if you observe to him that even in such a mystery as a woman's age, he does, once he has seen her, have a judgment concerning it. He may not know whether she is 29 or 40 but, to be a little ridiculous, he can look at any woman and tell if she is over 10 and less than 60. With that analogy, and bringing the limits of judgment closer together, it is not difficult to make the witness understand.

There are some devices the adjuster may employ to make the witnesses' task, and his own, easier. For instance, conventional methods of expressing distance in feet, yards, etc., may be difficult to apply. Although a rifleman or surveyor may describe a distance as "a thousand feet," they are about the only people who are accustomed to thinking about distance in such terms. Where the distance is greater than five or 10 feet, the witness's judgment in terms of feet is likely to be highly inaccurate. Therefore it may be better to ask the witness to compare the distance under consideration with the length of a football field, something with which he is probably familiar, and then express his judgment in terms of that object. It appears to the author that the use of "car lengths" probably in the end comes nearer to reproducing what is in the witness's mind than feet, although it is conceded that the four car-lengths referred to by witness Smith mean one thing if he had Volkswagens in mind, and quite another if he had Cadillacs.

The use of landmarks—as distinct from estimated measurement—(see again Smith's statement and the words "opposite a large banyan tree") is by all criteria much superior to the writing of Smith's judgment that he may have been "X car-lengths" or "X feet" from the corner. The location of the banyan tree can always be determined by going to the scene and using a steel measuring tape.

The beginning adjuster should be reassured that the experienced adjuster has the same problems to cope with and must be just as patient and tenacious as the neophyte. A statement may present from five to 50 objective judgments to be drawn from a witness, and it should be re-emphasized that the first such judgment should, within the limits of politeness, be made the point of indoctrination. Often it is desirable for an adjuster to make a slight issue of an item which he knows to be within the observation and judgment abilities of the witness. If he chooses his ground carefully, he should find that it is wise to stick with the first question until the answer is obtained. The rest should come more easily.

To re-emphasize: Patience is the watchword.

The Sense of the Accident—The "Real Reason"

Litigation tends to turn on "key points." It does not weaken this observation to concede that the point may be irrelevant (e.g., a dominant juror may react adversely to an attorney's personality). Accidents are likely to have one *real* reason for happening. It is not to be wondered at that this fact reflects itself in the ensuing litigation.

Highlighting this real reason might be referred to as bringing out the "real sense" of the accident.

These pages have suggested that it is not unknown for an adjuster to write several pages of statement without ever permitting the cars to collide. Admittedly this is a bit rare, but it is *not* rare for an adjuster to write a statement that fails to state a witness's observations on the one thing that is the root cause of the whole mishap. Blank's statement demonstrates this very shortcoming.

Some adjusters are gifted with better language sense than others. The process of reducing an accident to positions, speeds, distance—in short, writing it out—comes naturally to them. This type, along with his brother who has been trained by a supervisor who is a stickler for detail, is particularly prone to err in this regard.

For instance, two cars are headed in opposite directions on the same road. They hit, head on. It seems incredible to write a witness's statement about this accident without recording where the witness stands on the question of who was on the wrong side of the road. Yet this error falls only a little short of the designation "common." It should be unnecessary to observe that a statement on such an accident that fails to deal with this key point is nothing but wasted effort. In "wrong side of the road" cases, the real reason is obvious, but in other cases the reason may be less apparent. The author remembers a recent case that developed like this:

The insured was about to cross a main artery. She stopped at a stop sign. She started up when the other car was less than one-half a car-length distant from the curb to the insured's left.

Of course, the other car hit her squarely on the left side. There was, however, a reason for this accident a little deeper

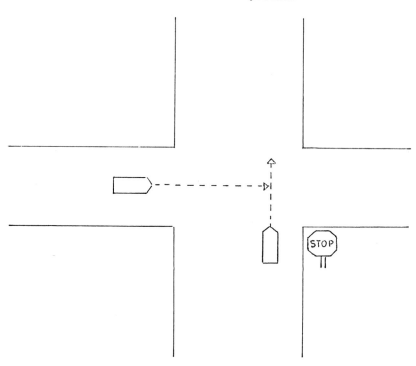

than what has been disclosed to this point. The adjuster uncovered it by asking, "And why did you start up with this other fellow bearing down on you?" The answer: "He had his right-turn light flashing and I thought he was going to turn before he got to me, so I was watching the other traffic." The outcome of this issue is irrelevant. The point is that the statement would have been inadequate had it not brought out the premature turn signal as the cause for the insured's error.

Many accidents are susceptible of two explanations, each compatible with the physical evidence. Pulling-out-from-the-curb accidents illustrate this. The "real reason" is usually that the emerging car starts up without looking and the passing car has nothing to do except hit or be hit. However, from time to time drivers do emerge carefully, see an approaching danger, stop, and sit helpless while the other fellow runs into them. If *this* is the witness's testimony, then this is what the statement should reflect.

Much of what the participants say about the "real reason" is little better than a lame excuse. Many such self-exculpatory stories are ridiculous on the face: "I stopped at the stop sign; there was nothing coming. When I got halfway out into the crossing, I stopped and his left rear wheel hit the front end of my car at a 'fast' rate of speed." (They never say a "high" rate of speed.) Opinion in the claims world is not unanimous as to the proper procedure when one is faced with such untenable statements from one's own insured. Some feel it better to leave him with his error; others think it better at least to point out his error and give him a chance to take a more tenable position. It is not the function of this book to make policy. Each adjuster will be instructed on that point by his employer.

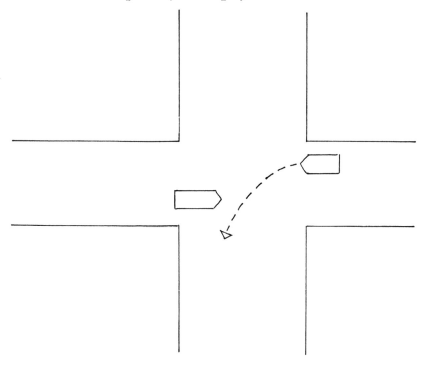

Turning-left-in-front-of cases (as illustrated above) tend to generate arguments over whether or not a signal was given and *whether the turning car started its turn at a time when there was sufficient opportunity to complete the maneuver.* Though most traffic codes place the burden on the turning vehicle, this does not relieve the adjuster of the duty of ascertaining, in such a dispute, where his witness stands on the point.

A statement must therefore bring out its maker's position in relation to the real sense of the accident. This is no less important than tying down the details. The real sense may be arrived at by giving the witness his head (see page 233, the Story About Lonzie); or by emphasizing the word, "why?" in the question, "Why did this thing happen?" If these techniques don't suffice, the adjuster is expected to foresee the issues on which the eventual decision will turn and bring them out by pointed questions.

A statement that fails to do this is a waste of time.

Stating Conclusions

The witness testifies to the facts. It is the *jury's* province to form conclusions.

A witness may relate to a court (or set out in a statement) information that he obtained by the use of his five senses. This is evidence. He may not testify with regard to his *conclusions*. Hence, with one exception, conclusions are not properly included in a statement.

The distinction between observed fact and conclusion may sometimes be tenuous. A witness may have observed that a man's face was flushed, his manner obstreperous, his breath reeking of alcohol, his gait unsteady, his speech thick and incoherent. Classically, the witness could tell all this to the court, and all of the things related above could be recited in a statement (should be, in fact, if they were the truth). Having said that, though, the witness could not take the next obvious step to say, "The man was drunk." Now (and this demonstrates that legal views shift with the times) in many situations the witness is permitted to come right out and make the obvious statement, "He was drunk."

A hostile witness may want to say in his statement that "X was to blame for the accident." This conclusion is inadmissible as such. However, if the witness seems to make this an issue, it is usually better to permit the conclusion to appear in the statement than to risk the loss of the statement. This exception to the rule is the only time that conclusions should appear in the statement. The defense counsel may elect to offer the statement, hoping perhaps to demonstrate bias (claimant witness), or try to introduce part of the statement, hoping to exclude that which is objectionable.

Many experienced adjusters admit to a fondness for letting witnesses make such statements as "He turned right smack in front of me." Certainly this is not objective, and it is perilously close to a conclusion. If it is the witness's own verbatim statement, the adjuster may be inclined to set it down in black and white and let the lawyers and the court cope with it as they will. But—and this is the important point—after he has done so, the adjuster should interrogate to the point, "What do you mean, 'Right smack in front of'? How close were you two then? Where was he? Where were you? How fast was he going? How fast were you traveling?"

An adjuster's job is to find and record the evidence. Observed facts are evidence. Conclusions are not. When, for whatever reason, a good adjuster admits a conclusion to his page, he harbors a small guilty feeling. He has not even begun work until he records the facts that underlie the conclusion.

Obvious Error—How to Cope With It

In the purest innocence, a witness may make an outrageous misstatement of fact. Possibly he has already gone on record in a statement to an adverse adjuster or attorney. This poses questions. Should the adjuster simply accept the situation? What can be done?

Judgment is involved. The insurer's real interest is in having the truth prevail, and so long as his effort is toward the truth, the adjuster is under duty to try to set the record straight. Some advice as to what he *can* do about it may be helpful.

One insured operator, a housewife, told the investigating officer, "I did not see the other car until I was 10 feet from the corner." The intersection was wide open. Each driver could see the other for as much as 200 feet. What the adjuster may do is to tell her to walk back and forth and stand where she was when she first saw the other car. The adjuster may then measure, or step off the distance, or in some other way acquaint his driver with an accurate, objective measurement of the subjective impression which she incorrectly stated as "10 feet." The information thus derived may be an entirely different story. Her statement then should be written as: "Since the accident, I re-visited the scene. I walked back and forth and reconstructed the accident in my mind. I measured the distance to the corner from the place where I remember that I was when I first saw the other car. I found that it was 60 feet."

The lady still may have a difficult time if the matter is litigated, but if this is objectively and carefully done, she stands a good chance of showing the jury that she is not being untruthful. She simply had a typical layman's inability to judge outdoor distances in terms of feet.

Taking a witness back to the scene almost always produces sounder judgments and stronger statements than if the interrogation takes place away from the scene.

Insisting on detail may uncover outright misstatements or disclose that what the witness is offering for observed fact may actually only be unsupported conclusion, surmise or conjecture. In general liability claims, a claimant states, "I was on the fourth or fifth step from the bottom when my foot slipped or I caught it on something and I fell." The adjuster asks, "Was it the fourth step or the fifth? Or perhaps the third?" Soon it is clear that the lady has no idea how many steps she fell, whether one or 10.

Questioning goes on—Did her foot slip? Did she catch it? A foot "slipping" and a foot "caught" are entirely different things. They don't feel remotely alike. It frequently develops that what the lady really means to say is that she has not the faintest idea of what happened. She knows only that she was walking downstairs and that she feel. If this is so, this is the way the statement should read.

Witnesses are prone to make long and unshakeable statements about accidents which they did not see. The adjuster is permitted to feel that he has advanced the cause if he terminates such a statement with the observation, "I was in Dominic's barber chair waiting for a haircut when I heard the crash, ran out and saw. . . ." It should be unnecessary to point out that an adjuster ought always to ask his witness, "What called this accident to your attention?"

Injury

Insured's statements, as such, concern themselves only lightly with injury.[17] The real evidence on this point lies elsewhere. The adjuster, though, does not neglect to record such observations as may later bear on the subject. A claimant who was the first to jump out of his car, who argued vigorously and intelligently with a gas station attendant, etc., should be noted. This or similar information may lead to a possible witness and may indeed be of value if the claimant later alleges that he was knocked out or suffered a post-concussion syndrome. It is the statements of claimants and potential claimants that are most likely to concern themselves with injury.

Claimants' statements should describe their injuries in complete detail. One of the less obvious benefits of this is that doing so reveals the statement as a fair-minded undertaking. Certainly the injured party is entitled to get his injury "on record," and it helps to get the statement signed. If there was no injury, the statement should be explicit. "I was not hurt" is preferred over "I did not receive any injury." It is desirable to retrace the facts and thinking, reinforcing the statement and avoiding misunderstanding, by stating, "I have noticed no pain or soreness. I have had no occasion to consult a doctor. I continued with my usual job and performed my usual duties."

Injuries should be described in terms intelligible to the layman. The adjuster may know that the claimant has a fractured tibia, but the injured man may not know his tibia from his fibula. He can say that his leg was bent back at an unnatural

---

[17] Because of the now widespread use of uninsured motorists coverage, an *insured* may become a liability claimant under his own policy. Thus, *his* statement about *his* injury could be important on that count.

angle, that it hurt, that he was sick to his stomach, that a cast was applied, and that his doctor has told him that he had a broken leg.

The recital of a claimant's injuries should continue until the adjuster is able to write some terminating phrase such as, "And the injuries I have described are the only ones I received," or "Except for what I have described in this statement, I was not hurt." Unless this is done, the adjuster has not covered the subject.

A witness seen soon after the accident may be concerned that a later injury may develop. This concern is reasonable. The adjuster may accommodate him with a phrase such as "The only injuries known to me at present include. . . ."

Often an adjuster may attempt to adjust a claim involving only a bruised elbow and find that his ideas of value and those of the claimant differ by several hundred dollars. Then to his amazement he may hear complaints of momentary unconsciousness, nausea, headaches, "whiplash," etc. The likelihood of being exposed to this embarrassment is minimized if the claimant's statement has *first* described and limited the injury.

If a claimant suffers from a prior condition subject to aggravation, information regarding his prior medical history, addresses, treatment, etc., should be included in the statement. It is only human for claimants to associate almost anything that happens after an accident with the accident. The importance of informed medical opinion in litigation on such points is obvious. The dependence of that opinion on lay evidence is easy to overlook.

An opinion in associating or disassociating injury and trauma often depends on the existence or non-existence of certain symptoms *immediately* following the trauma. For example, consider the question of threatened miscarriage, a question that always arises when a pregnant woman is involved in an accident. There is much strong medical opinion to the effect that unless trauma is followed within 48 hours by symptoms denoting disturbance to the pregnancy, a subsequent miscarriage cannot be related to the trauma. The critical symptoms are cramping and "staining."

For ages, scholars have pointed out in vain the fallacy of reasoning, "*After* this, therefore, *because* of this." Adjusters, too, commit this common error in logic, so it is not surprising to find that if a miscarriage is preceded by an accident, the attempt to establish a connection between the two will be routine. The adjuster faced with a pregnant claimant should realize that the chances are better than one in 10 that she will miscarry, for whatever reasons. If she does miscarry, he will have his claim. If a well-written statement from the claimant establishes, within a few days from the accident, the symptoms which she did and *did not* sustain, the testimony of her doctor and of any examining doctor has a great deal better chance of arriving at the truth than if the claimant is left to let her imagination play on her symptoms.

The above example is cited merely to illustrate that medical opinion on the cause of pathology often turns on symptoms observable to a layman. The medical situations that may turn on the presence or absence of some symptom complex, and how those symptoms should be approached in a statement, could be the subject of a book in itself. The point for adjusters to remember is that post-traumatic symptoms are vital to the later accurate formation of sound medical opinion. It is essential that statements describe completely and objectively the symptoms that did exist. The statement should make it clear that there were no other symptoms.

Negative Statements

Some occasions call for a statement from a witness to establish that he *did not* see the accident (or some phase of it). Adjusters refer to these statements as "negative statements." They should be secured if there is reason to suspect that a witness may later allege that he saw something which he did not in fact see.

On serious claims it is often considered good technique to take statements from all persons in a neighborhood (perhaps a court reporter should be used). There is the story of a conscientious young adjuster who received more than a little kidding. He had taken statements from almost everyone in Boston. Included was the attendant in the men's toilet on the Common, whose statement explained that when the accident occurred he had been inside, cleaning bowls. This adjuster had the last laugh when the attendant came into court with a strong "pro-plaintiff" story. The witness spent several weeks in jail for contempt of court as the result of his indiscretion, and the plaintiff's attorney very nearly bore him company.

Negative statements, by and large, are reserved for the serious cases.

Earlier it was observed that it is often harder to say that a witness *does not* know something than to write what he does know. It is not enough to say, "I don't know anything about. . . ." The accident referred to must be specified and the statement explicit in saying that the witness was not present, was in fact elsewhere, was in no position to observe, and did not in fact know that the accident happened until. . . .

VERBATIM STATEMENTS

This chapter has dealt with statements in their traditional form—that is, hand written and in narrative order. This has been done at length, for unless the technique necessary to this method is mastered [18] *verbatim statements* which are now about to be considered will not incorporate the desired information.

---

[18] The paragraph opening this section is unchanged from the first edition. In the short six years since it was written, the narrative "signed statement" has become almost a rarity. To the author's observation, better than 70% or 80% of the statements now taken by adjusters are recorded in question and answer form, but recently there came to the author's attention startling confirmation of the assertion above.

One of the major carriers had just purchased a smaller company which was quite big in our local area. The smaller company's staff was being absorbed under the direction of the executives of the acquiring company. The author had occasion to discuss the takeover with one of the executives.

Author: The last time we were together I think you told me you weren't letting your field men take recorded statements.

Executive: That's right. Two things disturb me. Unless you transcribe every statement in its entirety, recordings are almost impossible to supervise. Even if you do transcribe them, which is devilishly costly, they are so long that it is terribly time consuming to read and criticize them. But the real reason I made them go back to handwriting was because I found they weren't getting into their statements the things they ought to. And when I made them start writing I found that most of them didn't even know how to write a narrative statement. So now I'm making them learn how to block and tackle and when they master that I'll think about the fancy stuff.

Verbatim statements are simply another means of recording the same information as narrative statements; the same attention to detail is required. It is no less essential that the sense of the accident be established and recorded.

(Throughout this discussion of verbatim statements the story about Lonzie, page 233, an excerpt from a verbatim statement, will be referred to frequently. Its careful reading at this time will be helpful.)

Verbatim statements include those recorded by court reporters or other shorthand or stenotype writers, and statements recorded by adjusters on discs, belts, tapes, etc., by various mechanical and electronic means. Although each method presents some considerations peculiar to it, they are on the whole so similar in their problems and requirements that they will be discussed together. (An attempt will be made to identify and discuss problems peculiar to one or the other of these methods as they appear.)

Verbatim statements will first be considered from the standpoint of their *characteristics* and then from the standpoint of the *techniques* to be employed in procuring them. It should not be surprising that many of the desired techniques flow from the special characteristics of this class of statement.

Contrast with Narrative Statements

This chapter's comments about writing narrative statements emphasize the virtual impossibility of the adjuster following the witness word for word, hence the necessity of the adjuster's interrogating, organizing and composing himself a coherent account of what the witness has said.

Verbatim statements are the opposite. Every word uttered, whether by interrogator or witness, is recorded literally. In fact, this is the essential difference between the two types, and in the difference lie both the strengths and the weaknesses of verbatim statements.

Credibility and Persuasiveness

Verbatim statements are commonly regarded as possessing greater credibility or authenticity than conventional signed statements. This quality derives, for the most part, from their content. They are the witness's very own words. Since no witness can avoid putting a lot of himself into his utterances (putting his stamp on the statement, so to speak) statements of this type derive great authenticity from that fact alone. To the extent that the story is volunteered by the witness, the questioner's participation is kept to a minimum, and the statement is further strengthened.

Statements recorded by court reporters are, of course, supported by the testimony of the reporter himself, a person of unquestioned probity whose official connection with the court is not lost on the jury. On the other hand, statements recorded mechanically or electronically preserve the *voice, tone and inflection* of the witness and can be played back to the jury so that the jury *actually hears the conversation* that took place. Some counsel opine that this is even stronger than the testimony of the reporter. For further authentication the transcript may be taken back to the witness for signature, but this is rare.

In addition to their credibility or authenticity, verbatim statements are uniquely *convincing*. That is, they not only possess a high ability to satisfy the jury that they are the utterances of the persons who made them, but they also convince in the sense of persuading the jury to accept the testimony thus recorded as the *real* version of what took place. This convincing power derives from their sometime graphic qualities and is vividly demonstrated by the story about Lonzie. This point will be elaborated when appropriate *techniques* are discussed.

Ease of Procurement

On the whole, adjusters who have had broad experience in procuring all classes of statements agree that all forms of verbatim statements are more easily procurable from witnesses than handwritten signed statements. Too, the question of securing a signature (even though this may not be a major problem) is completely done away with.

Probably the technique which presents the very minimum of problems and the fewest refusals employs the court reporter, preferably writing shorthand rather than using a stenotype machine which is awkward and may frighten the witness into silence.

Although an adjuster meets with some refusals, more persons will consent to having a recording made than will agree to the signed statement procedure. Public officials and policemen may be reluctant to render signed statements but often offer no objection to the recorded statement. Many laymen, likewise fearful of being "tricked" into signing something they do not understand, do not hesitate to commit themselves to the truth in the form of a recorded statement.

THE STORY ABOUT LONZIE

Lonzie drove out of a private yard, through a dense hedge, across a shallow ditch, made a right-angle turn to his right, and collided head-on with a bus.

There were very many serious injuries. Among the injured was Lonzie's young lady, Velva Dee, who was interrogated in the hospital in the presence of a court reporter.

Adjuster: Can you tell us how fast Lonzie was driving as he drove through the hedge?

Velva Dee: Yes. And I can tell you something else, too.

Adjuster: (His heart in his mouth—he has no idea of what he is about to hear.): All right. You tell us.

Velva Dee: Well, Lonzie, he just went flyin' out of that hedge, and he swang 'way over on the wrong side of the road, and here come this bus a-bearing down on us, and I said, "Lonzie, you get back on your own side of the road or you're going to kill us all." And Lonzie, he didn't see that bus, or something, and the next thing we knowed—blammo! and there we was!

Please note:

1. The almost total lack of detail (a weakness)
2. The vivid quality (a strength)
3. The way the real sense of the accident comes out (a strength)

Graphic Quality

In the earlier discussion of handwritten statements, it was demonstrated that the search for detail, necessary though it may be, tends to smother or stifle the real sense of the accident. This conflict between the techniques necessary to produce two desirable but different qualities in the same statement is found to be more acute in the case of all forms of verbatim statement.

Had the adjuster who interrogated Lonzie wanted to deny himself Velva Dee's vivid outburst, he needed only to say, in answer to the girl's first response, "Wait just a minute. Now, give me, in your best judgment, your estimate of the speed in miles per hour . . ."

By his choice of the *mode* of questioning, the adjuster invariably makes an election. A similar choice, whether to give the witness his head or extract his story bit by bit, confronts him in every verbatim statement. His guide being his judgment, he is forced to consider when to press for detail and when to turn the witness loose, to recognize that there are two basic approaches to the witness, and to make an intelligent selection of the mode best suited to his purpose.

Economic Factors

Court reporters are highly trained, highly skilled persons. Only a few people master this rigorous trade. Therefore court reporters' statements are expensive. They are usually employed only in the more serious claims, where no expense may be spared to achieve the most effective results.

Statements mechanically or electronically recorded are very economical of adjusters' time. If transcribed, however, they require much clerical time. From a cost standpoint it is difficult to draw a comparison between adjusters' handwritten statements and mechanically recorded statements.

Pitfalls

Admirable instruments though they are, verbatim statements have their pitfalls. There is a story that illustrates this point, one possibly antedating the memory of those who may try to learn adjusting from this book.

The late Major Bowes presented in the early 1930's a radio program known as the Amateur Hour. A lady contestant once offered to sing *The Jewel Song* from *Faust*. The Major told her to go ahead, if her voice had any flaws, *The Jewel Song* would hang a red light on every one of them—and it did. She was a screecher.

A recorded statement will do the same thing to an adjuster that *The Jewel Song* did to the unhappy soprano. If there are any flaws in his technique, it will hang a red light on every one of them. They will screech.

Possibly the major pitfall is the danger of improperly using *leading questions*. Possibly less important from a technical standpoint but more embarrassing from a personal point of view, a verbatim statement mercilessly exposes any flaws in one's use of the English language. This text will offer no assistance on the second point. A way to avoid the first pitfall will be discussed in the technical paragraphs to follow.

General Procedure

In recording a verbatim statement, the interrogator *plans* his questions. He trains himself to follow an order of presentation so as to produce an arrangement of information similar to that which he would present in a conventional handwritten statement.

The witness is asked to identify himself by name, age, etc. To authenticate the statement, he should be asked such questions as his mother's maiden name, the place and date of his marriage, his driver's license number, Social Security number, and other items reasonably known only to himself. Then, as the accident itself is dealt with, the adjuster should check off mentally each of the items that he would have covered in a statement of the more conventional form, and see that each is properly considered.

He mentally constructs a diagram as the witness talks, holding the picture in his mind's eye until he has made all the necessary and significant entries. If the witness says that he put on his brakes without specifying where, he should be allowed to finish what he has to volunteer. Then the adjuster asks those questions necessary to clarify the picture of what took place. He asks him *where he was* when he applied the brakes. The statement continues in this way until the adjuster has developed all the information which he would have included in a conventional statement. At the end, it is desirable to ask the witness if there is anything he wishes to add and to request him once more to identify himself by name.

If the statement is mechanically or electronically recorded, the machine, once it has been turned on, should run continuously, during pauses for reflection and all, until the statement is finished. If it is a long statement and more than one belt, tape or disc is needed, the adjuster should announce the coming interruption *on the record* as the need to change belts approaches and request the witness to identify himself just as he would at the end of the statement. Then as the new belt is started, the witness should be asked to identify himself again, to confirm that this is a continued recording, and be asked if any conversation took place during the change of belts which he wishes to place "on record." The interrogation then proceeds to its end.

Choice of Locale

One of the pronounced advantages to working with a shorthand reporter is the ability to record in almost any environment, even while walking about as might be necessary in following a witness about on a job. Stenotype operators have an advantage in their ability to record with absolute ease in utter darkness.

If the recording is to be by machine, an attempt should be made to select a place for the interrogation as free as possible from echoes and background noises. Most machines can be used even under adverse circumstances by adjusting filters or other devices. Since there are many machines on the market, no attempt will be made here to explain the techniques by which each machine can be adapted to its surroundings; this information is available from the manufacturer. If a quiet location cannot be had, the best method is usually to get both adjuster and witness as close to the microphone as possible and conduct both sides of the conversation in a loud voice.

If a witness is critical and his spirit of cooperation is in doubt, the adjuster should consider handwriting a conventional statement or deferring his first approach until a time when he can meet the witness in more accommodating acoustical circumstances.

Preliminary Instructions

A statement should contain no mention of insurance; it may be gravely damaging to the defense counsel's ability to defend the case if such a mention is made. Caution the witness before starting that he should make no mention of insurance, that he will be at liberty to discuss that situation when the recording is ended, and be prepared to interrupt him firmly in the event he tries to open up such avenues of inquiry.

In the event a witness mentions insurance before he can be interrupted, consideration—if the witness is cooperative—may be given to starting again from the beginning. All the recording media which operate by creating an embossed mechanical sound track are very cheap—the cost of a new disc or belt is mere pennies—and the electronic equipment all erases automatically, the second recording automatically obliterating the first.

If the recording is to be by machine it is most helpful to give the witness a few preliminary instructions. He should be instructed to keep the level of his voice up. A simple hand signal may be arranged, such as a lifting gesture—palm upward—to tell him when more voice-power is desired. He should be cautioned to hold his answer until the questioner has finished his question, so that the transcriber will not have to listen to two voices simultaneously. The reason for this should be explained and another simple hand signal arranged (hand up, palm toward witness in the traditional "stop" position).

It should be added that if the signals fail to produce the desired result when the statement is under way, there is no harm in speaking up and asking the witness, on the record, "Will you please RAISE YOUR VOICE THE WAY I AM DOING? I am afraid your voice is so faint that my secretary will have trouble in understanding you."

Avoiding Leading Questions

While leading questions are not forbidden to adjusters in recording statements (as they are to lawyers in a courtroom examining their own witnesses) they should be avoided, if at all possible, since they must to some degree intrude the interrogator between the witness and the person who is eventually to read or hear the recording. And, to the extent that the interrogator intrudes, he diminishes the authenticity and possibly the graphic quality of his statement.

Few people realize that in day-to-day conversation, leading questions are the rule rather than the exception. Hence, almost every adjuster starting out to record statements must to some degree change long-standing habits. It will be wise, therefore, if the first few statements he records are non-critical. He should carefully examine these transcripts, observe where leading statements have crept in, and refine his techniques and habits to exclude them from future statements.

When this has been done he may consider adopting the following advice which has been recommended by a number of defense counsel. Almost certainly this procedure best suppresses the bad effects of leading questions, yet it yields a maximum of solid objective information.

1. By question and answer, take the witness through the necessary preliminaries until, in effect, he is on the street, approaching the corner and ready to have his accident.
2. Having taken him that far, give him his head. Invite him, "Now, in your own words tell me just what happened." (Be ready to interrupt when he starts to talk too long about what happened after the accident, as he almost certainly will.)
3. Bring him back repeatedly to the accident, with more and more pointed "Why" questions. Make these questions palatable by phrasing them tactfully. Do not ask, "Why didn't you stop when you saw the other fellow?" Put it this way, "The record should reflect your reason for not stopping. Will you state your reason, so that I may be sure I have your full story?"
4. During the above exchanges keep mental note of the items of information volunteered and developed. Then place specific questions to clear up points not yet covered, such as, "You have explained that you were about six car lengths from the corner when you first saw the other car. How fast were you going at that moment?"

In the end this style of interrogation should yield the same information that would have been incorporated in a good signed statement. If it doesn't, it's not a good recorded statement.

Just as under more conventional questioning, a witness may be inarticulate. In that event, the questioner should exhaust non-leading questions first, but in the end he may have to resort to a leading question to help the witness phrase what is on his mind. It is better to do that than to leave the point uncovered. As was explained earlier, a question can be leading in form but still, by offering the witness a choice of alternatives, avoid imposing the views of the questioner.

Now a further rereading of the vignette about Lonzie is in order. Note how this graphic account has none of the detail that this chapter recommends. Nevertheless, it was an immensely valuable statement and the cornerstone of a successful defense. It describes in subjective, graphic, and colloquial terms exactly what took place. No one hearing it read could fail to have a graphic picture of Lonzie's recklessness in bursting through the hedge and charging over onto the wrong side of the highway. *But after this outburst, the adjuster went back, picked up the threads and reduced the young lady's testimony to objective terms, as he had been taught to do.* He determined and recorded: (1) the speed in miles per hour as the car went through the hedge; (2) how far the car had proceeded into the road before the lady saw the bus; (3) how far beyond the center line Lonzie went; (4) the distance separating Lonzie from the bus when he crossed the center line; (5) the speed of the bus; and (6) all the other things that good statement-writing technique requires.

Diagrams (How to Use Them in Taking Verbatim Statements)

Earlier in this chapter it was strongly recommended that a diagram be used in preparing a narrative statement. It is now recommended that a diagram be used in taking most verbatim statements; however, the verbatim statement is a more sophisti-cated tool than the narrative statement. A diagram is used for much the same purpose as in a narrative statement, but in a very different way. Unless an adjuster knows *why* he is using a diagram when he records a statement and unless he guards him-self carefully, he can get himself into bad trouble.

First, it will be helpful to recall how this chapter recommended that the diagram be used in the narrative technique:

> Adjuster interrogates
> Witness responds
> Adjuster records fragments of information
> on diagram
> Adjuster organizes bits of information on
> diagram into coherent whole
> Adjuster writes narrative statement for
> witness's approval and signature

In the verbatim technique, every word the witness utters is immediately recorded and fixed in its ultimate context. The very technique forbids the analysis and organization by the witness himself, but the adjuster must be sure that all of the witness's knowledge is exposed and that all subjects pertinent to the accident are covered. The seasoned man turns again to the diagram but now he uses it in a different way. His technique, (and this is now recommended) is as follows:

> Before commencing to interrogate (possibly even before he is in the witness's presence), he draws a crude diagram.
>
> Knowing in general how the accident took place, he prepares the necessary lines to indicate streets and their boundaries. To jog his memory and to permit him to make quick, "one word" or figure notes, he prepares questions or key phrases. As the witness touches on or is interrogated about those points, the adjuster plans to and later does pencil in a quick word or figure to tell him two things:
>
>> that the witness has spoken to the point, and
>> what the witness had to say about it.
>
> He prepares himself, of course, on those points which are standard to the kind of accident he is concerned with. Pages 241 to 244 show standard preparation for four very common collision situations.
>
> He also prepares himself to cover points which are particular to the claim he is handling. Page 245 shows notes an adjuster might have prewritten to guide him in his interrogation of Velva Dee (See p. 233, The Story about Lonzie).

Right-Angle Intersection Accidents

Fill in desired items as witness volunteers story. Requestion for omitted relevant data.

Before recording:

Invite witness to take out and have ready: his driver's license, social security card, and car registration. Instruct witness as to hand signals.

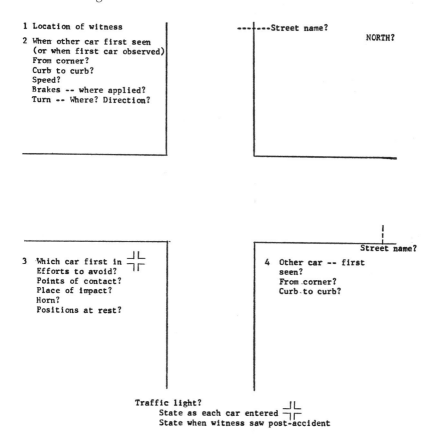

1 Location of witness

2 When other car first seen
(or when first car observed)
From corner?
Curb to curb?
Speed?
Brakes -- where applied?
Turn -- Where? Direction?

-------Street name?

NORTH?

Street name?

3 Which car first in
Efforts to avoid?
Points of contact?
Place of impact?
Horn?
Positions at rest?

4 Other car -- first
seen?
From corner?
Curb to curb?

Traffic light?
State as each car entered
State when witness saw post-accident

Rear End Accidents

Fill in desired items as witness volunteers story. Requestion for omitted relevant data.

Before recording:

Invite witness to take out and have ready: his driver's license, social security card, and car registration. Instruct witness as to hand signals.

1 Front car stopped or moving at impact?
  Where?
  Speed?
  How long stopped?
  Why stopped?
  How stopped?

2 Signal?
  How?

3 If witness attributes fault to front car -- why?

4 See rear car before bump?
  Speed of rear car then?
  Speed of rear car at bump?
  How far front car pushed?
  Skid marks?
  Horn?

5 Positions at rest?

6 Description of damage to each car

NORTH

------Street name

Head-On or Side-Swipe Accidents

Fill in desired items as witness volunteers story. Requestion for omitted relevant data.

Before recording:

Invite witness to take out and have ready: his driver's license, social security card, and car registration. Instruct witness as to hand signals.

```
                                          Nearest town or
                                          prominent landmark

                                               ▲
 1  When other car first noticed:              |        NORTH
       Distance separating the cars
       Locate, if possible, relative to
       fixed object
       Speed of each
       Position of each relative to center
       or side of road

 2  Did either car leave road?
       Where?
       Why?

 3  Course and changes in course and speed
    of each until impact?  Enter relevant
    data on diagram

 4  Where did collision occur (relative to
    center line)?

 5  If adverse car came on witness's side:
       Why not leave road to right?
       Why not avoid by going to left?




                                               |
                                               ▼
                                          Nearest town or
                                          prominent landmark
```

Turning-Left-In-Front-Of Accidents

Fill in desired items as witness volunteers story. Requestion for omitted relevant data.

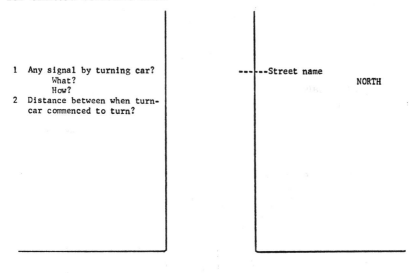

```
1  Any signal by turning car?
        What?
        How?
2  Distance between when turn-
   car commenced to turn?
```

----Street name

NORTH

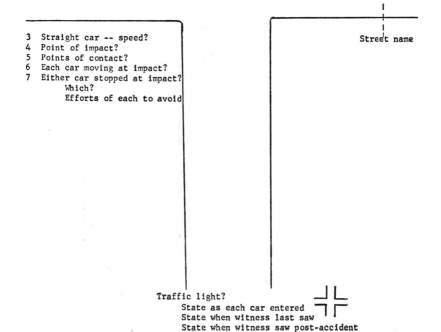

```
3  Straight car -- speed?
4  Point of impact?
5  Points of contact?
6  Each car moving at impact?
7  Either car stopped at impact?
        Which?
        Efforts of each to avoid
```

Street name

```
Traffic light?
State as each car entered
State when witness last saw
State when witness saw post-accident
```

Some Do's and Don'ts

Prepare a diagram or sketch before interrogation; make unobtrusive notes on the diagram while questioning him. While questioning, make only such notes as are necessary for guidance. If an attempt is made to construct anything more complicated while interrogating, the witness is likely to answer one of your questions: "I can't really say it, but he swung out just like this." (Meanwhile, he may be drawing a meticulous curve with his finger tip on your sketch. This gesture, will escape your machine.) Here are some notes one might prepare for questioning Velva Dee.

Note	The notes, interpreted
Sp @ H	Lonzie's speed when he went through the hedge
Sp enter rd	His speed when he hit the roadway
? VD knee	Was anyone sitting on Velva Dee's knee to block the view of the bus?
Stop	Did Lonzie stop?
Why no stp	Why did he not stop?
L to B @ #1 C	Distance from Lonzie to the bus when the bus was 1st seen?
How far out L @ #1 C	How far out had Lonzie gotten by this time?
L mph "	Lonzie's speed, then?
B mph "	Bus speed, then?
L re cen-line when hit	Where was Lonzie in respect to the center line when the bump happened?
B "	Same information for the bus

It may be (often is) alright to have a little conversation with your witness before you begin to record. This will give you some idea where the statement will take you, but it exposes the adjuster to two dangers:

Your witness may balk at some question in the middle of the interrogation. "But I told you that. Why do you ask me again?" The cure, "Yes, you did tell me that in the conversation we had before I turned on the machine. Will you now restate what you told me then so the machine can hear you."

The second danger. Having heard what a witness says on an important point, the adjuster may remember what he heard but forget that the witness was "off the record." Thus he returns to the office with a statement which fails to touch on an essential point. For this error, there are two remedies (precautions might be a better word). First, the adjuster might increase his life insurance.[19] The second precaution is for more cautious souls. See that the pre-interview notes on the diagram are set up as a reminder that an answer is wanted on the point. Then when the answer is obtained make an entry of a word or two which indicates what it is.

Do not worry about how the sketch looks or whether it makes sense to anyone else; it is not supposed to be intelligible to others. It exists to guide and remind the adjuster, to help him make a record and the record has to be in the words of the witness. The diagram exists to guide and to help cover the necessary ground; it has no other purpose.

If the adjuster has an excellent memory and is experienced, he may get away with dispensing with a physical sketch—and with the notes on it. But it will be helpful if he will at least carry a sketch of the scene in his mind's eye and do within his head, by imagination and memory, what this chapter has recommended be done on paper.

The Time Squeeze

Most recording machines use discs or belts which are designed to record for 12 minutes (which can usually be stretched to 13). While this is adequate for an experienced adjuster and a witness who sticks to the point, 12 minutes often is not enough time and changing belts is a nuisance.

To make most efficient use of the recording time available spot the rambling witness in the pre-recording conversation and explain that he should stick to the question. Help him to do

---

[19] His boss, of course, will kill him. The added benefits will do the *adjuster* no good, but that's not the point. Almost every significant social advance is marred by a certain amount of pouting and outcry from those who fancy their interests to be adversely affected. Odd though it may seem, some of his dependents may adopt this course. Life insurance proceeds tend to subdue this unseemly behaviour—and *that* will be appreciated by his colleagues at the office.

this by arranging a simple set of hand signals. Also explain that what happened after the accident is of only minor importance, but that if he wishes a second record to cover that will be made.

The best way to keep a witness from rambling is to know where he is going and to avoid questions that go over and over the same ground. To spot such tendencies have some of your statements transcribed and then study them. This eliminates the tendency, especially of young adjusters, to go round and round on the same point.

Each of the above suggestions can be adopted with little fear that an adjuster is courting the disapproval of his employer.

We now come to another technique which is approved by some and absolutely unaccepted by others. Therefore, this text makes no recommendation on this point. It is the employer's absolute right to determine policy.

Much of the verbage in a statement is routine and non-controversial. Items in this category include:

> Name
> Birthdate
> Residence
> Driver's license information
> Place of employment
> Ownership of vehicle
> Identification of passengers
> Date, time and place of accident
> Weather
> (Possibly) Origin, purpose and destination

To get a maximum amount of information onto a minimum amount of belt (providing always that the employer has no objection to the use now to be made of a leading question), all of the above items may be obtained in pre-recording conversation. Also at that time request to see witness's driver's license and registration certificate. Interrogation may then proceed along these lines:

> Adjuster: This is a recording made at Tampa, Florida Jan 15, 1970. My name is John Smith. What is your name?
>
> Witness: Joe Witness

Adjuster: During the conversation which we had before I turned
             on the machine you showed me your driver's license
             and registration. With your permission, I'll read some of
             this data into the record, along with some background
             information about an accident we are going to talk
             about. If there is any question about any of this or if
             anything comes out wrong, feel free to interrupt me.
                You live at 2411 San Pedro, Tampa, Florida. You
             were born March 10, 1943. Your driver's license is un-
             restricted and numbered 123456. It expires March 1971.
             You are a mechanic employed at XYZ Machine Com-
             pany. You own and have registered in your name a
             white, 1965 Buick, 4 door sedan, registration number 3-
             65432. The accident we are about to describe happened
             January 14, 10:00 A.M., at San Pedro and Lois Streets
             in Tampa; weather was clear; the roads dry. You were
             alone on your way from your home to the Publix Super-
             market to do the family shopping. Your direction was
             west on San Pedro. Now tell me, in your own words,
             what happened.

Trial attorneys, with whom this technique has been discussed,
find no fault with statements prepared this way, provided the
material covered in the long recitation (which amounts to a
leading question) *is not in controversy.* Just because most of
the items recited are usually routine, it should not be assumed
they are never in dispute. Weather conditions might be in
question, or the origin, purpose and destination may disclose an
agency relationship between driver and his passenger. In that
event, the subject should be covered by direct questions which
expose the subject without leading the witness but still permit
him to tell the story in his own words.

A final word of caution is perhaps in order. It was said that
the witness should be required to state the matter in his own
words if the subject is "not in dispute." This is too narrow a
criterion. The witness should not be lead over ground that may
later be in dispute or over any ground, in fact, which may be
important to the ultimate disposition of the case. An agency
situation, for example, may be openly admitted at the time a
recording is made, but, since the outcome of a law suit might
turn on the question, a witness might well decide to try to
repudiate his testimony later. Were this to happen, it would be

better for the witness to have divulged his information in answer to such questions as:

Where were you going?
Why was Jones in your car?
Did he tell you what he intended to do there? What did he say he intended to do? Etc.

The "It Hurts Here" Problem

Few people realize how much information they convey by gestures rather than words. This phenomenon should be anticipated by an adjuster who plans to take verbatim statements. He must be alert to convert the information thus conveyed into words which a machine can record or which a court reporter can translate into shorthand.

This will be referred to as the "It hurts here" problem.

A court reporter can write down what he hears and, if he is quick, some of what he sees. Thus, if the witness says "It hurts here" and points to his right shoulder, the reporter will usually add a parenthetical observation, "Witness points to right shoulder." *But a good adjuster makes it easy for his reporter; he asks his witness, "Was that your right shoulder that you pointed to?" and requires him to answer "Yes" or "No."* If the interrogation is to a machine rather than to a court reporter, this helpful courtesy now becomes an *absolute necessity.*

What is really the same phenomenon may be more recognizable in the field if it is seen now in two other contexts.

It is probably unwise to attempt to construct a diagram while interrogating a witness to a recording mechanism or to a court reporter. This is because the important thing is the record. Neither reporter nor machine can cope with a witness who points to a piece of paper and says, "Right there." The words will be recorded, but their significance is lost.

Since court reporters are employed most often on the serious cases, it is likely that the adjuster will sometimes visit the scene of an accident with a court reporter and his witness. He must use special care to be sure that all the information conveyed by the witness is put in a form that will enable the reporter to record it properly. If the witness states that he was "Right here" when he put on his brakes, the reporter can record the words "Right here" but that will be insufficient. Let the witness step off the distance to easily identifiable objects, and then have him reduce that information into verbiage for the benefit of the reporter:

Question: Have you identified the exact place where you put on your brakes?

Answer: Yes.

Question: Where was it?

Answer: In the middle of Highway 17 and 50 steps north of the north curb of B Street. I just stepped it off.

Assistance to Reporter or Stenographer

In taking any form of verbatim statement, never forget the problem of the third party who must listen and understand what is being said. Both adjuster and witness must maintain an adequate voice level. If the adjuster drops his voice, the witness will drop his, and vice versa. The adjuster must speak slowly and distinctly. The witness will tend to slow down to that pace.

When the witness mumbles anything, the interrogating adjuster should go back over the ground, speaking very slowly and very distinctly so that the witness can confirm that he has been heard correctly and so that the secretary or reporter can get a second chance to hear the word.

Witness: I was born in Playfee, New Jersey.

Adjuster: (Speaking very distinctly) Plainfield, New Jersey?

Witness: That's right.

Remember too that neither reporter nor machine can hear the witness nod or shake his head. The affirmative "Mm hmm" sounds much like the negative "Uh uh." Keep the witness, as much as possible, in Yes or No answers.

Be patient!

Controlling Transcribing Costs (Alleviating the Executive's Distress)

It is necessary to give the supervisor a reasonable insight into the contents of a statement at reasonable cost. There are two techniques to answer the executive's all too valid complaint that recorded statements are costly both in time and money. (See footnote page 230.) The first is so widely used that, even though this book does not endorse it, it deserves mention.

First Technique

Adjuster interrogates witness, records conversation on belt, tape or other medium. Later in his report or in an addendum to his report, he dictates a summary of what the witness has said.

Advantage: The summary is short, therefore not costly to transcribe. It is organized and coherent and gives a picture of the described accident.

Disadvantages: Some adjusters report that it is difficult and time consuming to dictate even a few days after the recording has been made. Others report that they have to take so much time listening to the recording to refresh their memories that they might as well have handwritten the report in the first place. Supervisors complain that they often wonder if the testimony recorded in the summary is actually covered, or covered well in the question and answer interrogation. Others report that they have had the unpleasant experience of ordering a full transcript as a case approaches litigation only to find the statements attributed to the witness by the summary are not covered at all, or are covered so carelessly that they might as well have been overlooked completely. All too often they report that the adjuster has summarized not what the witness said but what the adjuster hoped the witness said. Even with the best of intentions, it is easy to fall into this error.

The summary is devoid of internal authentication, that is, the witness's assent to it as a fair summary.

Second Technique

Adjuster interrogates and records. Before closing his recording *and while still in the witness's presence,* speaking in the conversational mode to the witness, he (the adjuster) summarizes what he has just been told. This is done after inviting the witness to correct any errors or misconceptions. When the summary is complete, just before the final sign-off, the witness is asked if the summary is a fair statement of what he has to say.

Advantages: It is easy to do—the adjuster's memory is fresh and clear and the summary can usually be done in less than three minutes.

It is short and coherent. A well done summary can usually be transcribed in one to one and one-half pages of double-spaced typing, and it is easy to type and read.

Errors are often exposed and eliminated. This gives the witness who has made a slip of the tongue or who is the victim of an honest misunderstanding a chance to correct the record; a right that would be difficult to begrudge him. It also provides authentication— the witness's own words accepting the summary are reproduced.

Disadvantages: It is still possible for important points to be overlooked or glossed over in the questions and answers, and assented to in the summary.

The summary is principally in the adjuster's words. It amounts to a long leading question. And, hence, it has the danger of putting words in the witness's mouth.

Preservation of Recording Medium

If statements are recorded mechanically or electronically, the recording medium should always be preserved in such a way as to enable its taker to identify it and testify from his own knowledge as to its unaltered character and that it is the record of the conversation that took place. Difficulty in introducing such matter is rare. If trouble is expected, the adjuster might strengthen himself by sending the item to himself by U. S. mail, thereby sealing it in a stamped, dated envelope, with his signature written across the seal, to be opened in the courtroom. Probably this refinement is necessary only in an extreme situation.

Bus Accidents

The subject of verbatim statements cannot be left without reference to their extreme applicability to such situations as exist in bus accidents—several witnesses to be seen in a hurry. With possibly upwards of 25 passengers, even in a minor accident, the problem is how to record in a hurry the "No Injury" statements, enabling the adjuster to concentrate at once on the injured. Court reporter or machine recording is the obvious answer.

MISCELLANEOUS STATEMENT PROBLEMS

Statements of Passengers in Claimant's Car

It has been observed that passengers in the "adverse" vehicle may have excellent recovery rights in spite of negligence on the part of their operator. In order for his operator's negligence to affect his passenger's claim, there must be some relationship between the driver and passenger so that the law will *impute* the driver's negligence to the passenger; that is, treat the driver's negligence as if it were the passenger's own, or view the passenger as if he himself had committed the driver's mistakes.

Usually the law imputes negligence only in cases involving an identity or community of interest. Note that the statement outline (on page 190) requires the adjuster to inquire about the origin, purpose and destination of the trip. The purpose of this query is to uncover any possible clues which might show a "community of interest." Inquiry on these points only opens the question—to suggest that there is a fact situation which needs further investigation. It is not too far-fetched to allude to "The Horrible Example" statement (on page 199) with its demonstration of the obvious error of opening up a subject, then failing to exhaust its possibilities.

It should be obvious that a witness's statement, "He was taking me from my home to 4100 North A Street" should be explored further. Why go to 4100 North A Street in the first place? What did the passenger intend to do there? Who requested the trip? Who selected the destination? Who chose the route? Who was to benefit from the trip?

The legal relationships which obtain when there is an identity or community of interest—agency, common enterprise, etc.—and which permit or require imputing of negligence from one to another, are complex. Adjusters waste much valuable time debating the fine points as to what is or is not agency. This time could be better expended taking more complete statements so that the facts against which the law will be applied are crystal clear.

The adjuster is not responsible for knowing the fine points of what may or may not be a close agency question. He is responsible for knowing that, if there is a possibility of an agency situation, his statement is probably his first and last chance to bring it into the open. If he is face to face with a possible situation of imputed negligence, he should proceed with his questions *until he is satisfied that he has exhausted the subject.*

Passengers in Insured's Car

Gross negligence, and the special problem it presents in dealing with guest cases, has been discussed previously.

In states having some form of guest law, it must be determined whether or not the passenger is a passenger for the benefit of the owner. If he is a paying passenger, he is almost without exception removed from the guest category. Sometimes it is difficult to know whether a guest is a passenger for a consideration, simply contributing his share of the cost of the journey, or merely observing social amenities.

Again, it is not the adjuster's function to make the distinction nor to decide the legal effect, if any. The decision itself is made easy if the adjuster determines exactly what was paid, why, by what arrangement, and in what manner. Adjusters are not lawyers. Lawyers should interpret the law and decide the significance of the facts.

In one way or another, the concept of gross negligence frequently encompasses the idea of a continued course of misconduct, often in the face of warnings or requests to desist. Therefore the passenger should be asked whether he had any objection to the manner of the operator's driving; if so, what was the nature of the objection, and how was the objection voiced?

The notion harbored by many adjusters that when a passenger has signed "I made no complaint," or "I did not make any objection," the matter is finished could hardly be farther from the truth. The presence or absence of complaint must be dealt with and exhausted, but it is only one facet of the investigation.

Assuming that the passenger being interviewed is clearly not a passenger for a consideration (and remember, the consideration may not be pecuniary), the question of gross negligence remains; there remains also the question of how to deal with it in the statement. The young adjuster should review the decisions in his own jurisdiction on the definition of gross negligence. If the jurisdiction recognizes ordinary negligence as grounds for recovery, he will inform himself on that point. Where gross negligence is required, he should attempt to rule out any specific acts of gross negligence which the circumstances make probable. In the end, though, an attempt to guard against a later charge of gross negligence by trying to rule out specific acts is almost certain to fail. This is because, no matter how thorough his scholarship and no matter how lengthy his statement, there will always be just one more bizarre story which he failed to negate. *Therefore the real answer to an anticipated charge of gross negligence is a statement so carefully and so thoroughly written, with such a complete explanation of* WHAT DID HAPPEN, *that there is no room for any other explanation.*

It should be made clear in the statement that the driver's hands were on the wheel at all times preceding, and at the time of, the accident. It should be made clear not only that he was not turning around to talk with passengers in the rear seat but that his attention was actively and exclusively directed to looking ahead and, to the best of the passenger's power of observation, his driver was limiting his actions solely to driving the car correctly.

Serious injuries have a singular propensity for arising out of one-car accidents. Therefore, a disproportionate number of serious injury claims turn on various aspects of what might be referred to as "the gross negligence situation."

Accidents of this type tend to climax an evening of happy pub-crawling. Someone yields to the thrill of a wild night ride. When cars travel at 80 to 90 miles an hour, bridge abutments develop a marvelous agility, and one of them may leap out at the wrong instant. The severity and number of injuries are often shocking. Perhaps the passengers were with the driver during the entire evening and were as drunk as he.

Perhaps the defenses of *contributory negligence* or *assumption of risk* apply. Where the passenger contributed to the cause of his injury, or where he assumed the risk of the insured's actions, he may not complain.

Therefore the starts and stops made by the parties, the places visited, and particularly the times when the car was at a standstill so that the passenger had an opportunity to leave, must be carefully established. Courts frequently take the view that no matter how culpable the driver's misconduct, if a passenger continues to ride with him after this misconduct is known to the passenger, he does so at his own peril. Possibly just stopping for a red light or a stop sign may have given the passenger an opportunity to dismount. In some jurisdictions, a protest and a request to be let out places on the driver the immediate burden of complying with the passenger's request. The point for the learning adjuster is the same as has been made many times previously—let him make a complete and accurate record while he can. But let him not forget that the fellow who passed out on the back seat may have been helped into the car like a sack of meal. The court will probably excuse him if he neglects to jump out at the first opportunity. He has to know what is going on to be held responsible for his inaction.

STATEMENTS SIGNED UNDER DIFFICULTIES

Many witnesses are unable or unwilling to sign for some reason or another. There follows a series of techniques for authenticating their statements.

Problems and Subscriptions which solve them

Witness can read but cannot write

John ^{his} × Witness
mark by W. N.

John Witness read this statement on
2 pages. He says he understands
it, that it is true and he makes his
mark.

William Neighbor

Witness can neither read nor write

John ^his x Witness
mark by W. N.

I, William Neighbor, read this statement
on 2 pages, out loud to John
Witness. He says he understands
it, that it is true, and he makes
his mark.

William Neighbor

Witness has an injury to his writing hand

John Witness

John Witness has read this statement on
2 pages. He says he understands it,
that it is true. His right hand is injured,
so he signs with his left hand.

William Neighbor

Witness does not speak the language

Evelio Hernandez

I, José Gonzalez, have read this
statement out loud in Spanish to Evelio
Hernandez. He says he understands it and
that it is true and he signs his name.

José Gonzalez

Witness refuses to read or sign

> I, William Neighbor, have read
> this statement on 2 pages out loud to
> John Witness. He says it is true; but
> he refuses to sign his name.
>
>   William Neighbor

In an extremity, if there are no witnesses, the adjuster may write subscriptions himself.

CHAPTER 7

Teaching and Learning about Statements

Almost any teacher will subscribe to the statement that the best way to learn a subject is to teach it. The author of this text now wishes to carry the idea a bit further: One doesn't really know how to take a statement until he is competent to teach statement taking—and a corrolary, one cannot really feel that he has mastered the statement taking technique until he is competent to teach it.

It seems that this is so in this phase of adjusting for a somewhat obscure reason—a great deal of the skill in writing statements depends on the development of a critical faculty.

This faculty is always at work. It listens in on the interrogation and helps the questioner decide whether his questioning has been complete. It guides him to his next question. It examines what has been written or recorded to see that it makes sense and that the necessary ground has been covered. It examines the work product minutely to see that each sentence (or question and answer) conveys its bit of information, and it sits in judgment on the whole job to see that the desired end has been accomplished, that is, that the knowledge in the witness's mind has been fully exposed.

Much of what will be said in this chapter bears on supervision rather than adjusting. However, all adjusters should aspire to be supervisors and managers and if learning how to supervise their own work helps them to take better statements, the thoughts may not be out of order, even in a beginning text.

Is the Writing Logical and Complete?

Please turn now to page 206. On lines two and three of that page there is a quotation beginning with the words, "to my best—." Please read it. Then, about this excerpt, from an actual field effort, consider: so far as the accident being investigated is concerned, the written words have no meaning. The author was writing to fulfill a preconceived notion of what a statement ought to say, not to make a logical statement about things—automobiles.

If the author of that statement had asked himself what that sentence means, he would have seen that it had no logical significance. This examination and evaluation must be applied to every written sentence and all utterances recorded in a question and answer statement. Now look back again and notice on page 195 the statement of Richard Smith. He says, "I was driving .... saw .... east on Second Street." This sentence was adequately criticized for logic and meaning.

As you continue in the text and meet the statements of Jones, Smith and Brown and the dismal "non-statement" of John A. Blank, read each sentence asking specifically whether it reflects adequate critical judgment on the part of the composer. It will be helpful, too, to consider what omissions might have been expected to result from lazy criticism.

Has the Questioning Been Complete?

The critical faculty is needed at another time. Since what is written is only the record of what has been covered in conversation, it follows that if the questioning has been incomplete, then the writing, which is its sequel, cannot possibly cover the subject.

The prime purpose of questioning a witness is to expose the knowledge buried in his memory. Incomplete questioning, therefore, results in insufficient writing and a statement that does not state. The disgraceful error, previously alluded to in Blank's statement (page 200), "I looked at my speedometer"—clearly discloses that this adjuster did not criticize as he questioned. (Neither did the criticize as he wrote; if he had, he would then have caught his error.) To make it worse, he discloses in the very next sentence at least one and probably two failures to criticize constructively. Failure to criticize one's interrogation is fatal in recording a witness's statement by verbatim techniques. This is the *only* opportunity the field man has to second-guess the sufficiency of his interrogation.

The Diagram—Its Place in Criticism

This device, the diagram, has already been met. Adjusters were advised to use it as a receptable for the information volunteered by and extracted bit by bit from the witness. Its use as a tool in the exercise of the critical faculty bears study. To illustrate: on page 197 there appears a diagram which might have been prepared prior to writing Brown's statement. Notice that the preparer of the diagram addressed himself to a complex of information. What should this witness know about the convertible at the instant when Brown first saw or became aware of it? These are the bits of information which he thought relevant. That diagram shows how he caught them and preserved them to guide his writing of the statement later.

Bit	How Recorded on the Diagram
On 2nd Street	Car symbol placed on 2nd Street
Traveling east	Direction indicated by pointed end on symbol
Car described as convertible	"Convertible" written in the symbol
Driver an elderly man	"old man"
Speed estimated at 20-30 mph	"20-30" with line to symbol
Convertible in middle of road	Symbol placed squarely in middle of area designated 2nd Street
Front of car ½ length west of stop sign	Bracket with the fraction "½" above it

The Tool (Diagram) in Criticizing Interrogation

The preceding paragraphs have demonstrated how a diagram is used to record the bits of information necessary to construct what a statement's author considered important to one phase of a statement. At the risk of stating the obvious, the reader should recognize that the interrogator, in order to exercise the critical function, had to have several questions in mind relating to the convertible. He recognized that he had not finished his writing about the convertible at the time Brown first saw it until he (the adjuster) had drawn out by questioning and recorded on his diagram some bit of information, some aid to memory to record and preserve each bit.

In any event, in one way or another, an adjuster interrogating a witness and preparing a record of the interrogation must constantly match the body of information which he is getting against standards of sufficiency. Some parts of those standards can be anticipated in advance, and by some device can be kept before him as he questions. Other standards have to do with logical description of types of information which occur and recur in all statements. Still other standards have to do with treatment of items which the adjuster has no opportunity to anticipate, and when this happens he must immediately construct his standards and examine the information on the spur of the moment.

To all new men and to any others who may feel that their technique is a little weak or who may find it a little difficult to accomodate to the swift pace of recorded statements, it is urged that a diagram such as is shown on pages 241 (pre-recorded questions) be prepared in advance.

A seasoned adjuster may omit this step even in recording a question and answer statement, but the author has yet to find a successful taker of recorded statements who does not admit that as the witness talks, he (the adjuster) is continually constructing a diagram, at least in his mind and noting thereon the items and bits of information which the witness should have covered but has not.

Making Critical Techniques Habitual and Three Techniques to Make Them Routine

Three critical techniques are applied so often that their use can be made a matter of habit. They should be learned and practiced until they require no more conscious thought than the act of stepping on the brake to stop an automobile. The first of these techniques is locating a point on a surface.

Tying Down Location

If the captain of a vessel in distress were to radio the Coast Guard only that he was at latitude "......" degrees, he would have a long wait for help and an angry Coast Guard skipper to reckon with if they ever did find him. To say that at a certain time a car was five car lengths from the corner without saying at the same time that it was in the middle of the east half of "X" Street (or in some other way showing its position between the curb lines) is the statement-making equivalent of giving latitude without longitude.

In the typical statement one expects to have to identify several locations and each must be defined in terms of information which corresponds to latitude and longitude. The need to identify many locations arises because cars travel a curving path. For all practical intents and purposes it is impossible to describe a curve objectively with words but its course can be fairly well indicated by locating significant points. The reason there are so many points is that in coming together the operators of two cars usually do several things—they turn, blow their horns, apply brakes. When each of these actions takes place it may be important, so each such location must be described. Therefore, each adjuster who starts to write a statement should anticipate that probably two to five times for each car he will have to go through a routine that corresponds to:

> Latitude
> Longitude
> Course
> Speed

If a field man will make it habitual to think about location in these terms, he will find that there is almost nothing else that he can do which will more markedly benefit his statements.

Objectifying Subjective Statement

Probably the second most important area in which the critical faculty must operate (and should be trained to operate) as casually as a reflex is in describing information in objective terms. It is quite foreign to the experience of most people to describe things objectively. Cars creep and crawl or they go "like hell." Furthermore, when asked to be specific and objective, a witness's first refuge is usually, "I don't know." An adjuster must not be surprised when this happens; it will happen and he should expect it on every statement. He can, if he wishes, cope with the problem when it comes up but it is easier to do this if he has a plan worked out in advance—a plan which he has so drilled into himself that his counter is automatic. Expect, therefore, that "how fast" or "where" will be answered "real fast" or "a long way off." Have the next question on the tip of the tongue, "I mean in miles per hour, how fast was?" or "Yes, I appreciate that he was a long way off but I need to know if by 'long way' you mean 50 yards or a quarter of a mile."

Although the requested data may now be forthcoming, one must be realistic; it probably will not. Instead, what usually comes is still some form of "I don't know," possibly with an embellishment, "It all happened so fast." This is where too many adjusters lose the thread of their questioning. There are several moves open to the statement writer at this juncture many of which will readily suggest themselves. Possibly the easiest route to take is to confront the witness with an alternative which he will be equally reluctant to take. "If you really don't know, then that is what I want to hear, but I don't think that this really does you justice. Don't know takes in a lot of ground, it means that you don't know if you were going 10 or 80 miles an hour and that you couldn't dispute a witness if he said one or the other. Now, is that what you really means to tell me?" The witness will almost always back off and then the adjuster asks him, "Were you going as slow as 10?, 20?" until he establishes some lower limit on the witness's judgment of the observed speed. The adjuster then repeats the process from the other end. "Was it your judgment that you could have been going as fast as 80?, 70?"

To apply this technique one must respect the layman's reluctance to overstate his knowledge and the questioner's tone should imply this respect. If the witness really feels that he has to say, "He was going somewhere between 20 and 50 miles an hour," but he cannot reduce the extremes from that point, this must satisfy the adjuster. But the statement, if written, or the record, if it is a recorded statement, must make it clear that it is the witness's honest judgment. It will be his best testimony and he cannot narrow the limits even to 25-45 miles per hour. At the risk of repetition, expect this problem to come up; do not be surprised when it does.

From an investigational standpoint it is about as valuable to demonstrate and tie down what a witness does not know as to show what he does know. The technique just described is almost ridiculously easy to apply, therefore, there is no excuse for letting a subjective judgment stand. No statement which fails to reduce subjective judgments to objective terms is satisfactory.

When the Witness Opens a Subject, Close It!

The final area of critical judgment where anticipation is helpful is demonstrated by the lines in the horrible example statement, "I looked at my speedometer" and the inexcusable failure to state what the speedometer showed.

A similar failure is demonstrated in the statement, "I looked down"—without following through to say, "and I could see for about one and one-half blocks" (or in some other way making it clear how far the witness did see). In each instance the statement writer neglected to criticize his interrogation and failed to realize that it was incomplete and that failure necessarily showed up again in what he wrote. Had either of these statements been in question and answer form, the failure to criticize would have had the same result—a body of information offered by the witness but with really important information still undisclosed.

It is impossible to anticipate the information a witness will volunteer but it is not only possible, it is mandatory to expect that the usual statement will open up several areas of inquiry, each of which must be followed until all reasonably pertinent information has been exposed. The need to use the critical faculty in this fashion occurs often in statements about auto accidents. It occurs even more frequently in statements dealing with liability (other than automobile) and workmen's compensation matters. Some examples follow:

Interrogating a witness who had made some observations relative to a claimant's disability status:

Offered: She was seated on the porch in a bathing suit.

Follow-up: Was the suit wet or dry?

Interrogating a claimant operator:

Offered: I looked both ways and saw nothing so I started up.

Follow-up: No doubt there was some reason why you failed to see the other fellow; let me give you a chance to explain your reason. And of course, how far could you see; were there any obstructions to your vision?

Or:

Offered: The container had liquid in it.

Follow-up: How much? Was the liquid clear, opaque or colored? What color? Thin like water or viscous? Clear or dirty? Also, how big was the container? Of what was it made? And maybe, Was it leaking? How fast? Where? Where were the drippings going?

A Supervisor's Tool

Having taken the liberty of showing that the diagram can be used as a teaching and supervisory tool, it is necessary to offer additional justification for such advanced material in a beginner's book.

1. All adjusters should aspire to become supervisors, managers and teachers of their craft.

2. In the last analysis a man is not taught to take a statement; he learns for himself. This should be apparent after an initial reading of this chapter about the critical faculty. The point of the section is that to take a good statement an adjuster must be his own critic. If he cannot learn to sense his own short comings as soon as they happen and immediately to apply adequate corrective measures, he will not take good statements.

To test the sufficiency of a statement, read it painstakingly in the office. From the written page construct a diagram. On it enter carefully the positions of the cars at each of the critical points at every position mentioned by the four characteristics:

Latitude
Longitude
Course
Speed given

Are all the important locations covered? Where was the witness's car when he first saw the other one? Where was the other car, etc., etc.? Doing this will accomplish these things:

It will show an adjuster many of his mistakes.
It will show him how he can guard against them by pre-constructing a guidance diagram by which to discipline his interrogation.
It will show him how, by using his diagram during the interrogation, he can spot omissions and rectify them before it is too late.

Helpful though this process is, it does not do much for the trainee or his supervisor in training a man to cover "the real sense of the accident." For that a different approach is required.

Supervising for "A Real Sense of the Accident"

To examine a statement for this quality think about the accident itself. What will the argument be about. Page 272 lists several common ways that automobiles bump into one another, and for each way there is cited a common dispute that should be expected.

For any accident about which you take a statement, expect the standard disputes, smoke out the non-standard disputes in the really ingenious stories people dream up to excuse themselves or to blame their accidents on someone else. Many accidents which seem stereotyped are really caused by unusual circumstances, alone or in combination with other circumstances. Do not close your mind to this possibility. Uncover these disputes, excuses and oddities by asking, Why? Why did this thing really happen? Why didn't you do (some obvious thing)?

In recording statements, err on the side of boldness rather than caution in giving the witness his head: "Now, in your own words tell me what happened—." After he has said this the adjuster must stifle his zeal to jump in with the next question until the witness has had his chance. While he is talking, the adjuster should ask himself, Why? Then, in addition to going back and filling in all the speeds and distances which will have been omitted, he should not forget to ask the question which will uncover the witness's position on the real cause.

It is no sin to come in with a statement from a witness showing that he saw things diametrically opposed to what the adjuster had hoped for. It is deadly sin, however, to come in with a statement that does not show where the witness stands on such a point.

Type of Accident	Typical Dispute
Two cars—opposite directions, same road, sideswipe	Each claims the other car came over on the wrong side of the road.
Two cars—opposite directions, same road, sidewipe. Position of cars clearly demonstrates that black car was on its own side.	(The white car's excuse.) He came way over onto my side so I turned to go to my left and at the last minute he turned back and hit me.
Rear-ender	(The rear car's excuse.) He stopped suddenly with no warning where he shouldn't have stopped. (It is probable that all adjusters will privately admit to a little too much of a tendency to blame the fellow in back and to feel that to attempt to defend him is hopeless.)

For rear end collisions, there is a phrase which may be used as a guide: "More often than not it's the guy in front who sets up a hazardous situation and the poor devil in back has nothing to do but hit him." Young adjusters should not let themselves get carried away with the notion that rear-enders are easy to defend, they are not. Almost any active office can find in its not-too-distant past litigated files where some overconfident claimant took his case to a jury after being rear-ended and went home empty-handed.

By and large, defending rear-enders is difficult, but if there is a germ of a defense and if an adjuster is taking a witness's statement, it is an unforgivable error not to disclose in the statement what the witness has to say to establish or refute the defense.

The adjuster who masters these techniques can deal with almost any check list, but no check list will do a thing for him if he does not master them.

CHAPTER 8

Determining Extent of Injury

One of the elements of a tort is "damage." Hence, if one were to ask what the claims business is all about, part of the answer would have to be the measurement of damage and the translation of that measurement into a dollar amount. Since bodily injury is, by all odds, the most important damage with which the liability insurance business is concerned, adjusters are necessarily involved with injuries, their cause, nature and effect.

Doctors (probably more to their surprise than their pleasure) have become involved in claims adjustments—not only as healers but as witnesses, as experts and, in some situations, virtually as judges. This deep and constant involvement makes adjusters in effect a liaison between the medical and the claims world. The adjuster is a translater. He translates medical fact, diagnoses, opinions, etc., into claims facts—which is to say evaluations and settlements.

This chapter will consider the importance to the claims business of developing sound working relations with the medical profession.

It will examine the role of the doctor as a witness and consider several of the problems involved in transferring to claims files the information and judgments with which doctors work.

It will also discuss briefly the procurement of hospital records and the adjuster's own modest part in accumulating information relative to injury independently of the medical profession.

The use of examinations to develop medical information, the development of a working medical vocabulary, and the cooperation which adjusters may extend to doctors will be considered.

Finally, since aggressive tactics in the exploitation of the opportunities inherent in litigation have shifted from emphasis on liability to emphasis on damage, some of the questions raised by malingering, exaggeration, etc., will be considered.

IMPORTANCE OF SOUND ADJUSTER-DOCTOR RELATIONSHIPS

It would not stretch the point to say that of the work an adjuster does in investigating, evaluating and limiting the value of injury claims—that is to say, translating the injury into settlement dollars—virtually everything he does somehow or somewhere involves him with the medical profession.

The nature of a doctor's opinions, despite some cynical thought to the contrary, cannot be purchased. The doctor whose opinion varies according to who pays him is rare. Seldom are doctors influenced by favors extended. Nevertheless, a doctor has unlimited opportunity to befriend the insurance business in innumerable ways which do not compromise his professional integrity. The welfare of the business demands that this friendship be encouraged. Just as the medical profession owes much to insurance (except for which a disproportionate amount of the doctor's work would still be on a charity basis), so does insurance acknowledge a debt to medicine. It seems not too much to say neither the business nor the profession could exist today in its present form without the other.

Few things can be more valuable to an adjuster or his principal than high standing with the medical profession. Conversely, almost nothing can more effectively handicap an adjuster than to be poorly regarded by the medical profession. Therefore it behooves him to consider his standing with the profession, and how he may enhance it.

Developing a Sound Relationship

So far as is possible, the adjuster should make himself known personally to the doctors with whom he deals. Although most of his contacts will be by telephone and mail, it is both possible and feasible for an adjuster to personalize this relationship. A call in person at a doctor's office when he happens to be in the vicinity and has a few moments to spare is well spent. If the call is *not* on a specific case, "I just wanted to make your acquaintance, since we will be phoning each other" is invariably well received. Where an adjuster is to operate in a small town or a rural area, a call in person on the principal doctors to introduce himself as soon as he is assigned to the territory is almost obligatory.

Medicine is a profession of the educated. Doctors do not expect to be, and ought not to be, dealt with in the same breezy informality as the proprietor of a body shop. This obvious point is often overlooked.

This chapter will discuss later the question of cooperation which adjusters may extend to doctors. Adjusters should be alert for opportunities to cooperate and extend this cooperation whenever possible.

THE DOCTOR AS A WITNESS

Doctors are constantly obliged to serve as actual or potential witnesses. In this they have two roles. When they report objectively on what they observe, they are in the role of any other witness. But when (in their second role) they exercise judgment and express opinion, they are *experts*. In their second role they go far beyond the average witness.

When a doctor reports that a patient suffered a fractured radius, he is in the first role. When he expresses his opinion that the injury has healed completely and without residual effects, he is in the second.

In whichever role he may speak—but especially the second—good adjusters carefully avoid trespassing on physicians' professional integrity. It may be permissible and proper to urge a doctor to express himself in regard to disability; to point out that sooner or later circumstances beyond his control will place him on the witness stand where he will be required to answer questions under oath; to urge him to come to a present opinion on the point at issue. It is never permissible to ask the same doctor to take a stand that a person is or is not disabled. As a man of conscience, the doctor may not be asked to compromise that conscience.

Getting necessary information from the doctor's mind into a claims file forms such a substantial part of an adjuster's work that several aspects of it require discussion. The conflict between professional confidence and the need of the insuring public that truth be known, requires an examination of the peculiar nature of medical information and the conventionally confidential treatment of this information contrasted with the need of the insuring public for a candid disclosure so that claims may be properly and accurately evaluated. The place of written reports must be considered as well as the value of written as against verbal information and the place in a proper scheme of things of each type of report.

A proper technique for interviewing doctors is helpful, so this point will be considered.

Confidential Nature of Medical Information

Some doctors interpret their Hippocratic oath as an absolute prohibition on the disclosure of any patient information whatsoever. However, when injury, the object of a doctor's treatment, is also the subject of a claim, a new and extraneous factor (the one who is going to have to pay for it) has been introduced into the once intimate patient-doctor relationship. Now the rule of silence may conflict with another obligation, the rule that requires all persons to disclose the truth (within their knowledge) in order that justice may be done.[1]

In this tug of war, many doctors feel that it is their duty to keep silence. Others feel their duty is to speak up. In some jurisdictions there has been legislation on the subject. In addition to understanding the basic conflicts involved, the adjuster must acquaint himself with the laws of his particular jurisdiction. It is still more important that he be conversant with prevailing local customs.

An adjuster who feels himself entitled to information which a doctor does not see fit to divulge should remind himself that the

---

[1] In the April 1, 1965, edition of *The Insurance Adjuster*, W. Karl Faust in his article "Medical Privilege—Shield or Bludgeon?" argues persuasively that medical information should be divulged in the public interest. He cites impressive authority for this view.

doctor's attitude is not mere stubbornness—he is conforming to the requirements, as he sees them, of a system he is bound to uphold. However, an adjuster must find some way to *overcome this refusal* and get the information he needs to properly evaluate a bodily injury claim. His problem is two-fold: He must satisfy the conscience of the doctor; he must also establish that his need for information is valid, even imperative.[2] Wherever possible adjusters release the physician of the burden of resolving his ethical conflict by procuring *from the injured party* written permission for the doctor to disclose information. A form for granting such permission appears on page 318.

A proper sense of proportion is always necessary. Important though adjusting may be, it is probably less important in the scheme of things than the work of healing the sick. The adjuster who bears this in mind will find that his standing with the medical profession does not suffer.

Written Reports—Verbal Reports

Ideally, medical information should appear in the file in the form of a signed, "sufficient" report of the doctor concerned. The adjuster does nothing to discourage this and as much as he can to encourage it. But among the many imperfections in the adjuster's world, these are permanent:

> Doctors are busy—they can seldom get reports out as quickly as they are needed for decision.
> Doctors may hesitate to give a written report.
> Doctors may write long reports, leaving critical questions unanswered.

---

[2] There is an interesting sidelight to this problem—one that opens the door to a means of satisfying both the adjuster's need for information and the doctor's reluctance to divulge it. Often what an adjuster wants is not really *information* but *insight* into the doctor's professional views.

Consider, for instance, the matter of causal connection. Although a doctor may be unable to satisfy his conscience that he is at liberty to discuss a given patient, he often feels no reluctance to discuss the problem presented in purely hypothetical terms. So, confronted with a question of causation, an adjuster might make an appointment with a doctor (paying, of course, for the time consumed) and present to the doctor a hypothetical question about a patient whose symptoms and history parallel the claim in which the adjuster is interested. This preview may be regarded as a probably accurate forecast of the doctor's testimony about the specific case.

Hence, as a practical matter, much of the medical information on which decisions are made reaches the file via the adjuster's dictated memoranda following conversations (usually by telephone) with the doctor.

Some insurers emphasize written reports to the point of virtual refusal to evaluate a claim without written reports in file. This procedure exposes them to the risk of missing settlement opportunities because of delay in procuring reports. Other insurers, perhaps concluding that the important things are information, early pricing and disposition, rely almost wholly on their adjusters' reports of what has been learned verbally from the doctors involved.

Clearly, the direction and extent of the emphasis one way or the other is an insurer's prerogative. But since even those insurers who place their main reliance on the written report must often require their representatives to seek supplemental information by phone or other verbal means, it behooves an adjuster to perfect and develop techniques for procuring written adequate medical information as early and as often as possible. But adjusters must also be practical. In this context to be practical means to recognize that often circumstances beyond an adjuster's control will make written reports impractical or impossible. Therefore, he develops his ability to acquire medical information verbally.

Procuring Written Reports

Written doctors' reports and hospital records almost without exception are available only with the written permission of the patient. There is a simple permission form on page 236. This complete form should be obtained from the patient on the first call and sent at once to the doctor. The preparation of reports is time consuming. It is galling to be at the point of settlement and then to have to wait weeks for a doctor to write a report which could have been completed earlier had he only been asked in time.

When a written report is requested, the adjuster should inform the doctor fully about all of the points which should be included. If the doctor must exercise judgment and *if in any part the judgment turns on lay information, the adjuster should be certain that the required information is made available promptly.* For example:

> A claimant alleged that he hurt his back in an automobile accident. The adjuster learned that three days post-accident the claimant participated in all normal activities. On the evening of the third day he participated in a basketball game and, near the end of the game, was involved in a pile-up and carried writhing from the floor. He was taken home, called his doctor, and gave him a history of severe pain dating from the accident.
>
> The adjuster acquainted the doctor with the real facts and the doctor hedged his report. When the truth came out in trial, the doctor, an honest man, was not only spared embarrassment, he was able without contradicting himself to ascribe all the claimant's troubles to the basketball injury.

The preparation of written reports requires much time; lost time is an expense to a busy doctor. As indicated previously, the request for written reports should be made as early as possible.

Realistic adjusters remember the demands on the medical profession and that doctors' time is at a premium. They recognize time spent preparing reports for what it is—an encroachment on doctors' earning hours—and they frequently offer to accept a small invoice to cover the cost of preparing the report. (The claims business usually recognizes this as a proper expense.) Many doctors decline to make such a charge but whether or not a doctor elects to submit an invoice the invitation to do so is usually appreciated. The invitation should be extended unless one is dealing with a doctor whose practice is already well known to the adjuster.

Procuring Verbal Reports

As indicated previously, it is desirable that the reports of attending physicians be in writing. However, written reports have their drawbacks. Sometimes it will seem to the harassed adjuster that doctors write reports covering all phases of the claim except those items that are really important to him.[3] To clear up doubtful points usually requires the telephone. For that reason, and simply because adjusters' operations are, in point of time, often well in advance of physicians' schedules for getting out reports, the working adjuster gains a high proportion of his medical knowledge from attending physicians by telephone. This common situation furnishes yet another reason why skillful adjusters learn to smooth their paths by sending to the physician, in advance of their phone calls, an executed permission slip.

The quality and amount of information gained will be enhanced if, as he phones his doctor, the adjuster has in his mind the recommended form for dictating medical information. (See page 356.) It will still further assist him if his scratch sheet has been set up in advance [4] with the subcaption headings around which he will later dictate:

Diagnosis
Disability
Permanency
Bill

Besides shortening the note-writing process, the outline serves as a reminder of the information needed. The adjuster will also gain more information if he avoids blurting out such general questions as, "What was your diagnosis on Mr. Smith?" a crudity sufficient almost to justify any doctor in hanging up. Questions should be specific. For example, of a patient with a cast on his left lower leg, an adjuster might ask:

Wrong question: "What's your diagnosis?"
Right question: "I noticed that cast—were both bones broken?"
Answer: "Yes, he got both the tibia and fibula."
Question: "He said you seemed a little concerned. Were they bad breaks?"

---

[3] More often than not in a verbal report—or verbal supplement to a written report—an adjuster learns the true *claims* significance of an injury. "Concussion," "broken back," "strain—sprain," etc., may be anything from trivial to highly serious.

[4] The illustration on page 279 demonstrates how an adjuster might organize a work sheet before calling a doctor and how he might devise a simple shorthand system to record information.

Answer: "Well, I'm keeping my fingers crossed; both breaks are down in the lower one-third." (Breaks in the lower third are "bad medicine" because of poor blood supply.)

Diagnosis	Translation
Multi C & L	Multiple contusions and lacerations
Str Cerv V	Strain cervical vertebrae
3" Lac L hand	Three-inch laceration left hand
Dis	Disability
2 W T	Two weeks total
4 W P	Four weeks partial
Perm	Permanent effects?
Prob 0	Probably none
$	Estimated fees
70.00 —to date	
125.00 —est Total	

Here is an example of how to deal with a questionable "whiplash":

Wrong question: "How long will Jones be disabled?"

Right question: "Doctor, I may be talking settlement with Jones tonight. I'd like to protect your bill. How much do you have invested in him?"

And then, later:

Right question: "He says he's going to be out of work a month. Do you find anything to justify that?"

In summary, the inquiring adjuster knows in advance the information he needs to obtain. He avoids general questions. Wherever possible, he asks specific questions. He progresses from confirming the known or obvious, to exploring the unknown. (He confirms the obvious cut on the hand, and then inquires,

"What else?") He volunteers an interest in the doctor's problems and offers his willing cooperation.

HOSPITAL RECORDS

Hospital records contain:

Admission data (date, time, history)
Objective findings on examination
Complaints
Initial diagnosis
Laboratory and X-ray findings
Daily log of visits by doctors in attendance, and medication and treatment rendered; daily log of significant symptoms displayed

---

To any doctor, hospital or organization whom this may concern: On presentation of this note, or photostat of it, please furnish John Smith, or the bearer, with a full report and/or a complete copy of your records concerning me.

Very truly yours,

_____

(Signature)

Note that this form is usable for doctors, hospitals or other entities who may later figure in the claim.

Note the omission of any mention of insurance or "adjuster."

The words "or bearer" are used so that if adjuster is transferred, this permissive authority may be used by his successor.

Discharge, diagnosis and appraisal of results obtained.

Any or all of these may bear on the value of a claim.

No great feat of imagination is required to recognize that the information on a hospital record, whether for an admission following an accident or _for an admission many years earlier,_ could be vital to a claim involving an alleged aggravation of an ordinarily non-traumatic disease.

A claim, on the other hand, may be such that the information contained in hospital records is taken for granted. A short hospital stay, for instance, following the application of a cast for the immobilization of a leg fracture would be unlikely to result in the recording of any information that would significantly alter the appraisal of what is already well known.

Only the smallest and most informal hospitals expose their records without written permission. Hence there is further reason for the adjuster to make it routine to pick up a medical permission slip on his first contact.

MEDICAL INFORMATION OBTAINED FROM CLAIMANT

In evaluating injury, adjusters play a modest part at best, but in some circumstances even this limited role acquires its own importance. Many wounds are visible to the naked eye, so a great deal of information about the claimant's condition communicates itself directly to the adjuster through his own powers of observation.

If a claimant is disabled and in obvious pain, this observation should be communicated by the adjuster through his reports to his principal. The same holds true for such shrewd observations as that of the adjuster who visited a claimant, supposedly disabled with a severe back condition, and found her in a *wet* bathing suit.

Doctors do disagree on questions of injury and disability. Therefore, the adjuster and his observations, in addition to being primary sources of information to the insurer, have their own intrinsic value in enabling the company to select proper strategy and make proper evaluations. Suppose, for instance, one doctor says a claimant is disabled and another says he is not. If the adjuster's own observations lead him to believe that the patient really *is* injured, this will certainly be given substantial weight by his home office. If an adjuster, inclined as he is toward skepticism, saw the patient and felt him to be disabled, is it not reasonable to assume that a juror will be apt to come to the same conclusion?

Occasionally, though rarely, an adjuster comes across outright fraud and malingering. Seldom shown by medical testimony, this situation is likely to be demonstrated by lay testimony. This may take the form of the discovery that a supposedly injured person was employed gainfully, or the not unheard-of finding that he was not in the car or even on the scene when the accident happened. Information of this sort should be made available to an examining physician. Whether or not it ought to be disclosed to a treating physician depends on the situation. Two factors that may bear heavily on disclosure will be the presence or absence of fraud [5] prosecution and the strategies of trial counsel.

The adjuster gains considerable information about the relative skills of the doctors practicing in his locality and, for a layman, acquires an astonishing familiarity with medical practices. He is sometimes tempted to advise injured parties. This temptation should be resisted. (The adjuster has some limited rights and real influence on medical matters in compensation claims. He has less influence and virtually no rights at all in liability claims.) Even if he is very sure of himself, the adjuster who feels that improper treatment is being given, to the detriment of the claimant's health and his insurer's interest, would do well first to get the advice of the insurer's examining doctors and then place himself under their guidance before even mentioning the subject to the claimant or his doctor. The old adage, "Unasked for advice is seldom welcome," is controlling.

By the exhibition of his obvious cuts and bruises, a claimant is the source of much information. More importantly, he is the source of information as to those parts of his body that are *not* injured. It has been noted elsewhere that after listing injuries known to him, a well written claimant's statement would always conclude with some remark such as, "I was not hurt anywhere else," or "So far as I know, the injuries I have described here are my only injuries." He should be asked outright whether he suffered any unconsciousness or other symptoms associated with concussion, such as headache, nausea and dizziness. Since it is possible for a person to be unconscious and then regain consciousness without realizing that he has been "out," it is desirable that the claimant's actions in the moment immediately succeed-

---

[5] An adjuster would never disclose information indicative of fraud to a doctor who might prejudice a fraud prosecution or a successful defense by giving the information to his patient.

ing the accident be described in such detail as to make it clear that he was conscious and observant during this period.

Again, permission to secure hospital records, reports from attending physicians, etc., should be procured on the first call. It is especially important that this item not be left until some dispute has developed. Permission then may be withheld.

EXAMINATIONS

To evaluate injury, companies often resort to the examination of a claimant by a physician other than the patient's attending physician. In many areas examinations are conducted almost as a matter of course on all bodily injury claims, regardless of whether the adjuster is dealing directly with an injured person or with his attorney. Even in areas where this is not customary, if an adjuster is negotiating directly with an injured claimant, it is prudent to arrange an examination before negotiations are permitted to come to a head. This precaution recognizes the obvious possibility that once controversy has developed it may be impossible to obtain an examination.

In some areas, most insurance companies have a limited number of doctors whom they patronize for examinations. In such an environment, the adjuster employs little discretion—it is a foregone conclusion that "Dr. White examines for us in this area." Nevertheless, since Dr. White may suddenly become incapacitated, or an adjuster may be required to select an examiner from a community in which Dr. White is not available, it is desirable that he be acquainted with the qualities of a good examining doctor.

An examiner should be a doctor qualified in his field. This means attendance at a medical school in good repute, membership in societies (American College of Orthopedic Surgeons, for example, if he is an orthopedist), and generally recognized competence in the field in which he operates. He should understand the substance and format of proper reports, write them promptly and have a staff capable of getting them out on time. He should have a good courtroom presence. That is, he should speak well, have a pleasing personality. In short, he should be able to *sell* a jury that his opinion on a disputed point is the *correct* opinion.

That he should be fair, objective, and given to calling them as he sees them, is almost too obvious to mention. This, however, may not be enough. If possible, he should not have been tagged with the label, "insurance doc." This may be difficult for him to avoid, since the less reputable consciously avoid a doctor such as described. It is usually better that he be forthright, almost dogmatic, rather than philosophical in his manner. He should understand the nature of "opinion" and be able to take a position and communicate that position. He should, when occasion demands, be able to say, "This is my opinion, and his condition is really . . . or I am wrong."

Many jurisdictions grant the right to examine as part of the pre-trial process, but this right is available to a defendant only after suit has been instituted against him. The court may permit the defendant to examine the plaintiff by a doctor of defendant's choice, or the court may appoint a doctor. The doctor so appointed may or may not be satisfactory. If the examining doctor so appointed is hostile or falls short in the qualities desired in an examiner, the insurer may wish that it had never requested the examination.

Since only a small minority of claims reach suit, most examinations are held by agreement between defendant's representatives and the claimant or his attorney. In some areas, examinations are commonly granted by counsel and are looked upon almost as a right. Even where this is so, the adjuster does well to remember that he is not claiming a right when he *requests the privilege* of an examination. Attorneys are only human and it is, after all, easier to grant a request than to yield to a demand.

A request for an examination may lead to a polite fencing match: "I'm willing to let Dr. White see my client but Dr. Black, never!" If the attorney is simply unreasonable, it may be better to drop the request, as an examination by an unqualified or biased doctor may do more harm than good. On the other hand, it may be altogether too easy to jump to the conclusion that an attorney *is* unreasonable. If by further inquiry it can be developed that both adjuster and attorney share a high regard for *Dr. Gray*, the result is well worth the effort.

The choice of an examining doctor involves still another decision. Ordinarily, orthopedic injuries are examined by orthopedic surgeons, and eye injuries by ophthalmologists. Many cases involve two or more specialties. Back cases, for instance, commonly involve *both* orthopedic surgeons and neurosurgeons. This presents a serious problem when only one opportunity for an examination exists. Whichever specialist the defendant employs, he has no way of gauging or, if necessary, rebutting the testimony of the other specialist. There is no answer except to consider all sides of the problem and make the selection that appears best under the circumstances. Consultation with trial counsel may be helpful. Usually the decision is based on an attempt to forecast where the real crux of the medical question lies.

One widely accepted maxim is: "Don't be the first to use a specialist." In other words, the claim may be for a lame back or a fracture, but if the injured party is treated by a general practitioner or a general surgeon, it will in most circumstances be wise to employ a doctor of the *same* qualifications to examine. The thinking behind the maxim is that if the patient had required a specialist, his own doctor would have had one in as a consultant. To use a specialist to examine may magnify the matter beyond its true proportions.

Timeliness has much to do with the ultimate value of an examination. The classic error in this regard is to have a fracture claim examined with the patient still in a cast. An examination, of course, should be held at the time when it will be of maximum benefit. In ordinary circumstances there will be several sources of lay information available to the adjuster to confirm and substantiate a claim of disability. There is seldom any point in examining to confirm what is already known. Usually, though not invariably, the best time to examine will be just as disability is drawing to a close.

If the injury involves a question of permanency, the adjuster may well let the question of temporary incapacity go by the board. In some circumstances, the later a doctor examines, the better able he may be to form an opinion relative to permanency.

COOPERATION—A DUTY AND A PRIVILEGE

A good adjuster regards it as his privilege to find ways to cooperate with the medical profession, and finds it good business as well as good manners to do so.

A physician's penalty for declining to support his patients in a claim of exaggerated or non-existent injury is often the loss of a patient and the patient's friends. Compromises are easy to make. He need merely rationalize, "I couldn't prove he wasn't hurt; therefore I will say that he was." Yet doctors stand up to these pressures daily. In the patient's decision whether to settle amicably or litigate, whether to try to settle with the adjuster or "go for broke," the doctor's attitude is often the deciding weight in the balance. Doctors, no less than other businessmen, have overhead to meet and families to feed. They have still other problems —many patients are less than grateful. Their claims settled, they let the doctor's bill wait on their convenience. Here lies the adjuster's opportunity to extend welcome cooperation to the profession. Cooperation may take the form of arranging for that portion of a settlement which represents a doctor's bill to be paid by a separate check, a practice known as "protecting" the doctor's bill. Similar courtesies are extended frequently to hospitals, nurses and other creditors who may have financed a course of therapy. This "bread cast upon the waters" is sound investment. How to draw a release so as to protect medical and other creditors is shown in Chapter 12.

DEVELOPING A MEDICAL VOCABULARY

In day-to-day operations the adjuster soon becomes familiar with much of what might be called "the inside of medicine." He acquires a shirt-tail familiarity with the standard treatment for common traumatic injuries, a fair working knowledge of standard disabilities, and a pretty good idea of who in his community is practicing honest medicine and who is a quack.

It is not expected that the adjuster should be either a doctor or an expert on anatomy. His purpose is not to pass medical judgment, but to translate the knowledge of the medical man into reports intelligible to his managers and examiners, and to understand medical terminology sufficiently to understand what is told him and to evaluate correctly the injuries with which he is dealing. Much of the adjuster's modest familiarity with common medical terms is gained "en route." Of prime importance to him, therefore, as this educational process blends with his work performance, is a willingness to confess his own honest ignorance by asking intelligent questions.

No one need be embarrassed when he comes across a strange medical term or a new disease. If he tries to bluff his way through, his bluff will almost certainly be obvious to the doctor. The more self-respecting way, and the way which will gain an adjuster more respect from the profession, is simply to acknowledge the gap in his knowledge and ask politely, "I'm sorry, Doctor, you said 'ecchymosis.' I'm afraid you were beyond me, what is an 'ecchymosis'?" Most doctors are patient, willing to explain, and generous in sharing their knowledge.

Since he must talk to doctors, an adjuster should learn as much of their language as is feasible. He should familiarize himself with the principal bones of the body. While it is unnecessary to know how the navicular lies in the wrist or its relation to the capitate, it is helpful to know that each is one of the carpal bones (and it will help him if he can remember that fractures of these bones are likely to mean trouble with a capital "T").

In order to converse intelligently, an adjuster should acquaint himself with the bones illustrated in the Appendix.

EXAGGERATION—MALINGERING

An investigation of an injury and the determination of resulting damages may be straightforward, an earnest search for the truth, or it may be something else entirely.

The point has been made that decent, restrained, forbearing people outnumber those who malinger or are grasping. There is a significant minority who, while they do not make a living out of claims, are quick and almost professionally skillful in making any mishap into a lucrative recovery. This minority, substantial and active, which furnishes most of the contention in the claims business, is an insult to every reasonable soul who refuses to consider a bruise an injury. Their demands constitute an unjustified tax on the buyer of insurance.

It was observed previously that distortions of fact, while still with us, might be somewhat less obvious and frequent than other aggressive claims tactics. If this is so, it is probably a matter of economics. It has simply become more profitable to "build" injury resulting from a clear liability accident (and safer) than to skirt the edge of perjury by tampering with the facts trying to make "liability" out of "non-liability."

Unfortunately, every sizable community has some doctors who are simply prejudiced. There are, too, those whose sympathy for suffering, real or feigned, simply outruns their judgment. The men who fall into either of these classes are well known to those whose business it is to press claims and to those who investigate and defend them.

The insurance industry owes a duty to the insurance buyer and the doctor of character to resist exaggeration and malingering in all their forms, and to be diligent in perfecting its techniques of resistance. If claims men suffer feelings of inadequacy, it is probably because of the difficulty in generating techniques adequate to this task.

Exaggeration or its equivalent may take any of these forms:

1. *Imaginary injuries.* The person with no injury who fabricates subjective symptoms may wind up convincing himself that he was hurt.
2. *Prolonged injury*—complaint and treatment carried on long beyond the normal healing period. Once treatment has gone beyond a few weeks, and if the treating doctor reports no objective findings to sustain the complaints, it is common for these complaints and treatments to be prolonged until settlement or trial. This leads to a paradox: The really dangerous injury is rarely the one with discoverable objective injury. Medical science can cure that. The ones who don't get well are those for whose continued complaints no reason can be found.
3. *Dubious causal connection*—an obvious injury or disease for which recovery is sought on the ground of aggravation. This is not to say that all aggravation claims are suspect but, whenever there is an underlying or pre-existing condition, the adjuster should expect that an attempt will be made to link up the condition with a recoverable injury by accident. It is sad

to report that his anticipations will usually turn out to be correct.

The real defense against these practices, as has been said before, is the ability to appeal to the streak of decency and self-restraint of which there is at least a little in everybody. Claims lore abounds with the stories of adjusters faced with claims from persons of known bad character, admitted gangsters, confessed burglars and the like, who have declined to stoop to take advantage of an insurer.

The notion that a rear-end tap is a heaven-sent opportunity to repair the family fortunes continues to be too widespread to be ignored. In his book, *Successful Handling of Casualty Claims,*[6] P. H. Magarick declines to distinguish between exaggeration, extortion and outright fraud. He says:

> Many articles . . . attempt to distinguish between falsification of the facts in an accident, as opposed to mere exaggeration of injury. . . . This seems to make an unnecessary distinction between a little evil and a lot of evil. To be blunt: malingering is fraud.
>
> You no doubt have heard these rationalizations: "There is a little larceny in all of us," and "It's only human nature to try to get something for nothing." These are half truths. The distinction between an honest man and a thief is that the honest man resists temptation. He does not deny that it exists.

Since, at heart, the author endorses every word of this, it is difficult to justify any distinction. Yet one has to be made. While the adjuster may share Mr. Magarick's (and the author's) deepest feelings, exaggeration, malingering and distortion, and the fact that a large minority of the public fails to consider these things reprehensible, are the real problems. The adjuster may even conclude from some judgments that juries find much to reward in these attitudes. Exaggeration *is* commonplace, and it must be controlled, but *to permit oneself the luxury of considering an exaggerator a thief not only clouds one's perspective, it destroys one's ability to negotiate and evaluate realistically. This emotion is a luxury; it may, in short, destroy one's effectiveness.*

---

[6] Prentice-Hall, Inc., Englewood Cliffs, N. J., 1955.

A story about a Parisian grandmother seems to make the proper point:

> She was asked for her views on the morals of the young. She refused to excite herself. She declined to pass judgment. "Men—they are incorrigible. And what have girls on their minds but the very same thing?" she shrugged. "Diligence! I shall simply chaperone my granddaughters, night and day *avec diligence.* And they will arrive at the altar, very, very happy and very, very virtuous."

The adjuster's job is neither to approve nor disapprove. In either event, he is wasting his time. His job is to control the loss and protect the insurance buyer. He will do well to follow the grandmother—accept the world as it is and protect that which is entrusted to him, as the grandmother proposed to chaperone her granddaughters.

CHAPTER 9

Reporting

Separation in time and place is inherent in the claims business. What does that statement mean? It means that over and over again in the insurance business important actions or decisions bearing on the settlement of an insurance claim are taken or made in places and surroundings far removed from the site where the claim originated—i.e., the place where the accident occurred. What is more, a claim may be finally settled weeks, months, even years after the accident or occurrence which gave rise to it. To bridge these gaps in time and place and to enable its functions to be performed efficiently, the claims business has developed a system all of its own. The heart of this system is the *claims file*. The information placed in this file consists in part of *evidence* (statements, photographs, estimates, etc.) and in part of *reports*.

In this chapter, we will discuss the critical role that *reports* play in claims settlement. Specifically, this chapter will describe the importance of proper reporting, the characteristics of good reports, techniques for producing proper reports, the various types of reports, and the subject matter of reports.

NEED FOR PROPER REPORTING

Information gained today governs decisions made tomorrow. Work done here depends on what was learned elsewhere by someone else. Management in Boston assists, judges, and often directs work done in Peoria. Trial counsel, long after the fact, must think, decide and act. They must have a *record* enabling them, in effect, to recreate the accident.

The *claim file*—the information, evidence and reports in it—is the device developed by the claims branch of the insurance business to cope with the necessary transfer of information from *place to place* and to preserve information from *time to time*.

Moreover, no claims department is an entity by itself. It is always a part of a larger organization which has a constant need for information regarding claims activities. For example, there is the need for apprising statistical divisions of the nature of the loss and the effect of relevant developments on its probable outcome.

Just as departments are parts of their companies, so the companies are parts of the insurance business as a whole, and the nature of the business requires an uncommon amount of pooling of information. Companies must therefore report to various agencies which are allied to but separate from them. Some of these are statistical, some advisory, and some combine both functions. Among them are: American Insurance Association, Index Bureau, Property Loss Research Bureau, and others. These organizations gather information pertinent to the industry as a whole and disseminate information and advice. Much of their information originates with adjusters.

An adjuster is responsible for many files. He cannot possibly remember all the relevant information he gets. He records information so that he may refresh his memory. He initiates the process of evaluation, so he must support his recommendation or decisions with fact and logic. The adjuster may transfer, resign, or be promoted. There must be a record to enable his successor to pick up where he left off. He may need to apprise adjusters in distant locations of his work and findings.

Each of the situations mentioned above reflects a need, and reports are the way adjusters discharge their duties in respect to these needs. It is not too much to say, then, that without reports the claims man could hardly function.

But, in addition to satisfying the necessities of the business, reports, it seems appropriate to add, affect adjusters. This book is written to help adjusters, so a private word of what is intended as helpful advice may be in order.

The conflict of interest between an individual and his society is classic. The soldier sacrificing himself at the pass, the politician who tells the truth at the loss of his career, the bureaucrat who continues to enlarge his empire long after it has outlived its usefulness—these are commonplace.

Starting with the first time he is late home to dinner, and growing in subtlety, an adjuster finds the same conflicts between his needs, desires and requirements and the requirements of the system which employs him. He must be ready to subordinate his interests to his employer's. He must consider the broader needs of the insurance business, and the still broader needs of the insuring public. The lesser interest always yields to the greater. Philosophers have repeatedly recognized this feature of life, but they have also pointed out that even the philosopher must eat, and the adjuster is permitted to exercise a modest regard for himself.

An adjuster should note that of all the ways to call attention to himself, there is no way more effective than by his reports. Over half of the judgments on which his progress depends will be based on his reports—and nothing else. *There is no surer way for a good adjuster to cut his throat than by poor or dilatory reports. Even a substandard adjuster may enjoy a reputation for ability he does not possess if only his reports are sufficient and timely.* When self-regard in no way conflicts with, but instead satisfies, his other obligations, the adjuster is indeed fortunate.

Neither eloquence nor self-inflation is called for—just plain, common, pedestrian prose. He is asked to be sufficient, simple, timely, and of these virtues, the greatest is timeliness. Life seldom offers a person such an opportunity to advance *himself* by conforming to the requirements of the system in which he operates.

CHARACTERISTICS OF GOOD REPORTS

The characteristics of good reports will be considered from the standpoint of "sufficiency" which will be contrasted with "completeness," the adaptation of reports to the philosophy of the company, timeliness, simplicity and coherence.

Sufficiency Contrasted with Completeness

Much that has been written about reports has stressed the words "complete" and "detailed." These uncompromising words may account for much of the difficulty adjusters encounter in their attempts to compose satisfactory reports. In their place, an attempt will be made to substitute what seems a more appropriate adjective, "sufficient."

Just as there is almost no limit to the extent to which a $50 fender-bending can be investigated, there is no practical limit to what can be said about the simplest of occurrences. The adjuster must therefore strive for *balance*. He has not the time to permit himself to over-report. If he does this, witnesses will not be seen nor cases settled. Neither, lest the whole system break down, may he neglect to report at the proper time and in appropriate detail.

Because his time is limited, the adjuster must report with discrimination. Not only for the sake of the adjuster, *but for the sake of the organization which must deal with his work product,* a line must be drawn between "enough" and "too much."

Over-reporting places on examiners a search and selection problem, that of extracting the necessary controlling information from surrounding detail. Therefore, to attempt to say everything about everything may, so far as the reader is concerned, be the equivalent of saying nothing about anything.

Attempting to be "complete" and to say everything that can be said on a subject often confuses adjusters to a point where they forget to mention the one simple item of information which may be of real importance.

The word "sufficient" implies both adequacy to a particular need and a *freedom* from surplus. This chapter will recommend that approach to reports.

Adaptation of Reports to Operating Philosophy of Individual Companies

Closely allied to the question of what is sufficient is the adaptation of the reporting requirements of an insurance company to its own management philosophy.

At one extreme might be a system which places a maximum responsibility on the adjuster. Management's intervention, reduced to a minimum, consists of coming in, looking for trends, and correcting unsatisfactory features.

The reporting system of such a company might dispense with home office files (although one may be called for if the claim attains a certain age). The files (depending upon circumstances) might consist *only* of accident reports, statements, property damage estimates, doctors' reports, releases and draft copies.

Reports as such may have been almost eliminated, but the needs of the system remain and have still been complied with. Post-settlement examination of these files may be reduced to spot checking, but from them management may still determine that its policyholder's money has been properly spent.

At the other end of the scale, an adjuster might be reduced to an errand boy. He is sent out to interview witnesses, procure statements, collect information and make reports. Upon these reports, his principal instructs him what to do next, when to deny, when to offer and how much. Reports are long and detailed. Initiative is at a minimum.

No designer can incorporate in the hull of a single boat maximum speed and the ultimate in seaworthiness. Every hull, therefore, is a compromise. It is scarcely to be wondered at, then, that the usual claims organization falls between the two extremes. The adjuster may be charged with a high degree of responsibility but still subject to upper limit. Required to report and explain himself in most matters, he may, in trifling matters, be relieved of all reporting duties except keeping a reasonable record so that a post-settlement audit may be made if desired.

In these ways differences in the structure of his organization and its management philosophy affect the frequency, scope and content of an adjuster's reports.

Timeliness

An ancient proverb has it, "The corn grows tall in the footsteps of the owner." Since the fields cultivated by management are as many as the claims at any time pending and as distant as the extent of this country, or even the whole world, and since management cannot directly inspect each operation, even though it may be vitally concerned, the operations must in some way have placed themselves before management. Unless this placement is prompt, *timely* and sufficient, management breaks down.

In theory, an insurance company's reserves are always accurate and up-to-date. The potential of any claim may change overnight. Reports therefore ought to be at least as frequent as developments. If not, management's reserve figures will be out of date.

Management has no way of knowing whether a silent file is receiving necessary attention. Even if there are no developments, this alone requires periodic confirmation.

Decisions on claims involving coverage questions usually take place at the home office level. Many departments may be involved. The adjuster's report is prerequisite to decision-making. Delay may prejudice the company or waive its rights. Therefore, *where coverage is at issue,* reports take precedence over almost everything in the office.

The adjuster's stake in reporting has to do not only with the content but with the timeliness of his reports. Because, overcoming the human tendency to procrastinate is often the biggest problem some adjusters face, a word on how to overcome this handicap may be welcome. Many adjusters find it easy to dictate while an item is hot, and almost impossible if even a few days are permitted to intervene between completing an item and reporting on it. If an adjuster finds himself procrastinating in reporting, he should consider whether or not he may find it easier to dictate more frequently than to "wait and do it all at once."

PRODUCING PROPER REPORTS

Planning

Reports should be planned in terms of the uses to which they will be put. What judgment will the examiner have to exercise? What facts will he need in order to exercise his judgment? What will he need to know in order to affirm that the adjuster has exercised *his* judgment correctly? What questions are raised by the claim? What information should be recorded as an aid to memory? What information should the file reflect to justify action taken and to guide another adjuster, should he be obliged to take over and handle the claim?

These are the questions implied by the word "sufficient." To answer them requires no flash of genius. The answers are usually obvious. A good adjuster analyzes his situation, puts himself in his examiner's shoes, anticipates an examiner's questions and sees to it that his report spells out the answers, producing a self-sustaining report which disposes of all the questions necessarily before the examiner. If a report is sufficient in content and sound in judgment it enables the examiner to respond, "I approve your recommendations." *To render reports of such caliber as to permit this response is the ideal.*

A good outline helps the adjuster to anticipate questions. A good outline, the willingness to invent or delete a caption or two, and a stern resolve never to procrastinate, will soon place an adjuster in the category of those whose reporting techniques are held up as models.

Planning involves the mechanics of arranging enclosures and exhibits, considering whether or not to discuss them, and the order and extent of the discussion. If the report is other than a "full formal" (to be discussed later in this chapter), a brief outline, limited to the listing of the captions to be employed, will help produce a brief, coherent and sufficient report. Failure to do this results in the examiner's complaint, "Three pages and I don't know yet what he is trying to say."

Dictation

The use of dictating equipment is almost universal in the claims business. For most people, learning to dictate requires overcoming a little mental block. Talking into an empty microphone does seem a little silly.

To overcome this feeling, come down to the office early or stay in at night, in order to dictate privately. Before attempting a report, warm up with a few paragraphs out of a book or a newspaper. (Spare yourself the burden of thinking what to say while you are mastering the technique of talking to a machine.) Listen to the play-back, put yourself in the transcriber's place, note and correct poor enunciation, failure to punctuate, failure to spell difficult words, and try again.

Good transcribers let dictation flow into their ears and out their fingertips. Typing, to them, comes close to being a series of conditioned reflexes. A transcriber should never have to correct grammar; punctuation and spelling should be furnished by the dictater. A new dictater will fall far short of perfection. In addition to suffering through a lot of self-critical proof-reading, he should confer with his typist. If he sincerely seeks advice, the typist transcribing his dictation has help to offer and will jump at the chance. He should make it a business to learn what his typist needs, then give it to her. His goal should be to prepare the cleanest, clearest, easiest-to-transcribe dictation in the office. Then his dictation will be done and on its way while the other fellows are making up lame excuses.

Simplicity—Coherence

Unnecessary striving for style handicaps many young adjusters.

Cultivate a simple style. Avoid long, run-on sentences. Short, declarative sentences may sound choppy and juvenile as they are dictated. They are firm and authoritative in the reading. This paragraph is an example.

E. B. White, long-time editor of the *New Yorker* and considered by some to be the foremost prose writer on the North American continent, recalls with downright affection his college text and the admonition, "Omit needless words."[1] If a writer of Mr. White's stature follows this pedestrian advice, adjusters can afford to follow his example.

A good dictator trains himself to think ahead from one caption to the next. He stays within his caption headings. His reports

---

[1] William Strunk, Jr., *Elements of Style* (Harcourt-Brace Company), p. 24. This is the famous "Rule 13."

develop logically, passing from coverage to the problem presented by the accident, to evidence gathered, to the conclusions arrived at. The eventual disposition can then hardly be avoided.

Captions

The use of captions has been standard procedure in reporting practice from the first days of our business. They endure for more than one reason. They are helpful check lists. Knowing that he will be obliged to report on a caption serves as a reminder to the adjuster to perform the necessary operations relevant to it when he is in the field. Thus a caption list may serve as an investigation guide.

Captions conserve adjuster's time. They capsulize information and permit summary reporting. Consider the following:

LOST TIME & WAGES
None alleged.

Then consider how much easier that is for an examiner to handle than 10 or a dozen lines buried in the midst of a four or five page narrative report.

Caption headings work for the good dictator by establishing the content of each paragraph. He stays within his caption. Having started out on one subject, he does not stray to another.

Captions economize on examiners' time. The volume of paper passing over examiners' desks is little short of incredible. They develop remarkable techniques to enable them rapidly to skim through reports that pass over their desks. They concentrate on those elements of the work which require their attention. They may disregard the remainder. In a long report captions enable an examiner to locate quickly just what he is looking for. Without captions, it seems no exaggeration to say that an examiner's efficiency would be reduced not less than 50%.

TYPES OF REPORTS

Preliminary Reports

A *preliminary report* enables the company to set up its file, assign file numbers, establish reserves; in other words, to make ready the clerical, statistical and supervisory machinery to handle the information which it will soon be receiving.

If the exposure is serious, there may be added supplemental information, a brief run-down of liability, a thumbnail picture of injuries, and the information called for under the item "claimant data and suggested reserves."

Company men, because they usually work at the same location where their accident reports are received, seldom make preliminary reports. Preliminary reports should issue from independent offices not less than 24 hours from the receipt of the accident report.

In a serious case, an adjuster can win the gratitude of his ulcer-ridden examiner by sending in immediately such items as statements, photographs, pertinent clippings, estimates, medical reports, etc. The cover letter for these items may be a check-off form or a mere listing of the attachments.

Full Formal Reports

Most claims involving injury require, at some time during their lives, the drawing together of all relevant information. The report that does this is commonly known as the "full formal." It is usually called for relatively early in the life of the case.

The time for submission of this report depends upon the policy of the adjuster's employer. Most procedures call for it from 10 days to two weeks subsequent to the initial accident report. A fairly complete preliminary report may justify some delay in submission of the full formal. By the same token, a sketchy, incomplete preliminary report usually calls for a full formal report as quickly as possible.

Requirements of examiners differ according to the needs of the insurers and their organizational setups. The wise adjuster recognizes that his examiners' requests and his organization's rules stem from the need for having information submitted at a certain time and in a certain way. He studies these needs and tries to anticipate them. In the more serious claims, the full formal report deals at considerable length with coverage and liability. The real extent and nature of injury may, on the other hand, take a long time to become known. Therefore, information relative to injury and pricing is often dealt with in *interim reports* which may follow the full formal by weeks or even months.

Full formal report outlines are exceedingly complete—so complete that it is a rare claim that utilizes all the captions.

Just as one must discriminate between the witnesses whom one needs to see and the witnesses to be disregarded, so the dictator selects necessary captions and eliminates others. Thoughtless following of over-long outlines creates such abominations as the three-page, neatly captioned report setting forth under each caption the jewel, "This item not completed because. . . ."

Following is a report of a fictional accident prepared according to the principles stated in this chapter.

AUTOMOBILE LIABILITY CLAIM REPORT [2]

```
RE:   CLAIMANT:        Richard Smith
      INSURED:         John Jones
      POLICY NO.       123456
      YOUR FILE NO.    Not Yet Received
      AGENCY:          ABC Agency, Tampa, Florida
      DATE OF LOSS:    4/1/63
      OUR FILE         200001-4
```

ENCLOSURES:

```
          Signed Statement - Claimant Smith
          Signed Statement - Insured Jones
          Signed Statement - Witness Brown
          Police Blotter Report
          Estimates - claimant car
          Diagram
          Photographs
```

COVERAGE:

Policy No. 123456, effective 1/1/63-64, limits 50/100/5, 2,000 Med Pay, ACV Comp. No collision coverage, Uninsured Motorists, 1962 Chevrolet Convertible, ID No. 21344321.

---

[2] Note that this example of a claim report relates to the accident discussed earlier in Chapter 5.

IDENTIFICATION:

Physical inspection at Sarasota Body Shop.   ID number correct, odometer reading 12,362 miles, '63 Florida registration 16 W1234

DATE, TIME & PLACE:

4/1/63, 4:00 p.m., Orange Avenue and 2nd Street, Sarasota, Florida.

DESCRIPTION OF LOCUS:

Right-angle intersection, Orange Avenue, designated through street, runs north and south. Second Street is controlled by stop signs at the intersection. Please refer to the diagram, attached, for measurements.

DIAGRAM:

Attached and self-explanatory.

DESCRIPTION OF ACCIDENT:

Assured headed east on 2nd Street. Struck the claimant who was north-bound on Orange Avenue. Although assured maintains that he stopped for the stop sign, there is reason, as you will see, to conclude that he is in error on this point.

CLAIMANT DATA AND SUGGESTED RESERVES:

Richard Smith, age 28, married to Jane Smith, 140 Siesta Key Road, Sarasota, Florida. Suggested reserve: BI - $2,000.

Smith Candy Company, 2900 South Tamiami Trail, Sarasota, Florida, a closely held Florida corporation, president Richard Smith. PD - $300.

S/S - INSURED, JONES:

Assured is age 79, retired. He apears senile and confused. He maintains that he stopped for the stop sign, looked but cannot explain how the accident occurred. In fact, he never saw the Smith car until after the accident.

At best, he would be a weak witness in his own behalf.

S/S - CLAIMANT, SMITH:

A well-spoken, well-mannered man, well known in
town. He makes a good appearance and would make
a credible witness.

Smith maintains that Jones came through the stop
sign at a speed of 20 to 25 and fails to disclose
any negligence on his own part.

S/S - WITNESS, BROWN:

This witness was located by canvassing the route
men of the Babee Dydee Service, Inc. He makes an
excellent appearance and would make a credible
witness.

He was a pedestrian on the south-east corner of the
intersection.
According to him, there is no question about it --
Jones ran the stop sign.

POLICE REPORT:

Attached and self-explanatory. Note our insured
was charged with failure to stop at the stop sign
and has posted a $25 cash bond.

PHOTOGRAPHS:

Photographs No. 1 and 2 are of the insured vehicle,
3 and 4 are of the claimant vehicle, and Photographs No. 5 and 6 are of the intersection. They
clearly reveal the point of impact on each car.

LIABILITY:

Probable liability on the part of the assured --
based on Brown's statement.

COLLISION LOSS:

No coverage -- no exposure.

MEDICAL PAYMENTS OBLIGATION:

Insured was not injured -- no exposure.

PROPERTY DAMAGE:

I personally checked the attached estimate against
the damaged car. Corrections and reductions are

noted thereon. As corrected, the estimate is in line and the Sarasota Body Shop has agreed to repair on this basis.

DR. U. R. GREEN:

In a telephone conversation 4/11/63 with Dr. Green (291-8080), I learned the folowing:

Diagnosis:

4" laceration on left forehead above the hairline.
Colles fracture of the right wrist.
Multiple minor lacerations and abrasions about the body.

Prognosis:

Excellent.

Estimated Disability:

One week – total.
Eight weeks – partial.
No permanent disability anticipated.

Bill:

Bill to date, $85. Estimate total bill $150, not including x-rays and hospital.

LOST TIME AND WAGES:

Smith returned to work on a partial basis after one week and advises that he is drawing his full salary of $200 per week as president of the corporation. Confirmed one week's loss -- $200.

SPECIAL DAMAGES:

White Funeral Home (ambulance)	$ 10.00	(verified)
Sarasota Hospital	82.50	(verified)
Dr. Keen - x-rays	35.00	(verified)
Dr. Green	150.00	(verified)
Lost wages	200.00	(verified)
TOTAL	$477.50	

CONTROL:

Arranged for a substitute loan vehicle through the repairing garage, thereby eliminating a claim for "loss of use". Mr. Smith appeared particularly grateful at this little assistance, and control seems good.

RECOMMENDATIONS:

  As to Value:

    Richard Smith - maximum value: $2,000.
    Smith Candy Company - property damage:
        $234.20.

  As to Further Handling:

    Obtain written medical reports (medical
        authorizations have been secured).
    Control and settle BI.
    Settle PD

_____
    Signature

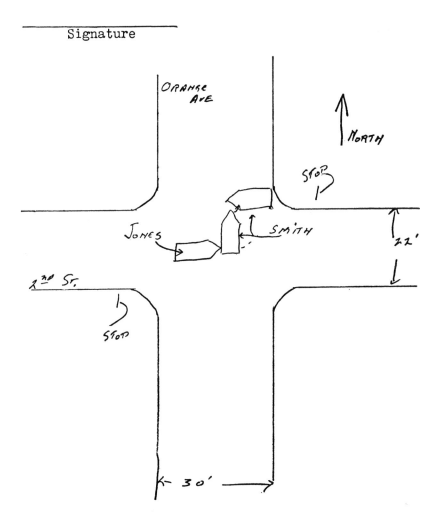

Interim Reports

If, in the reporting family, full formal reports are glamour girls, interim reports are the illegitimate stepchildren at the family picnic.

This is a pity, for full formals are a small minority of the reports an adjuster writes. Interim reports, on the other hand, update reserves, report developments, keep step with the progress of the injury and the accumulation of damages, and enable the supervisory staff to participate in control and settlement problems. When an examiner tears his hair, it is almost always over interim reports. *Without them, he simply doesn't know* what's going on. His plight ought to be understandable to the adjuster at the other end of the line. By his interim reports, an adjuster largely establishes his reputation.

The subject matter of an interim report may be determined by the full formal. It will be noted that the concluding item in the dictation check list on page 342 calls for an item-by-item list of recommendations—i.e., of proposed future activity. *The items thus listed should, then, reappear as paragraph captions in the next report.* An item uncompleted should be carried over to a still later report. Relevant developments, expected or unexpected, should be reported. Now an adjuster will frequently be called on to *invent* captions. Any list of situations that might arise and call for a caption would be ridiculously long. Yet if these reports are to be readable, they too should be organized and broken down into captioned paragraphs.

Proper frequency of interim reports is governed by the work done, the purposes served by the work items, and the reasons for early completion that attach to the work itself.

Liability investigation should be completed promptly. If the claim is urgent, its reports should be frequent. Lesser seriousness, lack of need for immediate decision, justifies delay in reporting the completion of liability investigation until several items accumulate. Delay probably ought not to exceed 30 days.

Because healing may be slow, and medical judgment correspondingly slow to crystalize, information on injury and damage usually trickles in over a long period. It reaches the file via interim reports. Recommendations as to value and request for authority are usually conveyed by interim reports.

To discipline his thinking and to assist his examiners, an adjuster may briefly recapitulate the liability situation and he should summarize information on medical and expenses at the time he requests authority.

Difficulty and drawn out negotiations permit one to err on the side of over-reporting. Examiners have no time to waste, but they usually are old hands and may have just the answer to the field man's problem. The more complete the report at this stage, the better the examiner's chance to visualize the situation. More than one adjuster has had cause to thank his examiner for a timely suggestion.

Final Reports

Final reports need carry no more information than is necessary to enable proper post-judgment to be passed. A properly reported case may, indeed, require no report at all other than a cover letter transmitting the release. If pertinent information not hitherto reported influenced the figure arrived at or the disposition of the case, it is to be treated factually and to the extent that its importance requires.

A Matter of Emphasis

Most of what has been written and taught about reporting in the claims field falls into two categories:

> Full formal report outlines with instructions as to what to say under which caption.
> The general exhortation that companies do not like big, long, windy reports; that adjusters should, therefore, wherever feasible, resort to check-off or other short-form reports or, if this is not feasible, hold their dictation to a minimum.

Such teaching, valuable though it may be, is wide of the mark and often misleading particularly if, as it it so often does, it suggests that it is really easier to write a short report. Sometimes the teachers as well as those being instructed are misled.

To ask an adjuster to be brief is a little like asking a high school boy to play center field like Joe DiMaggio or Willie Mays. To be brief is the highest skill in the craft of writing. It is doubtful if teachers or psychologists know why this seemingly simple goal is so hard to attain.[3]

Consider the familiar line:

"Tomorrow and tomorrow and tomorrow
Creep in this petty pace from day to day."

Brief, but it is one of the best remembered of its author's many memorable lines. Even though the author is 400 years in his grave, he is still revered as one of the greatest masters ever to write in our language.

Adjusters are not asked to be Shakespeares, nor is it expected that their reports will become "Macbeths," but it should enhance their pride in their work to know that the brevity they are asked for was also the great poet's goal. It is an honest goal, for almost any advance is rewarding of itself, and so a person may be proud of *worthwhile* accomplishment even if he has gone only part of the way. The result will be better than it would have been if he had never made the effort.

To be brief is a challenging goal. It is worth a person's best efforts as a story about Woodrow Wilson, then president of Princeton University and another acknowledged master of the language, demonstrates. Wilson was asked if he would honor a meeting by making an address. His answer was that he would have to know how long he had to get ready and how long his talk was to be. As he explained it, "If I'm to talk a quarter hour, I'll need two months to get ready. An hour, a month. Two hours, I'm ready now."

Reports—Other Than Full Formals

Chapter 4, "Reserves," emphasized the companies' need for information, a need so acute as to merit the adjectives "vital" and

---

[3] It pleases the author to know that some of the things that he has tried to learn in 35 years in the claims business have been worth the attention of the masters and that brevity has been the goal of the greatest writers.

"desperate." This need is especially acute in the first few days
after a file is opened. For reasons unnecessary to list, most accident reports are so lacking in information that the initial reserves are little more than a wild guess. Business strategy requires the officers of the company and the statistical department to keep constant pressure on claims departments for more
and more accurate reserve information. Thus as soon as he has
had a chance to size up the claim, an adjuster should immediately
let his principal know what the claim appears to be. Notice, in
the following examples, that the situation tells the adjuster what
to talk about, and that in every instance the captions employed
are lifted from the full formal outline. Note, however, that *only
a fraction* of the captions provided by the outline are employed.
Notice too, that although each report is brief to the point of
curtness, it says all that needs to be said.

Example 1

Accident report indicated questionable liability, probable injury
both cars.

Coverage: B.I., P.D., U/M, Collision Nil, Comprehensive Nil,
Medical Payments $500.

Enclosures:
Statement Black (Claimant)
Statement White (Insured)

S/S Black:
Admits his negligence. Plans no claim against us. Says he is insured.

S/S White:
Accident report was misleading. White says nobody in his car was
hurt.

Recommendation:
Close.

Example 2

Same background. Coverage: B.I., P.D., U/M, Collision $50
deductible, No Comprehensive, Medical Payments $500.

Enclosures:

S/S Black (Claimant)
S/S White (Insured)
Copy, White's medical authorization

S/S Black:

Admits his negligence. Plans no claim against us. Says he is
uninsured.

S/S White:

Firm (and probably correct) in insisting that he was on the
right side of the road. Notice that he complains of his left arm.
No other occupants in his car.

Collision Loss:

White's brand new Pontiac at DBC Pontiac dealer. We are going
to have problems with parts prices and parts themselves. Body
shop manager's estimate between $600 and $700.

Doctor Mathews (White):

> *Diagnosis:*
> Severe contusion left arm (X-rays negative for fracture).
> *Disability:*
> None.
> *Bill:*
> Will see him once more and probably release him (estimated
> bill $50 including X-rays).

Claimant Data and Case Reserves:

> Black —0
> White—Collision Reserve $700
> White—Medpay Reserve $ 75
> White—U/M Reserve $500

Remarks:

White indicates that although he is entirely familiar with U/M
cover all he wants is his car fixed and his doctor paid. There is
good reason to hope that the U/M claim may be CWP [4] or closed
with a small payment.

---

[4] CWP—closed without payment.

Example 3

Same background. Same coverage.

Enclosures:
S/S Black (Claimant)
S/S White (Insured)
Estimate, Black—$555.29

S/S Black:
He insists he was on his own side of the road. Alone in his car. Not hurt. Insured with _____ _____ _____.

S/S White:
At first tried to say he was on the right side of the center, but when I questioned him, I found he didn't know because he had turned his head away from the road while reaching into the back seat for his briefcase.

Liability:
Clearly a case to settle.

Comment:
Black seems to be friendly. In accordance with our recently established policy on advance payments, I have arranged for a rented replacement car. Black's car is at Fender Bender Body Shop. Their estimate, as I have revised it, is in order. I okayed Bender's incurring some expense for l.d. calls to expedite the delivery of new parts and hold down rental.

Example 4

Same accident report. B.I., P.D., U/M, $500 M.P., No Collision, No Comprehensive. To XYZ Insurance Company:

Liability is confused. Everybody is blaming everybody else. Everybody is mad at everybody and threatening to get lawyers. It will take me several days to get any sort of picture on the liability. In the meantime I'll try to get control and some medical authorizations. Claimant says he is uninsured, so we may have U/M claim. Injuries seem severe but so far I have only layman's observations to guide me. Look for formal report in about seven days.

Claimant Data and Suggested Reserves:

Black—B.I. $5,000; P.D. $1,500.
White—U/M B.I.—$5,000.
Mrs. White—U/M B.I.—$5,000.

These principles should be clear from the foregoing examples:

> That the adjuster directed his work efforts, as Chapter 5 suggests, according to the coverages exposed.
>
> That when he reported, he saw to it that developments involving (or releasing) his threatened coverages were covered in his report.
>
> That he anticipated his manager's (supervisor's or examiner's) need for knowledge and recognized that the "need to know" might spring from what was turned up in the field as well as from the coverages exposed. (Note Example 1. The adjuster learned that Black was uninsured and realized that his boss would be concerned about uninsured motorist cover, so he got the insured's no-injury statement and disposed of the subject in his report.)

This last principle is so important and is so persistent a thread in the claims business that it bears emphasis. The adjuster should never report without stopping to think, "What is there about this case that is going to trouble my reader? What questions will I raise by the things I have found out that he didn't know before?" If even very young adjusters were to ask these questions thoughtfully before reporting, they probably would place themselves at once in the upper half of all report writers.

To report in this way is quite a different thing from blindly following a check list. Reporting, like most other phases of claims work, is not a matter of learning what to do but a matter of making decisions. The decisions themselves are usually on the commonsense level—quite straightforward. The factors and circumstances change but the decisions continue to be quite obvious. The besetting sin of the hack adjuster, of whom there are entirely too many, is that he learns some procedure patterns and then applies them thoughtlessly to everything he does. There is no place where this shortcoming is more apparent than in his reports.

Returning to the examples, notice that in all but the last the captioned or topical form of organization is employed. This is a little awkward for the beginner until he gets used to it. It is, however, a great aid in the search for brevity and is well worth taking the trouble to master. Beginners or those given to wordy and poorly organized reports will benefit by deliberately injecting two thought stops into their procedure. The first stop should be before the first word is dictated. Then, if a man has trouble organizing his thoughts, he might refer to some such aid as a full formal outline and *from it select those captions—and only those*—which apply to the situation he proposes to describe. The second pause comes at the beginning of each captioned section. At that point, the dictator should consider what he needs to say, then say that—and only that. He should restrict himself to subjects within the scope of the caption.

Another helpful approach is to avoid claims jargon and to write as though the report is to be read by a dull, 12 year old.

It should also be noted that Example 4 obviously called for further report. Example 1 closed the subject and the author does not know of a carrier which would require any greater detail. Examples 2 and 3 are so written that if the claims they are written about close smoothly and within a reasonable time, the adjuster's closing report could probably be limited to a mere listing of the enclosures. At such a juncture, a checkoff form of report is ideal.

Examples 1 to 4 Handled by Check Off Form

Examples 1 and 2 are subject to short form reporting. Number 1 is treated on such a form (page 338) and Number 2 on page 339. Example 3 resists this method but can easily be handled by such a form plus a short dictated supplement which might read:

> "The real problem here is parts on a brand new Pontiac. White knows about U/M. Says all he wants is his car fixed. I am watching carefully as I don't want a delay on parts to antagonize him and put us into a U/M claim."

Example 4 is obviously not suited to short form treatment.

Actual Report

There follows the actual report of an adjuster on the claim of "R vs H." It is presented first as it was written by a competent field man trained in what we might call the "old school." Names and places, of course, have been altered.

Original

Claim of R vs H

This will acknowledge your telephone assignment of this loss received about 12:40 P.M. on the 13th of January. We immediately contacted the claimants by phone and determined that this case was not as serious as it could be and then proceeded with our investigation. You have since called our office and requested we contact the assured driver who resides in this area.

Insured: Robert G. H— of 743 Upland Avenue, Village State. Mr. H— is separated from his wife and family and the wife and two daughters reside in Townville, State area at the present time.

Insured Driver: Joan L. H—, white, age 23, single, lives with her mother at 200 Dayville Avenue,   , State She gives her legal home address as that of her father's your insured. She holds the State of — driver's license #79214. She is a student at the — School of Business, 50 Founder Circle West, Cityburg, State. We are at- taching her detailed statement which we feel is self- explanatory.

Insured Passenger: Mildred H—, age 17, also daughter of your insured and sister of the driver. We have not contacted this young lady for her statement and do not believe it is necessary at this time.

Coverage: You confirmed coverage for the above policy effective December 15, 1970 issued for six months pro viding the above assured with liability, property damage, $500 medical pay, comprehensive, $100 deductible colli- sion coverage on a 1964 Plymouth Fury, 4 door sedan, bearing identification number 3341188266. We have in- spected the car and find coverage in order. The assured car carries the State of — license tag L499K.

Accident Facts: This accident occurred about 2:00 P.M. on Sunday, January 10, 1971 in the intersection of Forest Street and Washday Road, Town, State. It was daylight; it was sunny; the weather clear and dry. This is a T intersection with Washday Street terminating where it intersects Forest from the east. We attach a rough sketch of the accident scene.
Your insured driver was westbound, downgrade, on Wash day Road, stopped for the stop sign waiting for traffic to clear on Forest and did not see the pedestrian who was on the west side of Forest south of Washday Road. When it was clear for the insured driver to go, she proceeded

into the intersection making a left turn and as she was straightening the automobile up heading south, her sister and passenger yelled "look out." At that point, the insured driver saw the claimant pedestrian about 2 to 4 feet in front of her car. She applied her brakes, but was unable to stop before she knocked the pedestrian down.

Police Action: We are attaching photostatic copy of the Townville Police investigation of the accident. You will find the police have placed the insured driver under $1,000 cash bond as it is required by the city ordinance particularly because an injured pedestrian is involved and the insured driver carried an out of state driver's license, driving an out of state automobile. There is no definite date set for the hearing and when we talked to Officer P— who conducted the investigation, he told us the charges would be dropped if the injured party did not prosecute. We understand the insured's mother has put up $1,000 cash to post the bond for her daughter.

Witness: We have not yet been able to locate any eye witnesses although we are told an attendant in the Atlantic Service Station some distance north of the accident scene called the local police and came to the accident scene to investigate. No one took this man's name and for the present at least we have not made any effort to get his statement.

Liability Aspects: We feel this is a case of negligence on the part of the insured driver. She alleges the sun was shining in her eyes, however, she did not see the pedestrian until it was too late. The pedestrian on the other hand saw your insured vehicle stop for the stop sign and started to cross the street having no reason to believe that the driver of the insured car did not see her.

Injured Claimants: Mrs. Evelyn R—, white, age 24, married to Larry R— and resides at 119 Lazy Street, Town, State. She is a housewife and works a part time job as a fountain girl in Lincoln Pharmacy, Town, State. She earns a total of $4.50 per day in her part time job.
We have medical authorization signed by this woman, although we have not taken her statement as yet. When we were in her home interviewing her, her two little children were so active and interrupted this adjuster to the point that it would have been impossible to take her statement. The mother, incidentally, made no effort to correct her children or to keep her children out of our brief case and papers. We thought under the circumstances a statement was not necessary as we are receiving 100% cooperation from this claimant.

Mrs. R— was taken in a police officer's private automobile to the Town State Hospital, where her left foot and ankle were X-rayed. She has a sprain of the foot although the swelling is gone she still experiences some pain while walking. She was off work from the day this accident occurred until January the 18th, when she returned to her part time job. She is under the care of her family doctor, Dr. B— of Town, State. She has seen the doctor once and is to see him again Friday, the 22 of January, at which time she expects to be released. We do not yet know what the X-ray bill is at Town State Hospital but would anticipate it would be at least $40.00 and the additional medical would be a couple of visits to the family doctor.

The other two pedestrians are Mrs. R—'s two children Lorie, age 4, and Lisa, age 2. Lorie got a black eye when her mother was knocked down into her, however, the insured automobile made no contact with either of the two children. The two children were checked in the emergency room at Town State Hospital and were released with no injuries.

Medical Report: We have requested a medical report from Dr. B— and have signed medical authorization so that we may talk to him after he sees the injured claimant next Friday.

Remarks: You will find in the statement, as I have told you on the phone, the injured claimant and the insured driver graduated from high school in 1965 together. They are friends and in addition to this, the injured claimant is employed at the same pharmacy as is Mildred H—, the passenger in the insured car. The claimant seems to be recovering from the bruise or sprain, she received in her foot. The swelling has gone down and she now has only a slight pain when she puts her shoes on and walks.

We believe we have full control of the injured claimant and expect to dispose of these BI claims within the next 10 days or two weeks for a nominal amount. Incidentally, the injured claimant's husband, Larry, took two days off from his work in order to stay home and take care of the children on the Monday and Tuesday after the accident occurred because the injured mother was unable to get around the home and was staying off of her foot as ordered by the doctor.

Reserve: We would suggest you maintain a $500.00 BI reserve for the 2 minor children and also the injured Mrs. R—. We do not expect to spend that much to buy these claims, but as soon as we get some indication, we will advise.

Enclosures:

Signed detailed statement of the insured driver
Photocopy of the police report
Photocopy of the statement secured by the investigating police officer from the insured driver
Statement from an independent witness, John M— secured from the investigating police officer
Sketch of the accident scene

Very truly yours,

Now consider the same report boiled down and organized as this chapter recommends. Note the use of lists and tabulations and how the captions work for the writer and help to carry the meaning.

The first writing consummed almost 1,400 words. That which now follows employs less than 300.

Dictation time at a leisurely pace for the original is fifteen minutes. Time for dictating the boiled down version at the same pace amounts to three minutes.

Claim of R vs H (Report reduced as to verbage.)

Enclosures:

Statement—Joan H—, insured's operator
Sketch of scene
Police report
Statement—Joan H— to police
Statement—Witness Murry to police

Coverage: Policy #—, effective 12/15/70 to 6/15/71, BI, PD, $500 MP, Comprehensive, $100 deductible Collision, no UM, '64 Plymouth #3341188266.

Identification: Physical inspection—serial number as above.

Description: Insured's operator made left turn, failed to see pedestrians until they were 2 to 4 feet from the car. There appear to be no mitigating circumstances. Her excuse, that the sun was in her eyes is reasonable but hardly a defense.

Witness: There have been rumors that an attendent at the Atlantic Service Station nearby called the police. Circumstances do not seem to warrant running down this rumor.

Claimant Status—Reserves: Evelyn R— (24) (Mrs. Larry)—Reserve $500; Lorie R— (4)—Reserve $500; Lisa R— (2)—Reserve $500

LTW—Mrs. R— part time fountain girl at Lincoln Pharmacy
$4.50 per day
? days per week
Losing time since 1/10
Probable RTW 2/22
Estimated wage loss $—

When we come to settle, practical consideration will have
to be given to Mr. Larry R— who took two days off to
nurse his injured wife and care for the children (his wage
loss $—).
Dr. Martin (Middleburg): I have not talked with him.
Mrs. R— says she expects to be released 2/22. She de-
scribes a sprain of the left foot and ankle now subsiding.
St. Francis Hospital: X-rays taken of Mrs. R—. Two chil-
dren examined in emergency room and released.
Control: Mrs. R— and insured's operator are friends and
were high school classmates. Insured's passenger works
in the same pharmacy as Mrs. R—. Friendship prevails.
I believe the claim is under control.
Recommendations:
As To Valuation—(Missing)
As To Further Work—(Missing)

Note how the abbreviated report makes the salient facts
stand out. It is easier to read and would be far easier to supervise.

Note too that the abbreviated report hangs a red light on
the adjuster's failure to do a number of things that he should
have done.

He had not talked in person with Dr. Martin despite being in
possession of a permission slip.
He had neither ascertained the charges to date nor estimated total
charges.
His only information as to the nature of the injury is lay information from the claimant himself.
The form of this report makes it quite evident that he should
have talked with St. Francis Hospital and picked up their bills.
The bare bones form of the report makes it further obvious that
he should have ascertained how many days a week Mrs. R worked
so that some computation of the total lost time and wages that he
expected to have to consider could have been made by him and
by his carrier.
Neither had he checked the wages of Larry R., in spite of his
obvious recognition that these would have to be taken into consideration.

This degree of condensation and organization is recommended. There is likely no examiner nor any company that would not prefer the second report to the first. However, this report can still be subjected to a great deal of compression. It could be put on a checkoff form, thus:

ADJUSTER'S TRANSMITTAL REPORT
For Automobile or Third Party Claims

( ) FIRST REPORT	(XX) INTERIM REPORT	( ) CLOSING REPORT

ADDRESS REPLY TO: Tampa	DATE: 7/30/71
CLAIM # 123456	OUR FILE # 666666
POLICY # 00PP23456	TERM	DATE OF LOSS: 7/2/71

INSURED: Joan H
ADDRESS:
CLAIMANT: Evelyn R et al
ADDRESS:
AGENT: Insure a risk agency
ADDRESS: Tampa, Florida
LIENHOLDER: GMAC
VEHICLE: 1971 Toyota

SUGGESTED RESERVES:

NAME	ADDRESS	INSD. OWNER CLMT.	INSD. DRIVER CLMT.	INSD. PASSENGER CLMT.	PEDESTRIAN	OTHER	BI	PD	MED	U M	COMP	COLL	OTHER
1. Evelyn R (Mrs. Larry)		☐	☐	☐	☒	☐	500						
2. Lori R (4)		☐	☐	☐	☒	☐	500						
3. Lisa R (2)		☐	☐	☐	☒	☐	500						
4.		☐	☐	☐	☐	☐							

WE ARE SECURING:

_____ CLAIMANT'S STATEMENT	_____ PROOF OF LOSS	_____ SALVAGE BIDS
_____ WITNESS STATEMENT	_____ REPAIR INVOICE/ESTIMATE	_____ RELEASE(S)
_____ POLICE REPORT	_____ MEDICAL INFORMATION ( ) EXAM ( )	_____
	_____ SPECIAL DAMAGES/BILLS	_____

ENCLOSURES: DETAILED STATEMENTS FROM:

_____ INSURED'S REPORT	X Joan H, Insured operator	_____ RELEASE
_____ CLAIMANT'S REPORT(S)	X Joan H, to police	_____ PROOF OF LOSS
_____ WITNESS REPORT(S)	X Witness Murray to police	_____ SUBROGATION/LOAN RECEIPT
X POLICE REPORT	_____ REPAIR INVOICE/ESTIMATE	_____ SALVAGE REPORT/CHECK
X DIAGRAM	_____ INSPECTION APPRAISAL/INVOICE	_____ MED. PAY PROOF
_____ PHOTOS	_____ MEDICAL REPORT(S)/BILLS	_____ SERVICE INVOICE: FINAL ( ) INTERIM ( )

DISPOSITION: PAYMENT:

			MAIL TO:	
			PAYEE	OUR OFFICE
_____ SETTLED AS INDICATED BY ENCLOSURES	_____ WE HAVE ISSUED DRAFTS PER COPIES ATTACHED			
_____ CLAIM DENIED	_____ PLEASE ISSUE DRAFTS PAYABLE AS FOLLOWS:			
_____ OFFER PENDING	$ _____ TO _____			
_____ WAITING ACTIVITY BY CLMT ( ) ATTY ( )	$ _____ TO _____			
_____ DIARY _____ DAYS	$ _____ TO _____			

SUBROGATION:

_____ WE ARE PROCEEDING TO ATTEMPT RECOVERY – COPY OF SUBROGATION NOTICE ATTACHED.
_____ WE ASSUME YOU WILL HANDLE OR REFER AS YOU DESIRE – WE ARE TAKING NO FURTHER ACTION.
_____ WE HAVE REFERRED ON YOUR BEHALF TO:

REMARKS:

From the foregoing, our liability is obvious. Claimants appear to be under control. To be conservative, I suggest reserves as outlined above, but actually expect to be able to move the group at substantially less than the suggested reserve figures. Look for another report in _____ days.

SR 21: FILED ( )   PLEASE FILE ( )   NOT APPLICABLE ( )

ADJUSTER

Or it could be boiled down to this:

Enclosures:

Statement, Joan H., insured's operator
Sketch of scene
Police report
Statement—Joan H to police
Statement—Witness Murray to police

From the foregoing, our liability is obvious.

The claimants appear to be under control. To be conservative, I suggest reserves as follows, but actually expect to be able to move the group at substantially less than the suggested reserve figures.

Evelyn R. (Mrs. Larry) $500
Lori R. (4)   500
Lisa R. (2)   500

Look for another report in —— days.

At this point, some editorial comment is in order.

Many companies, many examiners (possibly a majority) approve and prefer one or the other of the last two condensations.

The author's personal preference lies with the first condensation. This is so even though under pressure of time he has authored more than one report in the fully abbreviated style of examples three and four. Such a preference, having been stated, should be sustained.

A supervisor, manager or examiner reads reports for more than mere information. He reads:

To satisfy himself that the claim is receiving the attention it needs. The two final condensations give no clue as to the nature and extent of the injuries, hence, the reader is obliged to accept the adjuster's judgment as to value and reserves with no reasonable opportunity to test that judgment against other standards and prior experience. Each report lacks a description of the injury. It is true that the adjuster reports that he thinks he has control, but how much more solid it is to be told that claimant and insured were highschool classmates and friends and that the accident has not disturbed the relationship of the parties.

It is true that reader's time is valuable, but all desk men have their techniques for conserving time. One of these is to glance at the closing lines of a report and, if all seems headed in the right direction, to file it with no further time wasted.

Working with the adjuster in whom he has confidence from prior experience, a good desk man might spend no more than 30 seconds on the first condensation.

But, if the desk man did not know his adjuster or was working with a trainee who might need guidance, examples three and four would give him little information. As a desk man, the author prefers to see adjusters held to the discipline of the first condensation. If they need help or admonition, he can look above the closing lines and do something for them.

As an adjuster, the author prefers that an examiner who might not know the adjuster have enough information about the claim to know that the adjuster is on the right track.

This should not be taken as a blanket condemnation of examples three and four. They have their place, but an adjuster should realize that many factors affect his selection of the mode of report:

Adjuster's experience
Adjuster's degree of acquaintance and prior experience with his reader
Whether the duty of setting reserves has been ceded wholly to the adjuster or placed upon the reader, in which case the reader will need more facts to form his own judgment.

Finally, no adjuster should overlook the discipline value of knowing that he is obliged to report certain things in certain ways. Example two demonstrates that discipline at work in several ways.

It would probably take less than a minute to dictate the abbreviated example number four (a saving of only two minutes over example two), but it would probably take fully three minutes to prepare the short form (example three).

If the discipline imposed by example two forces the adjuster to organize his work better and to do promptly those items which might otherwise suffer from procrastination, it is probable that the discipline will, in the long run, save more field time than the additional time imposed in dictating in the pattern indicated.

In reporting, select the mode according to the criteria listed here and according to the desires of the employer or client.

Perfectionism and Early Reporting

Examples one to four (pages 309 to 311) share several common characteristics—they could have been written 24 to 48 hours after the claims occurred; they were written before the claims were ready to close; they were written before a full report was possible. They would each have been of substantial value to a carrier, and any field man who consistently reports in this vein will be well regarded, perhaps even if he is not a good adjuster. Nothing can be done about this injustice, except that if one is a good adjuster he ought not to neglect such an easy opportunity to bring favorable attention to himself.

Unfortunately, many dedicated adjusters neglect early reporting; in fact they have an almost pathological tendency to avoid it. The excuse usually is, "Well, I expected to settle it within a few days and I just wanted to wait until I had it all wrapped up," or, "I just wanted to wait until I had my investigation complete."

It is difficult to criticize these men. The desire to do a complete job is certainly one of the finer business attributes, but thrift carried to the extreme makes a miser. Similarly, generosity to the extreme makes a wastrel and the desire to do a complete job creates the sin of perfectionism.

Perfectionism, in this context, can prevent a good man from giving valuable service to his company. Good, quick, early reports permit prompt reserves, reserve adjustment, coaching and other advice which can be very helpful. Perfectionism can create a wrong impression of a man's ability and, worse yet, can almost destroy his value to his employer-client.[5] The condition can grow to chronic procrastination, a fault which makes a claimsman almost useless. It is probably the most common reason for dismissal known to claims organizations.

Procrastination grows out of laziness, too, and if that is the case, the man should leave the business at once. Procrastination growing out of perfectionism is a different story.

---

[5] This phenomenon is encountered when an adjuster has completed his investigation and preliminary work in timely fashion but then procrastinates about his report because he expects to close it next week, or has one more witness to see.

A man may overcome perfectionism if he teaches himself to take a broader and less selfish view of his work. It is something like the maturation process of a good student. Most of these start out as mere grade getters, but at some point in their progress they shift their emphasis from grades to learning for the value of learning.

The claimsman troubled with perfectionism needs to shift his emphasis, too. Instead of thinking, "I want to make a report on a closed file so that I can reflect credit on myself," he should think, "I am a vital part in the mechanism by which my company lives. My company lives on information (see the chapter on reserving). I wish to advance my company's interest so that I, too, may advance. Therefore, as quickly as significant information reaches me, I will make it available to my employer (client) in the quickest, clearest, most useful way I can."

The advice above is far from perfect. It has helped many perfectionists to control or eliminate the tendency, but many men, whose loyalty, dedication, ability and industry are beyond question, have been unable to put this teaching into practice.

Other Reports and Later Phases of a Claim's Life

There still remains to be considered a class of reports which by itself probably constitutes more than half of claims correspondence. These are reports on open claims. On most occasions, a full formal report or its sufficient substitute, perhaps in several installments, has gone to the carrier; sometimes liability investigation remains to be concluded. More frequently the problems are associated with accumulating information about damages; waiting for injuries to heal; waiting for people to make a decision (most people shrink from so conclusive a step as signing a release, particularly if they have thought about the decision for any length of time); waiting for lawyers to build their files before getting down to talking figures; waiting for cases to be placed in suit or to reach the trial room. These, for want of a better or more descriptive term are referred to as "subsequent" reports.

There are many things to be said about these reports to guide adjusters to better performance. Since, of all classes of reports, subsequent reports are those most frequently abused, it is worthwhile to identify the error which probably occurs most often and causes the most trouble. That error is rudeness—failure to reply promptly to specific questions. Again there is the sin of procrastination and, again, it is very possibly the offspring of perfectionism.

An adjuster has to get a statement from witness "X." He may be rebuffed or, conceivably, thrown out bodily, but the least he can do is try. Most attempts do yield something and courtesy requires an answer. A man's concept of courtesy and his feeling for his relationship with his correspondent will guide him as to the precise time limits he will set for himself. An excellent rule to impose is that all specific requests will be acknowledged (dictated) the day they are received unless the adjuster expects to be able to complete and *report* the item within the 48 hours. Adjusters should study their own performance and, if they find themselves abusing the 48-hour rule, impose the requirement of answering every specific request the day received. No harm is done if a second report follows a few days later.[6] There may be an excellent reason why the requested report may be subject to substantial delay, but courtesy calls for an *immediate* response and an explanation of the expected delay. If this simple courtesy were universally observed in the claims business, it might be the single biggest step that the claims fraternity has ever taken to improve its service to the insurance business.

Why do claims men neglect so simple and so obvious a thing? Probably laziness is the second biggest reason, and the first, the now-familiar sin of perfectionism—the sad refuge of the insecure and the immature.

---

[6] Answer immediately, even if you have to send in the desired information a few days later. This statement may seem to compound a complaint frequently heard—"The home offices are drowning in paper; don't write unless you have something substantial to say." There is, however, justification for the statement.

The biggest step that can be taken to alleviate home office paper jams would be prompt, efficient, and conclusive reports from adjusters. Any practice which strengthens his self-discipline is to be encouraged. Adjusters are prone to all the human weaknesses and procrastination is one of the worst.

Frequently people use silence to avoid the unpleasantness of acknowledging their shortcomings. Openly admitting the failure in writing, however, is a powerful incentive toward getting the job done and eliminating this weakness. It also increases the adjuster's self-respect and his pride in his work.

There is little room for sympathy for the adjuster who acknowledges his failure and *then continues to fail.*

Subject Matter of Subsequent Reports

In respect to earlier reports, claims against the carrier and the products of the work operations performed largely establish the nature of reports made and captions selected. This is just as true of subsequent reports. Carriers and the various layers of middle management who see an adjuster's reports, are just as eager to be told what the ultimate outcome of reserved claims will be.

Work operations performed and their product must also be reported. To a well organized man these operations (and hence, in a sense, the preparation of his subsequent report) started with the close of his last previous report. Notice the recommended treatment of the caption "Recommendations" in the full formal outline (page 305). Every well written report on an open claim should close with an outline as specific as possible of the work the field man intends still to do. This should be so, even if he intends to do nothing as in a situation which might call for the following:

RECOMMENDATIONS

As to Further Work

Nothing. I think this claimant is incapable of making up his mind. I'm going to leave him alone and if I hear nothing will close in 90 days.

RECOMMENDATIONS

As to Further Work

File seems to be in order. Plaintiff's attorney won't come off his asking price. I have exhausted everything I know to get him into what seems to me to be a reasonable range. Most of his cases are tried. I expect this will be no exception. It will be about a year before we are reached on the trial docket. I'll make no further report unless there is some unexpected action.

If further work does remain to be done, it should have been outlined item by specific item and then each item should become a caption in the subsequent report.

Some items which seemed important become less so as information develops. Sometimes adjusters have second thoughts. In such a situation, a man should never hesitate to report that he has scrubbed the item. This need not embarrass him, "Consistency is the virtue of small minds." [7]

Dealing With the Standard Stumbling Blocks

Some long term files stay open simply because the injury takes a long time to stabilize. These are relatively few. The two most common reasons for open files are claimants who are unable to come to a decision and attorneys who are unwilling to talk until they feel that they have accumulated their damages. If in either of these situations the file rocks along through several reporting periods, the adjuster should realize that for this file a static reporting situation has been reached. He is justified in telling his principal what the problem is and how he is handling it. From then on, unless the claimant's tactics change or the adjuster changes his, there is really nothing to report. This is so whether the situation is one which has settled down to a once-a-month telephone call or whether the adjuster calls at regular intervals and spends possibly hours reassuring a badly injured patient and giving the latter a chance to become at home with the adjuster's personality before the alienating process of talking money begins.

The general rule used to be that an adjuster ought to report at least once a month. Now the majority practice seems to be to expect adjusters to outline the situation when stability has been reached, indicate how long he expects it will be before he will have more to say and then to permit (better to say require) him to hold his silence until there is something *further* to report. [8]

Brevity in Subsequent Reports

Professor Strunk's most famous utterance, the Great Rule 13, "Omit needless words" is still the goal. However, there are ways to learn to be brief. Here they are:

---

[7] The author's friend, Stephen S. Bean of Woburn, Mass., paraphrasing Ralph Waldo Emerson.

[8] This technique was recommended as part of the Practical Casualty Claim Program—the product of country-wide conferences between claims executives and members of the National Association of Independent Insurance Adjusters. Their thinking appears now to represent a reasonable industry norm.

Order an extra file copy when dictating. Blue pencil this ruthlessly. Redictate and where possible have redictation transcribed to get both the sound and the sight of the reduced product. Enjoy the result.

Dictate as early in the day as possible.[9]

Keep some papers around as long term projects, second, third and fourth-cuts are often more productive than the first. Having gotten rid of several words, contemplate eliminating whole sentences and whole paragraphs. Doing this does not help the particular communication now being reduced (it is to be hoped that the original has long since gone on its way) but it does *teach* and that helps *the next communication.*

Look for and enjoy good examples of brief prose on incoming communications and be a shameless plagiarizer.

Avoid cliches, jargon and figurative language. Be sparing with superlatives.

Forget about trying to sound like an adjuster. There is no better way to clutter up your reports with meaningless, unnecessary phrases.[10] Try instead to write reports so they can be understood by a moderately bright twelve-year-old. This eliminates meaningless jargon for it is almost impossible to write in a simple style without having a clear idea of what to say. Imposing this self discipline makes a better report writer. The habit of clear thinking which it enforces will make a more careful, thoughtful purposeful and conclusive adjuster.

Study the following examples. In all instances the first draft was a field man's actual dictation. In each, names and places have been changed but otherwise the reports are exactly as written. Each is then followed by an edited version. The reduction in verbage is obvious. A reader should ask himself these questions:

Does the edited version convey its information more clearly?

Would it not—in the long run—have saved time for the dictator to have taken a few moments to organize his thoughts in order to produce the second version?

Finally would an adjuster prefer to be judged on the basis of the first or the second draft?

---

[9] The author finds that his early morning dictation can seldom be reduced by more than a 2 to 1 ratio. When he dictates late in the day, editing gives him a much higher reduction ratio—on bad days perhaps as high as 10 to 1.

[10] Trying to sound like an adjuster is a poor goal. There are, with one or two possible exceptions, probably no worse examples to follow.

Here is an example of a long report:

March 1, 1971

RE: Your File # xxxxxxxx
Insured: Albert S_____
Claimant: Mary Y _____
D/A: 12/6/67
Our File #xxxxxx

Dear Mr. S_____

ENCLOSURES:

SS of witness Lilly P_____

ACKNOWLEDGMENT:

This will acknowledge your letter of February 19, 1971 requesting that we contact the witness in an effort to secure her statement.

WITNESS:

Miss Lilly P_____, white, age 35 has never been married and lives with her mother, Helen P_____ at 924 Goathill Ave., Town, State, 23907. This young lady is employed as a secretary with _____ _____ University and has worked for them for the past four years. She is a small unattractive woman who appears to be very honest and cooperative.

Briefly, Miss P_____ states that she was sitting behind the driver about half way back in the bus resting, her eyes closed, when the accident occurred and she says she did not see what happened. She heard the plaintiff talking to the bus driver, H_____ H_____, all the way from the Oakland area of P_____ to M_____, P_____ where this accident occurred. After the bus stopped on S_____ St. at the intersection of R_____ St., Miss P_____ says she heard the driver tell the plaintiff to "Watch her step and be careful." A moment later she heard the driver say "My god she got hit—she got hit." At this point the driver and Miss P_____ ran across the street to render any assistance they could to the plaintiff. It appears to us that this witness was not too observant on the accident scene as she could not tell us where your assured car was stopped or where the plaintiff was lying after she was allegedly hit by your assured vehicle.

Miss P_____ tells us that she has ridden on H_____ H_____'s bus several times since this accident occurred and within a few days after this accident occurred, the bus driver was discussing this accident with her quietly. Miss P——— says that at the time the bus driver seemed to know everything that had occurred down to the minor details. As an example she pointed out that the bus driver said how far your assured vehicle was from the curbing, the distance from the bus to the point of impact and other measurements and details. She says she told Mr. H——— that she did not see any of the accident until after he shouted she got hit.

When we questioned, Miss P——— concerning another passenger on the bus she said she was completely unaware that there had been any other passengers on the bus at that time. She said off the record there was no one she recalled sitting between her and the bus driver and she doubted very much if there was any passenger on the bus after Mrs. Y——— got off except herself. We did learn from her however, that the bus driver, H——— H——— apparently thinks there was another passenger, but could not identify her.

He was asking Miss P——— if she remembered the alleged passenger in an effort to identify her.

REMARKS:

In reading your attorney's letter which was attached to yours, we see mention of an alleged witness who works at ———— Rest Home on N. First St., J———, P———, however, you did not suggest we make any contacts there. If you wish we can go to the rest home and make some inquiries and perhaps come up with the alleged witness, however, it appears doubtful.

By carbon copy of this letter, we are sending the original of Miss P———'s statement to your attorney in G——— as I am sure you will want him to have it as soon as possible. We trust you will agree with this procedure. If we may be of further service, please advise and in the meantime, we are giving this file a 30 day diary date.

Very truly yours,

JC/br

cc———— ————, Esq.

Attorney at Law

———— ————St.

————, ————34609

Now—the same report edited:

March 1, 1971

RE: Your File #xxxxx
Insured: Albert S_____
Claimant: Mary Y_____
D/A: 12/6/67
Our File #xxx xx

Dear M_____:

Here is:

ss Lilly P_____, witness—as you requested.

Unfortunately, she's no help. She was resting with her eyes closed when the accident happened. Even though she rushed out to help the injured claimant, Miss P_____ made no useful observations bearing on assured's or claimant's position.

I probed for other witnesses. Miss P_____ says she remembers no other passengers, thinks there were none although she tells me that the driver, H_____ H_____, seems to feel there was one other.

REQUEST FOR INSTRUCTIONS:

Your attorney mentions a witness at H_____ Rest Home, _____, _____. Since you say nothing about this lead, I assume you did not wish it to be followed. Please let me know if I guessed wrong; will close in 30 days if I don't hear.

Yours very truly,

cc _____, _____Esq.
_____, _____
_____, _____, 34609

Another long one:

January 18, 1972

RE: Your File # unprocessed
Insured: T_____M_____
Our File # xxx xx

Dear Mr. S_____:

This will confirm my telephone conversation with you on the 13th of January and acknowledge your confirmation of coverage dated January 15, 1971.

ASSIGNMENT:

We received this assignment by phone from the _____ Agency _____, _____,.

ASSURED:

T____ M____, 127 Cedar Blvd., _____, _____.
Mr. M____ is separated from his family and no longer
lives at this address.

STATEMENT OF YERVINA M____, WIFE:

We are attaching a long hand written statement of Yervina
____, wife of T____ M____ who resides at 127 Cedar
Blvd., _____, _____. Mrs. M____ confirms that she
has been separated from her husband since October of
1970 and that her husband has moved out of the home.
She also confirms that the automobile insured is actually
her daughter Josephine's, age 22, who lives at home with
her. This statement also confirms that Mrs. M____ gave the
permissive use of the automobile to the assured driver
to run an errand for her at the Bar they own in _____,
_____.

ASSURED DRIVER:

William C. Pittleway, white, age 17, a junior high school
student holding P____ drivers license #xxAxxJxx. He
lives at home with his parents, Mr. & Mrs. William T.
Pittleway at 621 _____ Ave., _____, _____. We
are attaching his detailed statement which is self-explanatory, however, we have some reasons to doubt this boy
is actually giving us the true facts and we refer you to
the comments under the claimant paragraphs and remarks.

COVERAGE:

You confirm this assigned risk policy #37999A099209
effective May 30, 1970 issued for one year providing BI
PD and Uninsured Motorist coverage on a 1970 Camaro
bearing serial #xxxxxxxxxxxx. The vehicle has been identified and we attach a photograph of it. Coverage appears
to be in order and permissive use confirmed.

DATE, TIME AND PLACE OF ACCIDENT:

This accident occurred approximately at 8:00 p.m., January 8th, Friday, 1971 in the 600 block of _____,
St., _____, _____. The weather was clear and dry
and it was night time. _____ St. is approximately 22
feet wide and runs up a steep hill to the north. We attach
sketch of the accident scene and one photograph of the accident scene to help you in visualising this accident.

ACCIDENT FACTS:

The assured driver confirms that he was driving south-bound downgrade on _____ St. and estimates his speed at 40 mph in a 25 mph speed zone. He alleges impact occurred on his own side of the street and after the impact with the adverse vehicle, he was knocked back over the right side of the street where he struck a pole breaking it off and continued down the road some distance.

CLAIMANT'S VERSION:

We are not permitted a signed statement from the claimant driver or his wife, who is a passenger in the car, however, verbally, Mrs. Brown says her husband was stopped with his right wheels up on the right curb of the street when the assured vehicle struck their car and crossed back over the street hitting a telephone pole.

POLICE ACTION:

We are attaching photostatic copy of the _____ police investigation of this accident, and may we call your attention to the description of the accident. You will see the numbers of the vehicles have been changed. The original report stated that vehicle #1, Brown's vehicle, was on the wrong side of the street when struck by your assured's vehicle #2. They have also changed the numbers of the vehicles to indicate and conform with their diagram which shows vehicle #2, the assured vehicle, on the wrong side of the street when the accident occurred. We interviewed Officer H_____, who was one of the officers conducting this investigation, and he confirms the change on the police report stating that a young clerk in the police department made the error. Officer H_____ confirms that the claimant vehicle was up on the right or east curb of the street when your assured vehicle struck him and confirms that the assured vehicle was on the wrong side of the street.

WITNESS:

The assured driver gives us the name of Kenneth Johnson who allegedly lives in _____ _____, exact address unknown, as a witness to this accident. He is to arrange for us to get Mr. Johnson's statement. We understand Kenneth Johnson is a 16 year old high school friend of the assured driver. Listed as a witness on the police report is a Mr. John Richard Jacobs of 42 _____, _____. We have been unable to locate this witness by phone, but have sent him a letter requesting a personal contact or for him to complete a witness report form.

Incidentally, your assured alleges that the witness, John Jacobs was a passenger in the claimant car and the claimants deny this.

LIABILITY ASPECTS:

From all indications, we would say we have a case of negligence on the part of the assured driver. All information thus far seems to point to the fact that the assured driver was on the wrong side of the road when the accident occurred. The assured driver denies this fact, but then he is not very definite with his denial. It is rather obvious that he is shading his statement to protect himself.

CLAIMANT DRIVER:

Mr. David Brown, of 40_____ Dr., _____ _____, _____. This man refuses to talk to us, but we have talked to his wife, who is listed in the next paragraph. We have no information concerning this man's employment and/or ownership of his automobile.

Mrs. Mary Jane Brown, wife of the claimant driver, says she was a passenger in the claimant car when the accident occurred. She denies there was anyone else in their automobile. She states that their automobile was up on the right curb or east curb of the street when the impact occurred and that your assured driver was driving at a high rate of speed. She refuses to give us a signed detailed statement and says if she is bothered anymore about this accident she intends to make a claim for her husband's condition.

INJURIES:

The insured driver was not injured and it is reflected in his statement. When we talked by phone with Mrs. Brown, she said neither her or her husband was injured, however, she alleges her husband has had cervical back injury in the past for which he is treating at the present time and if they are aggrevated any further because of this accident, they intend to have her husband examined to see if his injury was aggravated in this accident.

ADVERSE VEHICLE:

The only information we have thus far about the vehicle is that it is a 1971 Dodge station wagon owned by the driver,

David Brown. We understand the entire left side of this vehicle was damaged, but the claimants refused to give us an estimate and has referred us to their insurance company. We would suggest you maintain at least $700.00 PD reserve for this vehicle.

ADVERSE CARRIER:

The Browns allege they are fully insured with the _____ Insurance Exchange. We will attempt to confirm this and advise.

PROPERTY DAMAGE:

The assured vehicle sheared off a wooden telegraph pole which has been replaced before our investigation. The telegraph pole in the approximate center of the photo attached of the accident scene, is the one that has been replaced. There is no light on it, and we are assuming that it is probably owned by the telephone company but it could be from the _____ Light Co. At today's costs we would estimate approximately $650.00 for replacing this pole.

Also damaged was a concrete step into an apartment building at 601 _____ St. We have this item marked with an X circled on the attached photograph. We do not know who owns this property, but would establish PD reserves of approximately $100.00 as the steps are cracked and some sections broken off.

REMARKS AND FURTHER WORK:

Our first order of business will be to secure the statement of witness John Jacobs. Secondly, we will contact the _____ Insurance Exchange to see what their investigation reflects. While talking with Mrs. Brown, she said they have already received a bill for the telephone pole, but she had returned it to the sender and would not tell me whether it was _____ Light Co. or the _____ Telephone Co.

We will also attempt to get the statement of Kenneth Johnson, however, we have a strong impression that the assured driver is not telling us the truth and since this witness, Johnson, is a personal friend of his, we will probably find Mr. Johnson will confirm the assured driver's report.

As soon as we have any additional information we will, of course, post your file immediately. Incidentally, there is no collision insurance coverage on the assured car and the assured's daughter Josephine has retained an attorney

and asked him to file suit for her damages since she
believes what your driver said about the accident. I do not
believe that Miss M_____ is aware of the change in the
police report.

Very truly yours,

ENCLOSURES:

Statement of Yervina M_____
Statement of William Pittleway
Police Report
One photograph of assured car
One photograph of accident scene
Sketch of the accident scene

The same report boiled down:

January 18, 1971

RE: Your File # unprocessed
Insured: T_____ M_____
Our File # xxx xx

Dear Mr. S_____

ENCLOSURES:

SS Yervina M_____ (named insured's wife)
SS William C. Pittleway (operator—insured's car)
Police report
Photographs
Sketch of scene

COVERAGE:

Assigned risk #37999A099029, 5/30/70-71, BI, PD, UM,
Camaro serial # xxxxxxxxxxxx.

IDENTIFICATION:

By physical inspection _____, _____. Serial number
corresponds.

DATE, TIME AND PLACE:

1/8/71, 8:00 p.m., _____ 600 block _____ St.,
_____, _____. See photo and sketch for descriptive
detail.

DESCRIPTION:

Insured, south on _____ St., admits 40 mph in 25 mph
zone. Claimant heading in opposite direction. Claimant

maintains that *he* stopped at *his* curb. Insured says claimant crossed center line and hit him.

SS—YERVINA M_____:

She says that: she & T _____ are separated.

That the car actually belongs to daughter Josephine.
That she, Yervina, asked Pittleway to run an errand for her and gave him permission to use the car.

I am satisfied he had "permission."

SS—PITTLEWAY—Insured Operator:

Describes accident as I set out under "description."

SS—JACOBS—Witness:

Listed on police report. I have been unable to contact him but have not given up.

SS—JOHNSON—Witness:

Insured is arranging for this statement with Johnson which I intend to get even though it will probably have to be discounted heavily. He is said to be a 16 year old friend. He is a friend of Pittleway and, I dare say, hardly objective.

SS—CLAIMANT BROWN:

Saw Mr. & Mrs. Brown, _____, _____. Neither would give me a statement. Mrs. Brown expressed anger at being screened; says that neither she nor her husband were hurt, even though he is treating for pre-existing back trouble but that if she is "bothered" any more they will have her husband examined to see if his injury was aggravated.
I think these people are bona-fide. I intend to follow their wishes.

POLICE REPORT:

You will, I'm sure, be concerned at the obvious changes shown on the enclosed report. I discussed these with Officer H_____, one of the officers who made the original investigation. His answer seemed straightforward and it impressed me as probably true and a satisfactory explanation, i.e., the original entries were made by a clerk and later changed to conform to his (H_____'s) investigation.

PROPERTY DAMAGE:

Brown—71 Dodge Wagon—entire left side said to be damaged. I was referred to Brown's carrier (_____ Insurance Exchange). Recommend $700.00 reserve.

Utility Co: Wooden pole sheared off. I can not yet identify the owner—whether Telephone or Power Co. Recommend Reserve $650.00.

Unknown: Steps to apartment building at 601 _____ St. Owner not yet identified. Reserve___$100.00.

RECOMMENDATIONS:

As to value: Withheld until liability investigation is completed.

As to further work:

> Ascertain PD through _____ Insurance Ex-Exchange
> SS Jacobs
> SS Johnson
> and I will send in information identifying the owners of the pole and the apartment as soon as this data reaches me, as it soon will.

Very truly yours,

Short Forms (Checkoffs for Subsequent Reports)

Short forms are useful devices for subsequent reports; when there are enclosures to be submitted (with one exception to be noted); or when the file is being closed by release or other closing documents, all necessary supporting information having already been sent. Two examples of short forms follow.

ADJUSTER'S TRANSMITTAL REPORT
For Automobile or Third Party Claims

( ) FIRST REPORT   ( ) INTERIM REPORT   ( ) CLOSING REPORT

ADDRESS REPLY TO: DATE:

CLAIM #   OUR FILE #

POLICY #   TERM   DATE OF LOSS:

INSURED:

ADDRESS:
CLAIMANT:

ADDRESS:
AGENT:

ADDRESS:
LIENHOLDER:

VEHICLE:

SUGGESTED RESERVES:

NAME	ADDRESS	INSD. OWNER CLMT.	INSD. DRIVER CLMT.	INSD. PASSENGER CLMT.	PEDESTRIAN	OTHER	BI	PD	MED	UM	COMP	COLL	OTHER
1. White	100 A St. - City	X										700	
2. "	" " " "	X							75				
3. "	" " " "									500			
4.													

WE ARE SECURING:

____ CLAIMANT'S STATEMENT   ____ PROOF OF LOSS   ____ SALVAGE BIDS
____ WITNESS STATEMENT   X REPAIR INVOICE (ESTIMATE)   ____ RELEASE(S)
____ POLICE REPORT   ____ MEDICAL INFORMATION ( ) EXAM ( )   ____
____ SPECIAL DAMAGES/BILLS

ENCLOSURES: DETAILED STATEMENTS FROM:

____ INSURED'S REPORT   X _Black (Clt.)_   ____ RELEASE
____ CLAIMANT'S REPORT(S)   X _White (Insd.)_   ____ PROOF OF LOSS
____ WITNESS REPORT(S)   X _Med. Authority (White)_   ____ SUBROGATION/LOAN RECEIPT
____ POLICE REPORT   ____ REPAIR INVOICE/ESTIMATE   ____ SALVAGE REPORT/CHECK
____ DIAGRAM   ____ INSPECTION APPRAISAL/INVOICE   ____ MED. PAY PROOF
____ PHOTOS   ____ MEDICAL REPORT(S)/BILLS   ____ SERVICE INVOICE: FINAL( ) INTERIM( )

DISPOSITION: PAYMENT: MAIL TO: PAYEE | OUR OFFICE

____ SETTLED AS INDICATED BY ENCLOSURES   ____ WE HAVE ISSUED DRAFTS PER COPIES ATTACHED
____ CLAIM DENIED   ____ PLEASE ISSUE DRAFTS PAYABLE AS FOLLOWS:
____ OFFER PENDING $ ____ TO ____
____ WAITING ACTIVITY BY CLMT( ) ATTY( ) $ ____ TO ____
____ DIARY ____ DAYS $ ____ TO ____

SUBROGATION:

____ WE ARE PROCEEDING TO ATTEMPT RECOVERY – COPY OF SUBROGATION NOTICE ATTACHED.
____ WE ASSUME YOU WILL HANDLE OR REFER AS YOU DESIRE – WE ARE TAKING NO FURTHER ACTION.
____ WE HAVE REFERRED ON YOUR BEHALF TO:

REMARKS:

To maintain White's goodwill & minimize UM exposure, I have OK'd unusual expediting exposure to get new parts in.

SR 21: FILED ( ) PLEASE FILE ( ) NOT APPLICABLE ( )   ADJUSTER

ADJUSTER'S TRANSMITTAL REPORT
For Automobile or Third Party Claims

( ) FIRST REPORT	( ) INTERIM REPORT	( ) CLOSING REPORT

ADDRESS REPLY TO:	DATE:
CLAIM #	OUR FILE #
POLICY # TERM	DATE OF LOSS:

INSURED:

ADDRESS:
CLAIMANT:

ADDRESS:
AGENT:

ADDRESS:
LIENHOLDER:

VEHICLE:

SUGGESTED RESERVES:

NAME	ADDRESS	INSD. OWNER CLMT.	INSD. DRIVER CLMT.	INSD. PASSENGER CLMT.	PEDESTRIAN	OTHER	B I	PD	MED	U M	COMP	COLL	OTHER
1.		☐☐	☐☐	☐☐	☐	☐							
2.		☐☐	☐☐	☐☐	☐	☐							
3.		☐☐	☐☐	☐☐	☐	☐							
4.		☐☐	☐☐	☐☐	☐	☐							

WE ARE SECURING:

_____ CLAIMANT'S STATEMENT	_____ PROOF OF LOSS	_____ SALVAGE BIDS
_____ WITNESS STATEMENT	_____ REPAIR INVOICE/ESTIMATE	_____ RELEASE(S)
_____ POLICE REPORT	_____ MEDICAL INFORMATION ( ) EXAM ( )	_____
	_____ SPECIAL DAMAGES/BILLS	_____

ENCLOSURES: DETAILED STATEMENTS FROM:

_____ INSURED'S REPORT   X   *Black (Clt.)*   _____ RELEASE
_____ CLAIMANT'S REPORT(S)   X   *White (Insd.)*   _____ PROOF OF LOSS
_____ WITNESS REPORT(S)   _____   _____ SUBROGATION/LOAN RECEIPT
_____ POLICE REPORT   _____ REPAIR INVOICE/ESTIMATE   _____ SALVAGE REPORT/CHECK
_____ DIAGRAM   _____ INSPECTION APPRAISAL/INVOICE _____ MED. PAY PROOF
_____ PHOTOS   _____ MEDICAL REPORT(S)/BILLS   _____ SERVICE INVOICE: FINAL( ) INTERIM( )

DISPOSITION: PAYMENT:

		MAIL TO:	
		PAYEE	OUR OFFICE

_____ SETTLED AS INDICATED BY ENCLOSURES   _____ WE HAVE ISSUED DRAFTS PER COPIES ATTACHED
_____ CLAIM DENIED   _____ PLEASE ISSUE DRAFTS PAYABLE AS FOLLOWS:
_____ OFFER PENDING $ _____ TO _____
_____ WAITING ACTIVITY BY CLMT( ) ATTY( ) $ _____ TO _____
_____ DIARY   DAYS $ _____ TO _____

SUBROGATION:

_____ WE ARE PROCEEDING TO ATTEMPT RECOVERY – COPY OF SUBROGATION NOTICE ATTACHED.
_____ WE ASSUME YOU WILL HANDLE OR REFER AS YOU DESIRE – WE ARE TAKING NO FURTHER ACTION.
_____ WE HAVE REFERRED ON YOUR BEHALF TO:

REMARKS:

Closing.

No exposure.

SR 21: FILED( )   PLEASE FILE ( )   NOT APPLICABLE ( )

ADJUSTER

Resist the temptation to write anything but brief comments under "Remarks." Most of what is said there could be omitted altogether. If it is essential to write more than two short sentences or remarks, consider using the dictaphone—it will take less adjuster time than to hand-write and the result will be more quickly read by the reader. Do not let the dictaphone make you wordy. If the subject could have been covered in three short hand-written sentences, dictate those sentences—*no more.*

What Is Shorter Than a Short Form?

Answer: no form.

Often an adjuster picks up documents important to the file. These may be repair estimates, or medical reports about a long-

INITIAL MEDICAL REPORT
FLORIDA DEPARTMENT OF COMMERCE
BUREAU OF WORKMEN'S COMPENSATION
TALLAHASSEE, FLORIDA 32304

Original HOCe 3-1-72

FIC – SI OR CARRIER FILE NO. *WC-23456*

FAILURE TO SUBMIT THIS REPORT WITHIN TEN DAYS OF INITIAL TREATMENT WILL JEOPARDIZE PAYMENT OF FEE

1. EMPLOYER NAME	2. EMPLOYEE NAME			3. SOCIAL SECURITY NO.
4. CARRIER NAME	5. AGE	6. SEX	7. RACE	8. DATE OF ACCIDENT

9. PATIENT'S DESCRIPTION OF ACCIDENT

10. DATE DISABILITY BEGAN	11. DATE OF FIRST TREATMENT	12. SERVICES ENGAGED BY

13. DESCRIBE NATURE OF INJURY

14. DIAGNOSIS (INCLUDE X–RAY FINDINGS AND CAUSAL RELATIONSHIP TO INJURY)

15. IF PATIENT HAS PHYSICAL IMPAIRMENT DUE TO PREVIOUS ACCIDENT OR DISEASE GIVE PARTICULARS

16. DESCRIBE TREATMENT (INCLUDE DRUGS PRESCRIBED)

17. IF FURTHER TREATMENT NEEDED OR NORMAL RECOVERY DELAYED GIVE PARTICULARS

18. DATE PATIENT ABLE TO RETURN TO WORK	19. HOSPITAL NAME AND ADDRESS IF HOSPITALIZED
20. DATE OF MAXIMUM RECOVERY	
21. DOCTOR'S ESTIMATE OF LENGTH OF DISABILITY	22. REHABILITATION WILL BE ☐ NECESSARY ☐ PROBABLE ☐ UNLIKELY

23. IF TREATMENT COMPLETED WITHIN SEVEN DAYS – THIS IS THE ONLY FORM REQUIRED IF YOU REFLECT FEES BELOW.

DATE OF SERVICE	CODE NUMBER	MEDICAL AND SURGICAL SERVICES (ITEMIZE BY CODE AND DESCRIPTION LISTED IN NOMENCLATURE BOOK)	NO. OF SERV.	RATE	AMOUNT	DO NOT USE THIS COLUMN

24. DOCTOR'S NAME AND ADDRESS	25. DOCTOR'S I. D. NO.	DATE
	SIGNATURE	

term case. When there is nothing else to be said, a check off form is certainly better than a letter of transmittal. Even better though, many carriers prefer the document itself with no transmittal document. Page 340 demonstrates a doctor's report as it might have been prepared for transmittal. All it needs to get to its destination is written in the right upper corner. The entry in the upper right hand corner reproduced by carbon on the retained file copy tells the adjuster when he submitted the item.

Caution for Examiners

An examiner who wants short reports and who reads files from independent adjusters should realize that he may be his own greatest enemy. Reporting such as this chapter asks for, if it is full-heartedly followed, presents the examiner with a file that tells him *nothing* about how much time an adjuster did spend or should have spent on his work.

Ill-thought letters complaining that the file does not support the bill discourage the adjustor who has made the sincere effort to eliminate needless words. Unless necessary letters of inquiry are thoughtfully phrased, they tend to create misunderstanding on the adjuster's part and put the examiner in a self-made box from which he may find it awkward to remove himself if an explanation is forthcoming.

SUBJECT MATTER

Dictation Check List

A dictation check list is offered on page 343. It could, if one chose, be employed as a caption list for full formal reports, but it is not for that purpose that it is presented.

The outline of his full formal reports will usually be established by an adjuster's employer. All outlines have, in the main, the same purposes, i.e., to bring out the information called for, *and to arrange it in a manner convenient to the organization which will receive the report.* No matter what his outline, no matter what the order or what the arrangement of headings, sub-headings, etc., an adjuster should know, for each item, how to dictate about that subject.

The subjects listed on the item-by-item check list should, sooner or later, be made clear in a well-ordered file. Therefore, those items not conclusively dictated into a full formal may merit attention in subsequent reports. When these items *then* appear, it is even more important to deal with them clearly and suffi-ciently, for now, crucial decisions are about to be made. The check list, therefore, is a guide to subsequent interim reports as well as full formal reports.

After a quick run-down of the list, and to emphasize that its use is a judgment matter, it will be well to stop and consider the possibilities for condensing. For instance, from the outline exhibited, even a serious claim might well require of items 5, 6 and 7 only the use of Number 7 (if the information to be con-veyed under 5 and 6 is adequately transmitted by photographs).

Complete as is this list, it furnishes no caption by which to report on a canvass for witnesses, an investigative move which many cases require. For a canvass or for any other unlisted move, an adjuster will have to write an appropriate caption.

This list (or any list) is a crutch, with a crutch's limitations. It illustrates again the point made in the Introduction: "There are no absolutes in this business." Even in reporting, seemingly a mechanical function, an adjuster may not escape the duty of thinking for himself. Expansion and contraction of his reports are in the end a matter of his judgment.

While this list will not think for him, it will help an ad-juster. It will even guide him to the proper completion of some of his investigative items; of this, the treatment of medical infor-mation is an example. This list is intended primarily for claims involving *automobile* accidents.

Dictation Check List—Automobile Claims

1. Enclosures	12. Imputed negligence
2. Coverage	13. Liability
3. Identification	14. Collision loss
4. Date, time and place	15. Third party—subrogation
5. Locus	16. Property damage
6. Diagram	17. Medical payments claims
7. Description of accident	18. Doctor
8. Claimant data—suggested reserves	19. Lost time and wages
	20. Special damages
9. SS [10] witness	21. Settlement
10. Police reports—official records	22. Control
	23. Risk
11. Photographs	24. Recommendations

Enclosures

Listing enclosures at the beginning of the report permits an examiner to see at a glance what supporting matter accompanies the report. A review of these items as he commences his report gives the adjuster a bird's-eye view of the ground which the report will cover. It invites shortening the report by letting the enclosures tell the story when they will.

Start the battle against unnecessary words here. "I hand you herewith" is just as silly as it sounds.

The caption followed by a list is all that is required.

ENCLOSURES

SS Insured—Brown
Invoice, Tampa General Hospital ($465.21)
SS Claimant—Jones

Coverage

The claims to which a company is exposed by a given accident are determined by the circumstances of the accident *and by the coverage afforded.* Coverage, therefore, to an important degree, governs the scope of the adjuster's work. To review the exposures at the outset is helpful, both to the examiner (who is thus

---

[10] It is common practice in reports to abbreviate the word "statement" to simply "ss." The custom continues. Even though most statements today are recorded rather than "signed." They are still "ss."

enabled to forecast the items on which the report should inform him) and to the adjuster whose duty it is to see that all exposures are duly covered.

As with so much of the reporting procedure, this item is a helpful self-discipline, much like the "given" that the adjuster was required to set up when he first met simple problems in arithmetic.

Almost all report outlines call for a recital of coverage at the very beginning of the full formal. Examiners expect to find the subject summarized there. They must have a familiar place to turn to for a quick review after the file has gotten to be inches thick. Here is where they *expect* to find this information.

When coverage is not an issue, a bare recital of the policy details suffices. Sentence structure is not necessary. For example:

> 1 FAP—2492160, 50/100/10, 4/1/63 to 4/1/64, medical nil, comprehensive nil, 100 deductible collision, UM 10/20, '64 Oldsmobile, motor GAA730S2960, serial 12345678.

Notice the inclusion of the information that medical coverage and comprehensive are *not* afforded. Negative information should be recorded, for otherwise it may later develop, for instance, that a comprehensive loss is involved. Unless the record has been made in the manner recommended, a reader cannot tell whether silence on the point arose from lack of coverage or because it was thought that coverage was not involved.

Do not say, "By your policy number so-and-so, you insure. . . ."

A complex coverage situation may require two or more captions. For instance:

> *COVERAGE:*
> *QUESTION OF COVERAGE:*
> *SS INSURED (JONES) RE COVERAGE:*
> *CONCLUSIONS—RECOMMENDATIONS AS TO COVERAGE:*

Under "Coverage" policy information should be set forth as previously recommended. Under "Question of Coverage," the factual situation that brings up the coverage question should be outlined and discussed. Under the paragraph "SS Insured (Jones) re Coverage," what Jones has to say on the subject is summarized.

It is not hard to imagine a coverage question involving still more complexities and many more persons. To avoid confusion, as many captions as may be required should be used. Summarize, conclude and recommend in the final paragraph.

Identification

The decision to include or omit dictation on this item is related to the judgment exercised in performing or omitting the act of *identification.*

Unless the identity of the automobile involved in the accident is in issue (assuming that the report deals with an automobile case), the usual treatment is to omit the caption altogether.

If an adjuster has reason to believe that his company may want to know whether he did or did not make a physical identification, and if his election was negative, he may simply dictate: "Waived."

If the vehicle was identified, a positive statement concerning the act should be dictated as briefly as possible: "By physical inspection, 11/1/63, Smith's Garage, Brooksville, Florida, motor and serial numbers correspond with policy information." If examination has disclosed a discrepancy, expanded discussion appropriate to the question is called for.

Date, Time and Place

This item requires the adjuster to consider "When?" and "Where?" seemingly routine items that may conceal defenses easy to overlook (claims arising before the inception or after the expiration date of the policy, for instance). It also establishes at a definite place in the file, easy to relocate, information that the examiner responsible for thousands of files may have to refer back to, sometimes months later. This item is never omitted.

> Poor: "The accident with which we are here concerned occurred at approximately 5:00 p.m. in a residential district at the intersection of San Pedro and Lois Streets, Tampa, Hillsborough County, Florida, the 4th of April, 1963."

Better: "4/4/63—5:00 p.m.—San Pedro and Lois Streets, Tampa, Florida."

Verbiage other than the recommended minimum costs money to transcribe. It makes reports *harder* to supervise.

Locus

This item may be required *if an understanding of the locus is a prerequisite to understanding the accident.* Locus will usually be described in some detail if the claim is serious.

The real description may be by diagram or by photographs, which may reduce the need to dictate or permit omission of this caption altogether.

This item is probably omitted more often than included.

Care should be taken, in any event, to limit the dictation to a discussion of the locus. Careless dictators at this point tend to slide into the later caption, "Description of Accident."

Diagram

A claim of sufficient severity to warrant a full formal report probably warrants a diagram as part of the report. A diagram may substitute completely for dictation relevant to "locus." On the other hand, photographs may make a diagram unecessary. A diagram may reduce to almost nothing the verbiage necessary under "Description of Accident."

A diagram need not be to scale, unless a purpose is served by making it so. Artistic ability is not required; the contending vehicles and pedestrians may be shown as symbols.

Scale and detail will be determined by the nature of the information to be conveyed. It may be desirable to indicate by numbered circles the positions of witnesses, or, if photographs were taken, the positions and facing of the camera. Diagrams should be simple. It is better to have two or three diagrams, each covering a different phase of the matter, than one cluttered with too much detail.

Discussion of the diagram should be limited to those things which it is necessary to say to make the diagram understandable.

Description of Accident

The aim here is to say enough about the accident to support the conclusions arrived at or to outline the elements of the dispute.

Here, then, the accident is described *as briefly as possible*. Anything over five lines should be suspected of verbosity. Little more is necessary than to name the type of accident and outline the dispute or disputes that prevail. For example:

> This is a right-angle intersection collision, at a controlled intersection. The usual dispute prevails as to which party had the green light.

If the subject is too complicated to deal with in this summary fashion, consider whether or not a diagram might better accomplish the desired results.

This is not the place to explain what each witness had to say, to analyze their various contentions or to state conclusions. All of that will be dealt with later. Here, the discussion is factual.

If the accident is simple and leads to an obvious conclusion, the essence of the later paragraph, "Liability," may be brought forward and disposed of here:

> *DESCRIPTION OF ACCIDENT:*
>
> Insured, Smith admits his attention wandered. He hit claimant from the rear. Clearly, a case for settlement. I have dispensed with further liability investigation and concentrated on control and settlement.

Claimant Data and Case Reserve

The purpose of "claimant data" is to describe all of the exposures and possible losses arising out of the accident which is the subject of the report. One person may have a claim under more than one section of the policy. Each such claim should be separately treated and listed as a separate entity. Dictate in summary fashion; do not use complete sentences.

List name, age, address, status if pertinent, and an appropriate reserve for each exposure. For example:

John Claimant (Op. C.C.), (35), 3314 Paxton Avenue, Tampa, Florida. Reserve, B.I. $1,000, P.D. $350 [12]

Mary (Mrs. John) Claimant (P.C.C.),[13] (32), same address. Reserve, BI $1,000

William Policyholder (Op. A.C.), (50), 3315 Paxton Avenue, Tampa, Florida. Reserve, Collision $500

SS Witness

As to the caption itself, "SS Witness . . . ." is preferable to "SS Witness" or "SS . . . ." The caption should recite not only the name of the person whose statement is to be discussed but identify him as insured, claimant, etc. In other words, if it is Smith whose statement is to be discussed, and if Smith is the insured, then the preferred caption would be, "SS Insured Smith."

Possibly the first point to be made about this caption is a negative one. *This is not the place to repeat in exhaustive detail what the witness said in his statement.* If an examiner wants to know *that* he will read the statement itself. Instead, dictation should *summarize* the statement and report those things which an examiner cannot learn by reading the statement itself. Therefore dictation under this caption should do three things. First, it should recite in as brief a form as possible what the witness has to say about those points that form the crux of the case; then it should furnish whatever additional information may be necessary to make the statement understandable to the examiner; finally, it should comment on the witness's credibility, whether there were unusual circumstances surrounding the taking of the statement, delays, callbacks, etc. Typical dictation under this caption might be:

---

[12] It is unnecessary to list the same person twice, once as a claimant for BI and once for PD, but an indication of the separate reserves will be welcomed by the examiners.

[13] Most claim departments recognize and use the following "shorthand": Op. C.C.—operator claimant car; P.C.C.—passenger claimant car; Op. A.C.—operator assured's car; P.A.C.—passenger assured's car.

SS Witness Brown:

Brown's testimony is unfavorable. He says that our insured was travelling not less than 50 mph in a residential district. He is unable to state which of the two cars entered the intersection first.

As his statement makes clear, Brown saw this accident from the west window of his living room. However, I looked out of that window and found that trees completely block a person's view, not only of the intersection but also of the entire length of Ross Ave., the street on which our insured approached the scene.

Except for his story being obviously out of step with the facts, he would be an impressive witness. It must be conceded that he makes a fine appearance, speaks well and conveys a general air of credibility.

Use a separate caption or at least sub-caption for each witness from whom a statement is taken.

Any of the forms of verbatim statement call for greater detail in setting out what the witness had to say relative to the fact situation. This is so for two reasons—first, verbatim statements are usually much longer and it is harder for an examiner to extract the meat from them. Secondly, the transcript may be delayed. In dealing with a serious claim, the examiner needs to know early and in considerable detail what each witness is going to be saying, even though he will certainly read the transcript as soon as it reaches him.

Police Reports—Official Records

These records call for dictation only if it is necessary to *discuss* them or to call attention to some information therein. If the record was procured and its contents routine, a simple listing among the enclosures is all that is necessary.

Photographs

If the photographs submitted are truly self-explanatory, then this dictation may be omitted. If the examiner requires an explanation in order to understand the pictures, then the adjuster should identify photographs by number to enable the dictater to comment on them. Point out the significance of the pictures, saying no more than necessary for the examiner to understand them.

Consider carefully saying nothing at all about them, for pictures often speak for themselves. Let them, if they will, do the talking.

One pages 351 and 352, from an actual claims file, is an example illustrating the complementary use of diagrams and photographs. The adjuster and home office examiner were accustomed to working with one another. In this particular file, the diagram and photos described the liability picture sufficiently so that *no* dictation was necessary on the subject.

Also, note that the significance of the pictures would not be clear without the diagram. Note the circled numbers demonstrating camera location and facings. Note that detail and scale were not necessary to the information sought to be conveyed and were not a feature of this diagram.

Imputed Negligence

This is a "reminder" item. Its principal reason for being is to remind the adjuster that if he has passengers in a claimant car, he should have explored their agency or common enterprise relationship to their driver. Having explored it, this is the place for him to report his findings.

This caption is relevant and included *only* when dealing with claims of passengers in claimants' cars. Every adjuster, however, should include it in his personal check list, for, whenever he is dealing with injury to a claimant passenger, this question must be considered. When utilized, material captioned this way provides comment on the factual situation out of which agency (common enterprise) and the consequent imputed negligence does or does not exist. Brief reference should be made to the evidence upon which the adjuster has established his conclusions. This may call for reference to statements of certain witnesses and admissions in them.

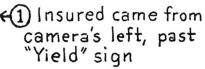
←① Insured came from camera's left, past "Yield" sign

Obstruction to ②→ insured's view

←③ Claimant headed same direction as camera faces

Obstruction to ④→ claimant's view

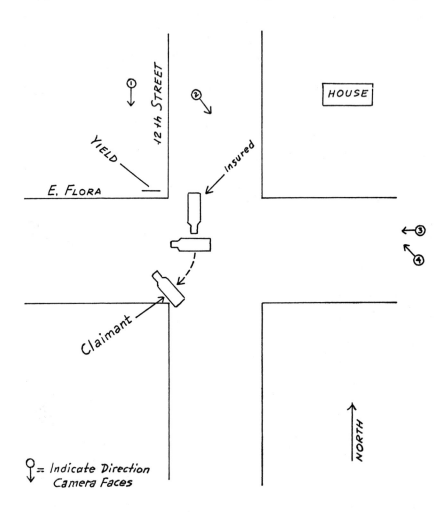

Liability

It has already been suggested that, if the conclusions are obvious, this whole caption may be dispensed with and the subject dismissed with a brief sentence under the caption "Description of Accident." If conclusions are not obvious, this is the place to bring together findings as to liability. The dictater should stop here to think back over what he has said under the captions of "Description of Accident," "Statements of Witnesses," etc. The report should have moved logically from the statement of the question under "Description of Accident" to discussion of the various versions in the statement of each witness. Now, under this caption, is the place to resolve the issues and state conclusions.

Resolution of conflict, even in serious cases, may be simple. For instance, an impartial witness pointing out the truth in the face of conflicting assertions by claimant and assured. Discussion in this situation is minimal.

Resolutions may require the weighing of irreconcilable factors or placement of a complicated fact situation against a complicated law situation; if so, discussion may be lengthy. If this is what confronts him, an adjuster needs to organize his thoughts carefully, possibly even outline them before he puts the microphone to his lips.

Collision Loss

This item is optional. If there is no coverage or no claim, it is often omitted entirely. In other situations, it may be well simply to remind the examiner that he has no exposure by a brief comment such as, "This loss is not insured."

If the collision loss is adjusted, no more is necessary than such comment as will enable the examiner to understand the submitted documents—estimates, proofs of loss, etc.

If it is *unadjusted,* the status of the claim will be reported (an insured withholding his claim pending attempts to collect from a third party, etc.). Items not easily knowable by the examiner should be mentioned if relevant. If, for instance, a garage was helpful and sold the insured on the idea that a slight scratch on an $80 face-bar did not require replacement, this should be stated, if for no other reason than to give the garage-man credit for good faith.

If the unit is a total loss or a potential total, the first full formal report should post the file and supply the examiner with the National Automobile Dealers Association (NADA) or "Red Book" figures applicable to the unit and probable salvage. He should be advised whether salvage bids have been solicited and, if so, from whom.

Third Party—Subrogation

If there is no collision exposure, this item will, of course, be omitted.

If in respect to a collision loss there exists a possibility of a subrogation right, identify the third party by address and comment on whether or not he is responsible in damages. For example:

> John Jones, 2231 Bird Street, Tampa, Florida, insured ABC Insurance Company
> Willie McGee, 710 Caesar Street, Abilene, Texas, uninsured

The company needs to know what steps are being taken to enforce subrogation rights, so steps taken or contemplated are reported here.

Contribution

Some full formal outlines call for this item. When they do, the adjuster is required to state whether there is other insurance contributing to the loss and to discuss arrangements and agreements made with the contributing companies. The basis for contribution should be explained and any required computations set out. If there is no other company involved, a simple statement to that effect suffices.

Liability insurance only rarely develops situations involving contributing insurance in the sense in which it so often appears in relation to first party coverages—that is, two or more policies applicable to the same insured and the same hazard. As far as the casualty adjuster is concerned, the more common situation is that involving two separate insureds each involved in the same cause of action (two cars, for instance, colliding and then one or the other or both striking an innocent bystander). Situations of this sort are quite common to casualty insurance, and they may be referred to as situations of joint responsibility or alleged joint responsibility. On whichever side he may be involved—that is, as representing the company which is trying to bring in another to contribute to the loss or as representing one company which another is trying to involve—the adjuster's tasks are to identify by name, address, etc., the other principal whose acts may have been jointly concerned with the acts of his own insured, to identify the other insurance company, and to relate the moves that have been made to enforce or avoid involvement as the case may be.

Dictation under this caption might read something like this:

CONTRIBUTION

John Staffman of Forever and Ever Insurance Co. has approached me to ask if we will contribute to the settlement with Claimant Lameneck. F. and E. insures Brown (identified elsewhere in this report). Staffman suggests that we pay $2/3$ and they $1/3$ of the settlement. He says that if we do not join, he will feel free to settle his obligation on a covenant.[14] I feel that his suggested division of the loss places too heavy a burden on us. I would be willing to contribute but on nothing more than a 50/50 basis. The facts bearing on liability and my views are set out elsewhere in this report. Please let me know if you agree with my views concerning our participation in the settlement.

Property Damage

In order to ascertain that the money entrusted to it by the public is properly disbursed, a company needs to be told what moves its adjuster has made in measuring the property damage.

Therefore if, in his discretion (and this is not to imply that such discretion may not have been properly employed), the adjuster has simply accepted one or more estimates as submitted,

---

[14] Covenants-not-to-sue, their effect, employment and the customs of the industry governing their use are discussed in Chapter 12.

his report should be unequivocal and should state his decision, and justify it if justification is called for.

Alterations or adjustments made in a submitted estimate are usually worked out on the estimate's face. If this is so, and if what was done is clear, no further explanation need be offered.

If an explanation is called for, or if a dispute rages, dictation at this point expands accordingly to enable the examiner or supervisor to assist, guide or criticize as need be. In short, dictation under this caption should be that which is necessary to let the examiner understand what has been done and to give it his approval or apply corrective pressure to forestall the repetition of error.

Medical Payments Claims

Information about medical payments claims is provided principally to enable the company to forecast the extent of the loss and to enable it to make sure that its obligations are being properly discharged. What is needed here is a summary description of the injuries for which the company has obligations under this coverage. If there is more than one medical payments claimant, it is desirable to use subcaptioned paragraphs naming each. Full sentences need not be employed.

The claim should have been set up so that no further active handling is necessary—nothing need be done except wait for the claimant to send in his bills.

The report should simply tell what steps have been taken in order to enable the proper submission of the bills and supporting reports to take place.

Doctor _____
(name)

It is elemental that a report on a claim for injury must set out an appraisal of the injury by a competent person. The usual person, of course, is the treating doctor(s). This information the company *must have.*

How he will be required to report has much to do with how an adjuster investigates the subject. The format of this part of his report, therefore, has to do with getting the proper information to the company's examiner and, because of the form required of him, it has to do, too, with assisting and even requiring a higher standard of performance from the adjuster.

The choice, then, of the caption, "Doctor ....," represents a deliberate holding of the adjuster's feet to the fire. It prevents his resorting to the vague terms, "Injury" or "Medical." Under *those* terms he might permit himself to escape with surmise, conjecture or hearsay. He *can't* do this if he follows the recommended form.

Vague terms may be resorted to *only when the adjuster is prepared to confess that he has been unable properly to discharge his duty to investigate by having talked with the doctor.* A good adjuster nourishes a sound reluctance to make this confession. He makes it his business to talk with the doctors and to report properly. Let this information be reported in outline form, as:

DR. JOHNSON
> Talked by telephone (935-2222) with the doctor 4/14 concerning John P. Claimant.

Diagnosis:
> Severe contusion of the left elbow
> Fracture left olecranon process
> Fracture head of left radius
> Fracture head of left ulna

Disability:
> Six months total (estimated)
> Four months partial (estimated)

Permanency:
> Since the fracture involves the joint space, there will probably be substantial permanency, the extent of which doctor cannot now estimate.

Bill:
> Estimated at $750

If the adjuster will keep in mind while he interviews the doctor, a self-imposed requirement of dictating in terms of the subcaptions, "Diagnosis," "Disability," "Permanency," "Bill," then his telephone interviews with doctors will be conclusive and informative.

There are other advantages to which a shrewd adjuster will not be oblivious. Reports set up in this form are easy to read. The monotonous march of the paragraphs is broken. Examiners appreciate information presented in this fashion. A further paragraph explaining doubtful points or elaborating on a discussion of causal connection may be added.

Managers and supervisors should insist on an outline form for this material, as an aid to supervision and as a means of requiring the adjuster to question doctors properly.

When an adjuster has a written report from his doctor (or doctors) he should consider letting them speak for themselves. A *complete* report would justify a reference to it in the enclosures and permit the waiving of all other comment. Unfortunately most doctors' reports are incomplete and require supplemental information, usually procured by telephone. The method suggested here is an easy, proven and sufficient method for getting the necessary information into the file.

Lost Time and Wages

Any reference to lost time and wages may be omitted if the claim involves no injury. However, *since it is always a feature of special damage in an injury case, a negative or affirmative report on the point is always needed even though no lost time may be involved.*

If one or more of the injured claimants is losing time from work, it is the adjuster's duty to verify this with the employer and determine the earning rate. This is the time and place to advise the insurer of these findings. If done early in the claim, this posts the file on an important feature of special damages and enables rapid computation of a claim's potential if and when an otherwise unexpected settlement opportunity arises.

No lost time alleged. Claimant admits in his statement that he is able to carry on his duty without difficulty.

If, on the other hand lost time is involved, the report may read:

Checked Garcia & Vega Cigar Company. Earnings average approximately $75 per week. Gonzalez losing time since the accident and continuing. Factory on full time, employee presumably would have worked had it not been for his injury.

Or:

Checked Garcia & Vega by phone 2/20. Lost time 2/1 to 2/14 inclusive. Wages $75 per week, total $150.00.

Special Damages

When a full formal report is dictated, special damages may be complete—this is rare—or incomplete. In either event, separate treatment of this item may be redundant, for the information dealt with under this heading ought to have appeared elsewhere. Nonetheless, and at the risk of repetition, a well-written full formal ought to draw together and list in one easy-to-find place the special damage figures, whether incurred or projected. The value of this technique in enabling management rapidly and soundly to forecast loss and establish reserves ought not to require pointing out.

Damages do take time to develop. It is the rule rather than the exception for complete medical information and expenses to trickle into a file, some now, some then, often months after the full formal report has been written. Then it is not only a kindness to examiners to consolidate, list and total the special damages, it is obligatory. Whether or not they have been seen before, special damages, listed, verified and totalled, should appear in that report which evaluates a claim or requests authority. Special damages are, after liability, the first thing an examiner wants to be informed on when he is requested to extend authority.

This information should always be tabulated.

Dr. Johnson (verified)	$ 750.00
Tampa General Hospital (verified)	400.00
Lost time and wages (estimated, still losing time)	1,100.00
M. Family Doctor, M.D. (verified)	35.00
TOTAL	$2,285.00

If special damages are known to have been incurred but the adjuster has been unable to check them, they too should be listed, and the adjuster's decision to accept them without confirmation noted. Judgment governs the decision whether to offer an explanation for failure to verify.

Special damages, crystallizing as they do on interim and subsequent reports, emphasize the dual role of the list on page 343, *a guide not only to the content of full formals but of subsequent reports.*

Settlement

Report any phase of the case settled to the date of dictation. No justification is necessary *unless the reason for the settlement is not clear from material already dictated.* Take care that this paragraph is not abused by a wasteful rehash of material already presented.

If checks or drafts are needed, request them. *For each draft desired, state clearly the amount in which it is to be written, and the exact designation of the payee.*

If problems are being encountered, explain them; supervisors or examiners "have been there." Their function is to help. Making clear the problem, in all of its ramifications, has often enabled an examiner to render valuable advice.

Control—Attorney

If any phases of the case are under control, discuss them carefully and in some detail. Examiners worry and wonder if everything possible is being done to maintain control of their cases. As long as an adjuster sticks to the subject, this is one caption under which he can give his tongue a little freer rein. Maybe he will put the examiner's mind at ease as to the direction and sufficiency of his fieldman's efforts.

If control is threatened, one of an examiner's functions is to assist. The adjuster, by explaining at some length, may open the door to valuable advice.

If control has been lost, name the attorney employed, inform the company as to his qualifications and tactics. Outline the moves made or contemplated to bring the claim to a head.

Risk

Although the occurrence of an accident does not, by itself, render a risk (as used here, risk means insured) undesirable, it certainly raises the question. It furnishes a convenient opportunity to gain new information about, and to reappraise, a risk.

At this place in his report, therefore, an adjuster should comment on the physical and moral qualities of the risk as he has been able to observe them. It is his duty to comment, not to judge. Rejection, cancellation, nonrenewal, etc, are the prerogatives of the underwriting department. Their decisions may embrace factors outside the range of an adjuster's knowledge, but *his* knowledge may influence an underwriter's decision.

It is the adjuster's duty to bring to the attention of his company, for underwriting attention if necessary, those factors observed by him which bear on an assured's probable future desirability.

Recommendations

An adjuster, in concluding his report, should think in terms of two different kinds of recommendations. These recommendations are concerned with both the *value* of the claim and the *further work* it may require.

Except in cases of fraud, almost all claims have some value, even if only a fraction of what they would be worth in a clear liability situation. Whenever possible, the adjuster should discipline himself to state the claim's present value in terms of dollars. It may be necessary to qualify this recommendation with an observation that further information may change the recommended figure. Recommendations are, of course, predicated on the facts available at the time of making the recommendation. (It is suggested that this section be reviewed after reading the chapter on evaluation.)

Recommendations should be stated in dollar figures. This book holds the opinion that values should not be expressed in terms of two figures. To say, "In my opinion this claim has a value of $350 to $500" means that the adjuster is ready to recommend and, if necessary, pay $500. If that is so, then it seems that $500 should be his recommendation. Although he may hope to settle for less, he should establish a limit to which he is prepared to go if he must, but beyond which he will not go.

Recommendations as to further work should be tabulated, listing each of the further items contemplated. Properly prepared, these recommendations serve as caption headings for future reports and a check list for examiners to assure the proper completion of outlined work. A typical dictation at this point might be:

> Secure opinions as to the valuation of motor scooter.
> Secure salvage bids
> Follow Dr. Johnson for discharge, diagnosis, and bill.
> Settle.

Dictation Check List—Falldowns

The check list used in dictating reports on claims involving *falldowns* differs somewhat from the auto check list just described. It includes these items:

Coverage	Ownership—control *
Description of locus	Maintenance *
Status *	Lease *
Date and time	Doctor (Name)
Description of accident	Lost time and wages
S.S. Claimant (Name)	Special damages
S.S. Companion (Name)	Disposition
SS. Store witnesses (Name)	Recommendations

* Items to regard as obligatory

This list merits much more rigid adherence than the automobile check list. It may be more rigidly employed than the auto check list because falldowns more nearly follow a consistent pattern than automobile accidents. No items should be omitted without conscious thought.

Not only is it a good dictation outline, it is an investigation guide. Except for those adjusters who operate in metropolitan areas and handle a sufficient volume of this type of claim to attain routine familiarity, claims from falls are rare. The list may be reviewed before starting an investigation. *Knowing what*

*and how one will be obliged to report encourages a proper con-
pletion of necessary work.*

Items marked with asterisks should be regarded as obligatory.
It is impossible to arrive at a proper decision on liability unless
the information called for is reported, affirmatively or negatively.

Treatment of many of these items has already been made
clear in discussion of the automobile check list. For each of the
new items there now follows a brief statement of the information
to be conveyed under it.

Description of Locus

Contrary to the practice in automobile claims, dictation on
this item or its equivalent is required almost without exception
in all types of general liability and falldown claims. The permissible exception is when equivalent information is conveyed by
photographs or diagram.

Stairs should be described by width of tread, height of rise,
depth of tread, number of treads, number of risers, location and
type of handrail.

Describe floors in terms of surface, repair, waxing, and
cleanliness.

If the scene was a floor rather than a stairway, cover neighboring counters and the items displayed on them by dictation,
diagram or photographs, as the situation may require. A liberal
use of a camera is urged.

Status

Information on the status of the claimant is a must in all
public liability claims. Relationship of the plaintiff to defendant
must be stated in terms of the invitee-licensee-trespasser concept.
The determined facts upon which a conclusion as to legal status
will be based should be set out along with the conclusions to
be drawn from them. The caption may be treated briefly:

Invitee—entered Maas Brothers to purchase sweaters.

A more complicated or borderline situation requires more
lengthy treatment.

Ownership—Control

In general liability claims it is essential to determine and inform the insurer as to the ownership of the property on which the fall occurred. Liability may hinge on this point.

Information should also be offered as to who was in control [15] of the premises. Physical occupancy, and use, have much to do with control. In the case of passageways, possession of keys, whether there are other keys, whether the doors are kept locked, is often determinative. The adjuster's findings on those points should be reported here.

Dictation under this caption should be factual. A tendency to theorize is often a tip-off that the adjuster is trying to cover up his failure to investigate the facts.

Maintenance

Investigation of every fall in a commercial establishment, and many in private establishments, includes a statement from the person in charge of maintaining that particular part of the premises. This is the place to comment on that statement. Dictation should record for quick reference the time at which the locus was last washed, swept or otherwise attended to. The general practice of the custodian, as well as the specific practice with reference to the place under consideration at the time of the accident, should be stated.

Lease

In commercial properties (and indeed in residential properties), the tenant is usually in almost absolute control. Unless an accident involves some defect in the premises, the lease is seldom an issue. To demonstrate that the matter has been considered and to discipline himself the adjuster should make an overt comment on this point.

If there was no written lease, he should say so, and give the source of his information.

---

[15] Note the word "control." Here it has its common meaning. Contrast this with its special meaning in claims work, as described in Chapter 12.

If the lease is in any way an issue, it is the adjuster's duty to ascertain at once whether there is a lease and to procure a copy of it. Ideally, dictation then would involve only a statement that a copy of the lease has been procured and is attached. Difficulty or delay in the procurement of a copy may be commented on.

Dictation Check List—Product Claims

Claims involving various types of *products* call for still another approach. The check list to be used in dictating a report on a product claim should contain these topics:

Coverage	S.S. Store personnel (Name)
Date, time, and place of purchase	Action over
Date, time and place of accident	Liability
Identification of product	Doctor (Name)
Foreign substance	Special damages
S.S. Claimant (Name)	Settlement negotiations—control
S.S. Companion (Name)	Recommendations

Close adherence to this list is recommended. Adjusters dealing with large numbers of product claims develop familiarity enabling them to cut dictation to a few sentences covering salient points. *This luxury is available only to the experienced man.*

Items whose treatment has not previously been explained are discussed in subsequent paragraphs.

Discuss the physical inspection of the product. Tell what the inspection showed. Identify the product by the brand name, if visible, wrappings, serial numbers, etc.

Record information derived from sales slip examination.

Describe any foreign substance observed or alleged. State size, shape, color, hardness, etc. Supplement dictation by photographs, as may be feasible or desirable.

Discuss by discovered fact each avenue of approach open to the claimant, whether tort or contract. Stick to determined fact, avoid theorizing. Leave theorizing to lawyers.

Discuss whether or not the insured is the party responsible, and inform the insurer whether or not "action over" letters have been sent. Inform the insurer as to other steps necessary or taken, to enforce the liability of other parties. (A copy of the action over letter, if any, should appear as one of the attachments.)

Landlord and Tenant Claims

Another type of claim encountered frequently is that brought by a tenant against his or her landlord. The items which should be considered when dictating a report about this type of claim include:

Coverage	Control (of locus)
Description of locus	Status
Date, time and place	S.S. Claimant (Name)
Description of accident	S.S. Tenant (Name)
Date tenancy began	S.S. Landlord (Name)
Description of rented premises	S.S. Witness (Name)
Details of tenancy	Liability
Lease	Recommendations

For the same reasons as were offered in respect to falldowns and products reports, this list should be closely adhered to. There follows a discussion of the subject matter to be offered under each of those items which are presented here for the first time.

State the date upon which *tenancy began*. State also the source of the adjuster's information. If there is any conflict, attempt to reconcile the conflict.

Ascertain and describe what the landlord did and did not rent to the tenant. In the case of borderline locations (a closet, for instance, in which the tenant was permitted to keep certain objects but physically removed from other premises), ascertain the facts, explain them, ascertain what each party says about them.

Leave theorizing to attorneys.

Explain requests made of the landlord and thought to bear on the subject of the claim, his responses, the obligations undertaken by him, and alleged oral modification of the terms of the lease or the usual landlord-tenant arrangement. Be factual.

CHAPTER 10

Miscellaneous Claims Problems

Many techniques are constant from one type of claim to another. Once a man learns how to write a good automobile statement, he needs only to learn the issues presented by a compensation claim to be able to write a good statement in that field. Medical is medical, and reporting—once one has grasped the idea of sufficiency and the techniques of clarity—is much the same, whether one is reporting on an automobile claim or a fidelity bond loss.

Some claims, however, present problems ("situations" or "issues" might be better words) peculiar to their class. Just as each challenge has its appropriate response, so there are special techniques for dealing with these situations.

In the sense of calling for specialized handling, the types of claim which have this quality of uniqueness include:

Automobile property damage claims
Death claims (automobile and general liability)
Fraud claims
Falldowns
Product claims
Owners, landlords and tenants claims

These claims will be discussed in the light of *their* challenges and the ways to meet them.

AUTOMOBILE PROPERTY DAMAGE CLAIMS

Automobile property damage claims call for their own approach in the following ways:

1. Unlike injury claims, they do not evoke emotions
2. In certain features of the laws that apply to them
3. In their several approaches to the question of measuring the amount of the damage
4. In a unique and very common claim for a type of consequential damage
5. And finally, in the infrequent involvement with simultaneous other insurance

Each of these features will be considered separately.

The Emotional Atmosphere

Sympathy, the emotional drive that makes it so difficult for a juror to let a badly injured claimant go uncompensated, is far less important in property damage claims than in injury claims. For this reason, in PD [1] litigation a defendant ordinarily receives a more sympathetic hearing on such a disputed point as contributory negligence than he is accustomed to receive when BI is at issue.

Some Legal Principles

Many jurisdictions follow what casualty claims offices commonly refer to as the "bailee rule." [2]

In its application this rule resembles the principle which deprives the defendant of the contributory negligence defense in respect to claims from claimant passengers. Where the rule is followed, the negligence of a claimant operator may not be argued as a defense against the claim of an absent owner unless there exists between the operator of a car and its owner some relationship which permits the negligence of the operator to be imputed to the owner. Upon entering a territory, it should be an early duty of the field man to ascertain the local holding in this regard.

---

[1] Just as "bodily injury" is frequently abbreviated to simply BI, so "property damage" is commonly expressed as "PD."

[2] The "bailee rule" is discussed in Chapter 2. It is suggested that that discussion be reread after this chapter's discussion of the application of the rule.

He should ascertain:

1. Whether negligence of an operator is imputed to an absent owner in the absence of agency or common enterprise, or whether mere possession is enough to accomplish this imputation.
2. The effect of the owner's presence in a car during its operation by another.

Where the bailee rule is followed, property damage claims of absent owners are usually considered open and shut liability claims and are settled as soon as possible. Where the bailee rule is followed it is common to find, too, an almost conclusive presumption that if the owner of the car was present in it at the time of the accident, the driver was the owner's agent, regardless of any factual testimony about the agency situation. In other words, actual physical presence of the owner frequently overcomes the "bailee rule."

Property damage claims raise two common questions. The first is quite prosaic: "Whose duty is it to protect this car from further damage"?

The second question often comes up by a claimant's aggressive assertion: "If you don't allow me a new fender (instead of straightening it) I'm going to rent a car and drive it at your expense till you see it my way." Each question finds its answer in a legal principle which may be stated simply, "It is the claimant's duty to minimize his loss.'"

Applying this principle to the first question supplies a prompt answer: It is the owner's duty to minimize his claim by protecting the property from further damage. Damage resulting from such failure to protect should be resisted. The cost of reasonable protection is an appropriate element in the claim. Although it is the owner's obligation to see that the property is protected, it is often necessary for an adjuster to encourage the owner to take proper steps. The adjuster should avoid taking steps to protect the property at the expense of his principal, and tact may be necessary in getting over to the owner the idea that the insurance company is not going to step into the owner's shoes and assume his duty.

The law will generally protect a defendant against the man who threatens to rent a replacement vehicle ad infinitum. Such a person's proper legal recourse, under the principle of minimization of damages, is to repair his car the way he wants it done—and then to sue to recover that which he considers to be a sum which will properly reimburse him.

The rule relative to minimization of damage works for the defendant whether the claim involves:

    a. a dispute over a proper method of repair;
    b. a dispute over the value of the damaged unit (in a total loss claim); or
    c. a damaged car whose owner is financially unable to repair it.

It should also be pointed out that while the rule may be (and usually is) "good law," the lower courts and small claims courts in which cases of this nature are tried are often loath to apply what they may regard as a harsh rule. Hence the conclusion that an adjuster who lets a case get to a crisis in respect to one of the above issues is already "in trouble." Good adjusting aims to prevent claims from reaching this kind of impasse.

DETERMINATION OF DIRECT DAMAGE

It often comes as a pleasant surprise to adjusters to discover that not only are there two approaches to the determination of the direct damage to an automobile, but that both approaches seem quite logical and practical. In contrast to what sometimes seems to be the illogic and guesswork of injury litigation, property damage may seem pleasantly rational.

The approaches to the determination of the value of a loss are: *Cost of repair* and *diminution of value*.

Cost of Repair

Most property damage claims are settled according to the cost of repair. To determine the cost of repair there are three principal techniques: *Appraisals, competitive estimates,* and *estimates, followed by adjuster's inspection* (or estimates written by the adjuster, if he is qualified).

Whichever technique he may elect to employ, an adjuster may become involved in subsidiary questions in respect to *depreciation, chrome items, doubtful causation* and *tow bills.*

Appraisals

Of the several methods of determining the cost to repair, appraisals are probably the most frequently employed. In many ways they are the most satisfactory to the problem. Appraisers operate in most sections of the country. These firms appraise principally damaged motor vehicles and, to a lesser degree, house trailers, dwellings, airplanes, etc.

Their employes usually have body shop experience or similar technical backgrounds. The usual method of operation consists of inspection of the vehicle, the expression of the appraiser's judgment in regard to such items as are not flat-rated (straightening of metal parts, etc.), reference to parts price manuals and flat rate manuals for the cost of parts and the cost of standard labor operations. Their report is in the form of an itemized statement of the cost to repair.

Appraisers are remunerated on a fee basis. Appraisal services have usually made prior arrangements with garages in their community to "back up" the appraiser's estimate, if necessary, by a willingness to repair on a "sight unseen" basis. The use of appraisers is an accurate and reliable means of ascertaining the cost to repair. There are, however, some drawbacks to their use.

The adjuster may have to guard against the tendency of an appraiser to see no farther than his immediate assignment. More than one serious bodily injury claim has been thrown into litigation by an appraiser insisting that a fender should be straightened rather than replaced. An adjuster may have to make it his business to learn whether his appraiser possesses tact and judgment.

Appraisers' duties do not include "adjusting" the claim or negotiating with the vehicle's owner. Some zealous appraisers overstep these proper bounds. The relationship between a garage and a car owner is often close. Statements to a garage owner or body shop proprietor are often tantamount to statements to the owner himself. An overly concerned owner may make it his business to be present when the appraiser is making his inspection. Therefore, if a claim involves both property damage and bodily injury, and adjustment of the property damage claim is likely to affect the injury adversely, the following practice may be adopted: The adjuster may instruct the appraiser to express no opinion in the presence of the garage or claiming party— simply to report in writing. Appraisers are technicians; they see problems in terms of things rather than in terms of people. Their natural tendency to be outspoken and to put all the cards on the table may make it hard for them to comply with these instructions. Thus, the adjuster may find it wise to be present at the inspection. He may then reserve firmly to himself the prerogative of deciding whether or not an issue is to be permitted to arise on a particular item. He may elect to waive appraisal entirely.

Competitive Estimates

Many evaluations are arrived at by competitive bidding. The principal advantages of this approach are economy and an occasional "bargain." There are pitfalls to be avoided.

Only where *real* competition exists can cost of repair be ascertained in this manner. Sometimes an outright bargain can be had without "short changing" the person whose property is damaged and is to be repaired. The key word is *competition*. Unfortunately, this is often nonexistent. It may be difficult, even when an adjuster is on the scene, to know whether supposedly competitive estimates are truly competitive.

Competition is often eliminated by furnishing what are known in the trade as "courtesy estimates," which work like this: The owner of the body shop points out to the owner of the damaged car that getting estimates is a time-consuming process and says, "Just leave the car with me—I'll take care of getting the other estimates." If the other garages then present estimates a little higher than the first, (and in the circumstances described, it may be taken granted that they will), these are referred to as "courtesy estimates."

It is unfair and incorrect to say that garages as a whole are collusive and dishonest; that is not so, but it is unrealistic to fail to recognize that a simple request for three estimates often produces something less than "no-holds-barred" competition.

Another drawback to this approach to damage is that, having gone to the trouble of picking up estimates, the owner is quite likely to be of the opinion that the insurer is morally obligated to accept *the lowest, which may still be far out of line.* This happens often.

If competitive bidding is to be employed, the adjuster should select the garages which are to compete and arrange for them to bid, rather than leaving it to the owner. It goes without saying that he should limit himself to competent shops. To insure real competition, he should consider a judicious mixture of dealerships and independent body shops. Personal knowledge of the town in which he operates is almost essential to the generation of real competition.

Adjuster's Inspection

Cost of repair may be determined by the estimate of a repairing garage *supplemented by an adjuster's inspection of the damaged unit.* This kind of checking imposes its own requirements. The soundness of its result is limited by the adjuster's technical knowledge. It is possibly the most common means of determining repair costs. Satisfactory determinations can be arrived at in this way.

Where possible, the adjuster prevails upon the insured to take his car to a shop of known reliability and reasonable cost. It is assumed that the adjuster has, in the exercise of his duties, acquainted himself with most of the shops in his area. If he has conducted himself properly in the past, he should have the confidence of the reliable ones. It is hoped that he has made it clear that he does not approach an estimate with the single-minded intent to reduce it, regardless of merit, in order to justify his activity. Garages quickly adjust to this self-defeating approach. They prepare for these adjusters in advance by building up the estimate so that the adjuster can have something to cut and thereby gratify his ego.

It is fatal for the adjuster to pretend to more knowledge than he has. Although he possesses reasonable knowledge of repair processes, he is not a technician in the field and he should recognize this. He must be as willing to recognize proper damage and cost factors as he is to question those which he thinks to be out of line.

Most damage is obvious, particularly after it has been pointed out. However, there will often be items that simply are beyond an adjuster's comprehension. This does not mean that he is helpless. His first move should be to ask the shop to point out the damage. He may ask that it be demonstrated to him by gauges or other means. He should avoid a challenging air. He may say frankly that he is unable to discern the damage, and he should indicate that he is willing to have it demonstrated to him and ask for help. The need for this kind of assistance grows less with experience, but only the rare adjuster reaches the state where he is not stumped on occasion.

The adjuster has other resources. He can call in a *competing shop* in whom he has confidence. He can call in an *appraiser*. If the questioned item lacks merit, the mere suggestion that one of the above techniques may be employed frequently leads the shop where the discussion is under way to concede the point.

Some differences between this technique and appraising should be emphasized. An appraiser starts with a damaged unit and, by inspecting it and applying his own experience, he forms an opinion of the proper cost of repair. Checking an estimate reverses the process. Having made the inspection, the repair agency has upon its shoulders the burden of ascertaining all of the necessary work. The adjuster's function is that of confirming these ascertainments and verifying the prices and costs.

An adjuster should never "authorize repairs," a prohibition which he will be wise to heed however he may have determined damage. Once he has agreed on the proper cost of repair, the adjuster should leave it to the owner to issue the order to repair. The adjuster should confine himself to the ascertainment of the proper money value of the damage, settle on that basis, and leave the repair to the garageman and his customer.

Failure to observe this precaution involves an adjuster in needless squabbles over the adequacy and skill of repair shops and may improperly obligate his employer or client.

Depreciation

Depreciation is an item that causes more trouble than it should. The practical rather than the legalistic approach goes a long way to keep the adjuster out of trouble.

Figuring depreciation means simply making an allowance for that portion of an object's useful life that has already been expended.

An unsophisticated laborer may have difficulty in grasping the idea that he has already enjoyed 75% of the useful life of the battery in his car. If a replacement battery is to cost him $16 he may resist violently and think he is being chiseled when the adjuster suggests that he can allow only $4 toward a new battery. He may have no difficulty at all, though, in recognizing that he is being treated reasonably when his garageman and adjuster together tell him that they propose to replace the damaged battery with a used one of like quality.

Most people, particularly businessmen, are aware of the theory of depreciation. An adjuster, nevertheless, is wise to approach the subject in this way: "You still had a quarter of its expected life to get from that battery; I will allow you $4," rather than to say, "I am going to charge $12 depreciation on this battery." This is an area in which an adjuster will pick up many helpful euphemisms; it will pay him to save them all for future use.

Almost without exception, depreciation is applied to tires, batteries, radiators and convertible tops. It is usually, but somewhat less frequently, applied to paint jobs, and seldom to sheet metal parts, hoods, fenders, etc.

What amounts to depreciation can be realized in respect to this last group of items by figuring repair on the basis of the employment of used parts. No unfairness to the owner is involved. If his car was five years old, every item on it was five years old. Used parts, however, should never be employed without the knowledge of the owner. The owner is entitled to insist that the parts employed be at least as good as those which were damaged. In actual practice, the adjuster and repairman usually see to it that used parts are somewhat better than the damaged ones. In figuring depreciation, the benefit of the doubt is invariably given to the owner.

Chrome Items

The usual car has anywhere from $75 to $300 worth of chrome on the front end alone. These items can be a real problem. Once a chrome item is damaged it may be almost impossible to repair it satisfactorily. To replace it is particularly galling when the damage is slight and the bumper may cost $100 or more. The adjuster has a number of alternatives:

1. He may offer a modest cash "defacement credit." (If this helps the insured to meet his deductible, it may be more than welcome.)
2. He can examine other areas of the bumper for similar damage predating the accident. (If a man has ignored chrome damage in one area, his position is inconsistent if he asks for replacement because of similar damage in another area. If the second damage causes the part to be considered a total loss, then it may be pointed out that the first damage had already rendered the bumper valueless. If an article's value is destroyed, it cannot diminish further in value.)
3. In many areas of the country, rechroming services are available. These concerns purchase damaged bumpers from salvage yards, straighten the metal and rechrome them. They may rechrome the damaged items itself. Experience indicates that the quality of the product is high. "Rechromes" are usually on the market at one-half the cost of a new chrome part.

Doubtful Causation (Property Damage Claims)

Although not so frequently an issue as is the case with injury claims, property damage claims may present problems revolving around damage the cause of which is obscure. A case in point is transmission damage. "My transmission never gave me any trouble before. Now just listen to that noise."

Even an automatic transmission will survive almost any collision unscathed, yet obviously there are times when the transmission *is* damaged.

The adjuster's best approach is the matter of fact, "I am ready to be shown." He should make obvious his position that, *if the facts support the claim, the claimant will not have to ask* for the transmission damage to be paid.

Where there is a question of doubt, it is often because all of the facts are not yet known. The transmission may indeed *not* function properly.[3] Until the unit is dismantled, however, it is difficult for the mechanic to know the real cause of the damage. Disassembling the unit may reveal a *worn* gear as the obvious cause of the malfunction. Disassembly may, on the other hand, discover a broken part, clearly the result of recent violence and presumably accidental. Finally, there is always that percentage of claims that never can be resolved. Again, the adjuster has alternatives:

1. He may resolve his doubt in favor of the claimant and agree that the claim should be paid. If the cost is modest and the adjustment otherwise satisfactory, this is often the best solution.
2. He can decline payment and risk litigation. If there is a collision insurer in the background, it will then step in and settle the claim, frequently being more inclined to accept the doubtful item as the price of satisfying its own customer. The subrogated collision insurer may then be willing to eliminate the questioned item from its subrogation claim as the price it knowingly paid to keep its customer happy.
3. Finally, the adjuster may inform the claimant that he will maintain an open mind but that it will be the claimant's duty to order the unit disassembled. *This should be done at the claimant's expense.* If disassembly discloses that the damage is accident-related, the adjuster may state his willingness to be

---

[3] Most transmission malfunctions are the result of damaged linkage or damaged motor mounts. Each of these is a minor item. Disassembly should never be seriously considered until the possibility of curing the complaint by attention to these items has been thoroughly exhausted.

The point here is not so much to make clear the *probabilities* relative to transmission damage as to point out that the adjuster's attitude should be open-minded (possibly more important, it should be *obvious* to the other parties that he is open-minded) and to emphasize that even technical points usually turn, in the end, on the presence or absence of physical conditions which a non-technical layman may affirm or refute, to his own satisfaction.

called back,[4] or may, if the garage is worthy of such trust, indicate that he will accept the repairman's findings.

The adjuster may compromise the matter while doubt
remains, but he should be careful about being the first to suggest
such an approach. Some people are prone to misread such
an offer as an attempt to "chisel."

Tow Bills

Reasonable tow bills are an acceptable part of a property
damage claim. In some areas, however, they are used as levers
to swing repair business to the shop operating the wrecker. An
outrageous tow bill may be charged if the vehicle is to be removed. This may, in aggravated cases, amount to nothing less
than holding the damaged vehicle for ransom. Although in some
cities law enforcement authorities are willing to exercise moral
pressure to bring an unreasonable tow bill into line. This is not
always so. If help from the law is not willingly forthcoming, the
adjuster had better realize that he is on his own to make the best
he can of a bad situation.

The adjuster's best defense against being placed in this pre-
dicament may not be what he does when he has a situation
staring him in the face, but what he has done in days past.
The owner of a damaged unit usually wants it repaired at whatever shop picked it up in the first place. If the adjuster has a
prior reputation for competence and reasonable fairness, his

---

[4] Many adjusters, mindful of the limitation of their technical knowledge, are
unduly reluctant to follow this technique. They fear that when the item is dismantled, they will still be unable to tell whether or not the condition disclosed is
accident-related. An adjuster who finds himself holding back because of this kind
of reluctance, would be well advised to plunge in and request disassembly, his
self-doubt notwithstanding. Unless his experience is quite out of the ordinary, he
will find that his fears have been mostly imaginary. Usually when the supposedly
damaged part is disassembled, it is quite obvious, even to a layman, whether its
malfunctioning is due to wear and tear, to accident-related damage, or to some
other cause.

The key to the successful handling of problems of this nature is to keep
them from becoming a contest of wills. If the adjuster makes it quite clear that
he is willing to allow the item if it *is* accident damage, he can usually persuade
a claimant to take a similarly objective view.

If disassembly still leaves an adjuster unable to satisfy himself as to the
cause of damage, then he may still elect to call in an appraiser or some other
technical person to resolve the doubt.

chances of agreement with the proprietor on the appropriate cost to repair are enhanced. It is better to come to a practical agreement, yielding a little bit to the owner and garage proprietor, than to let the matter degenerate into an outright dispute.

Diminution in Value

To be perfectly proper, the real measure of damage, even in a repair situation, is not the repair bill. It is the value of the unit before the occurrence, less its value afterward. In a less-than-total loss, diminution in value usually equals the cost of repair. Therefore, for adjustment purposes there is no harm in considering that repair cost is the real measure of damage. However, the value of the unit remains as a ceiling to limit the amount that may be properly allowed to repair. For example: Value before, $600; salvage value, $100; remainder, $500; estimated cost to repair, $550. This claim should be settled as a total loss. The damage is $500.

The value to be given to a damaged unit is a matter for judgment and often the subject of dispute. The NADA (National Automobile Dealers Association) Guide and the "Red Book" are available in all sections of the country. The adjuster should promptly acquaint himself with the use of these guides and with the significance of the retail and wholesale figures quoted. These publications enjoy no legal sanction. As his experience accumulates, the adjuster will come to respect them as reliable and realistic guides to the value of used automobiles. There can hardly be a better testimony to their realism than this: An adjuster seldom buys, sells or trades his own car without recourse to one or another of these publications.

A page from a typical issue of the NADA Guide is on page 380.

Cars decline constantly in value. Therefore, care must be taken that the guide book consulted is the book whose month of issue corresponds to the date of the loss.

A car in average condition should be classified according to the wholesale index. Argument that the prices quoted in local newspaper advertisements exceed even the retail quotations, as

This is a typical page from the N.A.D.A. Used Car Guide.[*]

4			1965-APRIL-1965					
Av'g. Wh'sle.	Ins. Sym.	BODY TYPE	Model	Fact. A.D.P.	Ship. Wgt.	Av'g. Retail	Av'g. Loan

BUICK

1964 BUICK Deluxe 4100 V6—continued

1690	J	Coupe 2D...............4127		$2457	2998	2025	1520
1935	J	Station Wagon 4D 2S.......4135		2787	3277	2330	1740
Skylark 4300-V6		Veh. Ident.: CK( )001001 Up.					
1855	J	Sedan 4D...............4369		$2659	3062	2210	1670
1905	J	Sport Coupe 2D...........4337		2680	3049	2270	1715
2025	J	Convertible..............4367		2834	3169	2410	1820
Standard 4000-V8		Veh. Ident.: OK( )001001 Up.					
1725	J	Sedan 4D...............4069		$2458	3016	2080	1550
1685	J	Coupe 2D...............4027		2414	2999	2030	1515
1910	J	Convertible..............4067		2676	3115	2295	1720
1940	J	Station Wagon 4D 2S.......4035		2760	3274	2325	1745
Deluxe 4100-V8		Veh. Ident.: 1K( )001001 Up.					
1800	J	Sedan 4D...............4169		$2561	3034	2150	1620
1780	J	Coupe 2D...............4127		2529	3014	2120	1600
2030	J	Station Wagon 4D 2S.......4135		2858	3293	2405	1825
Skylark 4200-V8		Veh. Ident.: 3K( )001001 Up.					
2165	L	Station Wagon Sport 3S.....4265		$3124	3689	2555	1950
2080	K	Station Wagon Sport 2S.....4255		2989	3557	2475	1870
Skylark 4300-V8		Veh. Ident.: 3K( )001001 Up.					
1950	J	Sedan 4D...............4369		$2740	3078	2315	1755
2035	J	Sport Coupe 2D...........4337		2751	3065	2425	1830
2115	J	Convertible..............4367		2905	3185	2505	1905
2290	L	Station Wagon Sport 3S.....4365		3286	3727	2685	2060
2190	L	Station Wagon Sport 2S.....4355		3161	3595	2585	1970
65		Add Power Steering......................$		97	28	80	60
110		Add Air Conditioning.....................		351	109	140	100
15		Add 300 Cu.in. 4 Bbl.....................		22		20	15
120		Deduct Std. Trans........................				150	110

YEAR ID'N: Grille

WILDCAT 4600　W.B. 123". Tires 7.60x15.　Veh. Ident.: 6K( )001001 Up.

2340	L	Sedan 4D...............4669		$3164	4021	2785	2105
2490	L	Hardtop Sedan 4D.........4639		3327	4058	2955	2240
2475	L	Hardtop Sport Coupe 2D....4647		3267	4003	2925	2225
2705	L	Convertible 2D............4667		3455	4076	3195	2435

YEAR ID'N: Grille
LE SABRE: As shown
ELECTRA: Four ventiports, massive chrome panel along bottom side

LE SABRE 4400　W.B. 123". Tires 7.10x15.　Veh. Ident.: 4K( )001001 Up.

2210	K	Sedan 4D...............4469		$2980	3693	2655	1990
2330	K	Hardtop Sedan 4D.........4439		3122	3730	2805	2095
2320	K	Hardtop Sport Coupe 2D....4447		3061	3629	2790	2090
2440	L	Convertible 2D............4467		3314	3787	2910	2195

PLEASE READ NOTE ON INSIDE FRONT COVER

[*] Reproduced with the permission of the publisher, National Automobile Dealers Used Car Guide Company, Washington, D. C.

they invariably will, may be countered with the explanation that advertised prices include selling expense, the repair of minor bumps, scratches, etc., cleaning, and often the mechanical work necessarily precedent to the furnishing of a limited warranty. It may also be explained that the "on the lot" price usually has been inflated to allow for an inflated trade-in allowance.

The claimant may invite the adjuster, "All right, you just get me one at your price."

There are at least two ways to meet this challenge. The adjuster may explain that the insurance company is in the insurance business—not the car business. (This must not be done defiantly. It does no good to inflame the claimant.) The adjuster then restates his cash offer and makes it plain that this is his final figure. Alternatively, he may elect to "shop the market." This technique is relatively involved, and before continuing with the general problem of dealing with and reporting diminution of value, it deserves explanation.

Shopping the Market

To shop the market, an adjuster must determine with maximum accuracy the exact unit that he proposes to replace, and he must have access to dealers who will quote him (and make available to the prospective purchaser) vehicles at the same price as they would sell to other dealers.

The adjuster begins by seeing to it that he has a complete and adequate description of the unit to be replaced. This means, of course, that the year and model must be identical, and either that the equipment be identical or that due allowance for differences be made. The car's relative condition, "cream-puff," "average" or "dog," should be determined and reported realistically to the dealers who are asked to quote.

Armed with this information, the adjuster then phones his dealers, taking care that he talks with the dealer direct (rather than the salesman—so that no salesman's commission need be figured), and procures from at least three dealers quotations to replace the damaged unit with an identical unit (or a similar unit, with due allowance for differences in equipment). Quotations should be secured on the basis of a "clean deal" (i.e., no trade-in). Provided that the prices thus secured are legitimate dealers' prices, the average of the quotations thus received may be taken as a fairly established "market value." This technique suppresses injustices which stem from the inability of "the book" to recognize special and possibly temporary market preferences.

An inexperienced adjuster, shopping the market, can waste a lot of time and can wind up with quotations no different from advertised prices.

It will pay a young adjuster, the first few times he applies this technique, to secure informal advice from a physical damage specialist such as the adjusters working with automobile finance companies. Not only do these men use these techniques skillfully—they have connections from whom wholesale quotations, which this technique demands, can be readily procured.

Another pitfall is that some claimants have no real interest in ascertaining market value. All they want is "more." These folks are likely to go to the quoting dealers, reject every car offered for trifling reasons (with a used car, one can always find some grounds for differentiating the substitute from the damaged unit), and so the adjuster may involve himself in a fruitless effort to find a car which "satisfies" the claimant.

Publications similar in purpose to the NADA guide and the Red Book are available for house trailers and, to a limited degree, outboard boats and motors. There is a lesser market for trucks than for cars. Book figures on trucks, therefore, are not so reliable as for passenger vehicles.

In dealing with prospective total losses, the adjuster should as promptly as possible post his file and advise his examiners with pertinent information from one of the standard guides for his locality. A photostat of a pertinent page from the guide will be appreciated both by examiners and by defense counsel should the matter wind up in a law suit years hence.

If the damaged unit is owned by a claimant accustomed to trading for a different car at regular intervals, realistic settlements can often be arrived at by what is, in effect, a depreciation technique. To do this, the adjuster may ascertain the price commonly paid by the claimant to "trade up" to a new car. This is then reduced to a "per annum" or "per month" figure. The cash price of a new unit of the same model on what is known as a "clean deal" (no trade-in) is then ascertained. For the last several years almost all American cars have been available on a "clean deal" basis for from $100 to $200 above dealer's cost. The cost of a "clean deal" replacement, less the per month cost to trade up to a new car, is often compatible with "book" figures at the wholesale level. The fairness of this method is obvious; on the whole it is an exceptionally satisfactory method of approaching total loss claims. It may require a claimant somewhat above the average in intelligence, but fortunately most of those who drive one, two and three year old cars fall into the upper intelligence levels.

Consequential Damage (Loss of Use)

In addition to the cost of repair (direct damage), the owner of damaged property is entitled to claim as part of his loss the added expense to which he may have been put in providing himself with *necessary* replacement facilities while the damaged unit is out of us. This type of claim is not limited to the automobile claim field but may be encountered when any piece of property is the subject of a legal liability claim. The discussion here will be limited to automobiles, but the recommended handling can be extended to corresponding action in respect to claims for other kinds of property. A claim for this type of loss is known as "consequential damage" because it is said to be a consequence of the direct damage to the property in question. In liability claim adjusting these are commonly referred to as "loss of use" claims.

Treatment of "loss of use" varies widely from company to company and from area to area. The following generalities are fairly universal. The claimant's obligation to minimize his damages, referred to earlier in this chapter, applies to all aspects of claims of this nature. In other words, merely because his car is laid up, a salesman is not licensed to stay at home and claim lost earning capacity until his car is repaired. He is expected to provide himself with a replacement vehicle and maintain his earnings. The claim must be based on *actual need to use, not mere inconvenience.* The measure of his loss in providing himself with the replacement vehicle is limited to the sum by which the cost of operating the replacement vehicle exceeds the cost he would have incurred in operating his own car. Courts will usually decline to make an award in reimbursement of the cost of a replacement for a period of time greater than that reasonably necessary to make repairs. The time that a car is laid up while a dispute regarding its cost of repair is ironed out is not regarded as recoverable.

Loss of use should not be allowed on "total loss" claims. (One can do no more than $10 worth of damage to a $10 bill.) If an item is so damaged as to be a total loss, the total amount that can be recovered is the value of the item before the damage, less salvage. The fallacy of permitting further recovery should be obvious, but adjusters frequently overlook it.

Adjusters may be asked to "authorize" the rental of a replacement car or even to guarantee the invoice of a rental agency.

Some insurers now permit this practice on the part of their representatives. The motive is usually the maintenance of good will and direct negotiation with a BI claimant. This is a risky tactic. Its risk is testified to by the adjusters who have found claimants unwilling to return a rental car until a "whiplash" is adjusted to their pleasure. Rental units should *never* be authorized except with the *express* permission or in conformity with the *stated policy* of the insurer involved.

With most adjusting problems the real solution lies in a practical rather than a legalistic approach, and "loss of use" is no exception. Many repair shops keep a number of cars around as "loaners." These are not necessarily the newest cars on the road. They are kept in reasonable operating condition. If Shop A is unwilling to provide a loaner, the situation can often be controlled by pointing out that Shop B would be glad to do the job at the same price and provide a replacement vehicle.

The adjuster should explain to the claimant that while "loss of use" is an element of his claim, a replacement vehicle must be procured at the claimant's expense and that his claim for this expense will be treated according to its merits when final settlement is discussed.

Property Damage Claims Involving Simultaneous First Party Coverage

The owners of damaged cars often have an election to make, whether to attempt to collect their damage from the liability insurer of the car with which they collided or whether to make a claim under their own collision coverage. (Owners of other types of property may have a similar election when *their* property is damaged under such circumstances as to create a potential liability claim.) Adjusters representing liability insurance companies have a corresponding election, an election which is usually made for the adjuster by the policy of his company. Some liability insurers generally decline to settle claims for property damage when the damaged property is covered by direct damage insurance (in the automobile field the direct insurance is, of course, the familiar collision coverage), preferring to let the direct insurer make its settlement—and then to deal with the direct insurer under the latter's subrogation rights. Other insurance companies, feeling that holding back unnecessarily complicates an otherwise simple claim, prefer to have their adjusters step in and make an immediate settlement without requiring the claimant to make his claim against his own direct carrier. Most insurers approach the problem on an "ad hoc" basis, stepping in immediately to make settlement when liability is obvious, and becoming reluctant to do so when liability is questionable.

Liability adjusters frequently make settlement with third party claimants on the basis of their injuries plus payment for the deductible but, by appropriate notation on the release, reserve to the subrogated collision insurer the right to assert *its* claim at a later time. This technique is particularly helpful when there are a number of passengers in the claimant car whose claims may clearly call for settlement, even when there may be a legitimate liability question regarding the claim of the owner-operator.

If the amount is large and if he has reason to suspect that the plaintiff-claimant had direct first party coverage, the liability adjuster must take this into account. Before settling directly with the claimant, he should take reasonable steps to ascertain that settlement has not already been made by the direct damage insurer. (The direct damage insurer, of course, is obliged to put the liability insurance company "on notice" of its possible subrogated rights.)

The availability to a liability claimant of simultaneous direct damage insurance may offer a distinct advantage to the liability adjuster. This is especially true if the property dealt with is not commonly handled by the liability adjuster. For example, an insured vehicle may strike a building, damaging the structure and putting its occupant out of business for some time, with resultant loss of revenue. Few liability adjusters are properly equipped to cope with structural damage, and fewer still are equipped with the knowledge of accounting techniques to enable them to determine the loss of revenue while the conduct of the business is interrupted. Neither problem is uncommon to direct damage insurers.

Many property insurance adjusters, particularly the senior men, are highly skilled in making determinations of this character. Therefore, even in the face of obvious liability, it may be desirable for the liability adjuster to rely on the adjuster for the property insurer to adjust structural damage and business interruption, relying on the latter's skill to hold the loss within reasonable bounds. Agreements with direct damage adjusters, however, should be entered into carefully. The first party adjuster and his client should never be led to expect that whatever they pay in loss will unquestionably be reimbursed to them. This may lead to loose adjusting, with the liability insurer left to pick up the chips.

Until he has had several such situations to cope with and knows the personalities with whom he is dealing, the field adjuster should look to his manager and supervisor for guidance.

Adjusting Techniques

The wise adjuster cultivates the support of and builds his reputation in honest and competent repair shops in his area. He may even dispense with an inspection if he knows a shop to be competent and honorable. This expedient may be employed, of course, only when it is consistent with the practices of the insurer involved. Independent adjusters should be particularly careful that, if adopted, this practice is not inconsistent with the instructions of their clients. In any event, an adjuster seldom waives inspection unless the amount is small, and never *unless he can and does report openly to his principal exactly what he has done and what he has not done.*

Photographs, usually by Polaroid or Brownie or the like, are helpful in enabling an adjuster to acquaint his principal with the true condition of the damaged unit. They may assist him in reducing his clerical burden, for one photograph may be worth several dictated pages of explanation.

Many owners of damaged cars are on the defensive and body shops are preoccupied with meeting payroll and overhead. If he approaches every estimate with a chip on his shoulder, the adjuster will find the trouble he is looking for. On the other hand, an experienced man making his first visit to a strange body shop frequently demonstrates his good faith by pointing out an overlooked item. This may seem "corny" but it works, having nothing but a beneficial effect on the body man's spirit of cooperation and the owner's willingness to be reasonable. Questions are raised courteously, considerately and with open recognition that, given the chance to explain himself, the repairman may have a perfectly sound reason for what may have seemed initially somewhat out of line.

DEATH CLAIMS

Many people live out their spans without ever sustaining a fracture, backstrain or any of the other common forms of accidental injury. *No one may hope to avoid the universal experience of death.* Viewed in this light, *the real loss in death claims is not the fact of death—but the premature end of a life.* In theory, these two thoughts underlie most of the thinking, legislative and judicial, on the subject of death claims.

Every state has enacted a wrongful death statute. Depending upon the jurisdiction, these statutes provide that a person's estate, surviving spouse, dependent children, or dependent parents may recover damages for his death caused by the negligent acts of others. These statutes and their interpretations vary considerably from jurisdiction to jurisdiction and each adjuster should familiarize himself with the statute of his particular jurisdiction.

Although the allowable damages vary considerably from state to state, as a general rule the amount awarded as damages in a death action depends upon those factors which determine the pecuniary loss to the beneficiaries. Some of the elements which control the amount of this loss include the life expectancy of the deceased, his earning capacity, the number and life expectancy of beneficiaries, the relationship of beneficiaries to the deceased, and the obligation and practice of the deceased in contributing to these beneficiaries. Many jurisdictions include, as a part of the award, an allowance for certain expenses and other damages which were recoverable prior to the death and which arose directly from the negligent acts of the defendant.

Some legislation has taken a mechanistic approach and has established arbitrary standards for the evaluation of death claims or has limited the awards for wrongful death.

Since there is a great diversity in the provisions of these several laws, no attempt will be made here to deal with the specific features of this legislation. Instead, discussion will confine itself to features of death claims reasonably common to all jursidictions. This section should be read in conjunction with the legislation and decisions in one's own jurisdiction relative to death claims.

In reading the statute of one's own state, attention should be particularly directed to its provisions as to those survivors *to whom a right of action may pass.* This seemingly technical feature is of very substantial practical importance because it happens frequently that adjusters, overwhelmed by an assured's having caused the loss of a life, have paid more than a premium price for the settlement of a death claim which, when carefully analyzed, would have had little, if any, value.

Since death claims present problems differing in kind as well as degree from the more common injury situations, an investigation check list follows. This list should be employed in the light of the legislative enactments of the jurisdiction involved.

1. Procure death certificate. (Most states furnish two forms of death certificate—a "short" form and a "long" form. The latter is sometimes referred to as the "death return." The long form usually has information as to the cause of death and contributing factors. The long form is preferred, and the insurance company's file should be supplied with a certified copy.)
2. Determine the age of the deceased and his life expectancy.[5]
3. Determine the earning capacity of the deceased.
4. Find out who was *dependent* on the deceased, and to what extent in terms of weekly or monthly contributions.
5. Estimate conscious pain and suffering.
6. Establish whether deceased died testate (i.e., left a will), or intestate (i.e., left no will). Identify executor or administrator.

The paragraphs to follow will make clear why this type of information is called for, discuss how it may be obtained and consider the unusual emotional climate of death claims—and how that climate affects adjusting.

Earning Capacity of Deceased and Expectancy of Survivors

The sum which an heir might have received from the deceased during his lifetime, as support perhaps (as a wife receives her support from her husband) is usually similarly considered as "damage." Life expectancy of the deceased is an obvious factor; the expectancy of the *survivor,* might be a less obvious point. To illustrate: The death of a breadwinner in his middle 30s is usually a more costly claim than that of a man about to retire— this is not hard to see. What may be less clear is that the death of a man in his 50s may be one thing if his dependent survivor is a wife of the same age with an expectancy of 20 years. The death of the same man would be quite another story in damages if he is a bachelor, his only survivor a widowed mother of 80; and the value might be still less if the mother suffers from a cancer and has a life expectancy of six months.

Ascertainment of the prospective earnings of the deceased is a matter of determining earning capacity, and it is the same as the checking of lost earning capacity in injury claims. Determina-

---

[5] To spare examiners and managers repetition of this labor, an adjuster's findings from expectancy tables should be promptly dictated to file.

tion of the deceased's prospective *ability to save* and the *value of his support to his dependents* involves an examination of the deceased's mode of life and his living, spending and saving habits during his lifetime. The best sources of information on those subjects are the survivors. If, of these, the law has designated one as the chief heir at law (usually a spouse), it will usually be found that the desired information, and access to the records from which such information may be derived, resides in that person. An early statement, along with written permission to examine records, should be secured.

Pain and Suffering

In death claims the investigation of pain and suffering involves features not met elsewhere. Many jurisdictions, it has been pointed out, place an arbitrary value or arbitrary limit on death claims. However, recovery for pain is a property right—a separate legal entity from the award for wrongful death itself—and is in addition to the award for death. It appears that in many situations, where the death statutes impose a limitation on recovery for wrongful death and a jury is desirous of granting a greater sum than the statute permits, the presence of *conscious* pain and suffering is seized upon as an excuse to award a sum which might otherwise have been given for the death itself.

Some jurisdictions have held that the smallest sign of consciousness—a sigh, a moan, a grimace—is evidence on which a jury may conclude that some degree of consciousness obtained. Once the evidence of consciousness, however small, is before the jury, courts are loath to interfere with the jury's evaluation of the suffering which the jury feels that the dying person was undergoing. The door to sizable awards has been opened by this device. The investigative duty that this possibility imposes should be obvious.

Testimony of those who may not be witnesses to the accident itself but who came to the scene later attains an uncommon importance in this class of case.

In addition to those whom chance may have drawn, the usual attendants upon the scene of the fatality include at least the police, wrecker operators, ambulance drivers and attendants.

Oddly enough, investigative problems of this nature occur in what might be termed a "middle range" of cases. Where the victim obviously lived, suffered and then expired, the question of whether or not he suffered is not at issue. It has to be conceded. Where, on the other hand, the victim was mercifully, undeniably and instantaneously killed, there is still nothing to investigate. Investigation of this type concerns itself with people who may or may not have died instantaneously, and of those who lingered briefly and then expired. It concerns itself with the question of the moment of death, whether or not signs of consciousness were evidenced; if there were no signs, it becomes the adjuster's duty to put himself in the position to *demonstrate* by testimony that there was no sign. (This again is the troublesome problem of proving a negative, which has been discussed at some length in the chapter on Statements.)

Promptness is more than usually important. An ambulance attendant seen in the first few days post-accident can recall whether his patient spoke, opened his eyes, etc., on the way to the hospital. Unless his testimony is preserved by recording it in statement form, he will almost surely have forgotten in a month. If there were signs, it is the adjuster's duty to ascertain what they were, their duration and their nature. The conclusions to be drawn from the signs are still a question of fact for the jury.

Young adjusters should be cautioned that the mere utterance of a sigh does not automatically confer astronomical or even substantial value upon the factor of conscious pain and suffering. It is equally possible for a jury to conclude that a patient's shock was so deep that he did not, in fact, know he was in pain, and to decline to make any award for this item.

Evidence and legal fine points notwithstanding, a jury's subjective view of what it wants to award is probably the controlling factor. Arbitrary legal limitations may control a jury's desires. Earnings and anticipated value to the estate, testimony on suffering and other concepts, will be influential or disregarded according to the mood of the day, the skill of the attorneys and sometimes outright caprice.

At the risk of tiresome repetition, the question of varying interpretations from jurisdiction to jurisdiction must be emphasized. It should also be clear that the foregoing paragraphs refer to *investigation* rather than *evaluation* and *settlement*. From an investigational standpoint the adjuster will occasionally do some unnecessary work, but on the whole be on the safe side if he conforms to the practice recommended in these paragraphs. Unless he knows that in his jurisdiction such a claim would not be allowed, he should always investigate borderline pain and suffering cases, but he should be cautious in assigning a dollar value to that feature of the claim until he has had competent advice or training in respect to the holdings of his jurisdiction.

Emotional Climate of Death Claims

It is not only in investigation that death claims present unusual aspects. While severe injuries may, in truth, be shocking tragedies, they are usually dealt with in an atmosphere of relative calm, compared to the tearing grief of the survivors which often characterizes a death claim. An adjuster is heartless, inhuman, and deserves the condemnation he will receive if he fails to recognize this. This factor governs his most pedestrian activities in handling a death claim. He may call promptly on survivors (not necessarily waiting until after the funeral), *but his manner must acknowledge* the unusual circumstances that prevail. In other than death claims, he usually makes a forthright approach, assuming that the parties are ready to proceed promptly to a discussion of the business at hand with no more than the common pleasantries about the weather which enable the parties to be at ease. This is the way the public expects to be approached. In death claims, on the other hand, a less casual approach is the order of the day.

Now an adjuster's manner should be deferential in the extreme (literally hat in hand). *Good manners dictate that which is also good tactics.* He will ask if he may come in for the purpose of presenting himself, to express his and his principal's sympathy, and to ascertain when it will be convenient to the survivors to meet him further. The restrained sympathy of one who acknowledges himself to be an outsider and who, therefore, defers to the personal grief of the survivors, keys the correct approach. To what may be his surprise, the adjuster will be invited in more often than not. Many survivors welcome the opportunity to discuss business as a relief from their emotional stress.

Mechanics of Settlement

Laws vary from jurisdiction to jurisdiction as to who has a right to make a claim in the event of wrongful death. Consequently, the persons from whom releases are sought are determined by the law prevailing in the jurisdiction. Home office legal departments are prepared to give prompt advice as to who may execute releases.

Investigation should routinely:

1. Disclose the presence or absence of a will.
2. Identify the next of kin.
3. Disclose whether an executor or administrator has been appointed.

So that the mechanism of settlement may be carried out, it is important to determine if the deceased left a will. If he did, he is said to have died "testate." One who does not leave a will is said to have died "intestate."

A will appoints a person whose duty it is to wind up the financial affairs of the deceased. He is known as executor—or executrix if female. This job must still be done for one who dies intestate. The person who then performs this function is known as an administrator (administratrix if female). Administrators are court appointed, usually upon the application of a relative of the deceased. If he is operating in a remote area and without recourse to expert advice, to be on the safe side the adjuster should have the release executed by the executor (or administrator) and all members of the immediate family. Many states *require* court approval of releases signed by executors or administrators. A phone call to the nearest county seat should clear up this question.

FRAUDULENT CLAIMS

Fraudulent claims means claims characterized by outright dishonesty, rather than exaggeration, malingering and distortion. The line is admittedly thin, not easy to see, and perhaps unrealistic. Nevertheless actual, downright, honest to goodness frauds (the staged accident, the passenger who wasn't there, the fracture sold and resold) are rare birds. Adjusters with a quarter of a century of experience often agree that they have never knowingly had personal experience with outright fraud. Adjusters who recognize as many as half a dozen in a lifetime are a minority.

Possibly the only thing to be said in favor of fraudulent claims is that they are possibly the one subject upon which the insurance business is in virtually unanimous agreement. Even those insurers which openly state that they will pay "nuisance claims" resist fraudulent claims to the utmost and summarily reject any thought of compromising, no matter how attractive the figure. The attitude of universal resistance that prevails is thoroughly justified. Not only is the fraudulent claimant an outright thief, he is a deliberate insult to claimants who are decent, reasonable and forbearing. The zeal with which he will resist frauds should not confuse the adjuster about the real problem, which is exaggeration and misrepresentation.

Fraudulent claims are frequently uncovered by an organization known as the Index Bureau. Subscribed to by most insurers, this is a central clearing-house to which all claims, falling within certain categories, are reported. Claimants are cross-indexed by name, location, mode of operation, etc. When the Index Bureau's files indicate that a certain claimant has "sold" the same broken arm in three or four cases, the insurance companies interested are notified immediately. This brings to bear on the claimant's current activities all of his past history.

Some companies place on field personnel the responsibility to report to the Index Bureau. In other organizations it is a home office function. The adjuster should be aware of the Index Bureau, with at least a summary knowledge of its functions. It goes without saying that he should give the Bureau's representatives his wholehearted cooperation in any requests made of him.

The making of a fraudulent claim is an attempt at larceny. Usually there are violations of several specific statutes. If the mails have been employed, a federal offense may have been committed. Therefore, a fraud claim must be investigated with the idea that criminal as well as civil action may eventuate. The adjuster should, at the earliest possible moment, coordinate his activities with whatever official body may be involved in the prosecution. He should be prepared to step aside in favor of "the authorities." He should be careful to undertake no operations that such authorities may prefer to perform themselves. The possibility that a crime may have been committed now influences almost every aspect of the adjuster's work. Particularly is this true of settlement negotiations. A frightened claimant may try to make a deal, "If I drop my claim, will you call off the prosecution?" Such an offer is *not* for the adjuster to deal with. Punishment of crime involves *all* citizens, not just the adjuster and his principal. To call off the prosecution is, therefore, the exclusive prerogative of law enforcement authorities. For this reason, and for the further reason that an agreement to forbear may in itself be a crime (this is known as compounding a felony), the adjuster should invite no such proposals. If any are made to him, he should refer them to "the law." At this point the matter is out of his hands.

There follows a list of certain things which may serve as tip-offs to the "fraudulent" claim:

1. The blind accident. (This means an accident which has occurred under such circumstances that there is no witness nor is there any possibility of a witness being able to say that the accident did not occur.)
2. The too-perfect story. This always bears careful scrutiny.
3. Important witnesses closely related to the claimant by blood or other ties.
4. Kinship or close friendship between the claimant and the insured.
5. History as a "repeater" reported either by the Index Bureau or by neighborhood reputation.
6. Anxiety for a quick settlement disproportionate to the apparent real value of the claim.
7. Refusal to submit to examination. The usual claimant, not represented by counsel, offers no objection to being examined. Refusal to submit to examination justifies raising a thoughtful eyebrow.[6]

---

[6] It should be recognized that many plaintiff's attorneys decline to permit their clients to be examined. This is simply a matter of tactics. Exaggeration or build-up may be in the wind. While these tactics may be deplored, they must, as a practical matter, be distinguished from outright fraud. If insurance companies were to tab as "fraudulent," and resist accordingly, every claim where plaintiff's counsel delayed or refused examination, there would soon be such a backlog of lawsuits that all the courts in the land would be unable to clear the backlog in the next 20 years.

When fraud is suspected, one of the best ways to deal with it is to slow down—wait to get medical information, talk to the doctor, request an independent examination, and stall the settlement. The "pros" usually do not employ lawyers, and fade away if they cannot make a quick settlement. In the meantime, check with police, other claims men locally, the Index Bureau and the Casualty Claims Bureau. Check out all addresses and alleged employers.

Fraud in Reverse—No Knowledge Claims

An interesting twist to the fraud question is the claim in which the insured "didn't know anything happened," "wasn't there," or claims that "the accident never took place." These are lumped under the term "no knowledge" claims. Adjusters are skeptical about these stories—with reason. The usual outcome is that the insured in the end admits that his story has been a lie. In the meantime, a claim that might have been settled has gone to litigation.

Adjusters are warranted in approaching these claims overtly expecting that the insured's story will turn out in the end to be a "cock and bull story." Rarely, however, will an assured break down under questioning. One technique is to press the question vigorously, pointing out that the truth always comes out in the end, and that a present admission will be easier than one wrung from him in the court house. He should keep up the pressure long enough for fatigue to set in, then relax, appear to accept the story, and turn the conversation to other channels. Then, upon rising to leave, the adjuster may ask again, in an almost confidential tone, "Now, isn't it true that you did hit him?" This has been known to produce immediate capitulation.

Another technique, which gives more dignity to the insured, is to take a *sworn* statement from him, reciting that any other version would be false. This may be supplemented by a separate agreement, also in writing, reciting that if the assured should thereafter change his testimony, or if it is adjudicated that his testimony is false, he understands and consents that the company shall be relieved of any obligation under the policy. A willingness to execute these documents indicates that the insured is probably honest.

No-knowledge claims often involve criminal complaints against the insured, since a charge of "leaving the scene" may have been made against him. If the adjuster has the claimant's confidence and hopes to maintain "control" of the claim, an effort may be made to persuade the claimant that the pending criminal procedures ought to produce a clear-cut answer concerning the insured's involvement. The truth is that the criminal proceedings usually do produce a clear-cut answer, not infrequently in the form of an open court breakdown and confession. Following this, the adjuster may proceed with the claim on its merits.

It goes without saying that insureds who thus evade their responsibilities are as false to the business whose duty it is to defend them as they are unfair to the injured party.

Although most no-knowledge claims turn out in the end to involve untruthfulness on the part of the insured, the possibility that an insured may have been telling the truth can hardly be discarded entirely. If he is telling the truth, he deserves a *vigorous* defense by his insurance company and his adjuster. Therefore, whether the end result is to be the vindication of the insured or the discharge of a reasonable obligation to an injured claimant, an adjuster is thoroughly justified in leaving no stone unturned to ascertain the truth in these perplexing claims.

FALLDOWN CLAIMS

"Falldowns" are considered here as claims for injuries allegedly the result of falls in premises where commercial operations, retail in nature, are being conducted. This purely arbitrary interpretation is made to avoid the complications which would be introduced by a discussion of the legal complications encountered in the investigation of falls (and other accidents) on private premises or on premises other than those where the common relationship of storekeeper to customer prevails between insured and claimant. Admittedly, the term "falldown" is redundant, but it is common to the claims business, possibly a little more common than "slip-and-fall," another term by which these claims are often

described. Adjusters should be familiar with both. An outstanding characteristic of falldowns is that almost all claimants in this type of claim are women.[7] This is so to the extent that it is common practice in claims offices to speak of the generalized falldown claimant as "she." That practice will be followed in this section.

Sidewalk falls will also be discussed in this section—not that the theory which underlies them bears any particular relationship to falls in commercial establishments but because adjusters are usually introduced to that type of claim at about the same time in their careers as they encounter store falldowns.

In many respects, the investigation of falldown claims repeats what has already been discussed in respect to the handling of automobile claims. Statements should be complete, objective, and the adjuster should try always to write a statement with such care and precision that its reading permits no interpretation except that which the maker of the statement intends to convey.

The handling of problems centering about the gathering of medical information is the same as in automobile claims.

Claims of this type will be discussed from the following standpoints: (1) the legal basis of falldown claims; (2) modification of conventional adjusting techniques (by the legal and social climate surrounding falldowns); (3) investigational aspects of falldown claims.

Legal Basis

The claimant's right to recover damages from an insured derives, as does the right of the claimant in an automobile liability claim, from the three elements of a tort discussed in Chapter 2, *duty owed, breach of the duty* and *resultant damage.* Investigation of falldowns differs from automobile work in two important respects. First, it emphasizes the concept of "duty

---

[7] The author's experience has included times when he handled nothing but falldowns and in 29 years he has always been exposed to large numbers of claims of this type. Of claims which may number in the thousands, he recalls only two men who fell. Another characteristic of falldowns is that of falls on stairs, the victim seems always to be going *down.* To add to this strangeness, one of the two male falldown claimants referred to, fell going upstairs—the *only* claimant whom the author recalls who fell on the way *up.*

owed." Secondly, in respect to falldowns emphasis more often shifts from argument about fact to argument about law. For instance, in automobile work, the facts more often than not are in dispute. Litigation turns less on matters of legal interpretation than on the question of whose version of the facts will prevail. Falldown claims reverse this picture. More often than not there is little dispute about the facts of the occurrence; dispute, if any, is likely to center about the legal significance of what everyone agrees took place.

What are known as "law defenses" [8] are more often available, and more frequently insurers take a hard and fast "no liability" position.

Since the law is the theoretical framework on which the facts of investigation are arranged, to understand their significance the law will be considered in these aspects: *status, acts of commission, acts of omission,* and *sidewalk falls.*

Status

The question of status is basic to all liability investigation. (Actually, it is a factor in automobile claims but is usually disregarded as an item of investigation, since the duty owed by one motorist to another so seldom varies.) The question arises from one of the elements of a tort, "a duty owed." In order to ascertain the duty owed by one party to another it is necessary to ascertain their relationships one to the other.

When a person controls property, other people may happen to come upon it. He owes them varying duties, depending on their purpose in being there. This purpose is what determines their status. To simplify they may be divided into three classes: *invitees, licensees,* and *trespassers.*

Invitees are those who come on the property by reason of an express or implied invitation for the purpose of transacting business by which the controller of the property expects or hopes to profit. A person coming into a store to make a purchase is an in-

---

[8] This term is a colloquialism of the claims business. Without getting into an involved discussion of "question of fact" versus "questions of law," it may be said that a claims man in speaking of a "law defense" means a case whose facts are such that the presiding judge may reasonably be expected to forbid the submission of the case to the jury by "directing" a verdict for the defendant.

vitee; a salesman entering a store hoping to make a sale to the proprietor is likewise an invitee. The benefit to the controller of the property need not be pecuniary. Social invitees are distinguished from business invitees. Therefore, when a store proprietor sees his neighbor passing by and invites him in for a cup of coffee in the back room to review the political situation, the duty owed the invited one may be less than if he entered for the purpose of transacting business. Many people enter stores for purposes other than trade. Possibly the most common such purpose is to use restrooms. These visitors are not invitees.

The duty owed invitees is to use ordinary care to keep the premises in a reasonably safe condition. The words "ordinary" and "reasonably" apply to the standards employed by the reasonably prudent man in similar circumstances.

Licensees are those whom the controller of the property does not forbid but whom he permits on his property (people coming in to use the restroom). The controller of a property has no hope of gain, pecuniary or otherwise. Most jurisdictions class social invitees as licensees. In most jurisdictions, the duty owed the licensee is only that of refraining from gross negligence.

Trespassers are those whom the controller wishes to, and does, forbid access to his property. They have no right there; the person in control does not want them there. He has probably posted signs or erected a fence to keep them out. The classic duty owed to such people is limited to that of refraining from setting a trap or pitfall.

Acts of Commission

Once the claimant is on the insured's property and has demonstrated that she has the status of an invitee, she has demonstrated that she is owed a duty of ordinary care. The next question is whether or not the duty has been breached. The breach of duty may be by the *doing of something which ought not to have been done* (an act of commission). Examples of an act of commission are:

1. Employe left a hand truck in the middle of the aisle.
2. Employe dropped a bean on the floor while loading a vegetable bin.

3. Storekeeper constructed a step or ramp in such a way that it was deceptive or dangerous.

In this class of act, the negligence consists in the actual *doing* of a wrongful thing. The act may be established by *testimony* (a witness testifies, "I saw that clerk drop a bean."); or the act may be established by *inference* (a bean was on the floor near a vegetable bin which had been filled by a store employe), from which it may be inferred that the employe dropped the bean in filling the bin. The distinction between acts of *commission* and acts of *omission* is vital, for, in respect to acts of commission by the storekeeper or his employes, the claimant does not need to show by testimony *how long* the condition which she alleges as the cause of her fall had prevailed. It will be seen, on the other hand that, when acts of omission are alleged that the ability to prove a time factor is vital to a claimant's case.

If the negligent act alleged is an act of commission, the claimant need not sustain the burden of offering evidence that the condition complained of had existed for any length of time. The negligence is in the act itself—not in the length of time that a condition had been permitted to continue.

Acts of Omission

The duty owed by a storekeeper to his customer may be breached by his failure to do something which he ought to have done (an act of omission). The great majority of falldown claims are alleged to arise out of this kind of negligence.

The most common allegation is that there was something on the floor which the storekeeper (or his employes) ought to have seen and ought to have removed. In order to demonstrate that that failure to remove was a negligent failure, the plaintiff must not only prove that the offending substance was on the floor—she must go further; she must offer evidence that the controller of the property *knew of the presence of the substance or in the exercise of reasonable care ought to have known of it and ought to have removed it.* The time factor which underlies the phrase "ought to have" is known as "constructive notice."

The classic example of a constructive notice attack and defense is based on a banana peel, described by a plaintiff as being old, withered, black and dirty, marked by many heel-marks. From this, her lawyer may argue that the banana peel had been in a position to be stepped on for a long period of time. The defense, usually sustained judicially, has been that the number of heel-marks upon a banana peel are as consistent with its having been walked upon by a great number of people in a short period of time as with its having been walked upon by a lesser number of people in a greater period of time. Some courts have offered the further observation that there was no evidence to indicate that the peel had not been in an old, withered, walked-on condition as the time when chance deposited it at the scene of the accident.

Clearly then, this dispute revolves around a *period of time* and, whether the foreign substance is a banana peel, water or something else, *time is still of the essence*. This emphasis on time therefore, requires that statements deal meticulously with all matters relating to time or from which an inference as to time may be drawn.

Almost the only way open to a claimant to surmount the hurdle of "constructive notice" is to offer evidence that the claimant or a companion had been by the scene earlier and had then observed the offending substance or condition. Interestingly, this may expose the claimant to the defense of contributory negligence since, if she already knew that the substance was on the floor, she ought to have stepped over it or walked around it. Almost without exception, inquiry discloses that neither claimant nor her companion had been past the scene of the fall on the day of the fall until the very moment of the fall. If this is the case, then the statements of the claimant and her companions should make the situation incontrovertibly plain, since second thought and backyard coaching often tend to "improve" testimony.

Sidewalk Falls

Although the rules vary from jurisdiction to jurisdiction, the owner and controller of a property is seldom responsible for the upkeep of public ways adjoining. Bluntly stated, this means that he has no obligation to remove slippery or dangerous objects on the sidewalk nor to keep the sidewalk in repair. This is the duty of the municipality.

It should not be thought that these claims do not impose investigative obligations. The question of what is "sidewalk," seemingly so obvious, may take more than a little digging. This is particularly true in downtown areas where the actual property line may fall in the middle of what appears to be "public way."

Bearing in mind again the danger of generalizing in a book to be read in more than 50 jurisdictions, it may be observed that the usual municipal ordinance holding an abutting property owner responsible for maintenance of the public way is not to be accepted at its face value. In many states it will be found that such ordinances have been subjected to judicial interpretation, and it has been held that the ordinances are a convenience to the municipality (a means of keeping the streets clean), and no duty to passersby has been created. Where ordinances have been so interpreted, failure to remove an offending substance does not constitute an appropriate allegation of negligence.

Modification of Conventional Adjusting Techniques

Because most falldowns occur spontaneously, that is, with no discoverable cause, and with no affective negligence on the part of the defendant; and for the further reason that the law is usually quite forthright in acknowledging this situation, falldown claims are probably more subject to disposition by outright denial than any other form of liability claim. In addition, while there are people who insist on thinking that the mere fact of a fall on the property of another is sufficient basis for a claim, there is an equally numerous class of persons who do not regard a fall as a proper subject of a claim for damages and who, to use their terms, "would never think of making a claim."

Since claims occur in a society which includes both classes and since handling techniques must reflect the legal obligations attendant upon this type of claim, adjusters, depending on the circumstances, vary their conventional tactics in two important ways—in the greater frequency with which they employ the "let rest" technique, and in their employment of a technique which will here, for want of any term generally recognized in the claims business, be called "exploratory denial."

"Let Rest"

Store help has been educated to report every accident, no matter how trivial. This results in the reporting of many matters as claims when really they are only "incidents." Improper handling can stir up a claim; proper handling can leave the matter in the "incident" class. It goes without saying that the adjuster should govern himself so that, if possible, the claim remains in the incident category. Therefore, adjusters generally prefer to introduce themselves as representatives of the store rather than as "adjuster" or by any other term associated with insurance. The claimant's voluntary remarks are often such as to indicate that she is not looking to anyone for reimbursement—that instead, she deplores the incident. This is the adjuster's cue to excuse himself and perform what has been referred to as "the classic naval maneuver": Getting the h - - - out as fast as he can.

The tip-off may come by way of a voluntary comment, of which an example might be, "Oh, wasn't it nice of the store to send you out to see me. I am going to be all right. Dr. X gave me two or three treatments and I feel just fine. I've always traded at ...." There are other tip-offs, more subtle, and the adjuster in appraising them should rely on his intuition, which he will find to be a remarkably reliable instrument. The feeling that "this person is not a claimant" is almost invariably correct.

If a statement is under way when the tip-off comes, the statement should nevertheless be finished. The handling of this question is closely related to the matter of the "exploratory denial" discussed below.

Exploratory Denials

The majority of falldowns are out and out no-liability cases. Many insurers deny them "all the way," up to and including death claims, and with a very high degree of success. The point has been made already that an adjuster's initial approach should be calculated to ascertain whether or not a claim really exists. Some people, of course, wish to enter a claim, and others, the adjuster's best efforts to the contrary notwithstanding, do not reveal their intent.

If the claimant's statement as written discloses an absence of liability, many claims should be denied on the spot. In addition to being the most effective time for making a denial, fairness to the claimant recommends this technique.

The problem may be particularly acute for independent adjusters, since some companies wish to litigate falldown claims on their merits, but others wish to dispose of them on "nuisance value" theories.

To enable him, in effect, to "test the ice" without committing himself to any particular course, an adjuster may, when he has finished writing the statement, deliver a brief discourse in which he explains that liability cannot exist without fault. He can go on to say that he has carefully considered the facts of the accident, including the claimant's story, and call her attention to her failure to allege any fault, shortcoming or misdeed on the part of the store. He may conclude with a statement that it would appear that the store is not liable to her for damages—that he assumes that she will understand that no claim can be entertained.

This often evokes expressions of complete agreement. The adjuster can then, with good judgment, close his file. If, on the other hand, resistance develops, the adjuster has an opportunity to explain that he is not the court of last resort, that he will explain the claimant's contrary views to his home office (or client) and will return at a later date.

Investigational Aspects of Falldown Claims

Some of the investigational aspects of falldowns will now be discussed in the following sequence: falls due to unknown causes, control—lease, companion witnesses, negligence in housekeeping, waxing, negligence in lighting, and negligence in construction.

And finally, some of the challenges to be expected from this type of claim having been pointed out, the section will conclude with a statement check list.

Falls Due to Unknown Causes

The typical falldown, if the claimant's statement [9] is secured before she has been coached, is found to have occurred for no known reason. Overwhelmingly, these ladies say that they have no idea why they fell. This does not relieve the adjuster of the duty of putting into the claimant's statement her affirmations concerning the state of the floor: whether clean, dry, free of obstruction, etc.

If, as is usually the case, the woman failed to make these observations, the statement should be equally unequivocal as to her failure to observe. The lack of knowledge should be brought out in general terms, and then should be carried through to the point of securing specific answers to specific question in "I don't know" form.

Control-Lease

Physical possession of the property and physical possession of the keys to it usually denotes *control*. The adjuster should be warned—it is unwise to become unnecessarily involved in vainly trying to fix liability on the owner of the property when the tenant is clearly in control.[10] Responsibility for accidents on property goes with control rather than ownership. Most store properties are under lease. The tenant is in virtually absolute control. Unless the allegation of negligence revolves around defective construction, the owner is probably in no way involved. It is a disservice to client or employer to attempt to bring the owner into the picture. (It is much better to concentrate on disposing of the claim on its *merits*.)

If there is a lease, avoid the common fault of speculating on lease provisions without having procured the lease. *Leases are seldom in actual issue but when they are the only acceptable handling is to make the language of the lease itself a part of*

---

[9] Discussion at this point assumes that the adjuster has received no tip-off to indicate that the claim may safely be "let rest."

[10] The reference here is to vain and ill-considered attempts to bring in the landlord as a co-defendant or to get him or his insurer to take over the claim entirely.

the file. This may be done by procuring a copy of the document itself and furnishing the file with photostatic copies.

Companion Witnesses

In respect to automobile claims, it must be granted that there is a tendency to assume that, right or wrong, companions will usually support one another with their testimony. This is a dangerous view in itself, but doubly dangerous when the attitude carries over into falldown claims. Here the public is not so sophisticated. Almost everybody knows how to blame an automobile accident on the "other fellow." Since the elements of liability are not so well known to the public in falldown claims, statements of uncoached witnesses incline more to the unvarnished truth. Therefore, it is of first importance to ascertain from any falldown victim whether she had a companion, and if so, to identify her. If there was none, the statement should make this clear. The statement of the companion takes a priority almost equal to that of the claimant herself. A plaintiff can as easily prove her case through the testimony of a companion witness as through her own.

For still another reason, the statements of companions to falldown victims are more important than in auto claims. In an auto claim the really important testimony is about an accident itself. Positions and conditions noted afterward are relevant but usually only in a minor way. In a falldown claim most of the really important testimony is about what was observed *after* the fall, specifically, the observation of the scene and of the things that caused the fall. Since the companions were not subjected to the upset and embarrassment of sustaining the fall, they may be better and more informative witnesses than the victim herself.

Negligence in Housekeeping

When negligence is alleged as the cause of a fall, the most common allegation has to do with a want of proper housekeeping; that is, the floor (or stair) was wet, dirty, slippery, or had on it some dangerous object which ought to have been removed and this failure to maintain the premises properly caused the fall.

Therefore, statements of claimants and witnesses should contain information as to the cause of the fall and should include affirmative statements as to whether there were or were not any objects on the floor (and if so, their nature), whether the floor was clean, dry, etc. If any degree of wetness is alleged, the statement should be specific as to the amount of water; whether simply damp, whether there was a film of water or whether there was an actual puddle of standing water. Describing the amount of water objectively is no easy task and if moisture is the problem, adjusters often have their hands full. At such a time an objective statement bearing on the subject can sometimes be obtained by asking the lady whether her skirt or other clothing was found to be wet or water-stained after she had fallen.

While the claimant is, more often than not, unable to surmount the hurdle of constructive notice, it is still prudent to be able to demonstrate affirmatively that housekeeping has, in fact, been properly accomplished. Therefore, it is often necessary to carry the investigation to the point of ascertaining whose duty it was to sweep (or mop) the floor and then procuring his statement as to when, prior to the fall, the operation was last performed and describing the manner of its performance. It is best, of course, if such a person can say, "I mopped 'B' area at 10:15 this morning." In actual practice, delay in reporting often results in an adjuster's having to investigate many days or even weeks after the fact. Then he may have to settle for, "I have no specific memory of May 7th, but my usual practice was to mop the floor daily. Attendance records show that I was on the job that day. I invariably pass through 'B' area, mopping as I go, between 10:00 and 10:15 a.m."

Waxing

Slipperiness due to over-waxing, improper application of wax, or the use of the wrong type of wax is often an alleged negligence factor. There has been so much judicial interpretation of this point that it is impossible to generalize. However, it should be noted that where waxing or slipperiness is an issue, the adjuster again has a problem in writing a statement in objective terms. How slippery is slippery? And then, how much more slippery must a floor be to be "too slippery"?

A convenient comparison is to the slipperiness of the housewife's own floor at home. An admission that the floor is of equal or less slipperiness than that which she maintains in her own living room leaves her in a poor position to allege that the store has behaved in anything but a prudent manner.

Many waxing claims stand or fall on the mode of application— the successful complaint being that the wax was unevenly applied, thick or lumpy in places, and "not all rubbed in." Hence statements attempt to bring out that the wax was evenly applied, well rubbed in, or at least to demonstrate that the witness made no real observaion from which inference or deduction as to the method employed to wax the floor can be drawn.

This again is a matter of getting to the claimant before her imagination has been stimulated.

Negligence in Lighting

Insufficient lighting may be alleged. To write an appropriate statement to deal with these claims is a real challenge. The problem is to describe lighting in objective terms. "Fairly well lit," "Quite dark," are obviously subjective and quite meaningless.

"Light enough to read a newspaper," "I was able to distinguish the features of a man on the other side of the room," are objective. With similar resourcefulness, some objective standard can usually be found.

Negligence in Construction

Negligence may arise by faulty construction, improperly built thresholds, steps difficult to see or in an unexpected place, etc. Photographs are of first importance in investigating claims involving these allegations. Second to photographs is inspection by a competent architect or engineer. The test of negligence is not so much whether the condition complained of is dangerous or whether better methods might have been devised but, rather, the standard of the ordinarily prudent man. Architects and engineers, therefore, in making their inspections, should be cautioned to compare the situation not with a theoretical "best" but with the standards commonly observed in like situations in the locality.

To illustrate this type of defense, the author recalls a case in which a woman tripped over a rather uncommon threshold. The inspecting architect pointed out that the threshold was higher than recommended under the best modern practice. However, the adjuster walked with him along the street for a block in both directions. The architect was thereby enabled to incorporate in his report the correct information that over half the stores in that area had identical thresholds. This supported the argument that this mode of construction was usual and common to store entrances in that locale.

Since the item complained about is more or less permanent, it may be thought that statements are of minor importance in investigating falldowns alleged to have occurred because of a fault in construction. This is not true. The statement is the time for the adjuster to bring out, if it is the fact, that the plaintiff had previously been at the scene, had mounted or descended the steps a number of times before sustaining her accident, and hence was on notice as to its existence and nature. *Most* supreme courts have been reasonably firm in applying the principle of contributory negligence to such situations.

An allegation of faulty construction has, for the claimant, the advantage of relieving her of the often insurmountable obstacle of demonstrating constructive notice, a factor that adjusters should bear in mind when weighing the liability aspect of the claim. In other words, an allegation of negligence based on faulty construction has the nature of an *act of commission* rather than the more common act of *omission*.

Statement Check List

Falldowns more nearly follow a pattern than do automobile accidents. Where a check list in the taking of an automobile statement may be a pitfall, deceiving the adjuster into thinking that he has taken a good statement because he has covered a lot of peripheral material not essential to the real issue, a check list of the subjects to be covered in a falldown statement creates less of that kind of trouble. Too, falldowns are not as common as automobile accidents; most adjusters see only a limited number of them and the use of a crutch is more forgivable.

A falldown statement includes the standard introductory information and conclusion, dealing particularly with injuries and special damages. Other items to be covered in the statement include:

Companions of claimant
Status of claimant
Location of fall
Constructive notice
Inspection (what the claimant
noticed before and
after her fall)
Cause of the fall

Cleanliness of premises and
fall area
Moisture
Obstructions
Need of repair
Construction defects
Lighting

PRODUCT CLAIMS

Product liability claims may, of course, involve merchandise other than food. Most of the features of the investigation and handling of all types of product liability claims which differentiate them from the more common automobile work are met with in *food* claims. Food claims are used here, therefore, for illustrative purposes in the confident supposition that necessary extensions of the principles involved will be made. (Once an adjuster has learned how properly to identify an allegedly harmful package of frankfurters, he will encounter no problems in making proper identification of an exploding wallpaper-removing machine.)

It will be convenient to discuss this class of claim in terms, first, of the legal background against which they are made, and then in terms of the activities of the adjuster which are unique to this class of claim.

Legal Basis of Product Claims

Legal liability for purchase or consumption of a product may be based on either of two alternative approaches. One of these routes is familiar, the demonstration of the elements of a tort.

The other is by a suit in "contract," alleging that there has been a breach of an implied condition of the "contract of sale" by which the product came into the possession of the consumer.

To proceed in a tort action a plaintiff must establish each of the familiar elements of a tort as he does in more familiar fields of litigation.

Simply stated, this means that he may attempt to establish by testimony or by inference that in some phase of the preparation, handling or sale of a product, a party responsible was careless and that the carelessness resulted in injury. The burden of establishing negligence by testimony of a witness was frequently more than a plaintiff could sustain (after all, the preparation and packaging of most products is hardly subject to the observation of the average claimant). Therefore, the law has provided claimants with another avenue by which to seek redress.

If the plaintiff elects the alternative route, he may then attempt to demonstrate that the offending product was, when sold, the subject of a warranty. To elaborate, the argument runs thus: The transaction by which the purchaser came into position of the object embodied a contract of sale; this contract held within it as an implied feature a warranty as to the fitness of the product for the purpose for which it was intended; finally, the product was not fit for its intended purpose and the plaintiff was injured thereby. Thus, the presence of a tack in a blueberry pie, so the argument runs, renders it unfit to be eaten. Since the pie is obviously *intended* to be eaten, this unfitness is alleged to constitute a violation of the implied warranty which was a feature of the contract of sale. These are the actions which are referred to as suits "in contract."

The ability of a plaintiff to sue in contract has been greatly enlarged by a series of recent decisions that the common law is only now in the process of starting to digest.

Whether a suit can be brought in contract, and if so, the allegations which must be made in order to sustain a cause of action and the defenses available to the defendant, are greatly affected by the presence or absence of what is known as the Uniform Sales Act as a part of the law of the jurisdiction in which the action is brought.

Many states have enacted a Uniform Sales Act. Many have not. No attempt is made, therefore, to set out here the governing features of the laws of the several states.

The adjuster should clearly understand, however, that in addition to the obvious and traditional route, the allegation of negligence, there is a possibility that another avenue of suit is open. If the threatened claim is substantial, a half hour with his local trial counsel, before starting to investigate, will be well spent.

Investigation Relative to Possible Contract Action

Because of the possibility that a claimant may attempt to bring his action in contract rather than in tort, product claims should routinely be investigated along the following lines:

1. Who made the purchase? A contract of sale may exist only between a buyer and a seller. If the purchaser and the consumer are different persons, there may be no contract obligation to the consumer.
2. Whose money financed the purchase? A wife may not be the breadwinner of the family. Possibly it was the husband's money with which the purchase was made. Possibly the contract of sale is with the husband rather than the wife. Does the wife earn or possess any money of her own?
3. Did the seller know whose money financed the purchase? Sometimes the rights of an agent acting for an undisclosed principal are different from what they would be if the identity of the principal were known to the seller. The right of the principal as distinct from the right of the agent may vary according to whether the seller knows who is the real purchaser.
4. Who made the selection? Did the customer buy directly from a shelf or did a clerk offer or recommend? This may govern the later decision as to whether or not there is an implied warranty. Was the product asked for by brand name? This, too, may influence a decision as to warranty.
5. Was the offending product returned by the customer? Did he get his money back? Did he accept a substitute product? Did he ever pay for the product at all? (When patrons find a harmful substance in restaurant food, it is common for the house to decline to submit a check.)

   Sometimes the acceptance of one or another of the above remedies will wipe out the possibility of any subsequent claim in *contract*. (There would be no effect on a claim made via the tort route.)

The caution is repeated that because of the diversity of law on the subject, the foregoing should not be used to attempt to decide whether a case is or is not a case of probable liability under contract. The foregoing are *suggestions* for investigation. An adjuster who covers them makes no mistake by doing so. The legal weight to be given his findings depends on the jurisdiction in which he operates.

Let Rest

Many accident reports of food poisoning claims, foreign substance claims, etc., are not really claims, only *complaints*. To identify and separate complaints from actual claims, the adjuster should approach each of these claims with this possibility in mind and shape his initial questions so as to discover the claimant's intent. If he senses that no claim is intended, he should get out as fast as he can. If an adjuster feels that in this departure, he may have taken an undue risk, he should promptly consult his supervisor. If the supervisor feels that the risk is too great, the adjuster can go back and repeat his call, this time making a complete inquiry, taking a statement, etc.

To avoid the possibility of stirring up a claim where no intent to claim damages exists, adjusters usually find it good practice to introduce themselves as representatives of the insured, rather than as representatives of the insurance company.

Identification of the Product

Remarkable because it is both so obvious and so frequently overlooked is the *duty of identifying the offending product*. The adjuster should ask to see both the product and the container. He should ask also for the sales slips, invoices and any other documents covering the transaction by which the item may have been sold or resold. Both in his notes and statements he should describe the product carefully. Size, color, freshness, spoilage, etc., are to be noted both in his notebook and in the statements. Identifying code or serial numbers, product names, etc., should likewise be recorded.

Often the product has been consumed—there may be no sales slip. Whether or not there is a sales slip the claimant should be required in the statement to record all of the details of the purchase known to him: the name and location of the store; the name or a description of any clerk dealt with and the substance of any conversation with him; the location at which the object was displayed in the store; etc.

Inspection of Product—For Fault

If there is a foreign object, ask that it be produced. Describe it carefully—length, breadth, weight, color, etc.—both in the claimant's statement and later in the dictated report. If a product itself is alleged to be defective (mouldy apple pie, for example) examine it carefully and record the results of the examination in the statement, bringing out those details which bear particularly on negligence. The resemblance of the substance to the product itself (or lack of resemblance) may be particularly important, as some courts have held that the presence of such an object as a small round brown stone in a can of beans is not evidence of negligence (the thinking being that the object so closely resembles the beans themselves that to find it would call not for the diligence of the ordinarily prudent man but for the skill and diligence of an *extraordinarily* prudent person).

Securing Possession of the Product—Foreign Substance

Both to identify it and to control the evidence, it is desirable to secure possession of the product which is said to have been the cause of a claimant's misfortune and the foreign substance itself, together with any supporting documents.

The adjuster should ask that these be exhibited to him. This usually takes place in the first part of the interview. He may put them down close to him and proceed with the taking of the statement. When he is ready to leave, he takes the product or the foreign substance and, without comment, puts it in his briefcase.

Objections are seldom offered. If the claimant demurs, offer to give him a receipt for the object.

When possession of the object has been gained, advice of home office or his counsel should be sought to determine the adjuster's obligation, if any, to preserve this evidence. It will usually be learned that the adjuster and his employer are under no obligation to the plaintiff to preserve the product, and unless it is to the insurer's interest to do otherwise, an election to destroy the substance may be made.

It goes without saying that any legislation or local decision imposing an obligation to preserve or return the product will be scrupulously adhered to. Of course, if called by the plaintiff, the adjuster must be ready to testify that he did, in fact, take possession of the product and truthfully relate the circumstances of the acquisition.

Actions Over

A unique feature of products claims is the divided responsibility that arises when the manufacture of the article may be by one party, its wholesaling by another and its retailing by yet another.

Product liability insurance for manufacturers is frequently written with what is known as "vendor's coverage endorsement." Vendor's coverage does not provide coverage under the policy of the manufacturer for any negligent act of a vendor (seller). It does provide coverage to a vendor for claims based on an allegation that a defect in the product is attributable to the manufacturer's negligent act or a harmful condition of the product as it came to the possession of the vendor. The presence or absence of vendor's coverage will naturally bear upon an insurer's decision as to whether or not to extend protection in the name of the ultimate vendor. Facts, too, bear on the situation, and manufacturers or their insurers frequently defend vendors when the facts call for such action, even in the absence of vendor's coverage.

If he represents the manufacturer, the adjuster should recognize that commercial interests as well as legal responsibilities are often involved. A failure to take over and defend, at the expense of a valued retailer, could well lose a valued customer for his insured.

The problem is usually met in its more acute form when the adjuster represents the insurer of a retailer, and the product sold and the allegations concerning it indicate responsibility on the part of a manufacturer. If there is reasonable ground for believing that the manufacturer (or wholesaler) is involved, immediate notice should be given to the person or organization from whom the insured purchased the object, by means of what is known as an "action over" letter. A suitable specimen of such a letter is in the "box" on this page. It is better that mention of insurance be avoided and, if possible, the letter should be written by counsel on counsel's letterhead.

Gentlemen:

This office represents (insert name of insured).

(Insert name of claimant) alleges that he sustained injury by reason of consuming or using a product (insert name of product) manufactured and/or sold by you.

On behalf of (insert name of insured), you are hereby called upon to take over the investigation in defense of this claim, and notified that in the event of failure to do so (insured), will hold you strictly responsible for all loss and cost incurred in respect to this matter.

Yours very truly,

These claims often—and unfortunately—tend to break down into long drawn-out affairs, each insurer and each adjuster gleefully trying to "stick the other," all to the injury of the good name of the insurance business. Rarely is there a real excuse for this, as the facts are usually quite clear. If responsibility clearly attached to the retailer, an attempt to involve the wholesaler or manufacturer or vice versa is a disservice to the institution of insurance and subjects it to justified but unnecessary criticism from the public.

If the adjuster represents the insurance company of the retailer he has an uncommonly powerful tool available to his hand. In addition to the legal means open to him, he may avail himself of commercial pressure. Any sizable retailer is a valued customer of his wholesaler or manufacturer. Simultaneously with the legal notice, the adjuster should see to it that his insured's assistance is solicited. Pressure from the insured upon the salesman servicing his account will be rapidly transmitted to that salesman's headquarters and has been known to work a remarkable change in the attitude of the manufacturer's insurers.

This type of action is not self-starting, but if the legal situation warrants such pressure the adjuster should institute commercial action, stay with it and drive it to a conclusion. Once he has seen the effect of economic power he will never overlook that weapon in the future.

Food Poisoning

Claims of alleged food poisoning are often rationalizations. Someone has been taken sick. He concludes that, in the classic phrase, "It must have been something I ate," and he picks on the most likely offending substance.

It has been noted frequently that the presence of an epidemic of virus intestinal upsets in a community always leads to corresponding increase in alleged food poisoning claims.

Medical support for such rationalization is often alleged but upon investigation it turns out that the doctor, overworked, tired, was asked by the claimant, "Doc, don't you think it was those hot dogs?" and the doctor, not realizing that he is planting the seeds of litigation, finds it easier to agree than to involve himself in a debate.

If the allegedly offensive product is privately consumed, the time of its purchase should be ascertained. The condition of the package, whether or not it was kept under refrigeration until the time of consumption and, of course, the identity of all those who consumed the product should be ascertained and tied down in statements. (It is not uncommon for one member of a family with an intestinal upset to have profound conviction as to exactly what food product caused his upset. There is reason to doubt his conclusion if there were six other people at the table with him, all of whom ate the same meal with no subsequent distress.)

The claimant should be required to state whether he observed anything unusual about the product at the time it was eaten. This exposes the claimant to a problem. If he admits that the food did not taste right, he may open himself to an admission of contributory negligence. At the first bite he should have accepted the warning of his senses and stopped eating. If he noticed nothing wrong, there is usually no evidence to identify the suspect product as the cause of his complaint.[11] It is fair for the adjuster to suspect, and with experience he will probably conclude, that most isolated food poisoning claims are mere rationalizations—people have been taken sick and are looking for someone to blame it on. However, these isolated cases are to be distinguished from what might be called the "mass poisoning" claims.

From time to time there arise food poisoning claims with a high degree of legitimacy which involve large numbers of people. A bakery or restaurant will have a number of customers all of whom are taken sick (or at least very many of them). Claims—often in the hundreds or even in the thousands—suddenly arise. When this happens, there is usually very little doubt as to the offending substance.

A frequent offender in mass food poisonings is found to be cream filling in pies, cakes and custards. These claims are much more frequent during hot weather. The resulting gastrointestinal upset is violent and has been known to end fatally, although usually the fatality occurs when the upset is superimposed on a preexisting cardiac condition or other weakness.

In dealing with mass claims, investigation must proceed rapidly with the policyholder to ascertain just what foods were

---

[11] Courts of certain jurisdictions have removed the requirement of *ingesting* a foreign substance before a plaintiff can recover damages. This applies particularly to those substances which could be considered so *repulsive* as to cause an upset.

served, what handling was given the foods suspected of having caused the outbreak. *Time is of the essence, for in a restaurant one day is like another and within two or three days of an outbreak, nobody can tell what was done with a certain batch of pudding on a certain day.*

The investigation of the actions of the insured and his employes should be completed within a matter of hours, if at all feasible, and a decision arrived at in regard to the insured's responsibility. If the insured is liable (and he frequently is),

---

CHECK LIST FOR SIGNED STATEMENT—PRODUCT CLAIMS

1. Details of purchase

   a. Who made the purchase
   b. Where
   c. When
   d. Surroundings
   e. Sales slip (secure possession)
   f. Source of money
   g. Price paid
   h. Vendor acquainted with the family (know who makes the money?)

2. Description of product

3. Description of foreign substance

4. Consumption

   a. When—and how—was the foreign substance or faulty condition noticed?
   b. Description of foreign substance
   c. Was the substance eaten, chewed or merely observed?
   d. Description of damage

5. (Food poisoning claims) Other foods at same and next preceding meal

   a. Who ate at the same meal?
   b. Onset of symptoms and chronology

6. Duration of injury or illness

7. Article exchanged or money refunded?

claims are then settled as fast as can humanly be done. Often a whole corps of adjusters is placed on the job.

Even in these situations, often so painfully clear, the sheep must still be separated from the goats. Claims of this sort are usually attended by wide publicity and there are always those who, even though they may not have been at the restaurant in question on the day when the poisonous substance was sold, will try to hop on the bandwagon and allege that they too were made sick.

Therefore, a statement should be secured from every claimant, including not only the time at which the substance was ingested and the subsequent chronology of his symptoms but also a careful description of what was offered on the day in question, what was eaten along with the supposed offending substance—if a cafeteria, what other foods were displayed, etc.

Many of the free-riders can be detected if their statements are inconsistent with known facts—facts which should have been known to anyone who patronized the restaurant on the day in question.

LANDLORD AND TENANT CLAIMS

Many accidents occur on other than store premises. Most— but by no means all—of these accidents are falls. For the purposes of this section, discussion will limit itself to falls, since there is a limit to the variety of circumstances that ought to be dealt with in a book about fundamentals.

A common locale for injuries of this type is the private residence. The law of landlord and tenant bears on this type of claim as it does on all injuries occurring on private premises.

Legal Background

In general, a landlord has very little liability in respect to rented premises. The rule is that a tenant takes the premises as he finds them. The thought behind that rule is that if a tenant did not like the premises, he did not have to rent them in the first place. An exception to this general rule of non-liability is that if there is a hidden defect whose existence is known to the landlord, he ought to have disclosed such a defect to the tenant. Another exception is that a landlord may be liable to his tenant if he makes repairs and makes them negligently.

Usually, however, there is no obligation on a landlord to make repairs or to correct defective or dangerous conditions even when he is admittedly aware of their existence.

Common Passageways

The landlord's duty with respect to common passageways is to use reasonable care to maintain the premises (passageway) in the same condition they were in or appeared to be in at the time of the letting.

If there is an unlighted stairwell and if this stairwell was unlighted at the time the tenancy commenced, investigation should bring that out by statement of the tenant. It should be shown that the stairwell was unlighted when the premises were first rented, even though that may have been years past.

The landlord's obligation to a tenant's invitees, whether social, business or otherwise, rises no higher than his duty to the tenant himself.

Questions Involving Leases or Other Contracts

It is a primary item of investigation to determine whether a lease is in effect covering the premises which are sought to be covered. The general rules applicable to the relationship of landlord to tenant may be altered by the provisions of a lease. Then again, there may be leases which *seem* to alter the duties and obligations but actually change nothing. It is not the adjuster's duty to decide unaided whether or not the basic rules have been changed, but it is very much his duty to find out exactly what the provisions of the lease may be. If there is a conflict between the general rule and a lease, or between the general rule and some oral understanding, it is not the adjuster's duty to decide the question, but it is his duty to get all the facts bearing on the situation so that an attorney or his home office *can* decide it.

If there is a lease, the adjuster's first order of business is to see that the file is promptly supplied with a copy. This is an item which tends to drag. People say they will locate leases and send them in. They just don't follow through. When an adjuster ascertains that a lease is in effect, the proper way to handle the situation is to go to the person in possession, stay with him until he locates the lease, borrow it, photostat it, supply the file, and return the lease. A half day spent in this operation is thoroughly justified and will save far more time at a later date.

A similar observation applies to any situation where a contract of one sort or another may be involved. If one suspects that a written contract is or may be involved, it becomes a priority item to secure the contract. Contracts have a way of getting into the most out-of-the-way places. They are often casually treated by the parties to the contract and, again, locating them is a task for the adjuster to get on and stay with until he accomplishes his purpose. *Inasmuch as knowing the provisions of a lease or contract is usually a prerequisite to other decisions that need to be made, procuring these documents is of paramount importance.*

Landlord's Oral Agreements

Usually a landlord's oral agreement to make repairs will not modify the basic law as to his obligation to pay damages. Nevertheless, if it is alleged that a landlord has made some commitment in respect to leased property, it is essential that the full details of that commitment be promptly recorded in the file. This has to be done *in the statement of the tenant and in the statement of the landlord.* The tenant must be required to state his full recollection of all conversations bearing on the subject with the landlord, and the landlord must be required to make a similar statement touching on the same subject.

Remember that the tenant is not necessarily the claimant. An adjuster may have secured a statement from the claimant, but *if the tenant is a person other than the claimant, the tenant himself is the person to speak about the tenant's side of the lease arrangements.*

Initial investigation should disclose all the facts, promises, undertakings and obligations bearing on a tenancy. As a practical matter, the claim can then usually be discussed informally with local trial counsel so that a sound understanding of the governing local law can be arrived at. Inability properly to assess legal responsibility more often hinges on failure to develop the necessary facts than upon lack of knowledge of the law.

Diagrams—Photos

As in almost all liability claims, it is not only important but it is essential to draw a diagram. A diagram of a stairway, for instance, would show the stairway, its construction, the halls leading from it, the apartments leading from the halls, etc. Lacking such a diagram, the supervisor may be unable to determine the exact relationship of the injured party to the insured.

Structural details are better shown by photographs than by diagrams. Photographs should be liberally employed. The usual practice applies of using commercial photographs in serious claims, and hand-camera photographs when the matter sought to be covered is for information only rather than for evidence.

Witnesses

Important witnesses in landlord-tenant claims are quite likely to be other than those who actually witnessed the accident itself. For instance, other tenants who may have left the property long before the occurrence of the incident may have information to give which is very helpful in determining facts as to long-standing or allegedly long-standing conditions.

Again, as with store falldowns, a witness who comes on the scene after the accident but who observes the surroundings may be in a better position to testify to important facts than the witness who comes on the scene of an automobile accident.

Control

In our parlance the word "control" usually applies to negotiations with an injured claimant. In general liability work the word "control" frequently occurs, but in *this* context it bears on the ownership or control of property, machinery or of a certain operation. It is important, always, to determine who is in control of a certain property or of a certain operation. Physical possession and possession of keys are usually germane to this point. It is a classic adjuster's mistake, however, to ascertain possession of the keys and to fail to find out whether the door is operated by those keys and whether it is kept in a locked or unlocked condition.

CHECK LIST FOR SIGNED STATEMENTS

The usual opening items—name, occupation, etc.

Exact location of accident.

Cause (describe specifically).

Any lease in effect? If no lease, the substance of all conversations dealing with details of letting, requests made to landlord, his responses, obligations undertaken by him.

Date tenancy began.

Description of rented premises.

If on a common passageway, describe the passageway and the premises leading therefrom.

Date condition complained of was first known to tenant.

Date condition complained of was first known to landlord.

How was this knowledge acquired by each?

Description of accident.

Usual closing items on damage.

CHAPTER 11

Evaluation

It is a tempting delusion to think of a claim as an orderly progression. Something that happens is investigated, reported, evaluated and in due time closed. Unfortunately, while this is part of it, it is far from the whole picture.

Even more unhappily, such an oversimplification fails utterly as a base from which to form an idea of a claim's value. Worse yet, it does not even help to show how one goes about thinking about a claim in order to form a realistic and useful idea of its value.

A claim is not static. It progresses from stage to stage. New information may enter the file at any time and the progression to another stage or the discovery of new information may increase or decrease value. Consequences at one stage may be one thing (perhaps the employment of an attorney); at another stage they may be something quite different as when the bailiff announces that the jury is knocking on the door and is about to disclose its decision. What is value today may not be value tomorrow.

To determine something so slippery as the value of a claim requires an approach that considers the factors of a claim, the pressures which exert forces on adjusters and claimants and how the factors and the pressures interact one with another. This chapter will approach value by that path. First it will be necessary to define some terms.

Definitions

When the following terms are used in this chapter they will have these meanings.

Verdict Value—the sum which a jury may be expected to award *if* it makes an award.

Judgment Value—this term is often used in the business and with substantially the same significance as verdict value.

Mathematical Value—verdict value multiplied by the plaintiff's expectancy of receiving a verdict. Thus: an adjuster might judge that a claim has a verdict value of $2,500, but if it were also his feeling that the chances of the jury returning a verdict in the plaintiff's favor were only one out of two, the mathematical value of the verdict to him would be one half times $2,500, or $1,250.

The term mathematical value is common enough outside of claims circles. It is met at a low level in mathematics, and while the concept is used in a multitude of situations,[1] it is seldom described by name by its users.

The claims business uses this concept constantly but there is no generally agreed upon term to label it. If there were such a term it would have been employed here. Lacking an industry term, the phrase mathematical value will be employed when it is necessary to invoke the concept.

Subjective Value—this is another term quite devoid of respectable ancestry. It has no industry sanction but it will be necessary in this chapter to refer to the ideas that people hold about what injuries should be worth in money before their ideas have been warped and distorted by inflammatory ideas and before the value of the injury has been enhanced by courtroom tactics and oratory.

Subjective value is the idea of value that reasonable people might put on a claim of one friend or neighbor against another, the claiming party having no desire for enrichment and the paying party anxious to discharge his obligation.

Settlement Value—this is a term frequently heard in the business usually (say 60% of the time) with about the same meaning as it will be given in this chapter.

Settlement value always has a high subjective component. For

---

[1] The concept can be employed (and usually is) without formally invoking its name, e.g.,

By a crap shooter to calculate the odds for or against making his point and particularly by those making side bets;

By a general to calculate the men and material he can afford to risk in an operation;

By an insurance actuary calculating rates.

instance, page 428 mentions an instance in which a claim is said to have a mathematical value of $1,250. Many claims might have exactly that mathematical make–up and many adjusters might feel that $1,250 is a proper settlement value for each of them.

It is more probable though that, of any given number of adjusters given the same facts bearing on liability and verdict value, some would place a settlement value of less than $1,250 on the claim and some would value the case at $1,250, and some would go higher.

This variance reflects two things: 1) the different personalities of the people making the judgment and, 2) that there are many factors other than injury, damages and liability which adjusters commonly take into consideration. These factors may make it wise to value a claim for settlement purposes at less than its mathematical value or they persuade a prudent adjuster to pay a premium (i.e. more than mathematical value) for a release.

The preceding paragraph embraces three concepts. The first is that decisions about price may be influenced by the personality of the person making them. The other two, the twin concepts, are that for any claim there is a limit beyond which one should not go (i.e., the release is worth *only* so much); or there are considerations *urging* companies to settle their claims. These considerations are sufficiently strong to require carriers to be ready— even anxious—to pay up to a certain amount. Settlement value is a point where the forces embodied by these twin concepts are in balance:

"It's worth this much and we had better pay it if we get the chance.

But, if we can't get it at that price, we'll take our chances."

Remembering the twin concepts is the key to understanding this chapter. Evaluating (or pricing, to use the term more common to the business) is a question of attempting to ascertain the point where the forces pushing one toward settlement are balanced by forces urging one to hang onto his principal's money. When this chapter refers to settlement value, this is what it means.

Forces That Urge, "Settle!"

In an order which roughly reflects their descending importance, and with the hurried qualification that circumstances sometimes alter the order of importance, the forces arguing "settle" might be listed:

> 1. If I don't pay "X" dollars now a jury is likely to award a greater sum.
> 2. If I don't pay "X" dollars now the elements of the claim may change and I may have to pay more later (the element most likely to change is the appearance of "the build-up").
> 3. If I don't settle now, my principal may be obliged to spend large sums of money defending the claim.
> 4. Political pressure, the intervention of a powerful agent or the controller of a large source of business.
> 5. The pressure to move cases.

The forces identified above operate not only to generate the imperative, "settle," but also express themselves in money—the same forces that urge a carrier to settle are obviously urging the carrier's representatives toward a higher view of settlement value.

Forces That Urge, "Don't Settle!"

There is really only one force that tells an adjuster not to settle (or not to pay more than a certain figure). It alone is enough to balance the formidable array of pro-settlement forces just cited. It is the obvious duty to the insurance company principal and the policyholder to minimize loss, preserve the company's funds and protect the rate.

Subjective Value

In Chapter I it was noted that "adjusting is not a process of determining what courts would award in a given circumstance and then delivering that sum to a claimant. On the contrary, disposition of a claim by litigation and verdict represents the failure of the adjusting process."

It was also pointed out that the majority of claims settle *by agreement* at a scale which bears no relation to the values set by the legal system. This statement is still overwhelmingly true and to set the stage for what is to follow, a re-reading of pages 2 to 7 inclusive is recommended.

For years, it has been an almost universally recognized phenomenon that very inexperienced adjusters secure releases that no one thought could be obtained and more often than not settle the claims at figures so modest as to defy belief. They have settled in a range which this chapter, for lack of a better name, calls "subjective value."

But young men are not the only ones who settle claims in this range. Consider the many claims that present these characteristics:

1. There are persons present in the claimant car.
2. The claim nevertheless settles for P.D. only.

These files alone outnumber files with asserted injury by about four to one. Everyone of these claims would have been a source of grave danger had it been exploited within the legal system, but each one settled at subjective value. That there were a few claimants who were innocently unaware of how to manufacture an injury claim is almost irrelevant. To think that many of them were so innocent is naive. The organization of many larger claims offices relegates the "P.D. only" claims to the inside staff and confines adjusters to asserted injury claims, a practice which gives adjusters a distorted view of the claims world.[2] There are many claimants who say, "I don't believe in that whiplash bit. Yes, I was shaken up but just fix my car, that's all I want."

Since a *sine-qua-non* of settling claims at subjective value is a knowledge of how many people prefer this route, any adjuster who doubts the existence or the size of this enormous body of claimants owes it to himself to spend a few minutes with the property damage supervisor or the P.D. payment clerk in his

---

[2] This is something like the distorted view of lame backs in compensation accidents that the author once harbored. Trained in compensation as a field adjuster, he saw only those lame backs that were questionable in origin or where the employe was resisting medical advice to return to work. When he became a supervisor he was perfectly astounded at the number of employes who suffer back strain, are out a few days to a few weeks, recover and go back to work peacefully.

office. Others whose work is not so departmentalized should sharpen their awareness of the many claims in this category passing peacefully through the office.

Being aware of the claims just described should make an adjuster more conscious of the claims he himself handles where, with no strife, he settles for out-of-pocket expenses or for expenses plus a modest sum, often with people telling him that they know that they could get more, "but this is all I want." Even where sums paid in excess of out-of-pocket financial loss are substantial, the difference between the sums so paid and what one might expect in a verdict are marked, but every such settlement represents an agreement—an agreement by a claimant voluntarily to accept the sum offered.

These characteristics mark settlements at subjective value.

1. The claimant does not desire to enrich himself nor view his claim as a means to that end.
2. The claimant usually identifies with:
   a. the adjuster, or
   b. the company against whom he has his claim, or
   c. the thought that insurance is a part of a general system of personal responsibility in which one tries to avoid shoving; a system where the claimant's view of value is as much motivated by his desire to behave in a manner recognized by himself as "responsible" as it is by a desire to gain funds, or
   d. the concept that when the outright desire to gain funds is a factor, claimant prefers a bird in the hand, or
   e. finally, (a less obvious characteristic of these settlements), that a claimant's idea of value is based on what *he* thinks the adjuster thinks about value.

It is quite possible that many adjusters fail to realize their service to the consumer by their successful adjustments at subjective value. It may be helpful, in recognizing this service, to contrast such settlements with an opinion about value obviously based on ideas derived from the legal system.

A young aggressive lawyer once said, "Any time one of my clients is even touched in the rear, somebody's going to pay him at least $1,200, whether he's hurt or not." This statement was made 10 years ago but even today if $1,200 were added to the price of each claim currently settled in the subjective range, the price of insurance would probably have to be multiplied by at least three.

To summarize, more claims by far settle at the subjective level than at values derived from the legal system. Encouraging subjective valuation keeps the business alive and serves the policyholder who has a right to expect that the claims which he pays for are not overpaid.

Adjusters should expect to be able to satisfy people by payment of their expenses or their expenses plus a modest allowance, and they should adopt negotiating tactics designed to create and maintain in claimants' minds the attitudes necessary to this level of settlement. The subjective level is where the adjuster really lives and works. The legal system awaits him (and his principal) if he is unsuccessful. That system is, by itself, another pressure forcing the adjuster toward the higher settlement figures at the far end of his subjective value claims.

Do not be misled by the comparative wordage now to be devoted to the legal system and to pricing influenced by it. The subjective value level is where the adjuster really lives and works.

Values—Within the Framework of the Legal System

Far more claims are settled by negotiation between claimant and adjuster than ever reach attorneys. Of the cases that reach attorneys, those on which suit is filed are a relative minority—most are negotiated to settlement by adjusters and plaintiff's counsel. Of the suits filed, only a small minority reach trial, the rest are settled or dropped by the wayside.

"Why, then, should the courts be considered at all? Why attempt to ascertain their scales of values? Why try to forecast a jury's award?" The reason is that the jury is always there in the background to curb an adjuster's natural skepticism and to enforce realism. In short, the study of judgment values reminds the adjuster of what may happen to him and to the interests he represents if he fails to bring about a settlement by agreement.

Factors Influencing Verdict Values

An adjuster is obliged to consider verdict values even though judgment values are almost never *settlement* values. He must weigh the many factors that come together in a court room to influence courts and juries and combine to form that dollar figure which a jury renders as its verdict. While some of these factors are recognized within the formal structure of the law, some of the most influential are not. They include *damages* in their many aspects, *liability,* and *location.* They include also other factors theoretically irrelevant and often emotional in nature but actually very important. Some factors, it will even be conceded, are completely irrational.

Adjusters use the terms "judgment," "verdict" and, to a lesser extent, "award," interchangeably and synonymously. Although adjusters should recognize these terms when they meet them in the field, this chapter, to minimize confusion, will, so far as is feasible, confine itself to the word "verdict" or the term "verdict value."

DAMAGES

Damages are the sums (in money) recoverable by a plaintiff as compensation for the injury sustained by him. Both because it is the custom of the business and because it is convenient to do so, damages may be considered as falling in two categories— "special damages" and "general damages."

Special Damages

Special damages, commonly spoken of as "specials," are out-of-pocket expenses or losses incurred by the claimant as the result of his injury. They are themselves recoverable but they may be only a fraction of a jury's verdict.

Special damages include: [3]

a. Doctor, dentist, and specialist charges;
b. Hospital, clinic or nursing home charges;

---

[3] *Future loss* in these categories, to the extent that it is reasonably probable, is also recoverable.

c. Nursing fees;
d. Charges for ambulance, medication and prosthetics;
e. Travel expense to and from doctors and hospitals (often a disputed item); and
f. Loss of earning capacity (from the date of accident to date of settlement.)

Of course, special damages affect verdicts, for they are themselves part of the damage sustained by a claimant and hence are included in the verdicts awarded. It is also argued by some plaintiffs' representatives that damages in addition to specials will be proportionate to the specials.[4] Because of this alleged proportion, plaintiff's counsel usually tries to demonstrate as much special damage as possible. The adjuster's duty to the insurance buyer requires that he must resist improper items. Many items frequently offered by attorneys as alleged special damages and deserving adjuster's scrutiny are *property damage, pain and suffering,* and *disfigurement.*

In order to show *why* these items should be resisted, it should first be shown *how* they get into special damages at all.

For example, attorneys frequently offer a listing of special damages something like this:

Repairs to automobile	$ 500.00
Dr. X	100.00
Hospital	200.00
Lost earnings	200.00
Total special damages	$1,000.00

They say in effect, then, "These are my specials; I expect to receive a verdict proportionate to specials of this order." It seems illogical to include the *property damage* in such a listing, for if there is any logic to the idea that the award for general damages varies proportionately to the specials, this, it would seem, would have to be based on the general premise that the more money it takes to cure an injury, the more painful the injury must have been. While this proposition seems dubious enough, it

---

[4] The arithmetic relationship and the factor to be employed to represent it varies according to who is trying to persuade whom. Counsel always tries to demonstrate as much special damage as possible.

is even more difficult to see how pain and other intangibles could be proportionately affected by the cost of repairing an automobile.

If this were so, then identical injuries sustained by an owner and a passenger would be worth more to the *owner* in general damages (because he could include his property damage as specials) and less to the *passenger*—because he would have no such figure to include in his specials. Were there such a relationship, then every claimant whose car was damaged but who was himself uninjured would, it would seem, be entitled to claim a sum in addition to the cost of repairing his automobile for his general damages.

Remember, it is the general view of the claims fraternity, in which this book concurs, that the notion that an award for general damages will vary proportionately to the special damage is incorrect. The thrust of these present paragraphs is simply to point out the *added* fallacy of considering property damage as special damage and to point out why its inclusion among special damages ought to meet a cold eye.

But property damage is not the only item that merits a cold eye. Pain, suffering, disfigurement, perfectly proper items of general damage, may also be offered as special damage and it is instructive to consider how they get into the picture and how they should be met. Some attorneys in preparing their cases, are prone to submit as specials something like this:

Dr. X	$ 100.00
Hospital	100.00
Loss of earnings	300.00
Pain and suffering (during three weeks of total disability at $100 per week)	300.00
Residual pain, not disabling (six weeks at $50 a week)	300.00
Total specials	$1,100.00

From this list the attorney then proceeds to argue that he expects to receive a verdict proportionate to the total specials shown—that is, some multiple of $1,100.

This offering embraces an obvious fallacy, for it is redundant to argue in one breath that special damages are worth a certain limited sum per week, and in the next breath to argue that the total which includes that sum should be increased by a further award to compensate the injured person for the pain *for which he has already asked a specific sum*. In other words, if a claimant asks $100 a week for his pain and suffering, it seems illogical to think that a jury will grant him a sum *in addition* to the $100 for the same item.

Disfigurement and *loss of consortium* (commonly but erroneously thought to be simply the loss of sexual relations) are also frequently offered as a weekly sum among the special damages. Such an offering embraces the same fallacy.

General Damages

General damages include such items as *pain and suffering, loss of consortium, inconvenience, disfigurement,* and *permanency*.

Their one common characteristic is that the money value of these items is related to no known standard. Since the money value to be assigned to each claim depends on the collective judgment of twelve jurors, this value is predictable only within a broad range. The amount of special damage sustained is almost always discoverable within reasonable limits by inspection of documents or reasonable inquiry, so forecasting a jury's view of liability and predicting the value to be awarded for general damages constitutes the main problem in estimating verdict values.

Pain and Suffering

Students once were taught that economics was "the dismal science." This was in part because few propositions in economics were subject to hard and fast proof. Economists saw a silver lining to their cloud for, just as they could not prove themselves right, no one could prove them wrong.

Adjusters occupy much the same position, for no one really knows what pain and suffering is worth, and when an adjuster holds an opinion, no one can really prove him wrong. Except for decisions turning on liability, the evaluation of pain and suffering is very nearly the heart of the problem of evaluating bodily injury claims. The courts in effect pass the duty down to the common man, the "jury of his peers." The common man, as we have already noted, is difficult to predict, but it is safe to say that his opinion of the dollar value of suffering, when he sits on a jury, has been enhanced by court room salesmanship. A layman's view of its value may range all the way from nothing ("I don't want any blood money," is a phrase often heard) to the outlandish.

When he prices a claim an adjuster must certainly consider pain. He must recognize the claim which generates high medical expense but little pain. Such an injury might be one involving internal bleeding. These injuries may be serious enough to threaten life itself but once the necessary surgery has been performed successfully, the path of recovery should be smooth and comfortable. Such cases should be distinguished from, for instance, causalgia—a disease in which pain is both the cause and the result. Even *conservative* medical men consider that its pain is excruciating, so, from the standpoint of pain and suffering causalgia would probably be evaluated more highly than a severe but completely controlled case of internal bleeding.

As his experience grows, an adjuster is involved increasingly in pricing claims. It is true that in the earlier stages of his training the actual pricing will probably be done by his supervisors; nevertheless, an adjuster should make it his practice to acquaint himself and advise his file of any unusual factors bearing on pain. Even at the stages when he does not have the actual pricing of the case in his hands, he should learn to recognize the unusual as a factor.

Pricing pain and suffering, therefore, presents major problems. To keep matters in proper perspective, it should be made clear that an adjuster's concern is only rarely with distinguishing one kind of pain from another. The injuries with which he deals are usually commonplace, and the question not so much whether one person's pain has been more intense than another's but, rather, what, in the situation presented, will a jury be likely to award? In other words, an adjuster's interest is only indirectly

concerned with the quality of the pain itself. What he is really
interested in is "for this injury, what will the jury award?"
In other words, an adjuster's interest is only indirectly concerned
with the quality of the pain itself. What he is really interested
in is "for this injury, what will the jury award?" Other factors
yet to be discussed—relative skills of opposing counsel, personality of the litigants, etc.—will probably have a greater influence
on the award for pain than the pain itself.

Disfigurement

Scarring and similar forms of disfigurement may be permanent
injuries. A court's evaluation of this type of injury resembles its
evaluation of pain in that the major factor in the determination
of the sum eventually awarded will be the subjective views of
the jurors as to the dollar value of the disfigurement. A court's
evaluation of disfigurement differs from its evaluation of other
types of permanent injury in that most permanent injury is in
one way or another susceptible to an objective pecuniary approach (reduction of future earning capacity, for instance). Disfigurement does have its objective components of value, a component known to claims men as "cosmetic value," a term which
refers not only to the objective characteristic of the disfigurement
itself but also to the idea that the damage done by a disfiguring
injury may be greater to one person than to another.

"Cosmetic value" refers not only to the appearance of the
scar itself but to its effect on the appearance of the injured and
takes into consideration such factors as masking by hair growth
(an astonishing number of scars occur on the eyebrow line; seen
in the hospital with the eyebrow shaved they are nothing less
than gruesome; with the eyebrow grown back they are often
invisible), and conformity of the scar line to a face's natural
pattern of wrinkles.

Of few men can it be said, "His face is his fortune." For that
reason men's claims for scarring and disfigurement generally
carry a lower value than the same injury to women. Scarring in
an unmarried woman calls for a higher evaluation than in a married woman. Generally, a scar is worth more on the face of a
pretty girl than on the face of her homely friend. This seeming

injustice is not by the decision of insurance people; it is an observation of the opinions of the average man as he expresses himself in a jury box.

In pricing scars, as in so many other aspects of claims work, the adjuster should bear in mind that the reality with which he is dealing is not so much the actual cosmetic value of the scar as *the opinion that the jury will hold* of the cosmetic value of that scar. For example, a scar located on the scalp and covered by hair would, logically, seem to have no cosmetic value. It would be a mistake, however, to assume that some clever and aggressive plaintiff's counsel might not demonstrate the scar to a jury and succeed in *persuading* them to make an award for it. To be realistic, the possibility of this improbable outcome should be recognized for what it is—one of those things which probably will not happen but which cannot be completely ignored.

The repair of scar damage falls to the field of medicine known as plastic surgery. To a layman not familiar with this specialty, the results are almost beyond belief. A young adjuster needs to be especially careful that he evaluates a cosmetic problem in the light of what it will be *after* plastic repair. Some attorneys have their scarred clients delay repair until after trial. The defense combats this by introducing testimony of a plastic surgeon to show the repair that can be made.

The best defense against this tactic is much like the defense against the forward pass: "Tackle the passer before he can get rid of the ball." The adjuster's best move is to conduct himself so as to merit and retain the confidence of the injured party and preserve direct negotiation with the claimant. The plastic repair may then be completed before settlement is undertaken. Financing this operation before the emergence of the industry's present attitude toward advance payments often presented a problem.

Now, plastic repair or any other medical or surgical intervention which repairs traumatic damage represents a type of claim to which advance payments are especially applicable.[5] Surgical intervention, whether financed by advanced payments or not, may have a profound influence on value here.

---

[5] For contrast, consider the first edition of this text published only six years ago which said, "Only upon explicit and rarely given instructions from the insurer will the adjuster be in a position to admit liability or underwrite expense."

Settlement tactics which might be employed in such a situation are considered in Chapter 12, Closing, page 516. A frank discussion with the claimant and the doctor, and a threeway agreement that doctor and hospital will be paid directly out of any settlement finally arrived at, may be sufficient to enable the desired repairs to be undertaken.

Pricing scars should recognize both the objective and the subjective components of value. The objective components are usually discoverable. Attorneys will usually permit representatives of the insurer to see their disfigured clients and will often cooperate by furnishing photographs. The effects of plastic surgery can, within limits, be forecast. Sound pricing of this type of claim requires the ascertainment of these objective factors as fully as circumstances permit.

After the objective factors have been recognized and ascertained, realism also recognizes the remaining subjective component—the jury's *evaluation* of the disfigurement demonstrated to them. In addition to other factors tending to enhance or depress value, the most important factor is probably the relative skills of counsel who may eventually try the case.

Pre-existing Physical Defects

It would seem natural to expect pre-existing weakness or predisposition to injury or disease to be a mitigating circumstance—that damages wrought on a body so affected would be worth less than those suffered by a sound body. This indeed is the popular view of the subject. The reverse, however, is true. The tort feasor who inflicts injury on a weakened or predisposed body is liable for the resultant condition, not for the condition that would have resulted had the injured body been a healthy one. A traumatic injury to a leg with varicose veins may result in formation of a stubborn ulcer. This claim must be evaluated on the basis of the resultant ulcer, not the bruise which on a normal leg would have healed in a few days.

Presence of pre-existing weakness or disease is widely recognized as a factor tending to *increase* value. This is particularly true in the early life of a case, where disposition tends to be based more on practical rather than on formal or legalistic considerations. An important result of this legal view of the question of aggravation is to open the way to an award for many conditions almost universally recognized as nontraumatic in origin. These may become the basis for an award if it is successfully contended that these conditions have been aggravated, accelerated or exacerbated.

Conditions that predispose to injury may be progressive in nature. In that event, the defendant *is permitted to argue that the injury's only effect may have been to bring the claimant somewhat sooner to an otherwise inevitable end result.* It is only realistic to point out that experience teaches us that such an argument is not easily accepted by a sympathetic jury.

Granting that the presence of a pre-existing injury or disease may enhance rather than depress a claim's value, nevertheless practical adjusting must attempt to make effective the reasonable view that an insurer is not held responsible for *all* of a claimant's infirmities. If, for instance, a retired person suffers a shoulder injury which lights up latent arthritis and leaves him with moderate limitation of motion, such an injury would almost certainly bring him less in damages than an injury with similar limitations sustained by an active major league shortstop. The adjuster's obligation is to recognize the potential inherent in pre-existing weakness or disease, but to hold such recognition within realistic financial limits. Therefore, while he recognizes that honest people do dream up connections between injury and disease, and find the doctors to support them, he does not conclude too readily that the basic trouble was neither accident-related nor accident-aggravated. He is in the familiar position of guarding against twin dangers. He may not open the company's treasury and lose all sight of the real injury sustained whenever he encounters a pre-existing condition; neither may he disregard the potential inherent in this situation.

Cases involving prior injury or disease *are* dangerous. The adjuster should bring them immediately to the attention of his supervisor and should avoid ultimatums, bending every effort instead to keeping open the channels of communication between himself and his claimant. Until his own experience enables him to form sound judgments, he should make it his business to consult the best brains among the supervisory personnel to whom he reports.

Permanency

A claimant is entitled to ask compensation for the future consequences of his injury as well as for those damages which have resulted up till the time of the settlement or trial. In order to sustain such a request he must offer competent evidence to the effect that the anticipated circumstances for which recovery is sought are "reasonably probable." Such evidence is usually supplied by the testimony of physicians, and if an attempt is made to refute it, it is commonly made by offering contradictory medical testimony. Many of the elements of future damage are susceptible to measurement in money (future medical expense and anticipated future loss of earning capacity, for instance). But, of course, some elements are *not* precisely measurable. An example is the slightly crippled arm which will not prevent a man from carrying on his usual occupation but which will always be a little bit of a nuisance, or, to consider a somewhat more common complaint, the allegation that a claimant will be subject to permanent recurring headaches. This combination of characteristics, some susceptible to dollar measurement and some not, highlights the often artificial distinction between special and general damage.

From the plaintiff's standpoint, no declaration in an injury suit is considered complete in these days without an allegation that the injury complained of is permanent, and this contention is usually disputed by the defense.

We are not at this time concerned with the obvious disputes that revolve around these contentions. Our concern is with the various aspects of permanency and their influence on value.

Among the continuing after-effects of injury are the need for medical care and the impairment of earning capacity. To each of these, a dollar value can be ascribed. Factors to be considered are:

1. Medical opinion on the extent and nature of necessary future care.
2. Past earning records.
3. Probable future earning capacity.
4. Medical opinion concerning the impairment of earning capacity.
5. The life and work expectancy of the injured person.

It is true of medical matters, as of almost everything else, that "anything can happen." Therefore the courts impose the test of "reasonable probability." A plaintiff is not entitled to recover for what "may happen"; he must offer medical evidence that the contingency for which recovery is sought is "reasonably probable."

Contentions relative to loss of future earning capacity and future medical expense are often bitterly disputed, and the testimony of one set of experts is found to be in violent conflict with that of another. An adjuster's evaluation of such a problem reflects his views of the probable outcome of the various contentions. He can hardly conclude that an award, if reached, could do less than reflect the findings of the most optimistic of available opinion. To be realistic, he should concede something against the possibility that the more pessimistic outlook will prevail.

To put it more plainly, if the company's own doctor informs an adjuster that he expects a plaintiff to suffer permanent loss of 10% of the strength of the right arm, the adjuster must, when he evaluates the claim, recognize that this opinion puts something of a floor under the view that the jury will eventually form about the injury. Moreover, a realist can hardly conclude that his doctor will be the only one to whom the jury will listen. If the adjuster knows that a respected doctor is to testify on plaintiff's behalf that the arm will sustain 25% loss of strength plus 10% loss of both extension and flexion, then he will, even if he honestly feels this view to be mistaken, almost certainly ask himself, "and what verdict will they find if they do adopt this more serious view of the injury?" He is very likely to raise his price to reflect the chances of such an outcome.

Pages 456 and 457 quote from actual correspondence and demonstrate an adjuster's attempt to apply the above idea.

Special Damages—Permanent Injury Context

Evaluating cases of permanent injury requires some shifting of mental gears to avoid being misled by illogical conclusions in respect to special damages.

Adjusters are accustomed to recognize *lost earning capacity* as "special damage." Therefore it is not uncommon for plaintiffs' attorneys to submit a list of specials something like this:

1. Medical expense .... $ 700.00
2. Lost earnings to date 2,000.00
3. Permanent injury, 20% permanent loss of function, left arm 20,000.00
4. Impaired future earning capacity based on 20 years work expectancy, earning capacity diminished by $1,000 per annum 20,000.00

Total special damages $42,700.00

This array of so-called specials may then be used to support a demand for three or four times $42,700. Granting that an argument can be made to the effect that the fourth item does not duplicate the third, it seems illogical to consider either item 3 or item 4 as acceptable special damages. If the concept that the total value of a claim should be some multiple of special damages has any validity at all, it springs from the assumption that the intangibles—pain, suffering, and the diminution of the other pleasures of life—are proportionate to the amount of out-of-pocket expense incurred, an idea that does not fit the example cited. It would probably be a very liberal jury in a liberal jurisdiction that would award anything remotely approaching three or four times $42,700 in the case cited above.

In this area, as in others, juries are difficult to predict. A realistic approach would seem to be one that recognizes that a claim for permanent injury involves also a claim for the temporary aspects of the same injury. In other words, the broken arm imposes its temporary effects—pain, cost of medical attention, loss of earning capacity, etc.—during the healing period, but if the fracture fails to heal perfectly, it imposes also its permanent effects which have to be anticipated and evaluated. In pricing such a claim it would seem realistic, then, to approach the temporary phase of the claim—specials, pain and suffering, etc.—just as though no permanency were involved. To consider the permanency one would consider those aspects of the permanency which are subject to dollar measurement and then attempt to forecast the figure which the jury will apply to the other general elements of the permanency. This forecast may or may not employ the anticipated dollar damages as a criterion of measurement.

In conclusion it should be noted that there are some injuries which are permanent but which neither impair earning capacity nor involve pain beyond the healing period. Such an injury might be the loss by a clean amputation of one or more phalanges by an elderly housewife. Here, the adjuster should be realist enough to recognize that no jury is going to fail to compensate the lady for her loss. He may, however, reasonably expect that her award will be less than it would be if continuing pain or impaired earnings capacity were a factor.

LIABILITY

"Liability" refers to the general complex of questions and arguments revolving about the question of fault—i.e., who was to blame for the accident? The influence of liability on value at the *settlement table* seems obvious, but discussion of this influence is deferred and dealt with when mathmatical values are considered. For the moment, consideration is directed solely to the effects of liability on the verdict.

The effect of liability on verdicts may be open and easy to recognize, as in those jurisdictions which recognize some form of comparative negligence. In jurisdictions which *do not* recognize comparative negligence, liability may influence the size of a verdict in ways not openly recognized. In the latter jurisdictions, it is necessary to acknowledge the possibility, possibly even the probability, that once a jury has made up its mind to *award* damages, it will dismiss the question of liability from all further consideration. This is certainly one of the things that can and often does happen. Indeed, in theory, this is what should happen.

On the other hand, the adjuster must consider—and in his pricing must make due allowance for—the possibility of some outcome like the following: A trial is to be held in a state where contributory negligence rules. The jury will usually be instructed more or less forcefully that they must either find a plaintiff free of negligence and award him full damages or, if they find him to have contributed in any degree to the accident, they must send him home uncompensated. They may even be instructed that they may not render what is known as a quotient verdict. (A quotient verdict is one arrived at by each juror's writing down the sum he desires to award. These figures are then added together and the result divided by the number of jurors, and that result, or quotient, is announced as the jury's award.) However, even in contributory negligence jurisdictions, liability situations may bring about what are in effect *compromise awards*—something quite close to a quotient verdict—although the process of arriving at them may be less rational. Such a result may occur when one or two jurors wish to make a defendant's finding, while all of the others wish to award damages. In such a situation the holdouts may eventually acquiesce in a verdict in a reduced amount, in order to let everybody get home in time for a good night's sleep. The converse, too, may happen—all but one or two want to find for the defendant and, to bring the matter to an end, the rest acquiesce in a small award. States which recognize the comparative negligence doctrine are in effect rationalizing decisions and attitudes quite similar to the above.

When a defendant's negligence is so glaring as to inflame a jury's wrath, this wrath may be vented openly or covertly by increasing the size of the award. This may be an open, rationally arrived-at decision, when the plaintiff sues for "punitive damages." The courts of at least one state, however, have held that *punitive damages*—because they are assessed with the attempt to *punish*—are not "damages" within the meaning of the insuring clause of a liability policy. This may result in the disappearance of pleas for punitive damages, but attorneys will still seek to inflame passions.

Claims people are inclined by nature and experience to be skeptical of punitive damages. The usual feeling is that whatever the liability situation, an injury is worth about the same amount—if a jury makes up its mind to find damages, its findings will probably not be influenced to any great extent by moralistic intent to punish. Where liability is so obvious as to invite punitive damages, counsel for the defense often admits liability and thereby confines testimony solely to the question of injury and damage.

Finally, liability may affect values—both judgment and settlement—according to the presence or absence of a cross claim for damages on the part of an injured insured. Experience forces claims people to recognize that of all the emotional factors bearing on judgments, a jury's reluctance to let an injured person go home uncompensated is probably the most important. When there is an injured insured pressing *his* cross claim for damages in an action to be tried simultaneously with the claim against him, the emotional factor is even. In such a situation, the insurer may hold a confident view of liability, for presumably the jury will be as anxious to award damages to the cross claiming insured as they are to award damages to the injured claimant. Hence, if an insurer feels that the liability situation is, on the whole, favorable to its insured, it may price the claim accordingly, feeling that the claimant has very little chance to recover—that the weight of sympathy being even on each side of the case, the jury will probably find in favor of the insured.

The insured may, however, persuade the other insurance company to make a settlement with him. Now the emotional factor is unbalanced. There will still be sympathy for the injured claimant. Most jurisdictions, moreover, require all knowledge of the settlement made with the insured to be kept from the jury. Paradoxically, therefore, the same insurance company which started out with a low idea of value because it expected to have its insured in court pressing his claim, may now have to raise its sights, even though—in fact, *because*—its own insured has been paid off.

Accident Location

Location as a variant in the makeup of value seldom concerns the field adjuster. It is a rare accident that is not adjusted and, if necessary, litigated in the same general area in which it happens. If an adjuster is familiar with values in his area, he has made the necessary adjustment to local conditions. He need only guard against the exceptional case that may be removed to another jurisdiction.

The federal constitution permits suits to be brought in a federal court if the parties to the suit have what is known as "diversity of citizenship, a condition which obtains when the claimant is a citizen of one state and the defendant a citizen of another. Then action may be brought in the federal courts. Some federal courts seem to render higher verdicts than state courts located only a few blocks away, but this is probably more the exception than the rule. The more common situation is for federal courts to be responsive to the prevailing local pattern. This is hardly surprising—they draw their jurors from the same areas.

The practical importance of the possibility of removal to a federal court is that the plaintiff's counsel may be enabled to bring his suit in a more liberal area. The involvement of a foreign corporation as defendant may open the door to a very flexible choice of jurisdictions, sometimes completely outside the state of the original happening. Matters of jurisdiction are extremely technical. Field adjusters should be wary of attempting to decide matters for themselves in this area. They should seek the advice of counsel.

At the same time that it is observed that diversity of citizenship presents opportunities to plaintiffs' attorneys to remove their claims to a more liberal venue, it should also be observed that most attorneys sue on their own home grounds. Travel expense, and a reluctance to split fees with counsel in the area of the suit, are influences tending to bring cases into court not far from their places of origin. Removal to a distant ground is likely to be "uneconomic," except in litigation involving very serious injuries, with all the other necessary ingredients of the shock verdict— that is, the availability of very high policy limits, or a defendant of unquestioned financial resources.

For practical guidance, the situation may be summarized as follows: The adjuster should be alert to recognize when diversity of citizenship prevails, and when it does, the opportunities it offers to a plaintiff. However, the opportunities notwithstanding, he should also recognize that attorneys usually sue on their own home grounds. The probability of the removal of a case to a more liberal jurisdiction is simply one of those possibilities to be held in mind. The consideration may be important in influencing adjusters or their examiners to include that last $100 or $200 in settling a bad claim.

Factors Irrelevant But Foreseeable

Courts sometimes respond to factors irrelevant to the merits of the case—factors that are nonetheless understandable, with an effect (if the adjuster is willing to admit that his vision may be a little cloudy) subject to some degree of anticipation, and even control.

The relative skill of counsel is such a factor. It ought not to be true that a given claim will bring more in the hands of one attorney than another, yet it is obvious that this is so. Hence plaintiffs' attorneys of real ability almost always command premium figures in settlement. The converse is equally true. Results attained by an uncommonly skillful defense attorney encourage his clients to be more restrained in their offers, and plaintiffs' attorneys facing such an adversary are more inclined to shave their demands.

Personalities of the parties also influence the final outcome. This is a point of great practical importance and one on which adjusters should promptly advise their employers or clients. Though it may seem a subtlety, the adjuster's approach to the question is practical in the extreme. He should realize that he carries a natural defendants' bias. If, then, the insured is unable to convince the adjuster of the merits of his case, this failure should be recognized and reported to the carrier as a danger signal. The jury will probably be similarly unimpressed. On the other hand, the ability of an injured claimant to convince the adjuster of the legitimacy of his injury and to strike a strong chord of sympathy should be recognized as handwriting on the wall.

Emotion is possibly the most important irrelevancy. No person old enough to be an adjuster needs to be told that a trial is at least as much influenced by emotion as by reason. To say, as has been said, "Serious injury to a plaintiff is evidence of a defendant's negligence," is an obvious overstatement, but only in degree. The adjuster who fails to recognize the sympathy factor is simply shutting his eyes to the facts.

Emotions may work for the defense. Once a jury gets the idea that a claimant is trying unfairly to capitalize his injury, its resentment is aroused. When a case that is seemingly hopeless from a liability standpoint is won by the defendant, it is usually won by the expression of this sentiment.

Further, juries are more inclined to generous verdicts if the defendant is wealthy. This is so peculiarly true of the large corporations that they are known to the trade as "target risks."

Important factors which color a case and thereby create an emotional atmosphere influential on value also include:

> The drunken driver
> The hit and run driver
> Remarks at the scene expressing inhumanity or repellent callous-
> ness
> A participant in the accident "out with the wrong spouse"
> One party a public hero in the community

Any of these seemingly irrelevant factors may influence the end result. The influence may be only one of the many factors leading the jury to its final verdict, or it may be so dominant as to override all the law and the evidence.

Irrational Factors

Efforts to understand verdicts risk complete frustaration unless there be accepted from the beginning the idea that much happens that *defies* understanding. Irrational factors *do* influence judgments. They may even determine them. *Racial prejudice* is a case in point. A jury might wrongfully deny a member of a minority his proper compensation, thus expressing its own prejudice. On the other hand, in the attempt to be impartial the jury might lean over backwards and make an award that it would never have given to a member of its own race. Adjusters see many miscarriages of both types, and while it is often possible to foresee that such a factor may operate, it is usually quite impossible to predict whether the net effect will be favorable or unfavorable. A way to forecast the direction in which these factors will operate has yet to be invented. They can only be accepted as part of the "unknown."

There are many more. A dominant juror takes a liking or a dislike to one of the attorneys. A snatch of courthouse gossip, overheard by a juryman, possibly out of context and completely misunderstood, may tip the scales. A jury may make three perfectly proper awards in a row, and then decide to even the scales of justice by sending an equally deserving plaintiff home empty-handed.

An amusing sidelight to this phase of justice is a classic story: Lawyer A spots a prospective juror whose appearance, occupation and manner convince A that the man should be kept off the jury at all costs. Despite all A's efforts, the juror serves, and, of course, turns out to be the one who, holding out against all his fellows, eventually persuades them to render a verdict in favor of Lawyer A's client.

Irrationality is not entirely to be deplored. After all, uncertainty is the spur that brings about settlements.

THE ATTEMPT TO FORECAST VERDICTS

A verdict consists of special damages, about which a great deal can be learned in advance of trial, and general damages, about which little can be learned. Forecasting verdicts is to a high degree a matter of forecasting what a jury will award for *general damages*.

Such a forecast requires claims men to:

    a. Attempt to place themselves in the shoes of the jurors;
    b. Consider whether such intangibles as pain have a dollar value per unit of time; and
    c. Consider realistically what is the most and least favorable of probable verdicts—and where the mean lies between these extremes.

Special Damages—as an Indicator of Verdict Value

Special damages are themselves part of a judgment—this factor ought not to be overlooked. If that statement is taken with the proviso that, even more than most, it is subject to the weakness of all generalities, then a very guarded additional statement may be made—that, taken as a whole, the judgment will probably vary somewhat in proportion to the amount of the special damages, a dim reflection of the reasonable proposition that an injury which required $1,000 to cure probably was more painful than one which required $50 to cure.

Beyond that guarded generality, it also seems proper to note that some categories of cases have low verdict values in relation to special damages. These are claims characterized by:

High special damages
Substantial lost earning capacity
Long hospitalization
Injury which does not excite unusual sympathy

On the other hand cases likely to develop high judgment value in relation to special damages include:

Small claims
Claims in which the only special damages are for medical attention
Claims where the healing period is long and disability short
Claims with a prolonged residual of pain

Forecasting the "General Damages" Element of the Judgment

Most attempts to forecast judgments come down, in the last analysis, to the attempt to forecast what a jury will award for pain and suffering or for those other elements of damage which are not readily reducible to dollars and cents.

Since any forecast is the attempt to predict what 12 men will think and do about an often disputed set of facts, it is hardly surprising that a really satisfactory forecasting technique has yet to be invented. The approaches to be considered have all been employed, and continue to be employed, by adjusters and attorneys. To the extent that they introduce a modest degree of order and discipline into an otherwise chaotic process, they have been found helpful.

To consider one approach, then, let it be supposed the trial is about to commence but negotiations are still in progress. The claim is one in which the claimant will probably recover, the insured being *clearly at fault*.

In awarding damages, a jury will certainly give this claimant his out-of-pocket expenses. It may be taken for granted that they will give him something with which to pay his lawyer (courtroom scuttle butt quickly informs the jury that lawyers' fees vary from 25% to 50% of the final verdict). The out-of-pocket expenses and the lawyer taken care of, the jury will then give the injured man something for his pain and suffering.

There, in a nutshell, is one of the soundest and most reliable means of predicting verdicts. A seasoned claims man, in pricing his case, may go through precisely this process. Putting aside his natural defendants' bias, and recognizing it to be an almost impossible feat of mental gymnastics, he nevertheless tries to put himself in the frame of mind of the average juror: "This man's expenses are $1,000. That fellow I talked to in the men's room before I was impaneled told me that lawyers' fees are generally one-third of the final verdict. Accordingly, if we give this fellow $3,000, the lawyer's fee will be one-third or $1,000, and that will leave him $1,000 for himself, which seems about right to me."

"X" Times Special Damages

The subjective factor in the approach to verdict forecasts has its obviously unsatisfactory features. To attempt to minimize these features, those who operate in the business have persistently tried to discover a mathematical relationship between the special damages, which are relatively easy to ascertain, and the general damages, which are not. To those who use this approach for the purpose of forecasting, there must also be added those who use the same approach as a tool of persuasion—that is, the attorney who says, "How can you make me such an offer? The jury will give me at least five times my specials," or the adjuster who says, "How can you even ask such a figure? Certainly you can't expect a jury to give you more than three times your specials."

There is simply no agreement as to what figure expresses the correct mathematical relationship between judgments and special damages. If there were such an agreement, the following examples would still raise questions as to the *universal* applicability of this approach.

An unemployed claimant, for instance, has "bumps and lumps." His doctor looks him over, tells him he sees nothing serious, says, "Call me if you have any trouble." Special damages are $10 for an office call. Multiplied by even such a generous multiplier as five, this case would have a value of $50, yet it would be a *conservative* adjuster operating in a conservative territory who would not agree that this was an unrealistically low estimate of the verdict value for this particular claim.

For the same injury, however, assume the claimant to be a mechanic netting $25 a day. He and his doctor agree that he should take three days off. His special damages, therefore, including the $10 doctor bill, total $85. If these specials are multiplied by five the resultant $425 would be high in some jurisdictions, low in others but most claims men would feel that at least it approached realism. As an adjuster gains in experience he will hear it argued that cases at the judgment level are worth anywhere from two and a half to 10 times the special damages. As he watches trial results he will find support for each extreme and for the figures between. Possibly the best that can be said for this mathmatical approach is that it one divides the amount of a verdict by the special damages, there will alawys be some kind of a quotient.

The conclusion simply has to be that no number for multiplying his specials has any validity as a predictor. The many influential factors *not related to special damage* mentioned earlier in this chapter point up the weakness of this approach.

Assigning Value to Periods of Disability

Another essentially arithmetical approach assumes that a jury will compensate for pain and suffering on the basis of a certain amount per day or week. In applying this approach, $100 a week is sometimes thought a proper figure for total disability and $50 for partial. There is no agreement as to what constitutes a "correct" figure and, if there were, no guarantee that a jury would act accordingly. This approach is probably erratic, and as misleading as the strictly arithmetical. It is a useful concept only if employed for what it is—one of a number of ways to predict.

Evaluating the Best and Worst Possible Outcomes

Litigated matters commonly are comprised of a number of elements about which there is substantial disagreement, and some elements about which there is no dispute at all.

It is helpful to approach such claims by attempting to consider the best and the worst that may happen in the jury room.

In this approach, one looks at the known facts—ignoring for the moment those still in contention—and attempts to form an opinion as to the least the jury may be expected to award on those facts. This he takes as a *minimum*. Then he considers the items in dispute—of these it must be ordinarily conceded that a claimant has at least an outside chance of selling his contentions—and, assuming that the claimant will be successful, the adjuster tries to estimate the *most* a jury might reasonably be expected to award. While it is true that he still has a wide range between his hoped-for minimum and dreaded maximum, he has at least narrowed the field of search.

This approach seems to introduce a note of worthwhile realism in claims of probable liability involving injuries, some features of which are admitted while others are in dispute. Its application is demonstrated by the following memorandum:

> I enclose:
>
> Mr. B's letter of 6/13
> Dr. W's letter of 2/1
> Dr. W's letter of 4/10
> Dr. K's letter of 2/20
> Mr. B's summation of special damages, with supporting bills and invoices

We have the familiar problem of a case with some very solid portions to it, and some parts more than a little shaky. Liability is obvious and we will get nowhere attacking those items of special damage that I have marked with "X."

To them must be added $260, the lost earning capacity ascertained by our Mr. G by checking with the County Board of Public Instruction. This case therefore should, at the very least, produce a judgment based upon special damages of approximately $850. You will understand, of course, that I am excluding property damage from the foregoing figure.

The big argument here, as I made plain to Mr. B, is a connection between the accident and the claimant's complaints referable to her thyroid condition. I was able to draw from Mr. B admission that he recognized that Dr. K had left the question of connection entirely in the realm of conjecture.

Mr. B took the position that he was frankly trying to get this woman in the hands of a psychiatrist but she was resisting him. I think I shook him up a bit when I pointed out that the psychiatrist would not have the free hand in this case that he does most of the time. Here we have a woman with a definite physical condition (a thyroid imbalance) which by itself is sufficient to account for her symptom complex. I believe that either with or without cross-examination, a finding of neurosis is not warranted. Nevertheless, while I am without reservation trying to tear down Mr. B's faith in that element of the case, realism requires that we recognize that, *after all, he may succeed in establishing it.*

If he does, we are faced with a major claim, one wherein Mr. B's suggested figure of $8,000 might well turn out to be reasonable, even modest.

When I price a case I try to look at it from two sides, first considering what is the most favorable result we can come out with. In that light, this case boils down to $850 worth of special damages that I see no way of attacking. Therefore I see a case that probably ought to settle for approximately $2,000. This I arrive at disregarding the possibility of involving the thyroid. Then I look at the worst side of the picture—the thyroid situation. There I see something that *could* make the case worth anywhere from $5,000 to $10,000 more, if Mr. B is succescsful in connecting it. If we are *completely* successful in combating it, we still have the minimum previously mentioned to reckon with. I think that the possibility of Mr. B's attaching the thyroid condition to the accident is certainly no less than one in 10; probably a little better than that. I recommend, therefore, a total price of $3,000.

Signed . . . .

(It might be mentioned that this memorandum is too long-winded. Boiling down would improve it.)

Adopting Approach that Fits Adjuster

This book has repeatedly emphasized that effective tactics and techniques vary from adjuster to adjuster according to the personalities and abilities of the individual. Some adjusters have a "two times two is four" approach to life. One who falls in that category estimates a claim's judgment value by applying one or all of the methods discussed here, and possibly others of his own devising. The results thus attained are probably not less in number than the number of methods employed. In the end, he is still on his own; possibly the figure decided upon is determined by that honored if somewhat confused entity, "good claims judgment." Other adjusters form their judgments intuitively. They go directly to the last step. Pricing to them is nothing more than an educated guess. The author has met both extremes and many in between. He fails to observe a significant advantage in foresight for any one type over any other.

In any event, in his attempts to forecast verdict, a claims man is on his own. To be a realist, he should at least consider each of the influential factors mentioned in this chapter. The weight he will give to each and how he will combine these elements into his forecast will have to be left strictly to him.

MATHEMATICAL VALUE DISTINGUISHED FROM VERDICT VALUE

Until now, this chapter has discussed *judgment* values—and has distinguished them from *settlement values.* It has been necessary to consider judgments before coming to settlements, because a sound appraisal of a case's settlement value cannot be arrived at except as that appraisal is based on a sound forecast of judgment value.

Another concept, mathematical value, has to be considered before one reaches settlement value. It is re-emphasized that the term "mathematical value" [6] is almost unknown to the claims vocabulary. It is employed only because the concept is in common use and this chapter has to name it to talk about it.

Essentially, two factors separate a claim's *mathematical value* from its *verdict value.*

1. *Uncertainty about liability.* Nothing is more uncertain than the outcome of a law suit. In many claims where liability seems obvious, juries refuse to make any award at all to the plaintiff and in other cases they go to the opposite extreme. Sound pricing at the settlement level considers the probability of either outcome.
2. *Uncertainty about damages.* Only rarely does a case reach trial without substantial conflict in evidence as to the nature

and extent of injury. (See the memorandum starting on page 456 for a case presenting a typical picture.)

Liability

Liability, as an influential component of verdict values, is of only limited importance (see pages 446 to 452). When it comes to mathematical value, liability (or uncertainty about it) is a prime factor.

A claim may, for instance, involve an injury of the greatest severity, yet, because the liability defenses may appear so strong as to be impregnable, sound pricing may lead to the conclusion that the claim has no value. (A denial of liability is essentially a conclusion that a claim has no settlement value.) In the claims business, as we have frequently noted, things are not black and white, but only different shades of gray. The fact is that the absolute "no liability" claim is relatively rare. Usually one has to concede that there is at least an outside chance that a claimant will prevail. More commonly, the issues could go either way.

The theoretical basis for pricing these matters is, like many things, simple to state but not so simple to apply. If experience teaches that a claim is of a class in which the plaintiff prevails only 50% of the time, then that claim has a mathematical value of only 50% of what it would otherwise be worth. By this thinking, then, in a fifty-fifty liability situation, a claim with injury (disregarding liability) worth $1,000, for settlement purposes would be valued at $500. The theory is simple, but applying it is far from simple, since claims do not come neatly labeled "50% liability" or "This claimant has precisely two chances out of 10 to prevail." In any event, the business is unanimous in considering that it is sound to lower one's sights for settlement purposes to reflect the extent that liability reduces the probability of a claimant's recovery. This excerpt from an actual file demonstrates an application of this principle: [6]

As I told you at the time of our last conversation, January 2, it is my opinion that your present authorization, $2,000, plus payment of the subrogated interest of Metropolitan ($1,106.16)

---

[6] The term "danger value" is in common use, but it has other meanings with which we are not concerned here.

is about all the claim is worth. I analyzed it in the following terms:

Disregarding for the moment the question of liability, I can't see a jury bringing in anything less than $4,000 (if they are to find damages), and I think it a little unlikely that they will go much over $10,000. Therefore I assume a median jury figure (disregarding the liability question) of $7,000.

We all know the accident was all the boy's fault. We all know, too, that when analyzed, all of our witnesses are weak.

As far as I am concerned, this case is a fifty-fifty one, both for the plaintiff and for the defendant. Half of $7,000 is $3,500; hence, I think your authorization represents a reasonable discount for settlement purposes.

Notice that the authorization in the correspondence just quoted asked for and extended for settlement purposes did not equal the mathematical value ascribed to this claim.

It should be obvious that both the adjuster and the examiner to whom he wrote considered mathematical value but did not mention it as such in getting to the figure they were really interested in, settlement value. Settlement and mathematical value may or may not be the same—but further discussion of settlement value is deferred until later in this chapter.

It would be a mistake to think that liability operates solely to depress the ideas of value of those charged with a claim's defense. It has a similar effect on plaintiffs' attorneys who, while they are obliged to try to secure for their clients the best possible return, must, if they are realists, warn their clients of the negative aspects of their claims. Thus, if an attorney felt that his client was not certain to recover—if in his heart he agreed, for instance, that the boy mentioned in the memorandum had only the fifty-fifty chance of recovery that the adjuster conceded him—he would be doing his client a disservice if he failed to advise accordingly. He probably would advise his clients to modify their demands proportionately.

Note the influence of the doubtful liability on the case's value. This adjuster and examiner were used to working with one another; the liability picture and testimony of the witnesses had previously been thoroughly discussed and analyzed; injuries were summarized in preceding reports; expenses verified by bills already submitted. In other words, the insurer was already in possession of virtually everything it needed except an expression of the adjuster's evaluation of the situation. Had this been the actual request for authority, special damages would have been retabulated and totalled.

Uncertainty About Damages

It has already been pointed out that most law suits develop some testimony about which there is little dispute and some testimony which will be strongly contradicted. The memorandum beginning on page 456 deals with such a claim. The outcome of such a claim would depend in part on the view that the jury adopts of the woman's nervousness and whether they regard it as related to her accident.

The outcome would also depend on the subjective evaluation which a jury might place on her condition once they had satisfied themselves as to what her condition really is.

An influential juryman may, for instance, have been exposed to some shrew with an over-active thyroid and vent his wrath on the claimant by persuading his fellows to a very low verdict. It is equally possible that a juryman may have had his heart touched by an over-active thryroid patient who made a brave fight to live with her complaint, and he may persuade his fellows to an unexpectedly generous verdict. Irrational factors are impossible to predict but they can, if one does not take the arithmetic of the thing too seriously, be expressed in terms of the dollar value of an outcome which embraces both possibilities.

Thus does uncertainty about damage affect mathematical value. Were it not for the predictive power of the concept, virtually all injury claims would have to be litigated to arrive at a disposition. It is a step on the road to settlement value. Whether or not he calls it by name, an adjuster will have frequent cause to consider mathematical value. From there he will go to settlement value.

Settlement Value

Early in the chapter, this term was defined as the point where the forces pushing an adjuster toward settlement are balanced by the forces urging him to hang onto his company's money.

The point was also made early in the chapter that the majority of claims settle for subjective values and it is repeated here that it is well that this is so. If it were not so, automobile insurance for a single year might well exceed the cost of the car.

Settlement value has to be remembered at all stages of a claim's life because it sets the upper limit to an adjuster's negotiations. Claims often pass beyond the stage of friendly negotiation and the claimant begins to evaluate his claim with the simple goal of getting as much as he can. The claims man must then form his judgment of the balance point of the claim for which he is responsible.

Many factors that bear on verdict predictions have been enumerated. The mathematical value of a claim is different from verdict value. The following paragraphs now consider additional factors which make settlement value something else again.

Nuisance Value—Cost of Defense

Cost of defense is often taken to be synonymous with "nuisance value," a term usually invoked in a derrogatory sense. Nuisance value is a restricted term deriving from the fact that defense of a law suit is a very expensive business. Some insurers admit that they pay nuisance value, considering it good sense to do so. Others refuse to pay nuisance value, even carrying their feelings so far as to forbid the term to appear in their files.

The logic (or fallacy, if you will) that underlies a nuisance value is: "It will cost me $500 to defend this claim. Even though I feel a defendant's verdict is certain, I will save $100 if I can settle for $400 or less." When the adjuster reaches such a management level as to become acquainted with the costs of doing business (in addition to the cost of paying losses), he understands the appeal of this thinking.

Those who refuse to pay nuisance value are moved principally by two considerations. They feel that to pay a nuisance value is, in effect, to yield to a threat of blackmail. It will only encourage bringing more groundless claims in the future. They feel, too, that the idea of nuisance value embraces a fallacy in logic. A dispute over a $10 claim might cost $100 to defend. To recognize nuisance value, they argue, concedes that it would be worth up to $100 to settle a claim for $10.

This is not the place to promote or defend either position. The adjuster will soon enough be informed by his employer or client as to *its* view of the subject.[7]

Nuisance value is usually used to refer to trifling claims, those where it seems inconceivable that a jury would find favorably to the plaintiff or where injury appears demonstrably absent.

Cost of defense, whether or not acknowledged as an element in pricing, is universally acknowledged in the business as a factor of major importance urging realism in pricing. It is for this reason that as early as Chapter I, page 5, there appeared the strong statement:

> There is nothing so futile as to try to explain an adverse verdict with the excuse, "It was a miscarriage of justice."

A quick look at costs explains why companies try to recognize value early. It costs from $500 to $1,000 in most jurisdictions to get the average so-called whiplash to the courthouse door. If the case does not settle there is usually costs roughly a similar sum to try it to a lower court verdict.[8] It is no wonder that even after getting a defendant's verdict, many claims managers have been heard to mutter about a pyrrhic victory. (Pyrrhus, in 279 B.C., lost the flower of his army in a savage battle with the Romans and his remark, "One more such victory and we are lost," made him famous to this day.)

For such reasons, a major part of claims management goes to making sure that a claim's potential is recognized early. It is

---

[7] It is the author's observation that a strong majority of the industry holds "nuisance value" to be a fallacy; a view which he is glad to share.

[8] Costs include defense attorneys' fees, court reporters' fees, fees for expert testimony and other lesser items, all essential to a vigorous defense.

expensive enough to litigate the claims one has to without wasting money resisting claims which can be settled within their settlement value.

Economics then—the sheer cost of contesting a claim—is a force which compels realism. It is a force inclining claims men toward the plus side in ascribing settlement value.

It was earlier suggested that a few competent claims men might value a claim at more than its mathematical value, but that others will probably price the same file at less than mathematical value. Why should this be so?

Economics works with the industry to bring down the price at which claims settle. It works when claims are in lawyers' hands and when claimants negotiate their own claims.

Economics—From the Lawyer's Standpoint

Lawyers are businessmen. Their secretaries and landlords are accustomed to being paid. Their wives and children prefer regular meals. A lawyer's problem, then, is to make his year's efforts yield as much revenue as he can. Settlement with lawyers thus becomes very much a matter of economics.

Most lawyers will agree that they make no money in courtrooms. A settled case on which he spent only a few hours, which brings him a fee of $1,000, may be more profitable to him than a $2,000 fee after trial. Preparation for a two or three day trial may require as much as a day or two on the books. It may require four to six days for interviewing witnesses, attending depositions, hearings on motions, and other conferences. Studies show that an attorney's hourly return for his effort on litigated matters can be as low as $5 an hour, because of the greater number of hours required from him in order to earn his fee. Economic pressure, therefore, often makes a negotiated settlement at a low figure more attractive to a lawyer than a larger judgment figure. At the risk of oversimplifying the situation, two examples may make this clear:

REVENUE PER HOUR—$1,000 SETTLEMENT

Item	Time Required
Conference with client	.50 hours
Conference with adjuster	1.00 ”
Phone call to client	.25 ”
Conference with client (to sign release and return it to adjuster)	.50 ”
	2.25 hours
Revenue (25% of $1,000)	$250.00
Revenue per hour ($250 divided by 2.25)	$111.11

This may be contrasted with:

REVENUE PER HOUR—$2,000 JUDGMENT

Item	Time Required
Conference with client	.50 hours
Conference with adjuster	1.00 ”
Phone call to client	.25 ”
Preparation of suit papers	1.00 ”
Answering interrogatories	3.00 ”
Conferences and depositions, two doctors	8.00 ”
Attendance at pre-trial motions and conferences ..	3.00 ”
Repeated conferences with client	8.00 ”
Conferences with two witnesses	3.00 ”
Research on law	10.00 ”
Trial (two days)	16.00 ”
	53.75 hours
Revenue (40% of $2,000)	$800.00
Revenue per hour ($800 divided by 53.75)	$ 14.88[9]

The fellow with the broken leg must also be considered, and economics affects him too. His interest will be taken into account by his attorney, for most attorneys conscientiously shape their decisions according to their clients' needs rather than according to their own economic interests. Attorneys' fees commonly vary

---

[9] The economics of settlements from the standpoint of the claimant and defendant are explored at length in *Better Settlements Through Leverage* by Philip J. Hermann, published by Aqueduct Books, a division of Lawyers Cooperative Publishing Company.

according to the distance the case has traveled on the litigation route. A common scale runs something like this:

25% if settled before suit
33-1/3% if settled after suit has been brought
40% if tried
50% if prosecuted through an appeal

A claimant would thus realize $2,250 on a $3,000 settlement before suit.

If the same claim were tried and resulted in a $4,000 verdict, his share of the verdict would be only $2,400, but from that $2,400 it is the plaintiff's obligation to pay several expense items, none of which is a trifle. For medical, courtroom testimony, $100 is almost a minimum. A $4,000 claim will probably involve two doctors, one a specialist. The cost of witness subpoenas is minor, but if the witness has cooled his heels for three days waiting to testify, he requires reimbursement for lost earnings and for his meals. (The effect on a case of the failure to guarantee such items is not difficult to forecast.)

Then, too, there are the fees of court reporters. With only a few pretrial depositions, these can easily go to $200 or more. Thus, a plaintiff might net $2,000 or less out of a $4,000 verdict. He would have been better off had his attorneys settled at the $3,000 level. Further, he would have been spared the risk inherent in any lawsuit—the risk of something going wrong. Experienced attorneys consider these things and advise their clients as to the most profitable time and level at which to settle. It should not be surprising that settlement values are therefore usually lower than verdict or mathematical values.

Attainment of a satisfactory settlement may bring into play the ancient art of horse-trading. Attorneys, of course, try to get as much as possible in settlement for their clients. This is not to be resented; it is simply the attorney doing his job by his client. The adjuster owes a similar duty to the buyer of insurance, and he must be no less zealous in *his* behalf.

Not only is it important for the adjuster to know that settlement values are usually lower than judgments; he needs to know why. *The economic reasons for this variation are some of the most potent sales tools available to him in engineering his settlements.*

Economics of Settlement at the Direct-Dealing Level

So far, discussion here has been limited to those negotiations which are assumed to be taking place with *attorneys.* It is necessary to consider negotiations with *claimants who are not represented,* for, as has been pointed out, more settlements are made at this level than with attorneys. It is desirable at this point to restate what has been said previously, that settlements made directly with injured persons often reflect value ideas in no way related to verdict values. While this is true in many instances, the influence of verdict values as a background factor, but modified by economic factors, continues to affect any adjustments made with claimants themselves. The adjuster may not disregard judgment values, for in the end they are what he will be faced with if he fails to come to an agreement. On the other hand he cannot justify wasting the public's money by paying more than his experience teaches him that a court would award. *In direct negotiation, therefore, the upper limit of value is the price the adjuster is ready to pay, and realistically ought to pay, rather than to permit the claim to advance to its next stage—that is, the entrance of an attorney.*

At this level the claimant certainly has it in his mind that the settlement will be paid directly to him. A lawyer's fee, no matter what its percentage, represents a substantial part of the claim. A settlement that in effect splits the lawyer's fee between the parties has much to recommend it to either side.

Adjusters have been stampeded into overpaying claims for fear that an attorney would be engaged. This is just as foolish as to fail to recognize that an attorney may be in the offing. If the claimant is uninformed and has wild, unshakeable notions of value, the adjuster is probably better off dealing with an attorney. Paradoxically, one of the best ways of bringing such a claimant down to earth is a tactful explanation that the claimant will be better off with an attorney who can spare him the trouble and danger of litigation by advising him realistically on value.

In pricing at the claimant level the adjuster should remember that a knowledgeable claimant may trade with him until he is satisfied that he has procured the highest possible offer and then take his case to an attorney. This leaves both the adjuster and the attorney in a hole. As a practical matter, the attorney has to procure for his claimant some net increase or the case will not settle. If the adjuster has offered everything the case is worth, he has no more to offer. The case has not increased in value simply because an attorney has been engaged. Therefore, there is a widely recognized principle: "Never spend your top dollar until you think you can buy something with it." This dictates caution and restraint in one's final offer to a claimant.

Whether a case's value at the direct-dealing level is less than its value at the attorney level is a matter for individual judgment and individual company practice. At this level an adjuster should weigh carefully such factors as these:

1. What attorney or type of attorney will the claimant be most likely to employ?
2. Will he be more or less reasonable than the claimant himself?
3. Are there factors in the case which an unscrupulous and aggressive attorney will magnify and which will be difficult to defend against? (For example, the claimant is stooped with arthritis. His doctor has assured him that his arthritis has not been aggravated, but the town contains an active lawyer-doctor team who always allege and exploit aggravation of this condition. In such a situation one must watch his footwork carefully, for possibilities can't be ignored, yet one can hardly open the treasury on the basis of what *may* happen.)

EVALUATION (TECHNIQUES TO MAKE IT EFFECTIVE AND ACCURATE)

Clearly the most accurate forecast of judgment values is of no use if it is not in the possession of the one who has both the authority and the opportunity to act on it. Pricing itself is so dependent on certain prerequisite findings that it often cannot take place until the proper investigational groundwork has been laid.

At its best, evaluation is highly subjective and therefore not as accurate as one might desire. There should therefore be a constant effort to improve the accuracy of one's forecasts. The practical side of evaluation—which is to say, a technique for developing accuracy, and several techniques by which the business tries to bring judgment and authority to act into play at a time when they can be translated into effective action—will now be considered.

Accumulating Information About Special Damages

Special damages are so integral to the pricing process that the claims business has, as has been pointed out, its own shorthand for them: "specials." Gathering information about specials may seem in many aspects to be an investigational function, but it is such an intimate part of the pricing process that it is both convenient and realistic to treat it as such.

If an award is made, *special damages themselves are part of the award.* Whatever their ultimate influence, the ascertainment of special damages starts early, continues through much of a claim's life, has much to do with reporting techniques, and does not end until all the elements forming special damages are known and confirmed.

On his way to the first call on a bodily injury claimant, an adjuster ought to make a few phone calls to provide himself with a brief rundown of anticipated hospital and medical expense. Unless he does this he will be unable to act on such a settlement opportunity as may present itself.

Much information about special damages comes to an adjuster without activity on his part. People are acutely aware of their out-of-pocket expense, so they are seldom backward about pointing out these items. Unfortunately these claims are not always accurate. Thus there is a constant need to confirm special damages and to require the exhibition of statements, invoices, receipts, and other confirmation of alleged expense. The adjuster should verify, at least by phone call, items not so supported. Minor amounts consistent with proven facts may be accepted without confirmation, i.e., a $10 ambulance charge from the scene of an accident to the hospital, when a man is known to have required hospitalization.

Attorneys will usually substantiate their positions in respect to special damages by bills or receipts—but not always. Most experienced trial men can relate several instances of plaintiffs' attorneys making firm assertions about lost earnings, or even doctor and hospital bills, only to be embarrassed by evidence disclosing that no time was lost or even that doctors and hospitals said to have treated the claimant never even saw him. The claimant's attorney who will make a deliberate misstatement of fact is almost unheard of but, strange though it may seem, they often fail to verify statements made to them by their clients. Hence, again, *before he gets down to talking money,* the adjuster must verify at the source, by phone, mail or personal call, any items he anticipates will be offered as part of the specials.

Ascertaining specials is neither difficult nor technical. An hour at the telephone enables the adjuster to tell his examiner, often long before either the claimant or the attorney is ready to price his case, what the special damages are, assures the examiner that the specials have been confirmed, and enables the two, adjuster and examiner, to come to a sound, even if admittedly provisional, opinion of value.

The adjuster's duty is, however, not confined to *confirming* expenses alleged. Since at any time his valuation should be realistic, he must recognize and ascertain items it may not yet have occurred to the claimant to present. Earning capacity is a case in point. An injured claimant may have said nothing about this item, but the adjuster who has done his homework will have learned from the doctor the expected period of disability, and from the employer the injured claimant's usual remuneration. A further reason for being beforehand with one's determination of specials will appear when the question of *authority* and the mechanics of its extension is considered.

The usual claimant knows nothing of specials as such, and cares less. When, therefore, he broaches the question of settlement based on his doctor bill, and the cost of repairing the leaky back porch roof, the adjuster should be prepared with his own realistic appraisal. Claimants often ask, and are paid for, many things not properly acceptable as damage. To get down to figures, assume that the adjuster has soundly concluded that the claim is worth $600 or more, and that the claimant evaluates his claim as:

Doctor bill	$100.00
Roof repair ...	500.00
Total	$600.00

The adjuster should be criticized if he does not walk off with the release.[10] He should be criticized if he has not checked specials and formed his opinion on value before making his call. *What is important is that the adjuster be prepared to act whenever he can attain a settlement justifiable on the basis of what he knows. Pricing is effective only when it can be translated into settlement; otherwise it is useless mental gymnastics.*

The converse of the situation demonstrated by the claimant with the leaky roof should also be recognized. The term "special damages" is part of the vernacular of the claims business. To the layman, *that is the claimant negotiating directly with an adjuster, the term "special damages" has neither meaning nor influence.* At the claimant's level, specials and their influence on value are concepts for the adjuster to hold in the *back* of his mind, if at all. If specials affect values at this level, it is probably only to the extent that the claimant picks up his notions of value from the adjuster with whom he is dealing. The reality of specials as a determiner of value, if it has any validity at all, comes into play only when the claimant retains an attorney. *At the level of direct negotiation,* most adjusters agree that the words "special damages" or "specials" should never be uttered.

When special damages are reported, it is helpful if they are summarized and totaled in this fashion:

Dr. Smith	$150.00
Dr. Jones (X-rays)	25.00
City hospital	250.00
Lost time and wages (four weeks at $75 a week, XYZ Manufacturing Co.)	300.00
Ambulance	15.00
Total	$740.00

---

[10] This is not to say that the adjuster should consider himself under an obligation to pay $600. His "value" may have been based in part on his knowledge that juries of the locality are notoriously inclined to disregard liability. He may be satisfied that the claimant's negligence contributed to the accident but doubtful that he can trust a local jury to perform its duty to protect the defendant. Therefore, though he may have "valued" the claim at $600, his duty to the public may require him to attempt to persuade the claimant to accept a lower figure. The claimant may be horse-trading with him and the adjuster may elect to respond in like fashion.

The adjuster should be able to follow such a listing with a statement that damages have been confirmed at the source, or if any were accepted on faith or not confirmed because of the difficulty of doing so, these should be identified along with the statement of the adjuster's recommendation as to their acceptability.

To summarize, then, special damages may or may not have an arithmetical effect on verdicts. They certainly affect attorneys' views of settlement values. The duty to ascertain them continues during the life of a claim. Ascertainment of special damages is a prerequisite to any theorizing to be done about them. Correct ascertainment is more important than the theorizing.

Discounting

The opportunity to settle does not necessarily time its appearance to suit the adjuster's convenience. It may come before he has finished his investigation. To enable adjusters to act effectively in such situations, a technique has been developed. When it is given a name, it is called "discounting." It can best be demonstrated by an example.

> Liability is disputed. An important witness is a serviceman who has been overseas since immediately after the accident. He may be out of reach for years. Upon consideration of everything known about the claim—excepting only the testimony of the missing witness—it appears to have a settlement value of $1,000. The missing witness is important but only as a part of the picture. Should he be a favorable witness, the insurer's chances of prevailing will, it is judged, be about two to one; if unfavorable, prospects will be two to one against the insurer. To *discount* the claim, therefore, it is reasoned that no matter how favorable the witness might be, the claimant's chance of prevailing would still be one in three. Therefore if offered a chance to settle at $333 or less the insurance company should not pass the opportunity (perhaps the adjuster should make an offer to find out if it will be accepted). The value thus arrived at is said to have been "discounted," because the insurance company has recognized that if the witness were located and did turn out to be favorable, the claim's value would be reduced accordingly by the betterment of the chances of the insurer's prevailing.

For another example, assume that the adjuster is called to a hospital within minutes of the accident. In his telephoned report, the assured admitted his liability. Claimant exhibits a leg with a bad case of varicose veins, and a minute bruise. Doctor assures all that the bruise is not bad enough to develop into a varicose ulcer. Claimant demands $50 for the ulcer that may develop. To discount the claim, the adjuster reasons, "It is a rare court that won't award at least $50 even for a simple bruise with no complications. Therefore even if the ulcer fails to develop, the claim has still a value of $50." While the adjuster does not settle claims for "what may happen," he would certainly be unwise in this situation if he did not settle the claim for $50.

These examples have been simplified deliberately to illustrate a point. The claims business is seldom quite so simple as the situations portrayed.

In either instance the adjuster might well have thought it wise to increase his evaluation to reflect the possibility of future developments being unfavorable. To return to the missing witness, he might have reasoned, "It's a fifty-fifty proposition whether the witness will be for us or against us. Therefore, I will price this claim at $500 and move it at that price if I can." He would thus have acknowledged the possibility of the witness's turning out to be unfavorable.

Considering the bruised leg, the same adjuster might reason that the chances of a varicose ulcer developing are remote but, if one developed, $50 would be "chicken feed." This might make him conclude that it would be the better part of wisdom to meet a demand of even $100. In either event he will have made a decision with relevant evidence still undisclosed. This is the process which is known as discounting. It is a way of thinking about claims and their value. It enables an adjuster to come to *limited* [11] conclusions about value before *all* of the relevant facts are disclosed. It enables adjusters to act effectively when settlement opportunities offer themselves.

---

[11] The word "limited" is used because it clearly reflects the idea that the disclosure of future information may justify an increase in price.

Other Insurance—an Influence on Value

The proceeds of other policies—often medical payments coverages and, less frequently, accident and health coverages—are frequently found to be applicable to the same injuries that give rise to liability claims. This raises the question of duplicate payment, and an obvious outgrowth of that question is whether the damages that the liability adjuster is obliged to consider are correspondingly reduced. Except for the exceptions to be noted later, the answer is "No."

Courts commonly take the view that if a man has been sufficiently prudent to protect himself and his family by the purchase of accident coverage, that purchase is irrelevant as far as the liability claim is concerned. Courts, therefore, decline to penalize the prudent man by reducing his damages.

When medical payments insurance first reached the market, it offered man one of life's few opportunities to eat his cake and have it too. An injured person could be reimbursed by his own insurer for his medical and hospital expense and then claim the same expense as an item of special damage in presenting a liability claim against the adverse party. Most jurisdictions even forbade the defendant to mention in a court of law that the injured party had already received some reimbursement. However, there is usually someone around to foul up a good deal, and this situation was no exception.

Medical payments began to be widely used by unscrupulous claimants to finance the "build-up" of bodily injury claims. In other words, such a claimant, knowing that the cost of medical treatment received by him would be paid by his own company, secured unnecessary and excessive treatment from his doctor or hospital, hoping thereby to increase his special damages and the value of his claim against a third party. This practice unfortunately is not yet a thing of the past—it is, in fact, with certain attorneys and doctors, the routine which one expects. It is hardly surprising that many insurance companies have now modified their policies to require a claiming party to assign to his carrier that part of his claim for which he receives medical payments reimbursement. Such assignment or subrogation prevents an injured party from collecting twice for the same item. The claims fraternity has, on the whole, welcomed this development.[12]

In other situations, the availability of medical payments may indeed assist an adjuster. His liability claimant may, for instance, have medical payments coverage on his own car. And, whereas, without this protection, this claimant might in desperation have put his claim in litigation for the sake of the temporary financial assistance available from an attorney; the sums recoverable under his medical payments coverage may provide welcome relief and enable the adjuster to maintain control of a claim that would otherwise go to litigation.

Many people have conscientious scruples against being paid twice for the same item, but it should be noted that such people ordinarily prefer to be paid by a liability insurer rather than to make a claim against their own company. Settling in such situations presents few problems. This type of person is usually forbearing in his demands.

The presence of other insurance affects adjusting tactics and adjusters' views of value in still other ways. This is particularly true when a claimant has been injured in such a way as to leave *two or more* defendants potentially liable to him under liability coverage. A claimant may, for instance, have been standing innocently on the sidewalk when two negligent drivers collided in the street with one or both cars leaving the roadway and striking the claimant. In such a situation the claimant, although he has only one injury, usually lodges his claim against one or the other or both of the two negligent drivers.

In such a situation, neither adjuster, of course, expects to see his company pay the entire claim. However, in their eagerness to see that their companies pay only a fair proportion of such damage, adjusters are prone to a strange form of intramural warfare. It seems, often, as if more energy is expended in trying to "stick" the other insurer than in negotiating with the claimant,

---

12 It is interesting to contrast these paragraphs with what the first edition of this text had to say on the same subject as recently as 1965. "Most jurisdictions forbid the defendant even to mention in a court of law that the claimant may already have been reimbursed for these expenses. However, there are beginning to be some exceptions to these general principles. In time, subrogating medical expenses may become the rule, although it is now the exception."

investigating the real merits of his claim, and attempting to make a friendly and reasonable settlement. If the energy expended by adjusters in trying to gain an advantage over one another were expended in better causes, the industry would profit.

It is almost universally conceded that it is to the insurer's best interests for adjusters to cooperate, the thrill of combat notwithstanding. It is also rather widely agreed that when more than one insurance company is involved, one adjuster should represent all interests in negotiating with the claimant. Before this is done, usually there is an agreement as to the division of damage, and almost any agreement as to the division of damage is preferable to letting the matter go into a lawsuit.

Workmen's compensation frequently enters the picture. In some states, the election to receive compensation requires a claimant to forego any other rights to seek damages at law he may have had. In other states, the claimant may accept compensation and simultaneously proceed at law against a third party. In still other jurisdictions, the right to proceed and control of these rights passes to the compensation insurer. In order to handle liability exposures properly, an adjuster must familiarize himself with the prevailing workmen's compensation laws in his jurisdiction as they pertain to subrogation.

With compensation and liability exposures simultaneously involved, adjusters should carefully consider the interests of their principals as they affect one another. Conscious thought should be given to the question of cooperation and a decision arrived at on the merits of the situation and the law of the jurisdiction.

In these interplays of coverage, legal rights and responsibilities are less important than reasonableness and common sense. The ordinary fair-minded person has an aversion to being paid twice for the same thing. This spirit may be brought to the surface if an adjuster permits a claimant to demonstrate the largeness of his character, but this spirit will be crushed if the adjuster tries to coerce the claimant into the same thing.

Able adjusters try to keep their principals out of trouble. They look for ways to agree rather than to disagree. They waste little time trying to convince a liability claimant that his medical expense should be stricken from his claim because it can be recovered from his own medical payments coverage. Neither do they risk a dispute by trying to reduce the settlement by trying to put off part or all of the claim on a personal accident insurer. In such situations, a too aggressive approach can be self-defeating.

Authorization

"Authorization" refers to *the amount to which an adjuster may commit his employer or client.* Along with many other words, it has two aspects. It implies the *permission* to act; this is obvious. It also implies—this is not so obvious, but possibly is more important—the *ability,* the *willingness* and the *responsibility to act.* It is the means by which an evaluation—which may have been a home office action—is transferred to the field, the only place where an adjuster's negotiations can transform it into a settlement.

A staff adjuster commonly carries *blanket* permission to commit his employer up to a certain amount. For sums in excess of this "blanket authorization," he is required to procure specific authorization in individual claims. An independent adjuster comes by his power to act in much the same way. From clients regularly and frequently represented, an independent firm will commonly carry a blanket authority. This is usually, but not always, subject to an upper limit. This authority is then supplemented by *specific* permission granted in respect to certain claims with a value in excess of the adjuster's blanket authorization.

When an adjuster is operating within the limits of a blanket authority he is not permitted to seek specific permission to settle. In fact, the shoe is now on the other foot. It is actually a dereliction of his duty for an adjuster to request permission to settle if he already has adequate authority. True, consistent with his principal's reporting practices, he should advise his file in timely fashion of all relevant developments, but the grant of authority to form decisions within a certain price range makes it the adjuster's *duty* to form those decisions. This may seem a heavy burden (in practice, an adjuster, especially a younger one, does have access to coaching), but the goal—the transfer of authority to decide and act in the field—is clear. Insurers don't need errand boys; they need men of discretion and judgment, armed with authority to act and with the courage to use that authority.

The Caine Mutiny [18] describes Willie Keith's growth to maturity: ". . . a junior officer, soberly reaching for more responsibility." This seems to crystallize what ought to be a conscientious adjuster's approach to the question of settlement authority.

The grant of blanket authority to an independent adjuster may be ambiguous. Representing one-time or infrequent clients, assignments may not make clear the limits within which he may act. He must then guide himself by his *judgment* as to his client's interest, with a healthy recognition that if he succeeds he's a hero, if he fails he's a "bum."

Procurement of specific authority on a particular case shows again the two-sided nature of the word. The adjuster receives permission to act, but on *him* falls the duty of requesting a timely extension of authority, proper in amount, and of producing the facts and reasoning to justify its extension.

The request for authorty to act is inseparable from evaluation, which begins almost with the first moment of an adjuster's knowledge of his claim and ends only with its disposition. *Ideally*, as soon as the adjuster discerns any value *in excess of his blanket authority*, he should request authority to act within the higher value which he now sees. *Practically*, this ideal is not attainable, but if he wishes to be in a position to act when opportunity knocks, an adjuster's reports, as soon as the outline of value can be sketched in, should request this authority. If he concludes his report with recommendations in respect to value, he will accomplish this desired result.

When an adjuster requests authority, his request should summarize, list and total the special damages, appraise the probabilities of winning and losing on the liability issue, highlight the nonpecuniary elements of damage and the evidence bearing on them, and should conclude with a specific recommendation couched in dollars.

If negotiations are prolonged, changes in influential factors should reflect themselves in altered recommendations. If this is

---

[18] Herman Wouk, *The Caine Mutiny,* Doubleday & Co. (Garden City, N.Y.), p. 317.

not done, the adjuster may meet a surprise opportunity and be unable to act because he lacks authority.

An initial grant of authority, while it may be less than the adjuster's considered opinion of value, nonetheless deserves his best efforts to settle within the limit imposed. If efforts fail, however, *the adjuster should be more than cautious about concluding that he should break off negotiations.* Not until every means at his command has been exhausted should the adjuster even intimate to a claimant any possibility of resubmitting the question of value —but before the last door is locked, the adjuster should, except in the face of the most explicit instructions, stall the negotiations in status quo, to give his examiner one more chance to reconsider.

This seemingly illogical procedure raises an obvious question: "If the case was worth more money, why wasn't it authorized in the first place?" The author confesses that he himself endorses the school of thought that an adjuster's *first* request for authority should consider *all* the facts and that an examiner's first grant should be sufficient—that it ought never to have to be revised upward. The author is convinced that supervisors and examiners in the main hold identical views. Unfortunately, what "ought to be" is not always so.

Years in the business, if they teach nothing else, teach that this is not an ideal world and that forethought is not necessarily the last word. To mix metaphors, an adjuster must stick out his neck and never hesitate to eat crow. He ought not to change his ideas except for good reason, but he ought not to fear to change his mind for good reason. Examiners, too, while they strive for 20/20 foresight, have the same problems and deserve the chance to second-guess themselves. Therefore, even though an adjuster may have exhausted all the authority which has been extended to him—that is, has offered every cent that has been authorized—it is still a safe rule to keep the door open until he is positive that his home office has had every opportunity to lay its last dollar on the line.

The exercise of supervision and the delegation of authority are inherently antagonistic. Their conflict is often acute in the claims business, where there are more claims than can possibly be seen by all the experienced adjusters in the world. Therefore there must be supervision. And where authority must be exercised in the only place where it can be effective—the field—authority must be delegated.

Adjuster's Duty to Form Opinions of Value, and Record Them

Settlement opportunities may arise at any moment. The adjuster should always be prepared to act on opportunity, or to give chance a helpful nudge. Therefore his reports should, as frequently as is feasible, terminate in an appraisal of value. This is the deliberate sticking out of one's neck. It is a practice the adjuster should discipline himself to follow, for:

1. Good mental discipline keeps him alert to the possibility of settlement taking place at any moment.
2. It enables the adjuster's supervisors to form reliable opinions of the soundness of his judgment.
3. It enables his supervisors to correct him when necessary.
4. Finally, and this is of the first importance, the adjuster exposes his value judgments to the real test—their effectiveness in action.

Too many cases getting into litigation, and too many verdicts coming down in excess of the value anticipated, are reliable indicators that values are being set too low. On the other hand, if all cases are being settled, there may be grounds to suspect that prices are too high. It will be impossible for the adjuster to satisfy all the opposing interests that operate through him. In the claims business no one is expected to approach 100% accuracy. One of the essential features of the business is the making of decisions. They way to learn to make decisions is to decide. The desire to avoid decisions is almost universal. The adjuster should be early and unremitting in his efforts to develop judgment and the courage to decide.

Summary

In pricing claims, investigation is a better guide than theorizing. Ascertain special damages. Ascertain by investigation the presence or absence of factors bearing on value. Enforce the constant discipline of forming and recording opinions on values, and of keeping authorization current and realistic. Study verdicts and subject previously formed opinions to the test of experience.

CHAPTER 12

Closing the File

"War," wrote von Clausewitz, "is the continuation of politics by other means." [1] Adjusting stands in the same relation to law as politics to the art of war. The analogy can be carried another step. It is said that in war there are no winners and when all has been said and done, this is true of many law suits. The resolution of differences by means other than the legal machinery climaxes the work which we know as adjusting. In that vein, therefore, it may be said that the real work of adjusting is closing claims without letting them get into the legal machinery.

This chapter, which deals with that climax, will, therefore, consider the way files are closed. Since claims, in the last analysis, are not paid with corporation money (the insurer being in reality a trustee), there will be some discussion of how adjusters close their files at acceptable figures.

Closing—And the Narrower Term, Settling

Many files are opened, sometimes to be reserved for substantial figures, and then closed *without release,* with no agreement with the injured party, nothing to protect the carrier against later assertion of a claim except the judgment of some adjuster that the claim probably will not be pressed. This phenomenon has already been alluded to under the general subject of "Fall-Downs" (page 397). In many instances claims—even those arising out of auto accidents, which have a remarkable quality of rousing a claimant's fighting spirit—die and are quietly closed with no formal closing document. In those claims,

[1] *On War,* Karl von Clausewitz, 1832.

the tip-off is usually prolonged inactivity on the part of a claimant or his attorney.

Traditionally claims have been closed by arriving at an agreement between a claimant (or his attorney) and an adjuster, this agreement then being acknowledged by the execution of a document (release). Although the mechanics are foreshortened, this is still essentially what happens when a carrier appraises a property damage claim and forwards a "release draft" to the claimant. To these closing techniques, which have been around almost as long as the liability insurance business, must now be added other techniques, claims paid but without release; a near relative, claims settled by release but after prior advance of some part, often very substantial, of the settlement amount; and claims settled on a release but with some feature, usually medical expense, left open.

These techniques are a major part of the insurance industry's laudable practice of looking first to its own linen in an attempt to mitigate the general public criticism which has been its recent lot. It is possible to take a broader view, to wit, that in its insistence upon closing files by release, the insurance industry somehow drifted into playing "the lawyer's game by lawyer's rules." Now a large fraction [2] of the claim industry goes about its business closing files under its own rules using humanely and aggressively its most powerful tool, money.

To consider how cases are closed, it may be helpful to look at it from what might be called a subjective viewpoint—i.e., to examine it almost as if one were trying to discover what goes on inside the adjuster. Since this chapter is going to raise questions about the extent and direction of adjusters' efforts to control the amount of money they spend, as well as their efforts to see that cases close at all, it is again requested that the paragraphs in Chapter I headed, "The Adjuster and The Insuring Public" be re-read. This chapter will have much to do about how the adjuster discharges the duty identified there.

---

[2] It would be officious and is unnecessary to attempt to discover whether the techniques referred to are the tactics chosen by the majority of the industry. To complicate the question, many home offices have laid down these techniques as the tactics of choice but find it difficult to overcome the resistance of the field staff.

The selling or persuasion aspect of adjusting will b
sidered—the development of a body of suitable working ~~~~,
whether or not there is such a thing as an adjuster's "feel" for a
given situation and, if so, its place in the scheme of things.

The Selling Component in Settling

In many aspects, arriving with a claimant at an agreement to
settle is a matter of persuasion. It therefore, has many of the
characteristics of salesmanship. Sales are made more by emotion
than by reason. The behavioral scientists are only now beginning
to understand how emotions are created and how people are
influenced by and through them. The persistent success of many
persuaders who defy (or at least seem to defy) all the rules
leads to the suspicion that much more remains to be discovered
than yet is known. The subject is therefore approached with care.
One man's success may be another man's failure. In the field of
persuasion, no one may be dogmatic.

Consider, for instance, a salesman selling a TV set. His work
is readily distinguished from the work of the factory which produced it. It is even probable that too much knowledge of its
inner workings is an actual handicap to the seller. It is true, the
adjuster did not "make" the claim in the same sense that the
factory made the TV set. He did do everything that was done
in relation to the claim. In that sense he is the producer as well
as a salesman.

When an adjuster raises a question about the cost of
straightening a fender, he is informing himself that he may come
to an opinion on value. But the way he asks that question may
build a wall between him and the claimant, or make final agreement a foregone conclusion. Similarly, when he writes a claimant's
statement, he is investigating—but he *cannot avoid creating at the
same time an impression of himself* which will aid or frustrate
his later efforts to close the file.

Cases may fail to settle because of an adjuster's failure to
recognize value, or they may fail because a claimant wants too
much. It is possible that one failure is no less prevalent than
the other. Any closing is the product of the agreement of two
minds. Procuring this agreement, persuading the claimant that

it is in his interest to accept the adjuster's thoughtfully derived concept of value, is related directly or indirectly to almost everything the adjuster may do in a claimant's presence, and many things that he does elsewhere.

The best salesmen recognize that for them there is almost no such thing as "closing the sale." If presentation has been proper, closing is almost a formality. This too is a feature of adjusting—many claims, whether they close by release on otherwise, flow so smoothly from what has gone before, from prior contacts and determination of damage, that they seem to adjust themselves. For an adjuster to recognize this and govern himself accordingly may be as important as anything else he may ever learn about the adjusting process. Property loss adjusters have a phrase that encompasses part (but not all) of this idea: "You have to adjust your insured before you adjust your loss."

The art of closing, then—if there is an art—is exercised simultaneously with an adjuster's other functions. Since it is at least as much the process of his making up *his* mind as it is the art of persuading a claimant to accept the adjuster's valuation, it is an integral part of everything he does. This involvement and interaction with his other operations notwithstanding, an attempt will be made to point out some things that experience seems to teach about adjusting in the sense of persuasion.

Developing and Expanding a Supply of Techniques

The personalities of successful adjusters are diverse. This point, mentioned in Chapter 1—that some are glad-handing extroverts, and others wear steel-rimmed spectacles and act the part—the young adjuster is invited to confirm by observing the several character types within his own scope of observation. What works for one type is not going to work for another. Nothing will be more suspect than backslapping by Mr. Steelrim. Nothing can be quite so ridiculous as a backslapper splitting hairs. Each type, if he is successful, has a manner that is consistent with his own personality. The successful attitudes and manners employed are those that "ring true" for the personality employing them. The adjuster should seek to develop, therefore, approaches in which he is comfortable; discomfort may be a sign that he does not "ring true" to others. But he may discover and mold to his own use *techniques* that work for others.

Claimants, too, vary. One man wants to be dickered with; the next wants a firm "no nonsense, one price" offer.

Incessant shop talk is the rule in any claims office. The adjuster probably learns as much from these vicarious experiences as he does from his own activities. He should note and preserve for his own use any tactics that strike him as potent. He should be ready to discard those that fail. The fault may not be in the tactic; the fault may simply have been in its use by the wrong person. The anecdotes cited on pages 487, 488 recite two actual attempts to learn from the example of others. The point is not that, second hand, one worked and one did not—for its imitator each tactic was successful and continued so in repeated use. The point is that any adjuster who keeps his ears open has a wealth of this kind of material offered him. He should cultivate a retentive memory, plagiarizing shamelessly any moves that seem promising, trying them but retaining or discarding them according to *his* success in employing them.

An adjuster should also realize that he may not be the same man today as he was yesterday. The extreme extrovert and the extreme introvert are each rare types. People (a category broad enough to include adjusters) are mixtures; at one time one phase of their character predominates; at other times, other phases. Therefore one has to acknowledge that the tactic which failed one day may work the next.

Efforts to enlarge one's supply of tested successful tactical moves should be conscious and continuous.

Developing a "Feel" for the Situation

In *The Human Factor in Insurance Claim Adjusting* [3] the authors, Willis Rokes and William E. Jaynes, point out non-verbal ways by which adjusters communicate and influence

---

[3] *The Human Factor in Insurance Claim Adjusting,* Willis Rokes, LL.B., Ph.D., professor and chairman, Department of Insurance, University of Omaha, and William E. Jaynes, Ph.D., professor and chairman, Department of Psychology, University of Omaha, Educational Program for Adjusters, Part ADJ. 2, December, 1964, and May, 1965, Examinations, Published by Insurance Institute of America, Inc., Bryn Mawr, Pa., page 37 forward.

claimants. This street runs two ways. At the same time that his behavior is creating attitudes and influencing responses, the adjuster is himself perceiving and sensing in many ways that he may not himself recognize as significant.

To illustrate, experienced adjusters all recognize "Won't you just make it X dollars?" for the tip-off that it is. The claimant has made up his mind to accept the figure last offered by the adjuster. Many young adjusters, and older ones looking back over their experience, recall that the first time they heard this phrase they experienced a feeling, hunch, intuition, call it what you will, that the claimant had made up his mind to accept the adjuster's figure, *but they did not know at that time why they had that feeling.* In other words, they got the message without knowing how they got it. Adjusting, particularly negotiating, is alive with instances when one has a "feel" or an intuitive sense that a certain course is the correct course of action. Adjusters often guide themselves in their negotiations by this intuition (they probably speak of it as "riding their hunches"), and intuition of this sort is often remarkably accurate. This suggests that there are other and less obvious non-verbal communications, and the frequency and surprising accuracy of adjusters' "feel" may mean that they are receiving messages the purport of which they grasp without recognizing that there has been a message as such. "Feel" may occur with respect to offers made and figures discussed. It may also occur with respect to the figure that a claimant will accept. This happens to young unsophisticated men as much or more than to veterans.

There are, however, two kinds of feel. There is the feel that an adjuster may have that a certain figure will be sufficient to settle a claim, and there is the feel that a given figure may *not* be enough. The first is seldom wrong, but experience teaches that the second should be suspect.[4]

---

[4] The author is unable to recall a single instance in 36 years of intense adjusting and supervisory activity when a field man told his boss, I think X dollars will do the job and failed to come in with the release.

Conversely, both from his own experience in the field and recalling many times when he sat in the supervisory chair, the author recalls un-numbered times when the boss growled, "Never mind, just go back and offer him—" (Perhaps a small fraction of the sum the field man thought would be required.) While memory recalls several instances when the boss was wrong, it also recalls a

However, if an adjuster finds that he is developing feel for his settlement situations, he should neither ignore it nor suppress it as silly superstition. He should give it a chance to work for him. If he finds these sensations to be accurate guides to developing events, he should blend them with the advice previously given—i.e., avoid trying to learn a set pattern, but instead adopt and adapt methods that seem appropriate to the claimant, the situation and *the adjuster*. It is part of the technique of developing a body of methods and tactics tried by him and workable in *his* hands.

Anecdote 1

A young adjuster found that he was at a disadvantage in dealing with claimants who wanted to horse-trade. There was no upper limit on the claimant's opening demand. Claimants could, if they chose, ask many thousands of dollars above a case's realistic value. This seemed to the adjuster to give the claimant a bargaining advantage, for while the claimant could get as far away from the claim's real value as he chose, the adjuster found that if he lowered his opening offer enough to compensate for the claimant's position, he (the adjuster) in effect ran out of figures. There was, after all, no way that he could offer less than zero—and the adjuster often wished there were a way.

This was the adjuster's frustrating position when, one day, an older man told him that he had developed a technique which he found effective. In pedestrian cases, the old hand pointed out, there was usually some vehicular damage. The adjuster shared the opinion, common to adjusters, that in a pedestrian accident the pedestrian is usually the party at fault. Therefore when the other adjuster suggested to him that in those claims it might be a good move to start out by asking the claimant to reimburse the insured for the damage to the automobile, this struck the adjuster as an excellent move—one certain to convince the claimant that liability might point in more than one direction. This was, in effect, a "less than zero" opening.

The first time the adjuster tried it, he was nearly thrown out of the house. He licked his wounds, took stock with himself, and

snowstorm of times when the boss turned out to be right after all. Why feel of one sort of hunch should be so surprisingly accurate and its opposite so unreliable will have to be left to the behavioral scientists. The author suspects that when they have finished mining this vein, they will have found out that in the first instance there probably *has* been some form of communication, but that in the second instance, fear of failure has garbled the message, if any.

concluded that his trouble lay in not having been sufficiently convincing. He practiced various phrasings of his opening offer (the demand for reimbursement) and waited for the next pedestrian. And this time only the most remarkable contortions enabled him to save the settlement.

The adjuster concluded that the ploy might work for some but not for him. It was no mistake for him to try this tactic but he was wise to drop it when it failed to work for him.

Anecdote 2

The settlement was a rough one, involving a substantial sum demanded by a claimant who showed every intention of making a killing and getting rich. Even the old timer who settled it at a sane price was elated at his success.

"How did you do it?" marvelled the young adjuster at the next desk.

"I got him to tell me his equity in his house, his car and his bank account," said the older man. "He didn't realize how much I was offering him till I showed him that what I had offered him represented several times his life's savings."

The young adjuster (no longer so young) is still using this one. It hasn't hurt him yet.

DIRECT NEGOTIATION WITH INJURED CLAIMANTS

For purposes of discussion, closing tactics divide themselves conveniently. Some claims are negotiated directly with *injured claimants,* and some are negotiated with their *attorneys.*

To consider the former it will be convenient to take up first *whether,* and if so, *how,* the adjuster may determine the range in which negotiations take place, and then how the actual negotiations may be conducted. Finally, a special kind of settlement will be considered, the "first call settlement."

Control

How an adjuster handles his claim has much to do with whether the matter is concluded by him directly with the injured party, whether with an attorney or, in fact, how far the case travels along the route toward eventual litigation. Since his own actions have so much to do with the outcome, an adjuster

should know something about some aspects of direct negotiation, the advantages to each of the parties, and how a direct
dealing relationship is attained and maintained.

Direct negotiation is usually a desirable state of affairs
whether or not the advance of funds is contemplated. Therefore, the points made in the following paragraphs are equally
pertinent whether one intends to advance funds or to obtain
a release.

Direct negotiation tends to avoid the "build-up." The adjuster remains in frequent personal contact with the claimant
and has direct access to correct, up-to-date medical information.
This may even lead to settlements higher than would have
resulted with counsel; this seeming oddity occurs because, faced
with a doubtful injury, the insurer has a full opportunity to
satisfy itself as to the legitimacy of the claim. Plaintiffs' attorneys
often restrict the availability of medical and related information
about their clients to adjusters. In practice, while they may
eventually make a full disclosure, there is often a tendency to
permit the release of *no* information until the attorney judges
the time for release to be advantageous to his client. It is not
the province of this book to approve or disapprove of this tactic
but, justifiable or not, it does have this unfortunate side effect
of creating considerable skepticism on the part of adjusters and
those whom they represent—skepticism which operates to the
disadvantage of a claimant with a legitimate injury.

Insurers, in the main, prefer to exhaust the possibilities of
direct negotiation before the intervention of counsel. Adjusters
are often judged by their ability to develop their skills at direct
negotiation.

The creation in a claimant of willingness to negotiate directly
is commonly referred to in the claims business as "control." This
is probably a misnomer, since the situation is the opposite of
"control." The claimant is free at any moment he chooses to
break off negotiations and engage counsel. Once he has engaged
an attorney, a claimant may not be able to settle or decline to
settle according to his own judgment. He may not be able to
discharge counsel without discovering that he has obligated himself for fees which he can only hope to pay by leaving the claim

in his attorney's hands. The claimant may find that he is indeed "controlled" by his own attorney. Be that as it may, control is the term common to the industry and it is in this sense that it will be employed here.

Of the means of attaining and maintaining control, the first and most effective step is an early meeting with the claimant. Therefore in most claims offices, a face-to-face contact with a bodily injury claimant is properly regarded as a priority item. The rule is that such persons are to be seen before the adjuster rests. Only a rare combination of circumstances justifies letting such a contact go overnight. An early appearance of the adjuster gives the claimant a chance to observe the kind of man with whom he will be dealing. Contact must be prompt, for there is never a dearth of backyard gossip to plant unjustified fears in a claimant's mind.

Possibly the next most important factor in controlling a claim is something that came into being long before the accident that caused the injury—the adjuster's reputation. Claims do not happen in a vacuum. Cars are damaged, and body repair men and wrecker drivers are not noted for their reluctance to give advice. Injured claimants frequently turn in confusion to them, or to their doctors, hospitals. or even to the corner druggist, for advice. If the adjuster's past has won him a reputation for integrity and basic decency, it now stands him in good stead. If on the other hand he has earned a reputation of being "hard to get along with," he is in trouble before he starts.

His own actions must now be considered.

To say that he must act so that the claimant is content to deal with him is to beg the question. What kind of a person does a claimant want to deal with? How indeed is a person to demonstrate that he is that kind? This again is a problem in behavior and persuasion. Emotion and a claimant's intuitive reactions probably count for more than logic or what is said. It is easier to enumerate the things an adjuster ought *not* to do than to state positively what he ought *to do*.

Many claims—probably a majority—are controlled from first call to release without the question of the engagement of counsel ever coming up. It is probable that the adjuster ought never to raise the subject, for, by his adherence to the agreement on respective rights and duties (Chapter 1), he has obligated himself not to dissuade a claimant from employing an attorney. If the claimant himself raises the issue, the adjuster may point out that although his principal is as willing to negotiate one way as another, the claimant may elect first to exhaust the possibilities of direct negotiation. He may also point out some of the advantages of direct negotiation and that most people prefer to exhaust this possibility before resorting to litigation. *Not only is this restraint proper, there is reason to believe that it is the effective tactic,* as will be explained later.

Young adjusters are prone to feel that they must make some kind of commitment in order to maintain control. This may take the form of ambiguity—some meaningless phraseology as "We will treat you right," or "You don't have a thing to worry about." or even "We are ready to admit liability." [5] More claims than not *are* controlled to an agreed disposition with no commitment whatsoever. Many such statements seem meaningless as far as control is concerned. They are simply things said because the adjuster feels the need of saying something, on the order of the meaningless phrases some people feel obliged to resort to in opening and closing letters: "We beg to remit," "Hoping you are the same," etc. It is possible that they are not only unnecessary but self-defeating, for such statements seem to strike a false note in a chord. In fact, an analogy can be drawn from the field of music.

In playing piano, the left hand creates chords. The notes played by the right hand, which carries the melody, must not be inconsistent with the chord created by the left. In settlement

---

[5] Premature commitments are to be distinguished carefully from an entirely different approach to the question of control and settlement—the non-conclusive advance of funds. Since this is an introductory text, the temptation to discuss this promising technique must be suppressed and discussion limited to the traditional approach; that is, settlements made by a single release with no payments or commitments until an agreement relative to the entire claim is consummated. The overwhelming majority of claims are concluded by this method.

This footnote, written in 1965, has been let stand, a dramatic demonstration of the rapid advance of the art. In 1971, so many claims are controlled by advance of funds that the technique considered a "promising" curiosity in 1965 may now have become the industry's standard. At the very least, change forces substantial restructuring of this chapter.

negotiations, the basic chords are the adjuster's obvious purpose, as clearly recognized by any claimant as by the adjuster. To suggest that a claimant refrain from the engagement of counsel, or to make premature commitments to him, *is in effect to indicate a fear that the claimant will go to litigation or will not accept an adjuster's valuation.* A claimant who may not analyze these statements to their ultimate significance may nevertheless be rendered uncomfortable by them, just as any listener can identify a false note without knowing the first thing about music.

The following statement is effective for adjusters who lack a basic charm of character, and has controlled many serious injuries. This statement is more often implied than expressed, but it is consistent with the adjuster's basic purpose:

> "It takes two to make a settlement. While I may be willing to settle, I don't know until you are ready whether your needs will be within what I can meet. I want you to believe any promise I make you. Therefore I will make you no promises except those that lie within my power to keep. I promise you only, then, that I will keep in close touch with you. When you are ready to talk figures, I will be ready to try to agree with you." [6]

Cold and forbidding though this may sound, it often evokes one or all of the following responses:

> "You sound like someone I can do business with." This is more often implied than expressed.
>
> "Well, I'd prefer to see if we can't settle between ourselves."
>
> Or even, "Well, when the time comes, I don't think we'll have any trouble getting together"—followed often by concrete statements indicative of modest demands.

The manner of an adjuster's making such a statement will vary according to his personality and his habits of speech. It bears repeating that the sense of the speech is probably more often implied than expressed. The adjuster's actions, statements, even his inner thoughts, should be within the framework outlined. If this is so, then there will be offered the claimant a character in the old country phrase, "with the bark on it—some-

---

[6] The foregoing paragraphs refer to tactics employed when the adjuster *does not* contemplate any advance of funds.

thing you can get hold of." It is felt that this is the essence of control. When control is lost, it is lost because claimants lose confidence in their ability to deal with the adjuster, not because of anticipation concerning the eventual settlement.

When management policies of the adjuster's principal or the circumstances of the case dictate that no funds may be paid except in satisfaction of a full release, claimants often seek a premature commitment from the adjuster, so a method for dealing with this move should be considered. The claimant's question, "I am not ready to settle today but I want to know what you will offer me when I am ready," or its equivalent, may be implied. The counter is, "I understand your concern, but the only kind of agreement that means anything to either of us is a settlement. If you are ready to settle today, I am ready to try to agree with you. I am anxious, however, to come to an agreement with you, not a dispute. It has been my experience that to try to agree in advance often leads to a premature disagreement. Therefore, unless you want to settle now let's wait until you are ready. Then if we fail to agree, it won't be for my lack of trying." Again, it must be understood that this will be phrased *in a style comfortable to the adjuster,* and in a vernacular that will be understandable to the person addressed.

The rapport of which control consists is readily felt by the adjuster. His "sense" or "feel" of a situation should be relied on. Most people are decent souls, and this includes adjusters. An adjuster, therefore, should have confidence in his purpose and in himself. He may then call as often as possible and expose his personality to the claimant as much as good manners permit, until he begins to feel the desired rapport. The more serious the claim, the more he will be justified in a heavy investment of time. In reading the anecdote which follows, note how the magnitude of the claim justified a lavish time expenditure and how much stress was laid on the adjuster's "feel" for the situation as it governed him in continuing or cutting short his efforts.

An adjuster was asked to handle an accident. Liability was obvious and the claimants, a young husband, wife and daughter, were very seriously injured. They were tourists from a highly claims-conscious territory. The grandfather's business involved him constantly with lawyers active in injury litigation. The adjuster was instructed to drop everything else, meet the grandfather at the plane, make no commitments whatsoever but spend as much time with him and the children as good taste and opportunity permitted. *He was told to stay with them until he felt that he was either harming his cause or until he felt that control was established.* The adjuster added a refinement of his own—he took along his pregnant wife. Three full days later the adjuster returned to the office, stating that he felt that in due time the claim could be negotiated to settlement. Two years later, the injuries having progressed to an end result, grandfather and son made a trip half the width of the continent to settle with the same adjuster. Jumbo limits were in effect. The initial demand was very large but, in the light of the injuries, modest—so modest, in fact, that the insurer met the first figure asked without delay.

In summary, then, an adjuster's ability to negotiate directly with injured parties is influenced by every contact he makes and by every claim he settles from the moment he enters a territory. To encourage direct negotiations, he should present a personality and pattern of statements that is consistent with himself and his real purposes. He should provide enough contact time to permit claimants to assess him. If his character and intent are right, control flows as much from the claimant's assessment of the adjuster as a person as from anything the adjuster says or does.

Negotiation

A settlement is the result of the meeting of two ideas of value—the claimant's and the adjuster's. Chapter 11 discussed settlement values and how they build backward from the anticipation of jury awards. Since it takes two to agree (as well as two to quarrel), it is necessary to consider the claimant's ideas of values. How they are formed has more than a little to do with settlement.

Claimants' ideas do not build logically backward from jury awards. Nevertheless, since he is so often obliged to resort to this method, the adjuster may make the serious mistake of assuming that a claimant's thought processes parallel his own. Worse, by discussing values as a backward extension of verdicts, the adjuster may wind up planting ideas that would never otherwise have been entertained. *Almost everyone's real ideas of value are much more modest than those entertained by the same person when he sits as a juror and is exposed to courtroom salesmanship.*

Claimants probably form more of their ideas of value from the adjuster with whom they are in contact than from any other source.

To demonstrate that there are other views of value (The subjective values discussed in Chapter 11), a simple experiment may be conducted. It involves one's wife or girl friend, mother, neighbor's wife, etc.; a few people will suffice to demonstrate the point. To these ladies may be described a claim, common enough in the business. An eager housewife, hot for a bargain, dives into a pile of merchandise in the dime store, and that pin that a careless stock clerk always manages to leave well buried, finds its accustomed mark. What is the housewife's scratched finger worth?

The answers will be small—very small to those of us inclined to think in judgment terms. There will certainly be at least one lady who indignantly says she wouldn't dream of asking for money for such a trifle. It is probable that some will value the injury in pennies, and the lady who thinks as high as $5 or $10 will probably be rare. Here, then, we have a scale of values no less vague than the court values an adjuster is accustomed to deal with, but clearly of an entirely different order of size, for experience tells us that it is hard-hearted court that will value the experience described at anything less than $50.

The same restrained approach to value is manfested by the person who gets shaken up in a collision. He is checked over by his doctor, who assures him that there are nothing but bumps and bruises, and he wants nothing more than to have his car fixed and his doctor bill paid. This again is a shocking departure from the awards to those whose doctors—for the same injuries—keep them under observation for six months, run up bills of three figures or more, and conclude with a "guarded prognosis." The housewife who wouldn't think of asking money for a pin scratch, and the man who wants only his doctor paid, not only have ideas sharply divergent from the conclusions courts are prone to arrive at—they are in the majority. The adjuster who in Chapter 1 was asked to be a person of conscience owes it to them and to the faceless man who finances the insurance business, to encourage this forbearance in as many ways as possible.

The best way to settle cases is to appeal to this streak of forbearance. If claims depend on a coming together of two ideas of value, then certainly *one of the most effective ways to settle is to arrange things so that the claimant's asking price is so reasonable that it can be met without difficulty.*

For the best adjusters, a high proportion of their settlements drop in their laps, seemingly without effort and possibly without conscious design. This is the best of all possible adjusting, and the ability to evoke the spirit that leads to this kind of settlement is the secret of the really good adjuster. This spirit is not evoked by a challenging manner. Neither is it nourished by treating every element of a claim with obvious suspicion. The psychologists have a term, "self-fulfilling prophecy," which, to oversimplify, means that hostility begets hostility and trust begets trust. Folklore, as usual, has a phrase for it—"Give a dog a bad name and he'll live up to it," or, "The way to make a boy honest is to trust him."

The millennium has not, of course, arrived and, although this book has repeatedly insisted that only a minority of claimants are dishonest or exaggerate, still, claims must be handled in a world where some *are* dishonest and some *do* exaggerate. The duty to the restrained and forbearing, as well as to the buyer of insurance who foots the bill, requires that every effort be made to control the grasp of those who try to take advantage of claims situations. Claims must therefore be investigated and expenses must be confirmed. The problem is to do this without demonstrating suspicion and arousing a self-justifying resentment in the claimant. The adjuster would be wise to have made no bones about his confirming investigation, but his manner should have reflected an inner conviction that he is being given nothing but the truth. He should have been forthright about bringing doubtful points into the open but ready to be persuaded by the facts. His manner should have made it clear that he is as ready to be persuaded as to resist the improper. A forthright attitude is more likely to be appreciated than resented. This again may be compared to the chord played by the left hand and the adjuster's attitude will, no doubt, be more often implied than stated. It will, therefore, be tempered to the quality of the claimant and the situation under negotiation. Frank recognition of why he is there and a pleasant willingness to recognize that there are two sides of a question will usually evoke the proper attitude in return.

Actions speak louder than words. The adjuster must satisfy the claimant that he is willing to be open-minded. A quarter of an hour of well-delivered statements may be helpful, but recognizing claimant's strong points may be a lot better.

Next to the failure to try to talk figures, more claims probably fail to settle because of the failure of the parties to attain an attitude of reciprocal respect than for any other reason. The adjuster, therefore, should enter negotiations recognizing that the claimant may have ideas of value other than verdict values. He should be prepared to encourage a modest approach on the claimant's part, or to respect him in his error if the claimant is overly demanding. So far as possible, the adjuster should think in terms of the scale exemplified by the pin scratch example. *His evaluation, derived from judgment experience, will be held in the background as an upper limit beyond which he will not go, but he will recognize that any opportunity to settle within that limit should be capitalized.* He tries to appeal to the best in the claimant and to order his investigation so that he does not destroy the rapport he has been trying to create.

However, the world has also its share of hard traders, and a high proportion of claims are settled by "horse trading." This tactic is often obligatory when an adjuster's instructions require that he make neither payment nor advance except in satisfaction of a full release.[7] Many claims departments indeed require an adjuster first to ascertain a claimant's "price" before permitting a counteroffer. (It may be that more claims are

---

[7] From this point to the bottom of page 499, discussion bears principally on negotiations with a release as the objective.

settled by an adjuster's first offer than the industry realizes.)
Horse-trading has its place and will always be a feature of the
business—at least, until there is in existence a clear scale of
imposed values binding on both parties. Horse-trading, in fact,
serves a useful purpose which deserves respectful recognition.

Horse-trading enables the parties gradually to expose their
minds and convictions. It recognizes that today's "rock bottom"
may in time be subjected to second thoughts, and it preserves
to each of the negotiators the opportunity of making another
small concession as a "face-saver" in the end. Adjusters ought
not to be self-conscious about horse-trading. In sending legislation to the Congress, Presidents of the United States have always
asked for more than they hoped to get. A technique that has this
high endorsement certainly has its place in the field of adjusting.
The adjuster therefore (and here his judgment and past experience will guide him) settles many claims by asking as gracefully
as he can the bald question, "What will you take?" and reconciles himself to offering less than he expects to pay.

Although many settlements may be better arrived at by the
adjuster's making the first offer, this should probably be considered a variation from the norm. The advantage of a first offer
lies in this: The biggest factor in influencing the claimant's idea
of value is the scale that he picks up from the adjuster. By
making the first offer, the adjuster may succeed in establishing the
range within which the negotiations take place.

A claimant's ideas may be ascertained by pre-settlement dis-
cussions. It has already been suggested that expenses be totalled
and the question asked, "Is there anything more to be taken into
account?" If the answer is in the negative, then some adjusters
proceed immediately to the writing of the release in the amount
of the total just arrived at.[8] If the claimant wishes to claim only
this amount and signs the release as it is offered to him, the
matter is settled. If on the other hand he does wish to claim
something for his other items (a claim which many persons are
honestly not inclined to make), the proffer of the release will

---

[8] This resembles the salesman's technique of "the indirect close"; instead of
"Will you buy this refrigerator?" he asks, "Do you prefer this in white or beige?"
Variations on this theme will suggest themselves.

certainly lead the claimant to express his views and, if they are within his judgment as to what he should pay, or close to it, the adjuster may settle or negotiate as the situation demands.

An opening offer by an adjuster may also help to avoid putting the claimant in a situation where "loss of face" is inevitable. Since the appearance of the Oriental idea of "face" may seem strange in this context, an explanation is in order. For instance, in a claim evaluated at $100 an adjuster asks a claimant what he will take. Expecting to be obliged to dicker, the claimant doubles his figure and asks $200. Now, for every dollar he comes down, he loses face. Resolving the many possibilities for disagreement that are inherent in any claim is enough of a problem as it is without creating further obstacles by permitting the matter of prestige or "face" to come into the picture. "Face" is not exclusively an Oriental phenomenon. Everybody's experience embraces many instances where someone has said, "I didn't want to knuckle under to him," or "I didn't want to seem to give in," or even, "He was perfectly right, but I just didn't want to admit it to him." These are simply the American expressions acknowledging the feeling which elsewhere is called "face."

Some people, however, regard dickering as a way of life; with them it is almost a breach of etiquette to make a firm price offer. "Face" here is not an issue, but the adjuster who fails to recognize this trait courts frustration until he does.

In summary, unless the adjuster's operational instructions forbid, he should experiment. In some instances he should try an opening offer. He will certainly settle some claims by the demand and counter-offer route. On occasion he will make a one-price offer and, if he has gauged the situation correctly, he may attain many settlements in this fashion. His opening offer, if he elects to make it, may well be based on clues derived from earlier conversations. If he knows he is going to have to horse-trade, his first offer may be very low, a frank opening move.

Opening the Negotiations

Many adjusters, particularly younger ones, find it difficult to get negotiations under way. This is a problem that bothers the assured, confident, salesman-type personality not at all. It is often a matter of real concern to the more methodical, formal person who is also found in the business.

If an adjuster finds he has difficulty in surmounting this hurdle he should prepare a list of perhaps half a dozen opening moves. These opening moves can be drawn from one's own imagination, from listening to shop talk, and by inquiring of one's supervisor. Those who have resorted to this technique report that they seldom use anything the way they wrote it down but knowing that a list was there seemed to give them confidence—in effect, seemed to assist their imaginations in developing opening statements appropriate to the situations with which they were confronted.

If an adjuster elects to prepare such a list for his own guidance, he should distinguish the strong moves from the weak ones, and will probably wish to arrange the list in some appropriate order so as to recognize the gradations of strength.

Probably the weakest opening move that an adjuster could make would be, "You don't want to settle today, do you?" "Do you want to settle today?" would be only slightly stronger. "How much do you want?" implies that there is no question but that the settlement is about to take place, and hence is stronger yet. Possibly the strongest opening one can use is to write out a release without any discussion of the amount and then tender it to the claimant implying by one's actions that he is to read it and sign it. This implies not only that settlement will take place on that day but that it is agreed that the claimant will accept the adjuster's evaluation of the claim. It is also a dangerous move. It should be employed discreetly—that is, when the time, place and type of claim are appropriate—and if the claimant demurs, the adjuster should be prepared to cope with his demurrer.

It should be unnecessary to add that if an adjuster equips himself with a list of prepared openers, he should select language, thoughts and ideas in which *he* feels comfortable and confident.

Persuasion and Some Aspects of Closing

When it comes to closing claims an adjuster is a salesman just as much as if he were soliciting applications for insurance. At this stage of the game motivation is what it is all about. One of the few qualified behavioral scientists [9] to have studied the claims situation feels that he has identified four stages through which a typical injured claimant passes:

1. Gratitude for medical services and, therefore, determination to pay for them.
2. "Thank God for insurance." At this point understanding of settlement procedures may fix claimant's attitude at the point of regarding the company as an ally working for his salvation.
3. "I've been paying for a long time, now's my time to get it back." This stage, Dr. Staton feels, is reached by claimants in whom there has not been created a feeling of confidence and trust. Dr. Staton feels that field men can inhibit this feeling (now's the time to get mine) by displaying interest in claimant's welfare.
4. Self-justification—a sequel to stage 3. Claimant develops excuses to justify an unwarranted or unrealistic claim which he intends to press. His guilt feelings convert to hostility toward the carrier by a phenomenon known as projection, i.e., he ascribes guilt to the company rather than to himself.[10]

Dr. Staton goes on to identify six significant determinants of claimant attitude:

1. Promptness of contact following the accident.
2. Thorough understanding of issues, procedures, and circumstances determining how the settlement offer was arrived at.
3. Adequacy of follow-through; the claim representative keeping up contact.
4. Attitude of the claims representative in explaining and discussing the situation with the claimant.
5. Prompt settlement when the time for settlement arrives.
6. Adequacy of payment.

The reservations (footnote 10) about stage 2 should be discussed. For each claimant and for himself, the adjuster is obliged

---

[9] Thomas Staton, PhD., Head, Dept. of Psychology, Huntington College, Montgomery, Ala. Another who has written on the subject is Willis Rokes, PhD., CLU, CPCU, Chairman, Dept. of Insurance, University of Nebraska, Omaha, Neb.

[10] The author recognizes stages 3 and 4; they confirm by objective observation what he has subjectively accepted. He has substantial reservations about stage 2.

to attempt to say and do those things which will best serve to bring the claim to an early, peaceful disposition.

Reservation # 1. That explanations of principles and procedures of claim settlement foster understanding and rapport.

It is the experience of many and a belief adopted by the author, but so far lacking in objective confirmation, that explanation of principles and procedures of settlement tend to create argument and controversy.

Reservation # 2. Is not so much a reservation as a "yes, but" thought.

Yes, the insurance company often is the injured man's ally and demonstration of the alliance by the adjuster can evoke gratitude, *but* in some situations the attempt to display the insurer as the claimant's friend is self-defeating because the claimant perceives these overtures as part of a confidence game. Moreover, claimants often do restrain their demands and moderate their attitudes not from any sense of gratitude but from what seems to be an attempt to identify with the carrier or possibly from an attempt to conform to the claimant's ideas of commendable and responsible behavior.

Reservation # 2 is also predicated on experience; experience which teaches us that in many instances the adjuster is required to do many things that are obviously not the act of an ally:

Expenses must be confirmed.
Witnesses who don't see eye to eye with the claimant must be seen and their statements taken. Their testimony will be given what seems to be its appropriate weight.
Most important of all, claimants' ideas of value must often be opposed and reduced.

To unreservedly cast the adjuster in the role of the ally, places him close to being a traitorous ally because of these activities. At the least they force the claimant, in mid-negotiation, to cast the adjuster in an entirely new role, a role which permits the activities enumerated and still permits the parties to relate to one another in terms of mutual respect.

It is entirely possible that further study will demonstrate that Dr. Staton's view and the expressed reservations are both right, or that they may be reconciled. In the meantime, some observations may help to apply Dr. Staton's six determinants, with a retreat available in case the reservations seem to control the situation.

Before offering these observations it is necessary to point out that Dr. Staton's observations appear to have been limited to a relatively limited class of claimant, i.e., those who are sufficiently hurt so that they can feel gratitude to those whose medical care seems to restore their health. This leaves adjusters with no guide to tell them how to handle the claimant they all know only too well—the fellow who is not hurt or is only slightly hurt. It is not difficult for this person to locate a doctor who will, up to a limit which usually cuts in at about $350 to $500, render as much treatment as necessary to incur expenses that the claimant or his attorney consider desirable. Yet many people elect not to travel this route. They know quite well what they could have done and what they could have claimed, but they simply do not want to do it. It is not only possible but probable that the way adjusters have handled themselves has influenced—maybe even determined—the claimant's election.

There are some procedures which may help explain how adjusters can develop this type of attitude. Prompt contact is one. The claimant is more cooperative when he is contacted by a person to whom he can relate. All things being equal, a personal contact is probably better than a phone contact, although the phone contact can work wonders. It is doubtful that such a relationship can spring from a mail contact.

An actual case illustrates this point. The claimant, a college student was injured and refused admission to a hospital. The claims manager in whose territory the accident occurred talked with the parents at their home 150 miles away to establish control. He secured entre for the adjuster in the young lady's home town and the claimant was returned home. Adjusters in the locale of the accident were never able to see her, but the field adjuster at claimant's home city settled a few months later with her parents. The adjuster reported that several times during the negotiations the mother observed that if Mr. Field Man was associated with Mr. Manager who called, he simply had to be reliable. The adjuster credits the settlement to the district manager who made one phone call.

The point is not that a phone contact is better than a personal contact; the point is that a contact which established a satisfactory rapport governed the entire further course of the claim. The important thing had to be the rapport, not the way contact was made.

How is rapport established? By offering the insurance company as an ally? It is doubtful that by itself this is a sufficient answer, but it cannot be disregarded for many adjusters settle many claims on the "I am your friend who has come to help you" theme. It appears that these adjusters are usually men of warm, outgoing personality, blessed with an irresistable smile, the kind of whom it is truly said that they can "talk the birds out of the trees." These men are particularly effective when injury is minor and claimant's principal concern is with his damaged car (his lost status symbol). When attention can be directed to the damaged car, and injury made relatively unimportant, the friendly ally role can be very effective. Other adjusters less generously blessed with charm, attain rapport but they have to go about it differently. Another anecdote should illustrate this technique.

The claim was for property damage ($500 more or less) to a van-type delivery truck. Driver was slightly hurt. Adjuster was trying to establish control of the B.I. and set up an opportunity to inspect P.D. He was talking with a tough, capable, lady office manager.

> The lady—"Why are you trying to make a federal case out of this? The last time we had a truck damaged A Insurance Company simply told us to send in the bill and they would pay it."
>
> Adjuster—"Well, I'm not responsible for spending A Company's money but I am responsible for my employer's and I intend to spend it just as carefully as you do Mr. "S's" (naming the owner of the lady's firm).
>
> The lady—"Well, you know when it gets right down to it, I didn't appreciate the way A Company handled us. In the long run, even though we weren't their insured's, it's still our money they are

tossing around. The truck is at X's body shop. Will it be okay if I have the driver in after lunch to see you?"

It is the adjuster's prime duty to spend his principal's money carefully, and his actions probably should imply this. If it becomes necessary to enunciate that duty, doing so usually enhances rather than diminishes rapport. Conversational leads in this vein which appear to have been successful include:

> My company gives me all the authority I need to be generous, but not 10¢ to give away.
>
> I want you to be comfortable dealing with me and to understand what I do. My job is to spend the company's money as carefully as you would want me to spend yours if I represented you. If you will remember that, there will be nothing that I will do or say that won't be perfectly clear to you.
>
> Many people in your situation are anxious to know how claims are handled. Anything you'd like to ask me, I'll do my best to answer.

To handle the surprisingly few questions that the invitation evokes, the following principles seem to have been reliable guides:

> Frankly acknowledge that investigation may disclose questions about liability that may put claimant in doubt or require compromise. This acknowledgment should be followed by the assurance that such questions can be openly discussed without rancor.
>
> Avoid the discussion of specific liability questions (i.e., "Witness A says.") Instead, "I understand why you feel as you do and I'm sure you know why I feel there is a question. The real question is whether you want to take this "X" dollars which I have offered you, or whether you would prefer to risk this sum in the hope that the judge will see it your way."

The claimant usually is not really interested in why the adjuster feels that liability is questionable. What he is really interested in is how confident the adjuster is of his position. The size of his offer, tone of voice, willingness to stand or fall on his appraisal will influence the claimant far more than logical arguments.

Treat the claimant always as a gentleman, even if there is reason to believe he is not. His actions may be surprising. If he thinks he is regarded as a gentleman, he will probably want to continue to be regarded so. This in turn will motivate him to act like a gentleman, which is what was wanted in the first place.

To summarize: the friend and ally approach may be self-defeating. It may be best to restrain the approach until a signal is obtained that tells how the claimant wants to be handled. Claimant may be strongly motivated by gratitude to the adjuster as a friend or he may view the adjuster as a figure (possibly a father figure) whose regard he wishes to retain.

Respect claimant's views but avoid discussion of specifics. If he insists upon the ally role do not resist it, but do not bet the whole case on the ability to maintain that role. Be ready to fall back into the role of the careful spender who expects to be respected for doing his job conscientiously.

Advanced Payments

Both the opening move towards settlement and the creation of that rapport which facilitates direct dealing and almost any kind of closing may, under present practices (always depending on the management policies of the insurance company involved), be considerably aided by advance of funds. Under such circumstances the execution of any kind of release may be at least temporarily and sometimes permanently waived. The way funds are advanced (documents executed or waived) is discussed later.

Almost any expense or damage suffered by the claimant may be the subject of an advance. In an order roughly indicative of the frequency of such advance, the following are often compensated by the advance of funds:

Property damage to claimant's car
Rental vehicle
Hospital expense
Medical expense
Lost income
Pain and suffering
Indemnity for permanent impairment

In short, just about any element of a claim may now be and frequently is the subject of voluntary advance.

Handling Advance Payments

The way companies want their adjusters to handle advance payments is still another field of activity in which practice varies between extremes. The variation represents differences in attitudes.

At one end of the spectrum are carriers who aggressively seek opportunity to advance funds as soon as liability appears probable. They are likely to do these things:

Make immediate arrangements for the repair of claimant's damaged vehicle—openly underwriting the cost of such repairs.
Place a replacement vehicle in claimant's hands at the carrier's expense.
Arrange for medical and hospital services to be billed directly to the carrier on a weekly or monthly basis as they are incurred.
Promptly institute payments for lost earning capacity.

The attitude of these insurers is characterized in these words, "just as quickly as possible we try to get some money into the claimant's hands, even if it's only re-imbursement of an ambulance bill." From a philosophical point of view, it might be said that their attitude is no longer that of trying to settle a claim—attitude has become that of making the claimant whole again (to the extent that money can do so).

If "make him whole" represents one end of the attitude spectrum, what is at the other end? At the other end are the many carriers who feel that companies *must* operate within the techniques of the legal system or face the possible collapse of the entire system of insurance. These people simply do not make advances. They really have no place in a discussion of advance payments except that it is necessary to show the opposite view.

In the middle ground, and with many shades of difference characterizing their practices are the many companies which do make advances but do so with the ultimate release as the obvious goal. Whether an advance is made is usually decided upon such factors as:

Will this advance assist us in maintaining control of the claim? Is the claimant co-operating with us? Is he making medical information available, etc?

Such an approach to advances might be referred to as a "guarded" approach.

As expected, there are many shades of opinion and consequent variations in technique. It is interesting to note that in negotiating with attorneys, one extreme development of the "make him whole" approach served the purposes of those who follow the guarded approach very efficiently.

Documenting Advance Payments

Two examples of documents follow which might be used in recording an advance. Again, there are many variations—a third widely used documentation being no documentation at all.

The second figure, page 509 demonstrates what is often known as an open ended release. It is used quite commonly in the guarded approach and is often very helpful in closing claims where the claimant is truly concerned about the possibility that he may incur further medical expense or additional lost wages. It is also helpful in closing claims where claimant has no real fear of further medical expense but wants a psychological face saver. Claims were the carrier is called upon to pay any more medical expense are infrequent.

Receipt

The undersigned acknowledges
Receipt of Thirty Five and no/100 Dollars in reimbursement of the Jan. 15, 1972 invoice of Emergency Ambulance Service, Inc., and the
Payment of Five hundred twenty five and 43/100 Dollars to ABC Body Shop, Inc.
It is agreed that these payments are to be credited against any settlement later made by the undersigned with John Policyholder of claim arising out of accident Jan, 15, 1972 or against any judgment arising out of said accident.
This is not a release.
SIGNED

The foregoing examples are *not* to be regarded as examples of the way it *should be done.* Many strongly and conservatively managed insurance companies, acting on the advice of their legal departments (and in some instances probably making a

AGREEMENT AND RELEASE

FOR AND IN CONSIDERATION of the payment of the sum of

_____ Dollars, the receipt of

which is hereby acknowledged, and of the promise of payment to the undersigned of benefits in accordance with the SCHEDULE OF BENEFITS set forth below, by the Company accepting this Agreement,

---

SCHEDULE OF BENEFITS

(1) To pay all reasonable and necessary expenses not to exceed $2,000 incurred for medical, dental or surgical treatment, ambulance, hospital, professional nursing services and prosthetic devices, furnished to the named beneficiary within 180 days of the date of this Agreement, as a result of the accident described herein, provided that such expenses are not paid or payable by any collateral source; and

(2) To pay $_____ for each day within 180 days of the date of this Agreement that said beneficiary is continuously and necessarily disabled and confined indoors under the care of a licensed physician other than himself, due to the bodily injury incurred because of the accident described herein (payable monthly); provided that the total of said per diem payments shall not exceed $2,000;

and, provided the total amount payable hereunder for this release, plus said expense payments, plus said per diem payments, shall not exceed the limit of liability for bodily injury to one person provided by the policy of insurance applicable to the releasee named herein,

---

the undersigned hereby releases and forever discharges _____

_____ , the Insurance Company accepting

this Agreement, and any and all other persons, firms or corporations liable or who might be claimed to be liable,

from any and all claims, demands, damages, actions, causes of action or suits of any kind or nature whatsoever,

both to person and property, and particularly on account of all injuries, known and unknown, sustained by

_____ ,

Named Beneficiary

which have resulted or may in the future develop as a result of an accident which occurred on or about

the _____ day of _____ , 19____ at or near _____ .

It is also agreed and understood that this settlement is the compromise of a doubtful and disputed claim, that the payment is not to be construed as an admission of liability on the part of the persons, firms and corporations hereby released, by whom liability is expressly denied. This Agreement and Release contains the entire agreement between the parties hereto, and the terms of this instrument are contractual and not a mere recital. It is further agreed that all parties to this instrument have carefully read the contents thereof and the signatures below are the voluntary and free act of each.

In witness whereof _____ have hereunto set _____ hand(s) and seal(s) this _____ day of _____ , 19____.

IN PRESENCE OF

_____(SEAL)

_____   _____(SEAL)

_____   _____(SEAL)

business decision to disregard the warning of the legal department) have simply done away with all documentation of advances. The cancelled check, they feel, is all that will be needed to secure credit for the advances. Those who follow this practice will either cross out the wording on the draft which makes it a release or will use a draft that does not include such wording.

Many carriers follow whole-heartedly a "make him whole" approach in clear liability situations but follow a guarded or no-advance approach when liability is in dispute.

It is not the province of this book to urge one approach over another. It is the prerogative of the company's management to do this. It should be pointed out, however, that many companies which have gone all or part of the way toward the "make him whole" policy have found their biggest problems have been with there own staff. Adjusters trained in the traditional approach have found it difficult to adjust their thinking; sometimes their attitude in applying the new techniques has boiled down to outright foot-dragging, certainly a perversion of the principle of personal responsibility.

Advance Payments—Plaintiff's Attorneys

Practice, of course, varies from company to company in this field of negotiating. The differences are what might be expected but it can be pointed out, by way of anecdote, how the "make him whole" approach in at least one instance served the most conservative ends of the guarded attitude.

The carrier had made several advances: repaired the claimant's car, furnished a replacement vehicle, advanced lost income, paid medical and hospital expenses. Claimant, who had demonstrated no spectacular gratitude, had made it clear from the first that he expected far more than his expenses and, as soon as the time for immediate cash outlay was behind him, engaged a lawyer. The company did not wait for the usual arm's length negotiation. Instead, it calculated the other sums which it felt proper to pay for general damage and sent a check to the lawyer with a letter explaining that the enclosure represented its idea of the remaining value in the claim, that it was paying that sum forthwith, and if the lawyer or his client wished to proceed further at law, they could do so. The lawyer's response was to call the claims manager, "Don't you ever do that to me again! You've paid so much that there's not enough left in the claim for me to make a decent fee on. I told my fellow to go home and forget it."

Perhaps this lawyer spoke at least half in jest, but maybe at least a small fraction of the attitude displayed was serious.

In its opening paragraphs, this chapter suggested that possibly the insurance industry had drifted into playing lawyers' games by lawyers' rules and that possibly the new approaches might represent a basic change of the game itself.

One swallow doesn't make a summer, and one anecdote hardly proves a point, but it suggests the possibilities which may lie in an entirely new way of thinking about claims.

First Call Settlements

Many injury claims are settled on the first call. This procedure has much to offer both parties. Not the least of the benefits are the reduction of uncertainty and the elimination of the cost of further handling. The buyer of insurance never relaxes his concern with the ultimate cost of claims, and his interests dictate that every claim that can be settled in this way should be closed at the first opportunity.

The first requisite to this kind of disposition is an adjuster's ability to act. It may be assumed that he has been provided by his employer or client with adequate authority. It is up to the adjuster to have equipped himself with such information as will permit him to exercise his authority sensibly. A quick series of phone calls ought to have provided him with, at least, sound estimates of the special damages. Thus prepared to evaluate the claim, he is in a position to open the door should opportunity knock.

The next requirement is the adjuster's expectation that he *will* settle. It is a foregone conclusion that he will not settle if he is afraid he won't. It may be helpful, then, to remind oneself that many claimants are better off for getting their claims behind them. This especially includes those who are nervous and inclined to hypochondria.

Too, the claims world includes those to whom a minor injury is simply the opportunity to try to hit the jackpot. This class, if seen promptly, is often willing to recognize the traditional value of the bird in the hand as against the two in the bush. People who have this opportunistic attitude towards claims are frequently people who simply like horse-trading. Certainly the adjuster can do no less than accommodate this tendency, particularly when it is in the interest of those he represents and to decline to dicker may expose him to the charge of lack of spirit.

The pleasantries that precede the taking of the statement and the conversation back and forth as the statement is written, provide clues not only to the claimant's intention but as to his evaluation of his claim. The adjuster should be alert to these clues; his actions should be guided in part by what he learns at this stage of investigation; and of course what he learns will determine and guide whether or how he goes about trying to negotiate a "first call" or any other settlement.

Going from the totaling of the expenses at the end of the statement to the question "Is this all?" is an effective technique for exploring the possibility of a first call settlement.

Even when the facts of the claim and the surrounding circumstances seem to indicate that a first call settlement is in order, the adjuster may still fail to settle. If this failure is from the claimant's reluctance, it is simply to be accepted. The mature adjuster has long since given up expecting to have his way in all things. The failure, on the other hand, may arise from nothing less his fear of raising the subject of settlement. This is nothing less than the salesman's common failure, the failure to ask for the order. If on any call, the first or subsequent, the adjuster feels that a settlement is appropriate, then he must raise the question. He may not be to blame if the case fails to settle, but he is certainly to blame if he doesn't ever give it a chance.[11]

A claimant's initial reluctance to talk settlement may not be what it seems. He may simply want to be coaxed. Within the limits of good taste and manners, the question, if the adjuster

---

[11] Sometimes even a serious injury can be settled on the first call, usually for reasons apparent from conversation or circumstance. Beware though of the claimant who talks settlement but is only on a "fishing" expedition.

suspects that this is the situation, may be presented and re-presented in a different form: "Well, if you *were* going to settle today, what would you. . . ?"

To get into talking money is not always easy, even for an adjuster whose business it is to deal in those terms. It is often equally difficult for a claimant to get down to brass tacks. The adjuster owes a duty to both parties to the transaction—the claimant and his principal. In settling situations, his function may be to provide the assistance to overcome reluctance to broach the subject. He may have to urge the claimant over the hump of that universally avoided duty—that of coming to a decision.

In summary, then, if he is to close on his first call those claims that call for that disposition, the adjuster should acquaint himself with the factors influencing value to the extent that it is possible to do so, by a few phone calls. He should *expect* to settle. If his insurer's practice and his judgment of the subject permit, he should shape the interview so as to lead smoothly to a release. The very least he can do is to make strong, and possibly repeated, efforts to urge the conversation into a discussion of actual figures.

Further Comments—Advanced Payments

Negotiations toward a release having now been explored, it is necessary, before considering how to proceed when claimant is represented by counsel, to consider some further aspects of the advance of funds. A closely related subject, the "walk away" settlement, also needs to be considered.

Documents to Effect Advances

Many carriers in many jurisdictions advance funds with no substantiating documentation. They simply forward the claimant a check or draft. The usual brief release printed over the space for endorsement may have been stricken because the company feels that the canceled check (draft) is all the substantiation needed to show what it has paid and to receive credit for the advance in the event the claim does go as far as a verdict. These carriers may also tell a claimant, doctor or hospital simply to send in periodic statements of expenses and then make payments directly to the creditors.

Other carriers, more conservatively inclined, require their claims representatives to confirm advances by letter to the claimant or his attorney describing the advance and indicating that it is to be understood that such an advance will be taken as an offset against any future settlement or verdict.

Some carriers require execution of receipts.

No attempt is made to demonstrate examples of such documents since they may vary by jurisdiction and by company and their selection is wholly within the management province of the particular insurance company making the advance.

Factors to Be Considered

As to the following factors, there is no unanimity as to how they will be weighted or the policy to be followed. It is, therefore, improper to attempt to identify any industry standard; however, almost all claims departments will consider the same factors and a plus factor in one office will usually be similarly regarded anywhere. Nevertheless, one office may respond by advancing funds while another may say, "Yes, I agree this factor makes the case a better candidate for an advance, but I'm still not going to pay anything until I get my full release."

Liability

The clearer the liability picture, the more likely a company is to advance funds. Very few insurers will advance anything on claims which have a strong likelihood of receiving a defendant's verdict. Many carriers will, however, advance funds where liability could go either way but injuries are substantial. Their attitude might be expressed, "Where there is a real injury and we know we are going to pay something, then we may advance anything up to a sum approximating the amount that we know we will eventually be ready to pay."

Injury

In general it is safe to say that severe injuries will more readily receive advance funds. From an injury standpoint, the most likely candidate for an advance is a claim for injury displaying the following characteristics:

The injury is serious. Its nature is such that there is substantial possibility that surgical or medical intervention will reduce disability or minimize permanency.

The injury is serious enough to cause one to expect substantial disability and consequent loss of earning capacity.

The injury is honest. Carriers are obviously more inclined to advance funds when they feel the injury is honest rather than feigned. It should, however, be noted that many carriers will advance funds even when they are substantially satisfied that the injury is feigned. Their motive in doing so is interesting and bears careful examination.

In many sections of the country, carriers are understandably doubtful of the ability of the courts to perform their duties in protecting defendants. Faced with what might be a built-up claim with a potential of, let us say, $2,500 to $3,500, a carrier might decide to advance funds or make a walk-away settlement in an amount somewhere between $1,000 and $2,000. Its purpose in doing so likely is to institute meaningful settlement negotiations or possibly to forestall a law suit.

In the instance cited for example, plaintiff's attorney possibly made a demand which the carrier was unwilling to meet, or the carrier doubted that its settlement offers were being transmitted to the claimant. The carrier might, therefore, select a limit it is willing to pay and send a check for that amount to counsel along with a release, describing the offer as a compromise offer and requesting counsel to have the release executed if his client elects to accept the check. This technique is often referred to as a "drop draft settlement."

Other carriers might go a little farther. They might send the same or greater sum and waive a release. In that event, the thinking is: it is difficult for counsel to charge a heavy fee on sums thus voluntarily advanced. The sums advanced bear a close enough relationship to the probable, anticipated verdict so there really is not enough left in the claim to justify the attorney going through the work of a law suit. The claim, therefore, settles without release simply because it is not worthwhile to press it.

The second type of tender—without a release—is often referred to as a "walk-away settlement." It is often used when attorneys represent injured parties but it is also used before the injured party has secured representation.

Almost always the selection of the sum to be tendered, whether by drop draft or walk-away release, is influenced by two factors:

The carrier's judgment of the settlement value of the case.

The desire to offer enough money so that there will be little economic incentive to claimant or counsel to pursue the matter further.

Scars—Advanced Payments Tactics

It may be instructive to consider a particular type of claim and the tactical opportunities that the advanced payment technique offers in managing it. This should help in understanding the tactical and strategic possibilities inherent in this technique.

Consider for instance, the claim of a child—serious facial scarring, parents of modest means, liability probable.

In dealing directly with the parents of such a child, immediate advance payments defraying such expenses as they are incurred may assist in controlling the claim.

Almost all scars can be substantially improved and many can be virtually obliterated by skilled plastic surgery. Plastic surgery is very expensive and since the child's parents are of modest means, plastic surgery is, at best, difficult for them to manage. An offer by an insurance carrier to finance surgery and attendant hospitalization may accomplish the following:

It will probably benefit the child by removing or lessening his disfigurement, a humane result.

By lessening the damage (child is less disfigured) it actually reduces the injury, thus parents may be willing to accept a lesser amount in settlement or a jury less likely to make an overly large award.

Child and parents may feel gratitude and identify with the carrier instead of being alienated and hostile.

The offer of plastic surgery may be beneficial in frustrating an aggressive attempt by counsel to capitalize on the child's injury. For instance, some attorneys will deliberately keep their clients away from plastic surgeons in an attempt to bring as disfiguring a scar as possible into the courtroom. The offer to finance examination, and if recommended, surgical procedure and hospitalization presents obvious problems to plaintiff's counsel.

NEGOTIATION WITH ATTORNEYS

Many people *will* wish to avail themselves of their right to representation by counsel. In dealing with attorneys, adjusters should take a lesson from the attorneys themselves. It will open an adjuster's eyes to go to the courthouse and watch two lawyers going at one another, fang and claw, until one can almost see blood on the courtroom floor. Then the court recesses. The adjuster goes across the street for lunch, and whom does he see at the next table but the same two attorneys breaking bread together and calmly discussing the problems of their children in college. The battle he saw in the courtroom was no sham—and neither is the friendship outside.

It is the adjuster's function to adjust, that is, to carry out his part in an essentially adversary relationship, without destroying sound personal rapport. He does the best he can to keep his cases out of litigation and to offer settlements which are attractive to the injured party. He makes no apology for a firmly held conviction that cases ought to be settled rather than litigated, for his views on value which may not be courtroom values, nor for his efforts to bring about settlements at figures which recognize the interest of the insurance buyers who have financed the system and the settlement. At the same time he is enough of a realist to realize that the attorney's function is just as legitimate as his, and when he must deal with counsel he does not regard him as a shyster. Instead he respects him for doing a good job for his clients. When he is new at the game and uncertain of his values, the learning adjuster should take care to consult with his adviser and manager to be certain that when he talks figures with counsel, they are realistic. An adjuster's standing with an attorney is not damaged by his failure to agree with him. If on the other hand an attorney gets the idea that an adjuster is unrealistic, arrogant, hostile or smart aleck, from that time on everything may be headed for suit.

When an attorney is on a case, the adjuster refrains from negotiating with or even contacting the injured party. As negotiations develop, if it begins to appear to the adjuster that there is little hope of the parties getting together, it may be wise for him to make a candid statement to that effect to the attorney. Negotiation implies that there is a reasonable possibility that the parties will be able to come to an agreement, and therefore implies the request that the attorney delay filing his suit pending the outcome of negotiations. An attorney may lose his position on the calendar by negotiating, so, in many situations, it is an act of decency for the adjuster to inform the attorney accordingly if it appears to him that there is no chance of arriving at a settlement. At the same time an adjuster should be careful how he conveys this information lest the attorney misunderstand him and think that what he is being told amounts to, "Sue and be damned to you."

Some attorneys are difficult to negotiate with and their initial demands impossibly high. It used to be thought that these situations presented no alternative but to wait until the courthouse steps were reached and until the exigencies of trial forced the attorney to face the facts of life. Often this is the only practical course. Modern practice, however, increasingly recognizes the desirability of making a substantial offer "of record." After all, money talks. Attorneys with blood in the eye have been known to confess, "I wanted to try this one, but your offer really put the heat on me. I just had to tell my client, and it was the old business of the bird in the hand, so we decided to take it."

It is difficult to lay down rules. The adjuster must consider each situation on its merits. He will withhold offers in some instances, offer all or very nearly all the full value of his case in others, and sometimes indulge in wild and furious horse-trading. A cardinal rule in dealing with attorneys is not to be carried away by the righteousness of one's own position. An attempt to preserve realism and one's sense of humor should be made at all costs.

The bar includes bodily injury plaintiffs' specialists, and a host of attorneys who see only four or five injury claims a year.

Of those who handle mostly injury claims, there are the seasoned trial men who are not only formidable opposition—they are usually realists in pricing. There are then the youngsters imbued with an abundance of drive and, frequently, outrageous ideas of value. The latter are by all odds the hardest to deal with. An adjuster may have to reconcile himself to letting some of their cases go to trial.

The seasoned specialist usually demands a premium for his client, based on his demonstrated ability to get "top dollar." Such men are usually realists and recognize that there are economic advantages to settlement. The price of doing business with them is a willingness to face the facts. If such a man has *demonstrated ability,* he can usually be settled with at a figure that puts a realistic but not necessarily exorbitant value on this ability.

Men who do not do a substantial amount of plaintiffs' work but who have an established practice in other fields are usually realistic in their appraisals, or at least they try to be. They are prone to check their own notions of value with the plaintiffs' men and defense specialists.

Some plaintiffs' specialists build their claims deliberately. The extent of this practice is not clearly recognized by those members of the bar who handle only an occasional claim. Thus, the man who handles small volume may be inclined to bring in a specialist who will later treat the claim in a manner that the first attorney would by no means condone if he understood what was going on. It is to the insurer's interest, and in the interest of the buying public, that it be made clear at once to these sometime injury lawyers that prompt and realistic settlements can be arrived at without delay. Many times, attorneys think the adjuster doesn't intend to settle because he doesn't make contact with the attorney—so the case goes to suit. Adjusters should learn to get in touch with attorneys as soon as their appearance is known. Willingness to settle is not a sign of weakness—and the attorney had better know that the adjuster is willing. Further, the best time for the attorney and adjuster to establish a personal relationship which will allow them to negotiate contentious matters to a successful agreement is before the contentions have arisen. In many ways negotiating with them can be likened to "controlling" a claimant himself. Many identical factors are involved.

RELEASES—NATURE AND PURPOSE

The usual closing document for a liability claim is a release. This is because the claim which has been disposed of results from an obligation imposed upon one party for the benefit of another, by the operation of law. For the purpose of disposing of these obligations, the law takes no cognizance of the insurer which has stepped in on behalf of and made the payment for the insured.

Consideration

A release is a contract and hence is not valid until the consideration called for in it has passed to the person signing the release. Consideration is usually demonstrated by a cancelled check or draft bearing the claimant's endorsement. Hence a case is often considered to be not really settled until the claimant has endorsed and collected the sums set out in the settlement draft.

Adequacy of consideration is one of the criteria by which courts decide whether to uphold or whether or not to uphold a release. To carry the illustration to the extreme, a $5 or $10 release can hardly be expected to be valid if the injury is of substance.

Execution by Claimant Who Reads and Writes

Under ordinary circumstances, the party releasing his claim is competent to read and write. When this is the case, the release should be executed by the technique demonstrated below.

The undersigned agrees, as a further consideration and inducement for this settlement, that it shall apply to all unknown injuries and damage resulting from said accident, casualty or event as well as to those now known.

Signed and Sealed this _____25th_____ day of_____January_____ 19_65_

in the presence of

at_____Tampa_____ _____Florida_____
(City) (State)

Address_____

I have read this release.

Robert N. Claimant (SEAL)

_____

Address_____

_____(SEAL)

The subscription "I have read this release" should be written in the hand of the party executing the release.

If the amount at issue is large, or if for any other cause he wishes to be especially conservative, the adjuster may engage a notary public as one of the witnesses. This assures that the release will be supported by a witness of "certified" impartiality. For smaller sums, and matters not in dispute, the adjuster often signs as a witness. Despite its obvious disadvantages, the practice is condoned because it saves time. Two witnesses are better than one, but one will usually be acceptable if the amount at issue is small and adjustment has been routine.

Execution by Husband and Wife

Whether male or female, if the releasing party is married, a husband-and-wife release should be executed. In almost all jurisdictions the husband has a claim of his own which derives from the injury to his wife. In many jurisdictions the law is cloudy as to whether the reverse is true; that is, whether or not the wife has a claim deriving from the injury to her husband. Since it is more practical to assume that this right exists and to write the release accordingly than to attempt to resolve the doubt, it is desirable for the release to be executed by both parties. In either case, the following form is recommended:

The undersigned agrees, as a further consideration and inducement for this settlement, that it shall apply to all unknown injuries and damage resulting from said accident, casualty or event as well as to those now known.

Signed and Sealed this _____25th_____ day of____January____ 19 65

in the presence of

at____Tampa____ Florida
(City)   (State)

We have read this release. (SEAL)

Address_____

Robert W. Claimant (SEAL)

_____

Address_____

Jane B. Claimant (SEAL)

The subscription "We have read this release" is preferably in the hand of the injured party.

Execution by Claimant Who Does Not Write

If a witness is unable to write his name he signs by "mark." Thus:

> The undersigned agrees, as a further consideration and inducement for this settlement, that it shall apply to all unknown injuries and damage resulting from said accident, casualty or event as well as to those now known.

Signed and Sealed this _25th_ day of _January_, 19_65_

in the presence of
Witness to mark
William W. Witness

Address _R.R. 4, Box 329,_
La Coochie, Florida

Address_____

at _La Coochie_, _Florida_
(City)   (State)

Robert X His Claimant (SEAL)
Mark by W.W.W.

_____(SEAL)

_____(SEAL)

In the case of a signature by mark, the adjuster should be more reluctant to let himself appear as a witness than in a situation where the claimant is able to read and write. Notice that William Witness, who wrote "Robert (His X Mark) Claimant" indicated that he did so by the placement of his initials.

Execution by Claimant Who Writes But Does Not Read

> The undersigned agrees, as a further consideration and inducement for this settlement, that it shall apply to all unknown injuries and damage resulting from said accident, casualty or event as well as to those now known.

Signed and Sealed this _25th_ day of _January_, 19_65_

in the presence of
I read this release out loud to Robert Claimant. He says he understands it and he is signing his name.
William W. Witness

Address_R.R. 4, Box 329, La Coochie, Florida_

at _La Coochie_, _Florida_
(City)   (State)

Robert Claimant (SEAL)

_____(SEAL)

_____(SEAL)

The subscription, "I have read this release out loud . . ." should be in the hand of William Witness.

Execution by Claimant Whose Signing Hand Is Injured

When the injured person's signing hand is injured, the following form should be used:

The undersigned agrees, as a further consideration and inducement for this settlement, that it shall apply to all unknown injuries and damage resulting from said accident, casualty or event as well as to those now known.

Signed and Sealed this _____25-th_____ day of _____January_____, 19 65

[In the presence of] Robert Claimant read this release and says he understands it. Since his right hand is Address injured, he signs it with his left hand.
William W. Witness
Address R. U, Box 329 La Coochee, Fla.

at _____La Coochee_____, _____Florida_____
          (City)   (State)

Robert Claimant (SEAL)

_____(SEAL)

_____(SEAL)

The subscription "Robert Claimant read this release . . ." should be in the hand of William Witness.

Execution by a Claimant Corporation

If the releasing body is a corporation, the following form should be used:

The undersigned agrees, as a further consideration and inducement for this settlement, that it shall apply to all unknown injuries and damage resulting from said accident, casualty or event as well as to those now known.

Signed and Sealed this _____25th_____ day of _____January_____ 19 65

in the presence of
Irma Secretary
Address 106 Resident St. Tampa, Fla.
Mary Fukelerk
Address 207 Residence St
Tampa, Florida

at _____Tampa_____ _____Florida_____
          (City)   (State)

Black + White Co. Inc. (SEAL)
By: William W. Quill, (SEAL)
          Treasurer (SEAL)

Any officer of the corporation may sign for it. If the amount is large or he feels the need to be especially careful, the adjuster may ask for the corporate seal to be affixed.

Execution by a Claimant Who Neither Reads Nor Writes English

When the injured person neither reads nor writes English, the following form should be used:

The undersigned agrees, as a further consideration and inducement for this settlement, that it shall apply to all unknown injuries and damage resulting from said accident, casualty or event as well as to those now known.

Signed and Sealed this _____ 25th _____ day of _January_ 19 65

in the presence of

I read this release and translated it from English into Spanish for Luis Fernandez. He says he understands it and signs his name.

Address _____

Robert W. Translator

Address _2345 E. Howard Ave., Tampa, Florida_

at _____ Tampa, _____ Florida _____
         (City)   (State)

Luis Fernandez _____ (SEAL)

_____ (SEAL)

_____ (SEAL)

The subscription, "I read . . ." should be in the hand of Robert W. Translator.

Conditional Releases

A conditional release is one by which the releasing party releases his claim at once, subject to the later performance of some other act or deed on the part of the person released.

This form of release is used rarely. The almost universal pattern is for the release to be immediate, final and binding; no other type of release should be accepted by an adjuster without the full knowledge of his employer. A special form is usually required. This type of release sometimes crops up in states having financial responsibility laws. They come into play when an uninsured wrongdoer is the object of a subrogation claim by a subrogated collision insurer. In order to preserve his driving privileges, the wrongdoer wishes to procure a release conditioned upon his making payments in the future. Experience with this type of release is spotty and, on the whole, unsatisfactory. Once the release is executed, the wrongdoer usually makes no more than one or two payments. In order to make its claim enforceable, the insurer may have to carry the matter to judgment.

A conditional release may also be taken to preserve a right of action or to release only a part of a claimant's rights. A general release may be made into a conditional release by reciting the condition. Knowing how to do this is a lawyer's province. The drafting of such a modification approaches, if it does not attain, the practice of law. This item can and should be left to counsel.

If the jurisdiction in which the adjuster operates holds that a payment to one's claimant may act as a bar to the litigation of an insured's claim, this too may require the modification of a standard release. Again, the modification should be made by an attorney, though in such a jurisdiction an adjuster would certainly want to provide himself with a standard language modification which he would use as a common feature of his day-to-day operations.

Policyholder's Release

A policyholder, by agreement or by error, may make his own settlement with the claimant. This type of settlement is frowned upon, but when the policyholder has acted in good faith and the insurer wishes to reimburse the policyholder, it may insist upon a policyholder's release. By the execution of this document, the policyholder releases the carrier from any further obligation to defend in respect to the accident or occurrence described. "Policyholders' releases," or "release under the policy" as they are often called, are used rarely.

Release Draft

For property damage claims of limited amount, usually not more than $250, the industry commonly dispenses with the signing of a release as such. Instead, once the carrier is satisfied as to the amount it owes, or agreement has been arrived at, a check or draft will be forwarded to the claimant, on the reverse side of which will appear a release substantially as follows:

> Received the amount specified in the draft on the reverse side hereof, paid by .... Insurance Company in full settlement, payment, discharge and release of any and all rights, claims and demands of the undersigned against .... Insurance Company and also against its insured named in said draft, for and on account of injuries and damage sustained as a result of the certain accident or loss occurring on or about the date specified on the reverse side hereof.

Sometimes, when the amount of property damage is in dispute, the insurer will forward to the claimant a release draft in the amount for which the insurer believes itself obligated. "Money talks" and usually, with the check in his hand, the claimant will conclude that the balance in dispute is not worth arguing over and will endorse the check or draft and the issue is at an end.

Nominal Releases

It is sometimes felt to be good judgment to buy releases for modest sums from persons slightly injured in clear liability situations, or more severely injured in "no liability" situations. This is a matter of judgment and management policy of the adjuster's employer or client. The practice is probably less common today than 10 to 20 years ago.

A release for a very small sum may be attacked for inadequacy of consideration, so its ultimate value, if put to the test, may be questionable.

If an adjuster can negotiate settlement in this range, he can certainly get a statement. Whenever the facts permit, nominal settlements should, therefore, be bolstered by non-injury statements and statements including admission of fault. A release bolstered by such a statement is a more formidable document than if it has to stand alone.

COVENANT NOT TO SUE

A release is a very specific document. It states explicitly that the person who signs the release is releasing one or more other persons who are named with equal specificity. Therefore it comes as something of a surprise to young adjusters to learn that in many jurisdictions a release means *more* than it purports to mean on its face.

Many (probably most) jurisdictions follow the rule that a release of one wrongdoer releases *all who may have been concerned in the same occurrence,* even though responsibility may be shared by two or more persons. Frequently there arise situations in which an injured person has rights against two or more wrongdoers. The common example is the innocent bystander who, waiting patiently for the light to change, sees two cars collide before his very eyes, and one of them alters course and strikes him. In states which follow the usual rule, the release by the bystander of one of the two drivers would act *also as a release of the other driver.* Thus, there may arise many situations in which one or more of the potential litigants find it not only desirable but justifiable to arrange the release of one tortfeasor but not of both. To cope with the problem thus presented, there has been developed a document known as a "covenant not to sue" by which an injured party may terminate his claim against one of the wrongdoers but preserve his right to proceed at law against the other.

The general feeling in the industry is that the insurers representing the two defendants should compose their differences in private, agree among themselves as to what share of the loss each will bear, and then make a united settlement with the injured persons. That having been done, a standard release would be executed, and the common practice is for all parties potentially liable to be named and released therein.

It is generally considered "dirty pool" for an adjuster to take a covenant from an injured party without disclosing his intent to other insurers at interest and inviting them to join with him. If they decline to join, he is then considered to be at liberty to make whatever deal he considers in the interest of his principal. Such a settlement would be consummated by a covenant not to sue, which would preserve to the claimant his right to sue the other tortfeasor whose insurance company declined to participate in the joint release.[12]

MEDICAL LIENS

Some jurisdictions give doctors, hospitals and the like a legal means of forcing insurance companies to protect their bills by permitting the filing of what is known as a "medical lien." Such a lien requires the persons or company on whom it is served to satisfy the bill which is the subject of the lien out of the proceeds

---

[12] Laws of some states expand the effect of covenants, or contract their effect to more or less than has been stated here, so an adjuster, before using a covenant at all, should find out if his jurisdiction conforms to the usual practice.

of any settlement that may be made with an injured person. Failure to observe a lien properly filed may result in the insurance company being required to pay the amount of the lien in addition to the agreed settlement.

The voluntary protection of creditors is recommended. Whether protection is voluntary or in compliance with a lien law, the technique is the same. Creditors may be protected in these ways:

1. By procuring a release from the claimant and drawing the settlement draft payable jointly to the claimant and all creditors whom it is desired to protect.
2. By procuring a release from the claimant and issuing a series of drafts, one payable solely to him, and the others payable jointly to him and to each of this creditors individually.

When disbursements are made in this fashion, the release simply recites a single consideration. The second technique has its drawbacks. The claimant may endorse and cash his own draft but withhold his signature from one of the others. The release may then be attacked on the ground that the carrier has not paid the full consideration recited in it.

To defend against this, the adjuster may procure the claimant's endorsement to the drafts for the doctor and hospital before leaving the claimant's presence and then personally mail those drafts to their ultimate payee.

The problem may also be avoided by wording the release so that its own language governs the distribution of the funds. This complicates the release but simplifies the drafts. An example of the wording of the release to satisfy this technique is on page 427.

Drafts to satisfy a release such as the above would be drawn as follows:

Payable to Robert M. Claimant $100.00
Payable to S. X. Bones, M.D. 250.00
Payable to Memorial Hospital 275.23

Choice among the foregoing methods will be governed, usually, by management decision of the insurer involved.

RELEASE

To be executed by Robert W. Claimant

an individual, of
(If Female, Married or Single)

Address 110 Residential Way, Tampa, Florida

𝕶𝖓𝖔𝖜 𝕬𝖑𝖑 𝕸𝖊𝖓 𝖇𝖞 𝕿𝖍𝖊𝖘𝖊 𝕻𝖗𝖊𝖘𝖊𝖓𝖙𝖘, that the undersigned does hereby acknowledge **receipt of**

One Hundred and No/100 Dollars _____ Dollars ($100.00),

and payment of S. X. Bones, M. D., not to exceed Two Hundred

Fifty and No/100 Dollars ($250.00) and payment of Memorial

Hospital not to exceed Two Hundred Seventy-Five and 23/100

Dollars. ($275.23).

which sum is accepted in full settlement and satisfaction of, and as sole consideration for the full **release** and discharge of, all actions, claims and demands whatsoever, that may now or hereafter exist against

---etc.---

_____ on account of injuries to the person of,

and damage to the property of the said_____

and the treatment thereof and the consequences flowing therefrom, as a result of an accident casualty or

event which occurred on or about the_____day of_____ 19____at or near

_____ for which the undersigned claims the above named

persons or parties are legally liable; which liability, injuries and damages are disputed and denied; and,

The undersigned warrants that no promise of inducement has been offered; that this release is executed without reliance upon any statement or representation by the person or parties released or their representatives or physicians concerning the nature and extent of the injuries and damage and liability therefor; that the undersigned is of legal age, legally competent to execute this release, and accepts full responsibility therefor; and,

The undersigned agrees, as a further consideration and inducement for this settlement, that it shall apply to all unknown injuries and damage resulting from said accident, casualty or event as well as to those now known.

Signed and Sealed this (1)_____day of_____19____

in the presence of

at_____
(City)   (State)

(4)_____

Address_____ (2)_____(SEAL)

(5)_____ (3)_____(SEAL)

Address_____ (3)_____(SEAL)

INFANT CLAIMS

Infant Defined

Who is an infant? In this context, "infant" means one who has yet to attain his majority. In most jurisdictions a person attains his majority at the age of 21, but the exceptions to the general rule and the possibility of an infant's "becoming emancipated," [13] thereby raising the question of whether he is or is not an infant, raise some complications. Rather than to attempt to outline the holdings of the several states, this section, in addition to outlining the techniques for closing the claims of those who are indisputably minors, will suggest a practical technique to be employed in questions of doubt.

In this section the words "infant," "minor" and "child" are used interchangeably.

Parents' Claims for Injury to Infants

Under ordinary circumstances an infant's claim for medical and related expense belongs, as a property right, not to him but to his parent. This reflects the usual situation, which is that few minors meet their own bills for these expenses. They are met by the parent as part of his parental obligation—and the law gives the parent the right to recover this loss. To the parent also belongs the right to assert in his own name the claim, if any, for the loss of the value of the infant's services to the parent. These claims are sometimes called "derivative" claims.

These elements of the claim are thus separated from the other usual elements of an injury claim. The separation may require special techniques in taking the releases by which these claims are closed.

Since the claim of the parents, which derives from the injury to a child, arises in part because of the parent's obligation to provide medical care, an adjuster, at the time he takes his release, may find it wise to ascertain that healing is complete, secure reports to that effect from responsible doctors (preferably the injured party's own doctors), and see to it that receipted

---

[13] In some states the emancipation of a minor gives him the right to sign a binding release in his own name. In other states, emancipation merely does away with the parents' derivative claim. The most common ways for a minor to become emancipated are to contract marriage and to live on a self-supporting basis away from the parental roof. The effect of emancipation and whether these or other criteria obtain in a given state will be for local determination on a state-by-state and case-by-case basis.

bills or checks payable to the doctor, hospital and other sources of care, demonstrate a full discharge of the obligation to them.

Infants as Claimants

In addition to the claims of his parents, an infant has, himself, a right to claim damages in respect to certain aspects of his injury. This right includes his claim for pain and suffering, if any, and for permanent impairment. To state it another way, that part of a minor's claim which belongs to him will generally be everything except the parent's claim for medical and related expense and for the loss of the value of the infant's services.

Control—Negotiation of Infant Claims

In controlling and negotiating infant claims, the involvement of both parents at an early stage will enhance the chance of success and avoid the possibility that one of them may feel himself to have been ignored.

Infant claims, more than those of adults, engage the attention of relatives and friends. All this advice may seem unwelcome to the adjuster but, more often than not, it works to his advantage. In any event, this array of advisors is a fact of life—to be accepted—so the adjuster had best perfect his techniques for operating in this environment.

The best move is to bring grandmother in from her bedroom where she has been talking, call the neighbor in from the porch, get them all together and go to it. The crowd will provide the usual division of hotheads and cool heads. As soon as the adjuster sees that one or two of the more responsible are beginning to see things his way, his move is to keep his peace and let them carry the burden of calming the hotheads. Life insurance salesmen know that, as they put it, "Someone else can always sell your wares better than you can." The wise adjuster should take advantage of this phenomenon.

RELEASE

To be executed by   John Smith, Father of _____

_____ John Smith, Jr. _____

(If Female, Married or Single)

Address   100 Residence Street, Tampa, Florida

𝕶𝖓𝖔𝖜 𝕬𝖑𝖑 𝕸𝖊𝖓 𝖇𝖞 𝕿𝖍𝖊𝖘𝖊 𝕻𝖗𝖊𝖘𝖊𝖓𝖙𝖘, that the undersigned does hereby acknowledge receipt of

__ One Hundred Fifty-Three and No/100 _____ Dollars ($ 153.00),

_____

_____

_____

_____

which sum is accepted in full settlement and satisfaction of, and as sole consideration for the full release and discharge of, all actions, claims and demands whatsoever, that may now or hereafter exist against

__ William Policyholder and any other person or organization responsible for the

__ ownership, maintenance or use of the automobile of the said William Policyholder

_____ on account of injuries to the person of,

and damage to the property of the said ____ John Smith, Jr. _____

and the treatment thereof and the consequences flowing therefrom, as a result of an accident casualty or

event which occurred on or about the _____ 5th _____ day of _____ January _____ 19 65 at or near

__ Tampa, Florida _____ for which the undersigned claims the above named

persons or parties are legally liable; which liability, injuries and damages are disputed and denied; and,

The undersigned warrants that no promise of inducement has been offered; that this release is executed without reliance upon any statement or representation by the person or parties released or their representatives or physicians concerning the nature and extent of the injuries and damage and liability therefor; that the undersigned is of legal age, legally competent to execute this release, and accepts full responsibility therefor; and,

The undersigned agrees, as a further consideration and inducement for this settlement, that it shall apply to all unknown injuries and damage resulting from said accident, casualty or event as well as to those now known.

Signed and Sealed this   _25th_ day of _January_ 19 _65_

in the presence of

Thomas Neighbor   at __ _Tampa_   _Florida_

Address _105 Residence St. Tampa_   (City)   (State)

Elizabeth Neighbor   _I have read this release._ (SEAL)

Address _105 Residence St._   _John Smith_ ____ (SEAL)

Tampa, Fla.   _____ (SEAL)

Releases—Infant Claims

The technical problems involved in procuring releases in infants' claims derive in part from the separation of the usual elements of the claim into the claim of the parent and the *separate* claim of the child.

Problems also arise from another factor. Releases are contracts and, since an infant may not make a contract, someone has to make it for him, which means that someone other than he must sign the release. Infants' claims are therefore settled with a parent or, as they are sometimes referred to, "the next friend."

PARENTS-GUARDIAN RELEASE AND INDEMNITY AGREEMENT

FOR AND IN CONSIDERATION of the payment to me/us of the sum

of_____ Two Hundred and No/100 Dollars _____ Dollars ($ 200.00),

the receipt of which is hereby acknowledged, I/we, the undersigned, father and mother and/or guardian of John Smith,

Jr., _____ .

a minor, do forever release, acquit, discharge and covenant to hold harmless William Policyholder and any other organization alleged to be responsible for the ownership, maintenance or use of the automobile of the said William Policyholder and his _____, _____

heirs, successors and assigns of and from any and all actions, causes of action, claims, demands, damages, costs, loss of services, expenses and compensation, on account of, or in any way growing out of, any and all known and unknown personal injuries and property damage which we may now or hereafter have as the parents and/or guardian of said minor, and also all claims or rights of action for damages which the said minor has or may hereafter have, either before or after___he has reached his/her majority,

resulting or to result from a certain accident which occurred on or about the 5th day of January , 19 65.

at or near   Tampa, Florida _____

_____

_____

I/we further promise to bind myself/ourselves jointly and severally, my/our heirs, administrators and executors to repay

to the said _____ William Policyholder _____

heirs, successors and assigns any sum of money, except the sum above mentioned that he/she/they may hereafter be compelled to pay on behalf of said minor because of the said accident.

It is further understood and agreed that this settlement is the compromise of a doubtful and disputed claim, and that this

payment is not to be construed as an admission of liability on the part of William Policyholder _____

_____by whom liability is expressly denied.

I/we further state that I/we have carefully read the foregoing release and know the contents thereof, and I/we sign the same as my/our own free act.

WITNESS ___our___ hand and seal this___25th___day of January _____, 19 65.

In presence of

_____ }   CAUTION: READ BEFORE SIGNING
_____ }   We read this release.
_____ }   ___John Smith___(SEAL)
_____ }   Mary Smith (Mrs. John Smith) (SEAL)

STATE OF_____ }   I approve of this release.
                         } SS:
COUNTY OF_____ }   John Smith, Jr.

On this _____ day of _____, 19___, before me appeared _____

to me personally known, and who acknowledged the execution of the foregoing instrument as_____free act and deed, for the consideration set forth therein.

My Commission Expires_____   _____
                                                         Notary Public.

The subscription "We read this release . . ." should be written in the hand of one of the parents, preferably that of the father.

This release should be witnessed by a notary public.

Unless the infant is of tender years, many companies require their representatives to secure also the signature of the infant, as shown. This signature may—in some situations—inhibit the assertion of a further claim by the minor when he attains adult status. It is a conservative practice, does no possible harm and if an adjuster is in doubt as to a company's requirements, he should secure the infant's signature.

The Latin phrase, "pro proprio amico," means "through his next friend" and in some jurisdictions this phrase, abbreviated to its initials, has penetrated claims jargon so deeply that children are commonly referred to as "p.p.a.'s."

All insurers have standard releases for infants' claims. While the signature of one parent, usually the father, may suffice, the standard and best practice is to procure the signature of both parents.

Some insurance companies, as part of their standard procedure, ignore the separation of the parent's claim from the infant's claim and, except in unusual circumstances, settle both parts of the claim with a combination release. Others follow what is possibly the more conservative practice and recognize the separation by taking two releases—one for the parent for his so-called derivative claim, and one from the parent in his capacity as next friend. In the latter capacity, as next friend he executes a release on behalf of the child for that part of the claim which belonged to the child.

Although practice is not uniform as to the taking of separate releases, this should not be permitted to obscure the areas where uniformity prevails. The release is always taken from at least one but preferably both [14] parents, or some other adult qualified to act as next friend on behalf of the child. An adjuster should not permit any person other than a parent to sign as next friend

[14] Investigation of the standard minor's claim should develop the name and address of both parents. If parents are separated, a statement should disclose the parent with whom the child resides and whether or not the absent parent contributes to his support. Under ordinary circumstances a settlement can be effected with *the parent who is responsible for the support of the child.*

except on explicit instructions from the company represented or upon the advice of local counsel as to the technique to be followed.

The releases on pages 532 and 533 illustrate the settlement of a claim in the total amount of $353 by the execution of the two releases so as to recognize the separation of the parent's claim from the child's claim.

The release entitled "Parents-Guardian Release and Indemnity Agreement" could have been filled out for the entire $353 if this was the only release taken. In many jurisdictions, and by many companies, this would have been regarded as sufficient. The separation demonstrated is probably the more conservative method and, in case of doubt, should be the method employed.

The form on page 533 is sometimes referred to as a "Parents' and Guardians' Release," and occasionally as a "Release and Indemnity Agreement." Both terms mean the same thing. The section which constitutes what is known as the "Indemnity Agreement" reads, "and also all claims or rights of action for damages which the said minor has or may hereafter have, either before or after he has reached his/her majority." Its meaning is obvious and it is a feature of most infants' release forms. Some states by legislation or decision have quite thoroughly emasculated indemnity agreements. In any event, if the parents are insolvent, the agreement is of doubtful value.

Releasing the Claims of Persons Who May or May Not Be Minors

Adjusters are often confronted with claims of minors in their late teens. Releasing their claims may involve a decision as to whether the claimant is still a minor.

The most common problem in this area is the one presented by a person who has reached his majority recently—or claims to have done so. In these situations the adjuster should not overlook the obvious precaution of requiring some reasonable proof of age. A driver's license record is usually sufficient. Other such demonstration might be by birth or baptismal certificate, school record or other permanent public or quasi-public record based on information recorded at a time when age was not an issue.

A similar problem may arise with youngsters in their late teens who have married, or with young persons still in their teens but self-employed.

Questions in this category, as well as questions hinging on age which cannot be demonstrated properly, can be handled by taking two releases. One release can be drawn in the assumption that the claimant is, in fact, "of age"; the claimant himself signs this release. The other, drawn assuming that the claimant is still a minor, is signed by the parents. The drafts drawn to satisfy the releases will then be made payable jointly to the claimant himself and the adult or adults (presumably his parents) who signed the minor's release for him.

In the event circumstances make this disposition of the question impractical, the adjuster will have to resolve his problem on a case-by-case basis, usually with the benefit of legal advice through his attorney or his company's legal staff.

Court Approval

Some jurisdictions provide for settlement of smaller claims involving infants by permitting claims up to but not in excess of a certain amount, to be settled directly by the parents without court approval. These settlements may have the same binding force as if they had been approved by a court of law.

Lacking such legislative enactments, the usual way to dispose of an infant's claim and to guard against the possibility of reopening it, is to employ the procedure known as "the friendly suit." The mechanics for carrying out this process differ from state to state, but the essentials are the same—the parties appear before the judge in a court of law, the facts are disclosed to him and, if he is satisfied that justice is done the injured child, the judge grants his approval and permits the closing of "the friendly suit" which has brought the matter to his attention. This method is employed to close the majority of infant's claims. Unless it is known that an insurer is willing to waive this procedure, a willingness which usually extends only to smaller claims, it should be assumed that a friendly suit is obligatory.

If the amount at stake is large, or if the infant's parents are irresponsible, the court may go to the length of appointing a guardian to receive the funds paid and to disburse them to the benefit of the child. The appointment of a guardian may be requested by the defendant's representatives. This request is usually not made unless the insurance company involved, for some reason, feels a need to be especially cautious.

SUMMARY

In the introductory portion of Chapter 1, and in chapters on investigation and medical aspects, it was pointed out that a substantial minority of claims involve questions that go deeper than mere differences of opinion. A re-reading of these sections might now be helpful.

An adjuster's duties include not only the disbursement of funds admitted to be due, readily determined and reasonably requested, but also the control of those who seek aggressively to capitalize the opportunity to make a claim. A person cannot escape forming personal opinions and judgments about these activities, but judgments, it will now be repeated for the last time, have no place in an adjuster's work. His duty is to deal with, determine, control, and to make his efforts effective.

No red-blooded American fails to rise to a challenge. In handling claims, what may well be the key technique is to make the necessary moves to control exaggeration and falsehood without, by those actions, suggesting the attempt to defend against those moves. In other words, statements must have been secured and allegations checked. If not, in some claims there will be exaggeration, coloring, and outright lying, against which possibility the more restrained claimant, and the public who pays the bill, ought to be protected. All this must be done without offending the claimant or challenging him to "beat the game." If the author were required to sum up adjusting in a single sentence, he would be tempted to say that *it is bringing out the best in a claimant while preparing to meet the worst.*

It should be clear from what has been said and implied throughout this book, but if it is not, it should once more be emphasized, that it is better adjusting to handle a claimant so as to bring out a restrained request than to frustrate an avaricious grab. The problem is that much of what an adjuster does in investigating liability and in controlling damages is inherently challenging. An adjuster must develop a way to do his work, to investigate, to do so thoroughly, and yet keep the challenge out of it. The development of this technique is the beginning of an adjuster's mastery of the technique for settlement, for, to pick up another thread that has been exposed at more than one place in this fabric, every phase of adjusting work affects every other phase, and settlement starts the moment a claim is assigned.

Each adjuster must develop those techniques that work for him. What works for one may not work for another. What works even for a majority may be all wrong for one.

In the end, key operations are usually those of persuasion, and the effect of personalities is inescapable. If a successful adjuster finds that he is defying all of the above suggestions, let him continue in his own way. The suggestions are for the benefit of those who find they have problems.

APPENDIX

STATEMENT of PRINCIPLES on RESPECTIVE RIGHTS and DUTIES of LAWYERS, INSURANCE COMPANIES and ADJUSTERS RELATING to the BUSINESS OF ADJUSTING INSURANCE CLAIMS

The following organizations are represented on the National Conference of Lawyers, Insurance Companies and Adjusters:

American Bar Association
American Mutual Alliance [now American Mutual Insurance Alliance]
Association of Casualty and Surety Companies [now a part of American Insurance Association]
International Claim Association
National Association of Independent Insurance Adjusters
National Association of Independent Insurers
National Board of Fire Underwriters [now a part of American Insurance Association]

On July 24, 1938, at the Annual Convention of the American Bar Association, an agreement was entered into reading, in part, as follows:

"As a result of a thorough study of the relationship between the fields of the adjustment of claims and of the practice of law, it has been unanimously agreed between the American Bar Association Committee on the Unauthorized Practice of Law and the Committee on Lay Adjusters of the Insurance Section of said Association, in conference with a special committee representing all types of insurance interests—life, fire, marine, and casualty—that laymen have a proper place in the adjustment of claims. There is hereby established a joint Committee composed of ten members, five of whom shall be representatives of the American Bar Association, and five who shall be representatives of the above designated insurance interests, to which complaints concerning insurance adjusters or attorneys handling insurance claims may be referred. Such committee shall be known as the Conference Committee on Adjusters. The Conference Committee, or a subcommittee thereof, shall investigate such complaints and recommend or take such action as is necessary to correct practices deemed contrary to the public interest."

The Conference Committee on Adjusters, as formed under the above agreement, having considered the business of adjusting insurance claims in its relation to the policyholder, the claimants, and the practice of law, has adopted the following statement of the matters with which it has thus far dealt, which it believes presents a correct description of certain of the rights of the interested parties and the general public.

The insurance business operates under sanction of law for the protection of its policyholders and the public. The terms of insurance policies are nearly all upon standard forms adopted or approved by state authorities in the interest of the public.

The Committee believes that anyone who has, or thinks he has, a claim against a company is entitled at all times to courteous, fair and just treatment from the representatives of that company. Claimant is entitled to an investigation of his claim and a reasonably prompt statement of the company's position with reference to it.

The Committee recognizes that, while the companies have a definite obligation to pay all just claims and to avoid unnecessary litigation, they have an equally definite obligation to protect the insurance buying public from increased cost due to fraudulent or non-meritorious claims.

1. Claims under insurance policies, for the purpose of this statement, are divided into two classes:

First—A claim in contract by a policyholder or beneficiary directly against the insurance company which issued the contract.

Second—A claim of a third person in tort against the holder of a policy of liability insurance.

2. In the first class the claimant and the insurance company each has the right to discuss the merit of the claim with the other, and to settle it.

3. In the second class, under a policy by which the company insures the liability of the policyholder, it is recognized that the company has a direct financial interest in the claim presented against the policyholder, and in a suit in which the name of the company may not appear as a party litigant, but which the company is obliged to defend in the name of the policyholder. Therefore the company has a right,

(a) To discuss with the policyholder or the claimant the merit of the claim, and to settle it.

(b) To investigate the facts, interview witnesses, appraise damages, consider and determine the liability of the insurance company and its policyholder in the factual circumstances.

4. In handling claims under the second class—

(a) The companies or their representatives * will not advise the claimant as to his legal rights.

(b) The companies and their representatives,* including attorneys, will inform the policyholder of the progress of any suit against the policyholder and its probable results. If any diversity of interest shall appear between the policyholder and the company, the policyholder shall be fully advised of the situation and invited to retain his own counsel. Without limiting the general application of the foregoing, it is contemplated that this will be done in any case in which it appears probable that an amount in excess of the limit of the policy is involved, or in any case in which the company is defending under a reservation of rights, or in any case in which the prosecution of a counterclaim appears advantageous to the policyholder.

---

* See footnotes to page 544.

5. Under both classes of claims—

(a-1) The companies or their representatives ° will not deal °° directly with any claimant represented by an attorney without the consent of the attorney.

(a-2) No lay person, lay firm, lay partnership or corporation serving as a representative ° of an insurance company, in the handling of a claim, shall engage in the practice of law.

(b) The companies may properly interview any witnesses, or prospective witnesses, without the consent of opposing counsel or party. In doing so, however, the company representative ° will scrupulously avoid any suggestion calculated to induce the witnesses to suppress or deviate from the truth, or in any degree affect their free or untrammeled conduct when appearing at the trial or on the witness stand. If any witness † ‡ making a signed statement so requests, he shall be given a copy thereof.

(c) The companies or their representatives ° will not advise a claimant to refrain from seeking legal advice, or against the retention of counsel to protect his interest.

(d) The companies will respect the disabilities of minors and incompetents, and agree that no settlement of a cause of action of an infant or an incompetent shall be presented to a court for approval, except under provision for an investigation of the propriety of the settlement either by the court or by counsel independent to the defendant.

(e) The companies will not permit their employees—whether laymen or lawyers—to collect for agents or policyholders claims or accounts in which the company has no interest.

(f) The companies recognize that the Canons of Ethics of the American Bar Association apply to all branches of the legal profession, and that specialists in particular branches are not to be considered as exempt from the application of those Canons.

(g) Lay adjusters will only be permitted to fill in blanks of release forms previously drafted by counsel, and they will be forbidden to draft special releases called for by the unusual circumstances of any settlement. All such special releases shall be prepared by counsel.

(h) The companies will undertake to be responsible for the conduct of their employees in observing and executing the foregoing principles, and will endeavor to see that their representatives,° other than employees, do likewise.

6. The Conference Committee will continue to meet for the further consideration of the foregoing matters, and of the problems not dealt with in this statement, and the Committee expresses the hope that all complaints of the conduct of lawyers or insurance companies in connection with claims under insurance policies may be referred to the Committee for its consideration.

°, °°, †, ‡ See footnotes to page 544.

THE NAME OF THE NATIONAL CONFERENCE OF LAWYERS
AND ADJUSTERS (CONFERENCE COMMITTEE ON ADJUSTERS)
WAS CHANGED TO NATIONAL CONFERENCE OF LAWYERS, IN-
SURANCE COMPANIES AND ADJUSTERS ON FEBRUARY 18, 1961.

---

* At a meeting on March 7, 1954, the Conference Committee adopted the following interpretation of this word: "The word 'representative' or 'representatives' means any person, firm, partnership or corporation, which is representing an insurance company in the handling of a claim."

** At a meeting on February 20, 1955, the Conference Committee adopted the following interpretation of this word: "The word 'deal' means to 'negotiate,' 'settle,' 'do business with' and 'negotiate for a settlement or a payment.' Any definition of the word 'deal' would not prevent a direct approach to a claimant for the purpose of checking his identification, or the bona fides of his representation by an attorney."

† At a meeting on February 20, 1955, the Conference Committee adopted the following construction of this word: "The word 'witness' shall be construed to include 'parties,' but this construction shall not authorize an interview of a party after he is represented by an attorney."

‡ At a meeting on March 7, 1954, the Conference Committee agreed: (1) that this language applies to all witnesses-plaintiffs, defendants and neutral witnesses; (2) that no time limit is placed upon the witness requesting a copy of this statement; and (3) that the obligation to furnish the copy of the statement runs only to the witness himself or herself.

MEANING OF "ACCIDENT"

This discussion of the meaning of "accident" is reproduced from the pages of *The Fire, Casualty and Surety Bulletins,* the monthly service described in Chapter 3. As indicated there, there are two reasons for showing this information here. For one, this is an important—vital, really—point of concern for the adjuster who deals with liability claims. Secondly, the article is an example of one type of approach used in the monthly service from which it is extracted.

Until recent years, most liability policies restricted their coverage to bodily injury or property damage "caused by accident." More recently, the phrase "caused by accident" has been dropped from many liability policies and coverage thus converted to what is spoken of as an "occurrence" basis. However, most definitions of "occurrence" include subsidiary reference to "accident" or use language the effect of which is to make "accident" still an important term.

Although there have been a number of court decisions, particularly during the past few years, on this feature of liability insurance, the courts do not seem to have agreed upon a definition of "accident" for the purposes of liability insurance coverage. A number of courts have quoted with approval the definition in *Webster's New International Dictionary,* "an event that takes place without one's foresight or expectations; an undesigned, sudden and unexpected event," but have applied this definition to achieve apparently contradictory results.

Recently, the Michigan supreme court in *Guerdon Industries, Inc. vs. Fidelity & Casualty Co., 123 N.W. (2nd.) 143,* quoted with approval the definition of "accident" in *Couch On Insurance,* Second Edition, 1962. That definition reads: "An 'accident' . . . may be anything that begins to be, that happens, or that is a result which is not anticipated and is unforeseen and unexpected by the person injured or affected thereby—that is, takes place without the insured's foresight or expectation and without design or intentional causation on his part. In other words, an accident is an undesigned contingency, a casualty, a happening by chance, something out of the usual course of things, unusual, fortuitous, not anticipated, and not naturally to be expected." (For a discussion of this case, see page 445.)

An important point, on which the courts at present do not seem to be in agreement, is whether, in addition to the injury or damage *not being intentional,* the incident, to be covered as an "accident" must be "traceable to a definite time, place and cause," so that notice of the *exact time and place* can be given the insurance company.

The case of *Howard vs. Massachusetts Bonding & Insurance Co., 6 C. C. H. (Fire & Casualty) 268,* was concerned with a schedule liability policy and presumably would apply to comprehensive coverage because of the similarity in policy language. The insured, who operated a summer camp, was sued by the father of two campers who had contracted polio there, on the ground that he had been negligent in *not closing the camp* before the boys became infected. He successfully defended the suit, but lost in an attempt to recover his legal expenses from the insurance company, the court holding that the suit was *not* based on bodily injury "caused by accident."

Repeated Exposure

A question frequently argued is whether injury or damage is "caused by accident" when it results from *repeated exposure* to some condition, without it being possible for anyone to prove the exact moment at which the damage was done. Many insurance men and attorneys have felt that a situation of this type is not an "accident" and a number of court decisions support this view. Recently, however, there has been some dissent.

This was held in *Jackson vs. Employers Liability Assurance Corp., 248 N. Y. Sup. 207.* Here the insured, who owned a tenement, was held liable for the death from disease of a child of a tenant, on the ground that he had been negligent in not providing heat. In a suit seeking to pass this judgment on to the insurance company writing liability insurance, the court held the judgment was not covered because it did *not* result from an "accident" within the meaning of the policy.

Although not involving a public liability policy, the New Jersey case of *U. S. Radium Corp. vs. Globe Indemnity Co., 178 Atl. 271,* is often cited in this connection. A number of employes of the insured had contracted radium poisoning from *gradual exposure* in the course of their work and recovered judgments against the employer. The court held that such exposure was not an "accident" within the meaning of the employers liability section of the old workmen's compensation and employers liability policy and hence that the insurance company was not liable. (At that time, the illnesses involved were not under the workmen's compensation law of the state.) Of similar effect is *Taylor Dredging Co. vs. Travelers Insurance Co., 90 Fed. (2nd.) 449,* which involved the claim of the insured's employe that he had contracted tuberculosis from unsanitary working conditions.

In *United States Fidelity & Guaranty Co. vs. Briscoe, 239 Pac. (2nd.) 754,* a road contractor had been held liable for both personal injury and damage to property of members of a family by dust from cement which the contractor had loaded into his trucks near the family's home over a period of *four months.* The Oklahoma supreme court did not refer specifically to the cases previously discussed, but held this was not an "accident," for substantially similar reasons, and hence that the liability of the contractor was not covered by his liability insurance.

Dissenting Cases on Exposure

A flatly contrary view was upheld in *Canadian Radium & Uranium Corp. vs. Indemnity Insurance Co. of North America, 108 N. E. (2nd.) 515.* An employe of a firm which used radium products supplied by the insured sued the insured—not her employer—for damages based upon similar exposure to radioactive emanations over a period of seven months and claimed the insured had furnished her employer with defective equipment and had not warned her of the danger. The insured defended the case and eventually settled it out of court. Reversing an appellate court decision, the Illinois supreme court held that this loss was "caused by accident" and that the liability insurer was liable for these expenses.

The court in the Canadian Radium & Uranium Corp. case refused to follow the U. S. Radium Corp. case and several similar cases, partly on the ground that the concept of "accident" in workmen's compensation laws is more limited than in the usual sense. It also pointed out that it was obvious that the injury could have been caused only by repeated exposure and hence was "caused by accident" in the commonly accepted sense of the term.

This view is supported by the later case of *Beryllium Corp. vs. American Mutual Liability Ins. Co., 223 Fed. (2nd.) 71.* The wife of one employe and the daughter of another died of beryllium poisoning contracted through handling work clothes during periods of five and eight years, respectively. Suits were brought against the employer, which were settled directly. Beryllium then sued to recover under its comprehensive general liability policy. A federal appellate court, affirming a lower court finding that the lodging of the beryllium particles in the lungs of the wife and daughter was a series of distinctive events, *whether noted at the time or not,* pointed out that while the insurer's intention might have been to require the accidental means to be one isolated occurrence, the policy did not read so. The court commented that there would be some justification for the argument that the policy was meant to cover a "single, unexpected distinctive event" if the policy language read "caused by *an* accident."

A still later case supporting the view that injury or disease caused by repeated exposure to a condition may be "caused by accident" is the Guerdon Industries case cited previously. A trailer manufacturer failed to equip a trailer with a proper drainage pipe and the sub-flooring of the trailer became saturated with water. Subsequently, members of the family which purchased the trailer developed arthritis (or their condition was aggravated) after continued and repeated exposure to dampness. The Michigan supreme court held that the illnesses were incurred because of improper drainage, and were caused by accident within the meaning of the product liability cover of the manufacturer.

Robert Hawthorne, Inc. vs. Liberty Mutual Insurance Co., 9 C. C. H. (Fire & Casualty) 237, which involved property damage, is somewhat similar to the Beryllium Corp. case. Here the insured did demolition work which lasted about two months. During this time debris fell upon the roof of an adjoining building and upon planks which the insured had placed there to catch debris. About three and a half months after the demolition was completed, the ceiling of a vault in the adjoining building fell and it was agreed that this was caused by the debris. It was obviously impossible to establish any specific date on which the ceiling had become weakened. A federal court held this amounted to "accident" within the meaning of the policy and also that the "accident" within the meaning of the policy and also that the "accident" occurred during the course of the operations, even though the ceiling did not actually collapse until later.

Property Damage—Natural Consequences

Particularly with cases involving claims for property damage, the argument is frequently raised that damage which is the *natural consequence* of performing some act, using some substance or failing to take proper precautions in the work is not "caused by accident" within the meaning of liability policies. There is no clear line of interpretation on this point, as the following cases indicate.

In *Cross vs. Zurich General Accident & Liability Insurance Co., 184 Fed. (2nd.) 609,* the insured had been hired to clean the exterior of a building. Although his employes used water on the windows, some of them were damaged by hydrofluoric acid. The insurer denied coverage on the ground that this was not an "accident," but the expected results of the insured not masking the windows with grease or heavy paper. A federal appellate court held that the damage was accidental and that liability for it was covered by the policy. The court said: *"Failure to take a proper or effective precaution does not prove intent to damage.* Plaintiffs [the insured] may have been negligent in not keeping sufficient water on the windows, but the very fact that water was applied to each window negatives any idea that plaintiff intended to damage same. And *lacking such intent, the damage was accidental,* even though caused by negligence."

While the Cross case obviously leaves many questions, it does seem to indicate that taking *some precaution*—even though ineffectual—makes resulting damage "accidental" within the meaning of the policy.

In *M. Schnoll & Son vs. Standard Accident Insurance Co., 154 Atl. (2nd.) 431,* a Pennsylvania court held damage from paint dripping onto the side of a house on which work was done by the insured *not* to be "caused by accident." The reasoning seems in harmony with the Cross case, the court here taking the position that it was virtually impossible to prevent this damage.

Dust and dirt deposits on the stock of a clothing merchant as a result of brickwork in the same building were held not "caused by accident" in *Casper vs. American Guarantee & Liability Insurance Co., 11 C. C. H. (Fire & Casualty) 579.* Upholding a lower court, the Pennsylvania supreme court ruled against the insured, a contractor, who had settled a suit brought against him by the clothing firm and brought this action against the insurer for the amount of settlement and legal costs. The court stated that the insured's conduct "was such that it was reasonably calculated to cause substantial damage." It also said, "If an occurrence is the ordinary and expected result of the performance of an operation, then it cannot be termed an accident."

A case which is difficult to categorize is *Moore vs. Fidelity & Casualty Co., 295 Pac. (2nd.) 154.* The insured operated a self-service laundry. Driers created *lint* which accumulated in floor drains. The clogged drains overflowed and caused water damage in neighboring premises. A California court held that this was an accident and that the liability policy of the laundry owner covered.

Failure to Protect Property

A question which arises frequently is whether failure on the part of the insured to take adequate precautions to *prevent injury or damage by other parties* or by the *forces of nature* amounts to "accident." There have been several conflicting cases on this point.

In *Rex Roofing Co. vs. Lumber Mutual Casualty Insurance Co., 116 N. Y. Sup. (2nd.)* 876, the insured was resurfacing the roof of an apartment building when a storm interrupted the work. Water leaked into the building, and the owner and several tenants sued the insured for damage to their property, claiming the insured had been negligent in not attempting to cover the incomplete work. A New York appellate court held that this damage was "caused by accident," and the insured's liability for it was covered by the policy. The court here did not attempt to define "accident," but based its decision on the principle that "the average man would consider the occurrence in question as an 'accident' in the common conception of that word." * The Alabama supreme court came to a similar conclusion in *Employers Insurance Co. vs. Alabama Roofing Co., 10 C. C. H. (Fire & Casualty)* 562.

Late in 1964, the North Carolina supreme court considered this problem in *Iowa Mutual Insurance Co. vs. Fred M. Simmons, Inc., 12 C.C.H. (Fire & Casualty)* 242. Damage resulted from rain leaking through a plastic covering placed over a hole in a roof which the insured was repairing. The court held that this *was* an accident, even though the damage was caused by the insured's negligence in improperly covering the hole. Both the Rex Roofing and Alabama Roofing cases were cited in support of this holding.

On the other hand, similar damage from rain was held not to be "caused by accident" in *Midland Construction Co. vs. United States Casualty Co., 214 Fed. (2nd.)* 665. This case is somewhat different from the Rex Roofing Co. case in that another contractor had the duty of closing the roof and the court may have felt that the likelihood of rain was more obvious. Basically, however, the two cases seem to be in conflict.

Several other cases also conflict with the Rex Roofing case, and follow Midland Construction Co. Among these are *Christ vs. Progressive Fire Insurance Co., 9 C.C.H. (Fire & Casualty)* 548. Again, damage by rain to an unroofed building upon which the insured was working was held not caused by accident.

Another recent case along this line is *Baker vs. American Insurance Co., 324 Fed. (2nd.)* 748, decided by the United States court of appeals for the fourth circuit. In the Baker case, a construction firm had done considerable grading—including removal of trees and other vegetation—on the site of a proposed shopping center. After the grading, there followed several months of abnormally high rainfall. Rain water ran off the denuded ground and caused damage to surrounding property owners. The court held that this damage was "caused by accident."

In *Neale Construction Co. vs. United States Fidelity & Guaranty Co., 199 Fed. (2nd.)* 591, the insured was a contractor doing construction work for a telephone company. His employes were negligent in splicing the cables and the insured was held liable for the cost of repairing them. A federal appellate court held this liability was not caused by accident and hence not covered by the insured's comprehensive liability policy. The

---

* The "care, custody and control" exclusion was involved in the Rex Roofing Co. case, the insured also winning on this point.

opinion cited the Briscoe case, but it seems to turn principally on the ground that the liability of the insured resulted from failure to perform a contractual obligation—to do the work satisfactorily—rather than from an "accident."

The Neale Construction Co. case can probably be distinguished from the Cross and the Rex Roofing Co. cases in two ways. First, it does not appear that the insured took *any precautions* to avoid the consequence of his negligence. Second, the case involved *replacement* of work actually done by the insured, rather than damage to other property. However, the opinion contains some far-reaching statements, such as "the natural and ordinary consequences of a negligent act do *not* constitute an accident," which probably will be quoted in arguments.

In *Town of Tieton vs. General Insurance Co. of America, 380 Pac. (2nd.) 127,* contamination of a well from a sewage lagoon was held not to be an accident. The insured municipality constructed the lagoon 300 feet from a residence, realizing that contamination of the well was possible. Seepage from the lagoon did contaminate the well and the owner got a judgment against the town. The town sued its insurance carrier for recovery under a general liability contract.

In reversing a lower court decision which held that the damage was "caused by accident," the Washington supreme court held that, though the damage was not intentional, it was not "caused by accident." To hold that such damage was caused by accident, the court said, the event must be unusual, unexpected and unforeseen.

"The evidence most favorable to . . . the town . . . supports no more than a finding that . . . the town . . . took a calculated risk that the residence property would not be damaged. From a business standpoint, it may have been wise to have taken this calculated risk and to have proceeded with the construction of the lagoon without first condemning the property or arranging to supply water to it by means other than the well. But, when, under the facts of this case, the possibility of contamination became a reality, it cannot be said that the result was 'unusual, unexpected and unforeseen.' "

A similar case is *City of Aurora, Colo. vs. Trinity Universal Insurance Co., 11 C.C.H. (Fire & Casualty) 1381.* A sewage system, inadequate for periods of prolonged moisture, backed up into several residences. The United States court of appeals for the 10th circuit excused the municipality's insurer from any obligation, holding that the damage was *not* caused by accident.

Mistakes of Fact

In *Hardware Mutual Casualty Co. vs. Gerrits, 65 Sou. (2nd.) 69,* the Florida supreme court held that a *mistake of fact*—inadvertently building over the property line—was *not* an "accident." This case was somewhat complicated in that the court seemed impressed by the fact that the insured had acquired title to a small strip of land for the money he paid as damages and that it would be "unjust enrichment" to require the insurer to pay for this. More recently, however, a federal appellate court reached a similar conclusion in *Thomason vs. United States Fidelity & Guaranty Co., 248 Fed. (2nd.) 417,* without any such complicating factor. Here the insured mistakenly ran over a property line doing excavation work.

For some time, the Hardware Mutual Casualty and Thomason cases were described in these pages as strong legal authority for the view that a *mistake of fact is not an "accident"* within the meaning of a liability policy. How this interpretation is affected by the more recent case of *J. D'Amico, Inc. vs. City of Boston, 186 N.E. (2nd.) 716* is difficult to say. A paving contractor, following stakes placed by the city engineers, removed three trees from the land of a property-owner. The property-owner sued both the contractor and the city. The contractor, who had standard premises and operations liability coverage under a manufacturers and contractors liability policy, notified the insurance company which at first agreed to defend under a non-waiver but subsequently withdrew altogether. The supreme court of Massachusetts upheld a lower court decision *requiring the insurer to defend,* holding that if it were proved that the trespass had resulted from mistake, the damage must be considered as having been "caused by accident."

An earlier and similar holding was *Haynes vs. American Casualty Co., 179 Atl. (2nd.) 900.* The Maryland court of appeals held that removal of trees through mistake was an "accident." This decision reversed a lower court holding. The appellate court held that even though injury or damage results from an *intentional act,* it may be an *accident* if unexpected, unforeseen or unusual consequences result.

RESERVATION OF RIGHTS

On .... (date) a report of an accident in which you were allegedly involved was received.

Investigation of this matter is being conducted with full and complete reservation of all the rights afforded us under the policy of insurance issued to you by this Company.

Very truly yours,
(name of company)

By: ....

NON-WAIVER AGREEMENT

——————————————————— 19____

THIS NON-WAIVER AGREEMENT, Made and entered into as of the above mentioned date, by and between _____ hereinafter sometimes referred to as the policyholder, irrespective of whether or not one or more papers or corporations are concerned, and the _____ _____, hereinafter sometimes referred to as the Company;

WITNESSETH: That in consideration of ONE DOLLAR ($1.00) this day paid the policyholder by Company, the receipt of which is hereby acknowledged, and for other good and valuable consideration, it is agreed between said parties as follows:

(1) That no action heretofore or hereafter taken, nor any information heretofore or hereafter received, by the Company in or while investigating and ascertaining the cause of injury, damage, loss or fire, the amount of loss or damage or other matters relative to the claim of, or against, the said policyholder for property alleged to have been lost or damaged, or persons alleged to have been injured, on or about the _____ day of _____, 19_____, shall in any respect or particular change, waive, invalidate, or forfeit any of the terms, conditions, exclusions, exceptions as to liability or requirements of the policy of insurance, Number _____ held by the policyholder, nor shall the doing of any of the things aforesaid prejudice or affect the rights of either party hereto as existing or fixed at the time of said loss, damage or injury.

(2) The intent of this agreement is to (a) save and preserve all of the rights of each party hereto as existing at the time of said loss, damage or injury aforesaid; and (b) permit by or through the Company on investigation thereof and any legal defense of the claim or claims, suits or causes of action arising therefrom, the ascertainment of the amount, if any, of such loss, claim or damage in order that the business of policyholder may not be unnecessarily delayed, without in anywise affecting the liability or non-liability of the Company on or under the aforesaid insurance policy, and without prejudice to any rights of the parties hereto at the time of the alleged loss, damage or injury aforesaid.

(3) Provided, however, nothing herein contained shall require any investigation or defense by Company, nor preclude policyholder from making an independent investigation and controlling any litigation which may be instituted pursuant to or by reason of the alleged loss, claim, damage, or injury aforesaid.

Signed and sealed in the presence of   _____(SEAL)

_____   _____(SEAL)

As to Policyholder

_____   _____

As to Company   By_____(SEAL)

THE SKELETAL SYSTEM

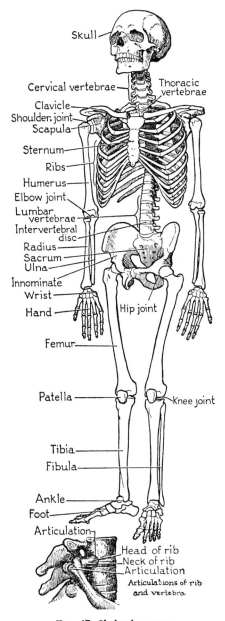

FIG. 47. Skeletal system.

From *Structure and Function of the Human Body*, Ralph N. Baillif and Donald L. Kimmel. Reproduced with the permission of the publisher, J. B. Lippincott Company, Philadelphia.

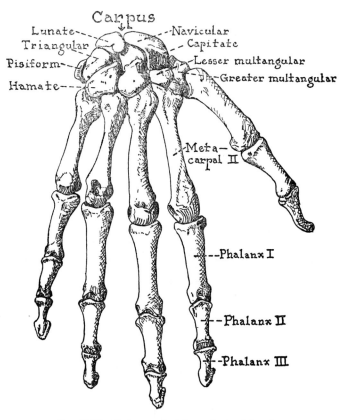

FIG. 100B. Skeleton of right wrist and hand.

From *Structure and Function of the Human Body*, Ralph N. Baillif and Donald L. Kimmel. Reproduced with the permission of the publisher, J. B. Lippincott Company, Philadelphia.

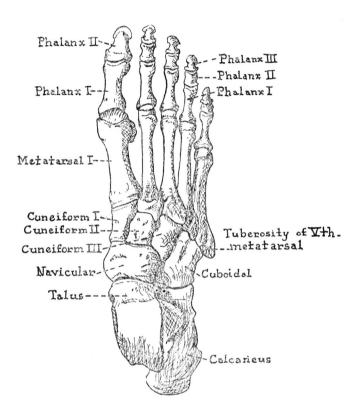

Phalanx II
Phalanx I
Metatarsal I
Cuneiform I
Cuneiform II
Cuneiform III
Navicular
Talus
Phalanx III
Phalanx II
Phalanx I
Tuberosity of Vth metatarsal
Cuboidal
Calcaneus

From *Structure and Function of the Human Body,* Ralph N. Baillif and Donald L. Kimmel. Reproduced with the permission of the publisher, J. B. Lippincott Company, Philadelphia.

INDEX